The History of the Church
in Carpathian Rus'

CLASSICS OF CARPATHO-RUSYN SCHOLARSHIP

Published under the auspices of the Carpatho-Rusyn Research Center
Patricia A. Krafcik and Paul R. Magocsi, editors

1. Pavlo Markovyč, *Rusyn Easter Eggs From Eastern Slovakia* (1987)
2. Aleksei L. Petrov, *The Oldest Documents Concerning the History of the Carpatho-Rusyn Church and Eparchy, 1391-1498* (forthcoming)
3. Alexander Bonkáló, *The Rusyns* (1990)
4. Athanasius B. Pekar, *The History of the Church in Carpathian Rus'* (1992)

Athanasius B. Pekar, OSBM

THE HISTORY OF THE CHURCH IN CARPATHIAN RUS'

Translated by
Marta Skorupsky

Bio-bibliography by
Edward Kasinec and Richard Renoff

EAST EUROPEAN MONOGRAPHS
Distributed by Columbia University Press, New York

1992

EAST EUROPEAN MONOGRAPHS, NO. CCCXXII

This volume is a revised and updated translation of the original Ukrainian-language version that appeared under the title, *Narysy istoriji cerkvy Zakarpattja,* Vol. I: *jerarchične oformlennja,* and was published by the Basilian Fathers, Rome, 1967.

Publication of this volume was in part made possible through the support of the Byzantine Ruthenian Metropolitan Province of Pittsburgh during the episcopal reign of Archbishop Stephen J. Kocisko. D.D.

Typesetting and composition courtesy of the Greek Catholic Union of the U.S.A., Beaver, Pennsylvania.

ISBN 0-88033-219-0

Library of Congress Catalog Card Number 92-81808

Editorial Preface

The series entitled Classics of Carpatho-Rusyn Scholarship is intended to make available in English translation some of the best monographs concerning Carpatho-Rusyn culture. These monographs deal with one or more scholarly disciplines: history, language, literature, ethnography, folklore, religion, music, and archeology.

The studies included in this series were first published for the most part during the twentieth century and were written in various languages by authors who may have had definite attitudes and preferences regarding the national and political orientations of the indigenous Carpatho-Rusyn population. Such preferences are often revealed in the varied terminology used to describe the group—Carpatho-Ruthenians, Carpatho-Russians, Carpatho-Ukrainians, Ruthenes, Ruthenians, Rusyns, etc. In keeping with the policy of the Carpatho-Rusyn Research Center, the inhabitants and culture which are the subject of this series will be referred to consistently as Carpatho-Rusyn or Rusyn, regardless what term or terms may have been used in the original work.

The appearance in this series of scholarly monographs whose authors may favor a particular national (pro-Russian, pro-Rusyn, pro-Ukrainian), political (pro-Czechoslovak, pro-Hungarian, pro-Soviet), or ideological (pro-democratic, pro-Communist, pro-Christian) stance does not in any way reflect the policy or orientation of the Carpatho-Rusyn Research Center. Rather, it is felt that the availability in English of scholarly studies representing a variety of ideological persuasions is the best way to improve our understanding and appreciation of Carpatho-Rusyn culture.

As in other publications of the Carpatho-Rusyn Research Center, placenames are rendered according to the official language used in the country where they are presently located; therefore, Slovak in the

Slovak republic of Czechoslovakia; Ukrainian in the Transcarpathian oblast of the Ukrainian S.S.R.; Polish in the Lemko Region of Poland; and Serbo-Croatian in the Vojvodina (Bačka) of Yugoslavia. The international transliteration system has been used to render words and names from the Cyrillic alphabet.

We are grateful to the editorial staff of the Basilian Order in Rome, the publishers of the original Ukrainian-language edition of the volume, for permission to prepare this English translation. They also agreed to our change in this edition of the name Ukrainian (which appeared in the original text) to Carpatho-Rusyn, or simply Rusyn. We were also very pleased to be able to consult throughout the editorial process with the author, the Reverend Athanasius B. Pekar, OSBM, who carefully reviewed the translation, made some necessary corrections in the original text, added new material to the bibliography, and brought some of the biographical data up to date, especially pertaining to recent developments of the church in the United States. We are particularly grateful to Professor Raymond M. Herbenick and Linda McKinley of the University of Dayton, for preparing the excellent index on Wordperfect 5.1, and to Janet L. Helterbran of the Greek Catholic Union for the composition of the entire volume. In the end, we are pleased to present this revised edition of an important work.

Patricia A. Krafcik
Paul Robert Magocsi

Contents

Bio-bibliography of Athanasius B. Pekar

Teacher and mentor, popular writer on religious and spiritual themes, and historian of the Church are all epithets that characterize the more than forty years of the Reverend Athanasius Pekar's career in the United States.

Pekar was born on March 1, 1923 in the village of Perečyn, then in Czechoslovakia's eastern province of Subcarpathian Rus', now the Transcarpathian oblast of the Ukraine. Pekar received his high-school education in Užhorod, and then left his homeland to continue his higher education in Rome, at the Pontifical Urban University (Pontificia Universitá Urbaniana), where he was awarded a doctorate in theology in 1947. He was ordained to the priesthood a year before on March 24, 1946.

Like many of his colleagues, the young Father Pekar immigrated to the United States and immediately began to serve the large community of Carpatho-Rusyn immigrants living in North America. One of his first assignments was assisting in the publication of one of the major publications for the Carpatho-Rusyn Americans, *Holos Svjatoj Makriny* [*Voice of Saint Macrina*]. During the early 1950s, he served as a professor at the Saints Cyril and Methodius Seminary in Pittsburgh, where his profound knowledge of Carpatho-Rusyn language and culture was much appreciated by his students, many of whom today serve the faithful throughout North America.

In 1955, Father Pekar made a dramatic move in his life by entering the monastic Order of St. Basil the Great. His assignments over the next decade were connected with the needs of the Order as a teacher and spiritual guide in the United States and Canada. Beginning in 1967, and continuing for the next decade, he returned to Pittsburgh as Professor and Spiritual Director of the Saints Cyril and Methodius Seminary, while carrying on pastoral work in nearby Carpatho-Rusyn parishes. The next five years also saw him work as a writer and broadcaster for Vatican Radio. Since January 1983, Father Pekar has served as Professor and Spiritual Director at the Ukrainian Catholic Seminary in Washington, D.C.

Despite his heavy duties as teacher, mentor, and spiritual director, Father Pekar has always displayed extraordinary personal discipline in pursuing his own research and writing. He is the author of more than twenty works dealing with some of the prominent figures in the history of the Basilian Order, the Church in Transcarpathia, and the Byzantine Catholics in the United States. His major work, published in Latin (Rome, 1956), dealt with the canonical establishment of the eparchy of Mukačevo. Other notable works deal with the eparchy of Prešov/Prjašiv (Pittsburgh, 1968), and his translation from the Latin of Aleksander Duchnovyč's history of the eparchy of Prešov (Rome, 1971). In his many other writings, Father Pekar has done great service by writing histories in English of both the Carpatho-Rusyn jurisdictions in the United States, as well as biographies of some of that church's notable ecclesiastical personalities in Europe.

His major work, however, is, the one translated in this volume, *The History of the Church in Carpathian Rus'*, first published in Ukrainian in Rome in 1967. It still remains the only modern summary of the *res gestae* of this institution. Since 1980, Father Pekar has also served his confreres as the editor of the learned journal of the Basilian Order, *Analecta Ordinis Sancti Basilii Magni* [*Analects of the Order of Saint Basil the Great*], three volumes of which have already appeared under his editorship.

Several features are striking to those who have been privileged to know and admire Father Pekar. First, there is his extradordinary self-discipline and great attention to detail. Second, there is his commitment to the writtern word and his desire to make better known the history of both his own people and that of the monastic order of which he is a member. Finally, there is his sincere encouragement and support of younger scholars seeking to learn more about the culture and history of Carpatho-Rusyns. All of these features are manifest in his life's work, most especially in the volume offered to the reader with this translation and republication.

The History

No complete history of the Carpatho-Rusyn Greek Catholic Church in Europe or America has appeared in the English language. Until now, literature in English has included a general history of the ethnic group,[1] and an earlier popular work on Eastern-rite Catholicism which contains one chapter on Carpatho-Rusyns.[2] Other contributions to Church history have addressed topics that are narrower in scope,[3] among which are also biographies of individual bishops.[4] Even the major mongraph by Paul Robert Magocsi, *The Shaping of a National Identity*, treats the clergy mostly as members of the national intelligentsia rather than as ecclesiastical officials.[5] Happily, this lacuna has been filled with the publication of Volume I of Athanasius Pekar's monumental work, *The History of the Church in Carpathian Rus'*.

The scope of the work and the source material used are vast. It begins with the introduction of Christianity during the time of Saints Cyril and Methodius in the ninth century and carefully carries us to the post-World War II suppression of the Greek Catholic Church in the homeland and developments in America during the 1980s. Latin, English, French, German, Italian, Hungarian, and various Slavic sources are utilized. Archivists will laud Father Pekar's use of the Secret Archives of the Vatican and the Archives of the *Congregatio de Propaganda Fide*. General readers will be greatly interested in the references to early and more recent Rusyn-American newspaper and *kalendar* (almanac) articles. This is the most thoroughly documented work on the Carpatho-Rusyn church that we have seen. However, the author does have a rather specialized perspective consistent with volume one's subtitle: *Hierarchical Structure*. In essence, this volume is a comprehensive history of the Greek Catholic hierarchy and its relations with ecclesiastical and secular leaders.

Father Pekar's monograph is a chronicle of the perennial religious struggles in the historic regions of his ill-fated homeland as well as among the diasporas settled in North America and Yugoslavia. According to him, these struggles were precipitated often by religious and secular officials in Budapest, Moscow, Rome, Vienna, and even in Philadelphia, Pittsburgh, St. Paul, and Minneapolis.

A primary example of such external influence occurred in the seventeenth century. In 1646, a group of Orthodox priests united with Rome during the Union of Užhorod, and this resulted in the administrative subordination of the local Church to Roman-rite authorities. For over a century, Protestant princes, Roman-rite prelates, and Orthodox hierarchs battled for the allegiance of a few hundred thousand Carpatho-Rusyns who were mostly unaware of these machinations. Habsburg support finally resulted in the solidification of the Roman connection which, while latinizing and magyarizing some priests and other members of the intelligentsia, did not end the religious conflicts in Subcarpathian Rus'. Generally, outsiders tried to determine the confessional affiliation of the region, but they were only superficially successful.

Pekar's work, which focuses mostly on the activities of ecclesiastical and government officials, treats the Carpatho-Rusyns as an oppressed people continually resisting domineering Magyar bishops and magnates. Since the Rusyns were placed under the Roman-rite ordinary of Eger and the primate of Esztergom, latinization of their canon laws and rite was virtually inevitable. Nonetheless, their religious culture flourished for a time due to Austria's benevolent monarchs, Maria Theresa (reigned 1740-1780), her son Joseph II (reigned 1780-1890), and the sympathetic pope, Clement XIV (reigned 1769-1774), who created the Mukačevo Eparchy in 1771. The dedicated Bishop Andrij Bačyns'kyj of Mukačevo (reigned 1773-1809) promoted this development. Thus, the Rusyns had patrons as well as opponents and the emphasis of both types are consistent with the "great man" approach which recurs throughout Pekar's book.

Another action by Church and governmental authorities was to have consequences which have lasted to the present day. In 1816, Emperor Francis II (reigned 1792-1835) created the Prešov Eparchy, a maneuver ratified by Rome two years later. In effect, this divided the Carpatho-Rusyn people, because the division became a cultural as well as administrative one. For instance, a century later, clergy from the Prešov Eparchy became pitted against clergy from the Mukăcevo Eparchy during the so-called "celibacy struggle" in twentieth-century America. An earlier and more positive development in Prešov was the fostering of a local Rusyn identity (albeit sympathetic to Russia) that was part of a cultural awakening and a fledgling literary movement led by the Greek Catholic priest, Aleksander Duchnovyč (1803-1865) and the secular leader Adol'f Dobrians'kyj (1817-1901). In contrast to many writers, Pekar contends that it was Bishop Josyf Gaganec's (reigned 1843-1875) convocation of the first synod of the Prešov Eparchy in June 1848 that initiated the Carpatho-Rusyn religious and cultural renaissance. On this point, he seems too particularlistic, because there were similar national awakenings among other European peoples during that year which conceivably influenced the Rusyns. Gaganec' was a true patriot, and it now seemed that Rusyn destiny might be controlled by Rusyns themselves.

The *Ausgleich*, or "Compromise" of 1867, which created the Austro-Hungarian Dual Monarchy, was a disaster for the Carpatho-Rusyn people. Rusyn schools were magyarized and their newspapers eventually eliminated. Magyar became the official language, and before long Hungarian was being introduced in some parishes as a liturgical language despite Vatican opposition. The cultural awakening would continue, but only in politically-free America among émigré priests and later among American-educated clergy, nuns, and lay people.

Pekar's interpretation of the American experience is that of a loyal Byzantine Catholic, united with Rome. He is supportive of Bishops Soter Ortynsky (reigned 1907-1916) and Basil Takach (reigned 1924-1948), both of whom ruled during periods of external manipulation and internal factionalism. Significantly, Pekar does not condemn Father Alexis Toth (1853-1909) for his conversion to Orthodoxy in 1891, but he does consider American Roman-rite bishops such as Archbishop John Ireland (reigned 1888-1918) of St. Paul to be intolerant of the "foreign" ethnic church of the Rusyns. Needless to say, Pekar is not pleased with the resulting loss of fifteen parishes to Orthodoxy. Other contributing factors were, according to the author, the "Orthodox movement" promoted among Carpatho-Rusyns by the Russian Orthodox mission as well as "Hungarian political influence."

At this point, Pekar also finds institutional blame *within* the Rusyn community in the form of the Greek Catholic Union (Sojedinenije). The oldest of Rusyn-American fraternal organizations is blamed for its opposition to Bishops Ortynsky and Takach during the celibacy controversy. It is probably because the monograph's scope is Carpatho-Rusyn ecclesiastical history that Pekar omits discussing such positive functions of the Greek Catholic Union, including its resistance to the encroachments of Roman-rite bishops at the parish level.[6] Pekar is unreserved in his criticism of this fraternity. In contrast, the achievements of the Byzantine Ruthenian Metropolitan Province of the United States are emphasized. The Province increased the number of its sees beginning in 1963. A seminary was opened in 1950, new religious houses were built, and its fourth eparchy was erected on the West Coast in 1981.

On the eve of the publication of this English-language edition, the political and religious situation has improved dramatically in the Prešov Region of Eastern Slovakia under the post-Communist

Czechoslovak government with the installation of Bishop Ján Hirka (b. 1923) as Ordinary of the Greek Catholic Eparchy of Prešov. In fact, a very valuable part of Pekar's book is an appendix containing brief biographies of every documented bishop of the Mukačevo and Máramaros eparchies prior to the Union of Užhorod, of all post-Union bishops of the eparchies of Mukačevo, Prešov and Križevci; and all administrators and bishops of the Byzantine Ruthenian sees in the United States.

No previous author has so thoroughly compiled a record of the persecutions and sufferings of the Carpatho-Rusyn people for their faith. The record of their ecclesiastical history contains numerous instances of deception, assertions of power, sins of omission, and spitefulness meted out against them. Even readers already suspicious of the Roman-rite clergy in their dealings with the Rusyns may be shocked to learn that married priests "were barred from saying Mass" (p. 388) by American Roman-rite ordinaries and that the Roman-rite hierarchy pushed for an American Byzantine-rite seminary "to institutionalize celibacy and Americanize [their] Church" (p. 403). These realities of history and life, which have produced a national consciousness buttressed by belief in the inseparability of the true faith and rite, are best summed up by Father Pekar's own words in this volume:

> Sensing the threat from both Protestantism and Roman Catholicism, the Carpatho-Rusyns grew even more strongly attached to their Eastern rite and their customs, thereby hoping to preserve not only their faith, but also their national identity. A great transformation occurred in the spiritual life of the Carpatho-Rusyns. Their rite became for them not only 'the external expression of their faith', but also the vehicle of their self-identity and the bulwark of their cultural and religious heritage. The Carpatho-Rusyns thus began to identify their rite with their faith and their faith with their nationality. Their Church became for them the Rusyn Church, and their faith the Rusyn faith (p. 28).

Edward Kasinec
Richard Renoff

Notes to the Bio-bibliographical Introduction

1. Walter C. Warzeski, *Byzantine Rite Rusins in Carpatho-Ruthenia and America* (Pittsburgh: Byzantine Seminary Press, 1971).

2. Stephen C. Gulovich, *Windows Westward: Rome, Russia, Reunion* (New York: Declan X. McMullen, 1947). See also his "The Rusin Exarchate in the United States," *Eastern Churches Quarterly*, VI, 4 (New York, 1946), pp. 459-486.

3. See particularly the work of Michael Lacko, *The Union of Užhorod* (Cleveland and Rome: Slovak Institute, 1966); and his "The Forced Liquidation of the Union of Uzhorod," *Slovak Studies*, I: *Historica*, 1 (Rome, 1961), pp. 145-185.

Other specialized studies include: Keith S. Russin, "Father Alexis G. Toth and the Wilkes-Barre Litigations," *St. Vladimir's Theological Quarterly*, XVI, 3 (Tuckahoe, N.Y., 1972), pp. 128-149; Thomas F. Sable, *Lay Initiative in Greek Catholic Parishes in Connecticut, New York, New Jersey, and Pennsylvania (1884-1909)* (Thesis, Graduate Theological Union, Berkeley, Calif., 1984); Richard Renoff, "Seminary Background and the Carpatho-Russian Celibacy Struggle," *Diakonia* X, 1 (New York, 1975), pp. 55-62; and Jaroslav Roman, "The Establishment of the American Carpatho-Russian Orthodox Greek Catholic Diocese in 1938: A Major Carpatho-Russian Uniate Return to Orthodoxy," *St. Vladimir's Theological Quarterly*, XX, 3 (Crestwood/Tuckahoe, N.Y., 1976), pp. 132-160.

4. Father Pekar has published several popular biographies of Greek Catholic bishops in Europe (see the bibliography below, items 036, 037, 039, 068, 189, 212, 213, 223, 293)

Other biographies of interest are: Lawrence Barriger, *Good Victory: Metropolitan Orestes Chornock and the American Carpatho-Russian Orthodox Greek Catholic Diocese* (Brookline, Mass.: Holy Cross Orthodox Press, 1985); Bohdan P. Procko, "Soter Ortynsky: First Ruthenian Bishop in the United States, 1907-1916," *The Catholic Historical Review*, LVIII, 4 (Washington, D.C., 1973), pp. 513-532; and Basil Shereghy, *Bishop Basil Takach, "The Good Shepherd"* (Pittsburgh: Byzantine Seminary Press, 1979).

5. Paul Robert Magocsi, *The Shaping of a National Identity: Subcar-*

pathian Rus', 1848-1948 (Cambridge, Mass.: Harvard University Press, 1978).

6. Cf. Thomas F. Sable, S.J., "The History of Early Greek Catholic Parishes in America (1884-1909) and the Role of Fraternal Societies in the Creation of Local Parishes," paper read at the Conference on Carpatho-Rusyn Studies, Philadelphia, University of Pennsylvania, April 19, 1986.

A favorable treatment of the role of Slavic benevolent societies during the early twentieth century is found in Margaret Byington, *Homestead: The Households of a Mill Town* (New York: Charities Publication Committee, 1910), pp. 161-164.

7. Consecrated February 17, 1990 at Prešov, reported in *Eastern Catholic Life*, March 4, 1990, p. 1.

Works by Athanasius B. Pekar on the Carpatho-Rusyns

This bibliography is only a portion of the more than six hundred works Athanasius B. Pekar has published in the course of his scholarly career. It contains only those works he has published on Carpatho-Rusyns and their culture. The bibliography is arranged in chronological order, and within each year alphabetically by the title of the article or book.

The careful reader will notice a discrepancy in systems of transliteration. Titles of items published in Ukrainian are transliterated according to the Library of Congress system, with modifications. Titles of items published in Carpatho-Rusyn using the Latin alphabet are, of course, given in the original form in which they appeared; practically speaking, this means the International Scholarly System, also with modifications. With few exceptions, each item in the bibliography was examined *de visu* in the rich Slavic and East European collections of the New York Public Library. Those few items which we were unable to see are indicated with an asterisk.

Because of its length, and some of the other inherent difficulties in its compilation, the compilers turned to a number of individuals for assistance. First and foremost, they are indebted to Father Pekar himself, who provided some of the initial notes for this bibliography. Further appreciation is extended to: the Reverend John Ball, St. Andrew's Byzantine Catholic Church, Westbury, New York; Professor Thomas E. Bird, Queens College; Reverend Sister Demetria, O.S.B.M., Librarian of the Episcopal and Heritage Institute Libraries of the Byzantine Catholic Diocese of Passaic; the Most Reverend Michael J. Dudick, D.D., Bishop of the Byzantine Catholic Diocese of Passaic; Reverend Stephen Veselenak, O.S.B., St. Nicholas Byzantine Catholic Church, McKeesport, Pennsylvania;

Reverend Phillip Sarnak, O.S.B.M., St. Josaphat's Basilian Monastery, Glen Cove, L.I.; Robert H. Davis, Jr., New York Public Library; and Luba Wolynetz, Librarian of the Ukrainian Catholic Diocese of Stamford.

Abbreviations

Analecta OSBM	*Analecta Ordinis Sancti Basilii Magni* (Rome)
BCW	*Byzantine Catholic World* (Pittsburgh, Pennsylvania)
ECL	*Eastern Catholic Life* (Passaic, New Jersey)
HHSM	*Holos Hory Sviatoi Makriny* (Uniontown, Pennsylvania)
P-E	*Prosvita-Enlightenment* (McKeesport, Pennsylvania)

1949

001 "Bor'ba za derevl'jannu cerkov," *Nebesnaja Tsaritsa*, XXIII, 3 (McKeesport, Pa., 1949), pp. 7-8.

002 "Borot'ba za derevl'anu cerkov: pamjati svjaščennika-mučenika prisvjačeno," *HHSM*, II, 1 (1949), pp. 9-11.

003 "Dovkola Staroho Kraju—položenije cerkvi v Starom Kraju," *Nebesnaja Tsaritsa*, XXIII, 7 (McKeesport, Pa., 1949), p. 7.

004 "1948—maj 13—1949," *HHSM*, I, 9 (1949), p. 6.

005 "Pered pjatdesjat' rokami," *HHSM*, I, 6 (1949), pp. 10-11.

006 "Pročto peresl'idovanije duchovenstva," *HHSM*, II, 3 (1949), pp. 11-12.

007 "Sl'idami sribernoho juvileju," *HHSM*, I, 8 (1949), pp. 11-12.

008 "Uže čas klasti osnovanije: dovkola sribernoho juvileja dieceziji," *HHSM*, I, 11 (1949), p. 6.

1950

009 "Ikona Materi Božoji Neustajučoji Pomoči," *HHSM*, II, 11 (1950), pp. 2-4.

010 "Počatki slavjans'koho obr'adu," *HHSM*, II, 11 (1950), pp. 6-10.

011 "Preosvjaščennyj vladyka v Rimi," *Nebesnaja Tsaritsa*, XXIV, 12 (1950), pp. 4-6 and 11.

012 "Seminarija—naša budučnost," *HHSM*, II, 12 (1950), pp. 3-5.

013 "Slidami mučenikov," *HHSM*, II, 12 (1950), pp. 7-9.

014 "Za želiznoju zaslonoju," *HHSM*, II, 6 (1950), pp. 6-9.

1951

015 "Počitanije Sv. Kirila i Metodija," *Nebesnaja Tsaritsa*, XXV, 6 (McKeesport, Pa., 1951), pp. 4-6 and 11.

016 [With Vasilij Shereghy]. *Vospitanije Podkarpato-Ruskaho Svjaščenstva: The Training of the Carpatho-Ruthenian Clergy.* English text of this bi-lingual edition translated by Josif Jackanich. Pittsburgh: n.p., 1951. 126pp.

1953

017 "Apostolskij delegat meži nami," *Nebesnaja Tsaritsa*, XXVII, 6 (McKeesport, Pa., 1953), pp. 8-10.

1954

018 "Posl'idnyj odpust u Mukačovi," *HHSM*, VII, 1 (1954), pp. 16-19.

1955

019 "Preosvjasčennyi Kir Nikolaj Elko vysvjačennyj v Rimi," *HHSM*, VII, 8 (1955), pp. 14-16.

1956

020 *De Erectione Canonica Eparchiae Mukačoviensis (anno 1771)*.
Analecta OSBM, Series II, Section 1: Opera, Vol. VIII. Rome,
1956. 157pp.

021 "Nad hrobom Episkopa-mučenika," *BCW*, November 4, 1956, p.
8.

022 "Testimony to Our Loyalty," *BCW*, October 14, 1956, p. 10.

1957

023 "Bačvans'ki rusiny," *BCW*, February 3, 1957, p. 9.

024 "Vizantiis'ko-madiars'kyi obriad?," *Ameryka* (Philadelphia, Pa.),
August 15, 1957 p. 3.

025 "Episkop Stojka—Otec bidnych: 25 lit od konsekraciji, 1932—12
julija—1957," *BCW*, July 7, 1957, p. 6.

026 "Herojs'ka vira našich divčat v Stalino," *BCW*, January 20, 1957,
p. 8.

027 "Kir P. Gojdič 30 l'it Episkopom: Episkopskij juvilej u vjaznici,"
BCW, March 24, 1957, p. 9.

028 "Na osnovi dokumentov: Jak sudili pr'aševskoho episkopa Pavla
Gojdiča?"
(1) Episkopa sudili za 'zradu' i špionstvo," *BCW*, April 21, 1957,
p. 7.
(2) "V čom pol'ahaje 'zločin' Greko-katolikov?," *BCW*, April 28,
1957, p. 7.
(3) "Pod'iji kotri poperedili arest Vladyki," *BCW*, May 5, 1957,
p. 7.
(4) "Zahraničňi podoroži Vladyki na sud'i," *BCW*, May 12, 1957,
p. 7.
(5) "'Samopriznanije' Preosvjaščennoho," *BCW*, May 19, 1957, p.
7.
(6) "Vladyka 'neprijatel' bidnoho naroda'!," *BCW*, May 26, 1957,
p. 7.

(7) "Kollaboracionist hitlerovs'koho imperializmu!," *BCW*, June 2, 1957, p. 7.
(8) "Slovac'ka vlada i Vladyka," *BCW*, June 9, 1957, p. 7.
(9) "Exkommunikacija komunistov," *BCW*, June 16, 1957, p. 7.
(10) "'Meždunarodnyj špion'!," *BCW*, June 23, 1957, p. 7.
(11) "Pomoč biženc'am," *BCW*, June 30, 1957, p. 7.
(12) "Podryvna d'ijatel'nost' Vladyki!," *BCW*, July 7, 1957, p. 7.
(13) "Vladyka 'propagator novoj vojny'!," *BCW*, July 14, 1957, p. 7.
(14) "Zasud na Vladyku," *BCW*, July 21, 1957, p. 7.

029 "O. Monsinior Avhustyn Vološyn: Bat'ko Sribnoï Zemli," *Ameryka*, March 15 and 16, 1957, p. 2 and p. 2.

030 "Holos iz Karpats'koï Ukraïny: zapysky na sluzhebnyku v Ostryhomi," *Ameryka*, January 23, 1957, p. 3.

1958

031 "Dolia monakhiv i monakhyn na Priashivschyni," *Svitlo*, XXI, 6 (Toronto, 1958), pp. 15-16.

032 "Hde Prjaševskij Vladyka Kyr Pavel Gojdič?," *BCW*, February 23, 1958, p. 10.

033 "Katedral'nyj chor v Užhorod'i," *BCW*, November 23, 1958, p. 11.

034 "Smutno v Starom Kraju pod Karpatami," *BCW*, February 2, 1958, p. 11.

035 "Vozroždenije cerkvi pod Sovitami?," *BCW*, October 12, 1958, p. 10.

1961

036 *Vasylianyn—Ispovidnyk Ep.P.Gojdych, ČSVV.* New York: Basilian Fathers Publications, 1961. 96pp.

037 *Vladyka-Muchenyk, T. Romzha 1911-1947.* New York: Basilian Fathers Publications, 1961. 64pp.

1962

038 "Preosv. Kyr A. Horniak, ČSVV v Anhliï," *Ameryka*, July 1, 1962, p. 3.

1963

039 "Bishop Peter Gebej—Champion of the Holy Union (1864-1964)," *Analecta OSBM*, Series II, Section 2, IV (X), 1-2 (Rome, 1963), pp. 293-326.

1965

040 "Bishop Gebej—A Beloved Shepherd: the 100th Anniversary of His Birth," *America*, March 18, 1965, pp. 2, 4.

041 "Iepyskop D. Niaradii: cholovik Provydinnia," *Svitlo*, XVIII, 9 (Toronto, 1965), pp. 354-357.

042 "Mytropolyt Andrei, Blahovisnyk z"iedyneniia," *Svitlo*, XXVIII, 11 (Toronto, 1965), pp. 447-448.

043 "Pam'iat' ioho iz rodu v rid: iz nahody smerty iep. Pavla Goidycha, ChSVV," *Svitlo*, XXVIII, 7-8 (Toronto, 1965), pp. 308-310.

044 "Tserkovna polityka madiariv na Zakarpatti," *Svitlo*, XXVIII, 4 (Toronto, 1965), pp. 170-173.

045 "U piatylittia smerty iep. Pavla Goidycha, ChSVV," *Ameryka*, July 7, 1965, p. 2.

1966

046 "Communists Condemn Bishop's Faith," *ECL*, March 6 and 13, 1966, p. 7 and p. 7.

047 "First Byzantine Bishop in America: Most Reverend Soter S. Ortynsky, OSBM," *ECL*, March 20, 1966, p. 8.

048 "In Commemoration of Bishop Romzha"
     (1) "Defender of His Church," *ECL*, November 20, 1966, p. 12.

(2) "He Became a Bishop During Crucial Times," *ECL*, November 13, 1966, p. 13.

(3) "He Died for his Faith," *ECL*, November 6, 1966, p. 12.

(4) "He Offered His Life for his Faith," *ECL*, November 27, 1966, p. 9.

(5) "A Martyr of Our Times: He Suffered for the Name of Christ," *ECL*, April 3, 1966, p. 8.

(6) "He Bore the Marks of Christ on His Body," *ECL*, March 27, 1966, p. 7.

049 "The Mock Trial of Bishop Gojdich...," *ECL*, March 20, 1966, p. 7.

050 "Naš Vladyka Ispovidnik: Preosvjaščennyj, P.P. Gojdič, ČSVV (1888-1966)," *HHSM*, XVIII, 6 (1966), pp. 22-24.

051 "Smert' Jepiskopa Teodora Romži," *HHSM*, XIX, 2 (1966), pp. 30-32.

052 "Ternystym shliakhom Vladyky—pionera Ortyns'koho," *Svitlo*, XXIX, 3 and 4 (Toronto, 1966), pp. 100-102 and p. 147.

1967

053 "Bishop Basil Hopko Modern-Day Martyr of Iron Curtain Communism," *ECL*, April 30 and May 7, 1967, p. 2 and p. 12.

054 "Bishop Manuel M. Olshavsky, OSBM," *ECL*, November 12, 1967, p. 2.

055 "Bishop Romzha—A Byzantine Martyr," *ECL*, October 29, 1967, pp. 1 and 5.

056 *Narysy istoriï tserkvy Zakarpattia*, Vol. I: *ierarkhichne oformlennia*, Analecta OSBM, Series II, Section 1: Opera, Vol. VII. Rome, 1967. 241pp.

057 *"Nash Ispovidnyk—Vladyka V. Hopko," *Shliakh* (Philadelphia, Pa.), May 7, 1967, pp. 1-2.

058 "Our First Historian: Father Joannicius Basilovits, OSBM," *ECL*, December 10, 1967, p. 8.

059 "Our Martyred Bishop Theodore Romzha," *BCW*, October 29, 1967, p. 13.

060 "Testimony to our Loyalty—Bishop Romzha," *ECL*, October 15, 1967, p. 9.

061 "Twentieth Anniversary of Bishop Hopko," *The Way* (Philadelphia, Pa.), May 7, 1967, pp. 1-2.

062 "20-ročnyj juvilej Jepiskopa Hopka," *BCW*, May 7, 1967, p. 8.

1968

063 "Bishop Alexander Stojka (1932-1942)," *ECL*, June 2, 1968, p. 12.

064 "Bishop Basil Takach," *BCW*, May 5 and 26, 1968, p. 9 and p. 7.

065 "Bishop Hopko Active Again," *ECL*, June 23, 1968, p. 7.

066 "Bishop Hopko Attends Velehrad Meeting to Establish Rights of Eastern Catholics," *ECL*, June 23, 1968, p. 2.

067 "Bishop Joseph Gaganets (1843-1875)—Shepherd and Leader," *ECL*, June 16, 1968, p. 8.

068 *Bishop Paul P. Gojdich, OSBM*. Pittsburgh: [Byzantine Seminary Press, 1968]. 51pp.

069 "Blessed Shepherd of his Flock: Bishop Basil Takach," *BCW*, May 12, 1968, pp. 8-9.

070 "Body of the Late Bishop Gojdich Transferred to Prjashev," *BCW*, November 24, 1968, p. 10.

071 "Commemoration of Bishop Gojdich," *BCW*, July 21, 1968, p. 8.

072 "Finale of a Great Life," *BCW*, August 18, 1968, p. 7.

073 "Greek Catholic Church in Czechoslovakia Recognized," *ECL*, July 14, 1968, p. 6.

074 "He Drank Courageously from his Cup: Bishop Basil Takach (May 13, 1968)," *BCW*, May 19, 1968, pp. 8-9.

075 *Historic Background of the Eparchy of Prjashev.* Pittsburgh: Byzantine Seminary Press, 1968, vi and 83pp.

076 "Historic Background of the Prjashev Eparchy"
(2) The Concept of a New Eparchy," *BCW*, September 29, 1968, p. 9.
(3) "The Establishment of the Eparchy," *BCW*, October 6, 1968, p. 8.
(4) "Bishop Gregory Tarkovich Defender of the People (1818-1841)," *BCW*, October 13, 1968, pp. 8 and 15.
(5) "Great Shepherd and Leader—Bishop Joseph Gaganets (1843-1875)," *BCW*, October 20, 1968, pp. 8 and 19.
(6) "Bishop Scholar Nicholas Toth, S.T.D. (1876-1882)," *BCW*, October 27, 1968, pp. 8 and 17.
(7) "Obscure Greatness of Bishop John Valyi, S.T.D. (1883-1911)," *BCW*, November 10, 1968, pp. 8 and 18.
(8) "War Time Bishop Stephen Novak, S.T.D. (1914-1918)," *BCW*, November 17, 1968, p. 9.
(9) "Administration of Canon Nicholas Russnak, STD (1918-1922)," *BCW*, December 1, 1968, pp. 8 and 14.
(12) "Bishop Dionysius Nyaradi—'Man of God': 1922-1927," *BCW*, December 8, 1968, pp. 8 and 18.

077 "Historic Meeting in Czechoslovakia," *ECL*, June 16, 1968, p. 2.

078 "Last Days of the Martyred Bishop Romzha," *ECL*, November 3, 1968, p. 10.

079 "U 50-richchia sviashchenstva o. Vasylia Laria," *Ameryka*, June 26, 1968, p. 3.

1969

080 "After Twenty Years," *BCW*, October 5, 1969, pp. 12-13.

(2) "Liquidation of the Eparchy of Mukachevo," *BCW*, November 12, 1969, pp. 12-13.
(3) "The Disposal of Bishop Romzha," *BCW*, October 26, 1969, pp. 12-13.
(4) "The Loss of the Basilian Monastery," *BCW*, October 19, 1969, pp. 12-13.
(5) "The Uzhorod Seminary," *BCW*, October 12, 1969, pp. 12-13.

081 "Apostolic Administrator—Very Rev. John Hirka: Twentieth Anniversary of Priesthood," *BCW*, September 7, 1969, pp. 6 and 19.

082 "Composer Father John Bokšay (1874-1940): The Author of the Prostopinije," *BCW*, July 27, 1969, pp. 8 and 18; and *ECL*, August 10, 1969, pp. 9-10.

083 "Constantine Matezonskyj (1794-1858)—Tribute to the Father of Our Choral Music," *BCW*, July 20, 1969, p. 16; and *ECL*, August 3, 1969, p. 9.

084 "Establishment of Our Metropolitan Province of Munhall," *BCW*, May 11, 1969, pp. 5 and 19.
(2) "Rights and Obligations of the Metropolitan," *BCW*, May 18, 1969, p. 5.
(3) "Our Hierarchical Growth," *BCW*, May 25, 1969, pp. 2 and 19.

085 "Father Anatole A. Kralickyj, OSBM (1835-1894)," *ECL*, June 15, 1969, p. 3.

086 "Father Andrew Popovich (1809-1898)," *BCW*, August 3, 1969, p. 9 and 17; *ECL*, August 10, 1969, pp. 11-12.

087 "Historic Consistory in Prjashev," *ECL*, October 12, 1969, p. 3.

088 "Masterly Pen Abruptly Broken: Tribute to Monsignor John S. Kocisko," *BCW*, June 8, 1969, p. 14.

089 "Nezlamnyi dukh bortsia zadoliu i prava svoho narodu," *Svitlo*, XXXII, 5 and 6 (Toronto, 1969), pp. 178-180 and 218-220.

090 "Our Church in Czechslovakia," *ECL*, September 14, 1969, p. 2.

091 *Our Slavic Heritage.* Pittsburgh: Byzantine Catholic Seminary Press, 1969. 44pp.

092 "Our Slavic Heritage," *BCW*, March 9, 1969, pp. 8 and 16.
(2) "Cyril and Methodius, Our Slavic Apostles," *BCW*, March 16, 1969, pp. 8 and 18.
(3) "Our Slavic Language," *BCW*, March 23, 1969, pp. 8 and 20.
(4) "Our Slavonic Rite," *BCW*, March 30, 1969, pp. 8 and 17.
(5) "Our Slavonic Liturgy," *BCW*, April 6, 1969, pp. 8 and 14.
(6) "Our Slavic Bible," *BCW*, April 13, 1969, pp. 14 and 19.
(7) "Veneration of SS. Cyril and Methodius," *BCW*, April 20, 1969, p. 14 and April 27, 1969, p. 12.
(8) "Cyrillo-Methodian Ideals in Carpathia," *BCW*, May 4, 1969, pp. 8 and 14.

093 "Pastyrs'kyi lyst Priashivs'koho Vladyky V. Hopka," *Shliakh*, July 20, 1969, pp. 4-5.

094 "Recent Pastoral Letter of Bishop Hopko," *ECL*, June 29, 1969, p. 11.

095 "Reverend Alexander Pavlovich (1819-1900): Tribute to Our Bard," *BCW*, September 21 and 28, 1969, pp. 14 and 16, and p. 14.

096 "Spiritual Renewal in Czechoslovakia," *ECL*, October 19, 1969, p. 6.

097 "Tribute to Bishop Hopko on his 65th Birthday," *ECL*, April 20, 1969, pp. 2 and 11.

098 "Tribute to Father Eugene Fencik (1844-1903)," *BCW*, November 9, 16, 23, and 30, 1969, pp. 13-14, pp. 11-15, p. 14, and p. 14.

099 "The Beauty of the Slavonic Rite," by Father Eugene Fencik, translation from an article originally published in *Listok* (Uzhhorod, 1889), pp. 1-2, *BCW*, November 30, 1969, p. 14.

100 "A Tribute to Father John Silvay (1838-1904)," *BCW*, July 6, 1969, pp. 14-15.

101 "Waited 19 Years For Their Ordination," *BCW*, July 13, 1969, pp. 14-15.

1970

102 "Father S. Papp's Song Book *Duchovňi Pisňi*," *ECL*, August 23, 1970, p. 3.

103 "Imprisoned Bishop Gojdich Tried to Please God," *BCW*, July 12, 1970, p. 16.

104 "Golden Jubilee of Msgr. A. Chira in Exile: 1920—December 19—1970," *BCW*, December 13, 1970, p. 14.

105 "Imprisoned Bishop Gojdich Tried to Please God: Died on his Birthday in Prison for his Faith," *BCW*, July 19, 1970, pp. 16-17.

106 "Let us Remember our Great Prelate: In Commemoration of Canon George Shuba (1869-1930)," *BCW*, June 14, 1970, pp. 16 and 19.

107 "New Irmologion of our Liturgical Chant," *BCW*, September 13, 1970, pp. 16 and 18.

108 "Our Great Historian and Ethnographer, Rev. George K. Zhatkovich (1885-1920)," *BCW*, November 8, 1970, p. 14.

109 "Rev. Cyril Fedeles: A Modern Confessor," *ECL*, September 20, 1970, p. 8.

110 "The Songbook *Duchnovňi Pisňi*: Great Achievement of Father Stephen Pap," *BCW*, August 23, 1970, pp. 9 and 18.

111 "300 Years of Weeping Icon in Klokochovo," *BCW*, September 6, 1970, pp. 8 and 14.

112 "Sumni naslidky slovakizatsiï tserkvy na Priashivshchyni," *Nasha meta* (Toronto), December 19, 1970, pp. 1 and 4.

113 "Tribute to a Great Son of Our People: On The Eightieth Birthday of Father Emilian Bokshay," *BCW*, April 19, 1970, pp. 14 and 19.

114 *"Z tserkovnoho zhyttia na Priashivshchyni," *Shliakh*, October 27, 1970, p. 2.

1971

115 "Basilian Reform in Transcarpathia," *Analecta OSBM*, Series II, Section 2, Vol. VII (XIII), 1-4 (Rome, 1971), pp. 143-226.

116 "Bishop Basil Takach (October 27, 1879—May 13, 1948)," *P-E*, May 1971, p. 4.

117 "Holy Union as Our Heritage: 1646—April 24—1971," *P-E*, April 1971, p. 4.

118 "In Memory of Bishop Basil Takach (October 27, 1879—May 13, 1948)," *P-E*, May 1971, p. 4.

119 "Let us Remember our 200th Anniversary—1771 September 19th 1971," *BCW*, December 26, 1971, p. 15.

120 "The Lasting Witness of the Union of Uzhorod," *ECL*, June 27, 1971, p. 10.

121 *"Likvidatsiia Tserkvy na Zakarpatti i Priashivshchyni," *Nova zoria* (Chicago), May 2 and 9, 1971, p. 3 and p. 3.

122 "Long Awaited Book Finally Published," *P-E*, January 1971, p. 3.

123 "Lucina—'Lourdes' of the Prjashev Eparchy," *BCW*, August 8, 15, and 22, 1971, p. 14, pp. 14 and 17, pp. 14 and 19.

124 "Our Spiritual Heritage in Holy Union—1646 April 24 1971," *BCW*, December 26, 1971, p. 15.

125 "Prof. Joseph Bokshay: Our Great Artist and Octogenerian (1891-1971)," *BCW*, October 17, 1971, pp. 10 and 20; *ECL*, October 31, 1971, pp. 6-7.

126 "Rev. N. Petrashevich—Promoter of Our Music: On The 30th Anniversary of his Priesthood," *BCW*, April 18, 1971, pp. 14-15.

127 Translation of Alexander Duchnovich, *The History of the Eparchy of Prjašev*. Analecta OSBM, Series II, Section 1: Opera, Vol. XXV. Rome, 1971, viii, 102 pp.

128 "Vasyliiany—nosiï uniïnykh idei na Zakarpatti," *Svitlo*, XXIV, 4 and 5 (Toronto, 1971), pp. 137-139 and pp. 184-186; *Analecta OSBM*, VII (XIII), 1-4 (Rome, 1971), pp. 272-282.

1972

129 "Chirotony of Bishop Bachinsky," *P-E*, July 1972, p. 4.

130 "Duchnovich's *History of the Eparchy of Prešov* Published," *ECL*, January 30, 1972, p. 5.

131 "Our Tribute to Bishop John Bradach, 1732-1772," *BCW*, July 19, 1972, pp. 15 and 19.
     (2) "Bishop Bradach Renews the Fight for Independence," *BCW*, July 9, 1972, pp. 15 and 19.
     (3) "The Imperial Court in Support of Our Cause," *BCW*, July 16, 1972, pp. 15 and 19.
     (4) "Bishop Bradach Victim of Our Cause," *BCW*, July 23, 1972, pp. 15 and 17.
     (5) "Vindication of Bradach by Bishop Bachinsky," *BCW*, July 30, 1972, p. 10.

132 "V oboronï chesty Vladyky Goidycha," *Ameryka*, September 1, 1972, p. 2.

133 "Blazhennoi pamiat'i o. Polykarp Bulyk, ChSVV," *Svitlo*, XXXV, 1 (Toronto, 1972), pp. 25-27.

1973

134 "Bishop Basil Takach Devoted Shepherd," *ECL*, May 13, 1973, pp. 6-7.

135 "Restoration of the Greek Catholic Church in Czechoslovakia," *The Ukrainian Quarterly*, XXIX, 3 (New York, 1973), pp. 282-296.

136 "Tribute to Our Martyred Bishop Romzha (Twenty-Fifth Anniversary of his Death)"
(1) "Political Situation," *BCW*, March 11, 1973, p. 15.
(2) "Early Vocation to the Priesthood," *BCW*, March 18, 1973, p. 15.
(3) "Plans to Become a Missionary," *BCW*, March 25, 1973, p. 15.
(4) "Consecrated Bishop," *BCW*, April 1, 1973, p. 15.
(5) "Defender of the Church," *BCW*, April 8, 1973, p. 15.
(6) "A Good Shepherd—He Laid Down his Life," *BCW*, April 15, 1973, p. 15.

1974

137 "Anatolii Kralyts'kyi ChSVV, iak istoryk (1835-1894)," *Analecta OSBM*, Section II, Series 2, IX (XV), 1-4 (Rome, 1974), pp. 276-292.

138 "Bishop Hopko Septuagenarian," *BCW*, April 28, 1974, p. 9.

139 "Bishop Peter Gebey: A Beloved Shepherd," *BCW*, August 25, September 1, 8 and 15, 1974, p. 9, p. 5, p. 9 and p. 9.

140 "Bishop Nyaradi— 'Man of God'—110th Anniversary of his Birth," *BCW*, November 10, 1974, p. 8.

141 "Canon Joseph Djulay Dead 1882-1973," *BCW*, July 7, 1974, p. 3.

142 *"Nekroloh o. Liudovyka L. Min'i, ChNIz," *Lohos*, IV (Saskatoon, Sask., 1974), pp. 277-280.

143 "100th Anniversary of the Birth of Msgr. Augustine Voloshin," *BCW*, April 12, 1974, p. 8.

144 *Our Past and Present—Historical Outlines of the Byzantine Ruthenian Metropolitan Province in the USA.* Pittsburgh: Byzantine Seminary Press, 1974, viii and 60pp.

145 "Pam'iati Ieromonakha L.Min'i, ChNIz," *Svoboda*, December 18, 1974, p. 4.

146 "Vladyka Dionysii Niaradi: storichcha ioho narodzhennia (1874-1940)," *Shliakh*, December 12, 1974, pp. 2-3.

147 "Vasyliians'ki protoihumeny na Zakarpatt'i," *Analecta OSBM*, IX (XV), 1-4 (Rome, 1974), pp. 152-166.

148 "Virnyi syn i bat'ko Sribnoi Zeml'i," *Svitlo*, XXVII, 3, (Toronto, 1974), pp. 97-99.

1975

149 "Bat'ko Voloshyn v oboroni prav Hreko-Katolyts'koï tserkvy," *Svitlo*, XXXVIII, 10 and 11 (Toronto, 1975), pp. 324-330 and 383-384.

150 "Canon Alexander Mikita, S.T.D.: Our Liturgist (1855-1910)," *BCW*, May 25, 1975, pp. 8 and 10.

151 "Father A. Kocak, O.S.B.M.—Author of Our First Grammar (1737-1800)," *BCW*, April 13, 1975, p. 9.

152 "Father Kralickij—Awakener of Our People: 140th Anniversary of his Birth, 80th of his Death," *BCW*, February 16, 1975, p. 8.

153 "Father Kralickij—Our Historian: 140th Anniversary of his Birth, 80th of his Death," *BCW*, February 23, 1975, p. 8.

154 "Ignominious 'Synod' of Prjashev (1950—April 28—1975)," *BCW*, April 27, 1975, p. 8.

155 "Iz sviatymy upokii: pam'iati o. d-ra Liudovyka Min'i," *Svitlo*, XXVIII, 3 (Toronto, 1975), pp. 94-96.

156 "Our Academician—Reverend Basil Dovhovich (1783-1849)," *BCW*, June 1, 1975, p. 8.

157 "Our Pride—Artist Hric-Erdelyi (1891-1955)," *BCW*, July 20 and 27, 1975, pp. 8-9 and pp. 6-7.

158 "A Tribute to Our Martyred Bishop Gojdich," *BCW*, September 7, 1975, p. 8.

159 "Tribute to Our Norwegian Friend, Björnstjerne Björnson," *BCW*, June 8, 1975, p. 4.

160 "25th Anniversary—Forced Liquidation of the Eparchy of Muka-chevo, 1949—August 28—1974," *ECL*, March 9, 1975, p. 6.

161 "The Union of Uzhorod Liquidated," *BCW*, February 23, 1975, p. 4; *ECL*, March 2, 1975, pp. 11-12.

1976

162 "At the Trial of Bishop Gojdich," *BCW*, February 26, 1976, p. 8.

163 "Father Kubinyi Observes His Silver Anniversary," *BCW*, May 16, 1976, pp. 1 and 3.

164 "Father Peter Oros—Our Martyr: He Died for the Faith in 1953," *BCW*, July 25, 1976, pp. 11 and 13.

165 "From the Diary of Our Underground Priest," *BCW*, August 22, 29, September 5 and 19, 1976, p. 8, p. 5, p. 5, and p. 8.

166 "Higher Education in Humility—Or How A Bishop Mended Mattresses," *BCW*, September 12, 1976, p. 8.

167 "Historical Background of Carpatho-Ruthenians in America," *Ukraïns'kyi istoryk*, XIII, 1-4 (New York and Munich, 1976), pp. 87-102 and XIV, 1-2 (1977), pp. 70-84.

168 "In Blessed Memory of Our Bishop-Confessor Basil Hopko," *BCW*, August 15, 1976, p. 3.

169 "Liquidation of the Greek-Catholic Church in Subcarpathia," *BCW*, October 17, 24, 31, November 7 and 14, 1976, p. 8, p. 8, p. 4, p. 8 and p. 8.

170 "Pamiati Vladyky stradnyka Vasylia Hopka," *Shliakh*, August 29, 1976, p. 2.

171 "Pomer ispovidnyk Viry, Vladyka Vasyl' Hopko," *Ameryka*, August 6, 1976, pp. 2-3.

172 "Rev. Emil Bokshay Fell Asleep in the Lord (September 15, 1889—May 9, 1976)," *BCW*, May 30, 1976, p. 3.

173 "Stately Burial of Bishop Hopko," *BCW*, October 10, 1976, p. 4.

174 "They Died for their Faith," *BCW*, July 18, 1976, p. 3.

175 "Tribute to Archdean John Flenyko (1872-1976)," *BCW*, February 1, 1976, p. 8.

176 "Tribute to Irene Nevickyj-Burik (1876-1965)," *BCW*, June 3 and 20, 1976, p. 8 and p. 8.

1977

177 "Artist Ihor E. Hrabar of Ruthenian Descent," *BCW*, October 23, 1977, p. 5.

178 "Bishop Andrew Bachinskyj (1743-1809)," *BCW*, November 27, 1977, pp. 9-10.

179 "Bishop Firczak's Legacy on the 65th Anniversary of his Death," *BCW*, September 11, 1977, p. 10.

180 "Bishop Michael Manuel Olshavskyj, OSBM (1743-1767)," *BCW*, November 20, 1977, p. 7.

181 "Canon Andrew Baludianskyj—Our Historian (1807-1853)," *BCW*, October 2, 1977, p. 2.

182 "Canon Theodore Rojkovich—Defender of the Ruthenian People," *BCW*, September 25, 1977, p. 10.

183 "A Great Jubilee for the Eparchy of Krizhevtsi (1777-1977)," *BCW*, July 31, 1977, p. 7.

184 "In Commemoration of Bishop Basil Popovich," *BCW*, September 18, 1977, pp. 10 and 12.

185 "In Memory of Bishop Dudas (1902-1972)," *BCW*, October 30, 1977, p. 10.

186 "Most Reverend Anthony Papp (1912-1924)," *BCW*, December 4, 1977, p. 10.

187 "Msgr. Alexander Chira—Our Confessor Octogenarian," *BCW*, May 1, 1977, p. 8.

188 "Msgr. B. Shereghy's Literary Contribution," *BCW*, July 24, 1977, p. 8.

189 *Our Martyred Bishop Romzha*. Pittsburgh: Byzantine Seminary Press, 1977. 30pp.

190 "200 roku Kryzhevskoho Vladychestva (1877-1977)," *BCW*, August 7, 1977, p. 4.

191 "Silver Anniversary of Bishop Bukatko," *BCW*, August 14, 1977, p. 8.

192 "The 200th Anniversary of the Chapter of the Eparchy of Mukachevo," *BCW*, August 28, 1977, p. 8.

193 "Tribute to Our Artist Nicholas Jordan (1892-1977)," *BCW*, September 4, 1977, p. 8.

194 "Fiftieth Anniversary of the Eparchial Synod in Prjashev," *BCW*, October 16, 1977, p. 6.

195 "Fly Our Ruthenian Song, Fly (Tribute to our Musician George Kostiuk)," *BCW*, December 11, 1977, p. 6.

196 "Tribute to Rev. Emillian Mustyanovich (1877-1947)," *BCW*, December 18, 1977, p. 9.

1978

197 "Bishop Alexis Pocsy—A Romanian," *BCW*, January 15, 1978, p. 6.

198 "Commemorating Our Historian, Rev. John Dulyshkovich (1815-1883)," *BCW*, February 26, 1978, p. 9.

199 "Father A. Duchnovich Ruthenian, Not Russian!," *BCW*, April 23, 1978, pp. 5-6.

200 "Fine Tribute to Rev. Michael Luchkay on the 135th Anniversary of his Death," *BCW*, May 7, 1978, p. 9.

201 "In Memory of Bishop A. Stojka on the Thirty-Fifth Anniversary of his Death," *BCW*, May 28, 1978, p. 9.

202 "In Memory of Father Alexander Mitrak-Materyn (1837-1913)," *BCW*, January 23, 1978, p. 8.

203 "In Memory of Vicar Michael Balog of Maramorosh," *BCW*, October 8, 1978, p. 7.

204 "The Most Reverend Basil Takach, D.D.: First Carpatho-Ruthenian Bishop in the U.S.A., 1924-1948," in Basil Shereghy, ed. *The United Societies of the U.S.A.: A Historical Album Compiled on the Occasion of the Seventy-fifth Anniversary of the United Societies.* McKeesport, Pa: n.n., 1978, pp. 27-34.

205 "Most Rev. John J. de Camillis, O.S.B.M. (1689-1706)," *BCW*, May 21, 1978, p. 9.

206 "The Most Reverend Soter Stephen Ortynskyj, O.S.B.M., D.D.: First Byzantine Catholic Bishop in U.S.A., 1907-1916," in Basil Shereghy, ed. *The United Societies of the U.S.A. A Historical Album Compiled on the Occasion of the Seventy-Fifth Anniversary of the United Societies.* McKeesport, Pa., 1978, pp. 23-27.

207 "SS.Cyril and Methodius and the Christianization of the Slavs," in Basil Shereghy, ed. *The United Societies of the U.S.A. A Historical Album Compiled on the Occasion of the Seventy-fifth Anniversary of the United Societies.* McKeesport, Pa., 1978, pp. 88-97.

208 "Tribute to a Great Carpatho-Ruthenian, Archpriest Basil Hadzhega, S.T.D.," *BCW*, March 12, 1978, p. 10.

209 "Tribute to Our Outstanding Educator, Rev. Demetrius Popovich (1899-1968)," *BCW*, August 6, 1978, p. 8.

210 "Tribute to Professor Augustine Stefan on his 85th Birthday,"
BCW, February 19, 1978, p. 8.

1979

211 "Administrator of the Mukachevo Eparchy, Nicholas Murany,
Died," *BCW*, February 25, 1979, p. 5.

212 *Bishop Basil Hopko, S.T.D.: Confessor of the Faith (1904-1976).*
Pittsburgh: Byzantine Seminary Press, 1979, 36pp.

213 *The Bishops of the Mukachevo Eparchy, with Historical Outlines.*
Pittsburgh: Byzantine Seminary Press, 1979, vi and 88pp.

214 "Centenary Celebration in Honor of of the Most Reverend Basil
Takach," *BCW*, September 30, 1979, pp. 6-7.

215 "Liquidation of the Mukachevo Eparchy in 1949," *BCW*, September
2, 1979, p. 8.

216 "Priashivs'kyi vladyka Iosyf Gaganets'—Vizytator oo. Vasyliian,"
Analecta OSBM, Series II, Section 2, X (XVI), 1-4 (Rome, 1979),
pp. 379-393.

217 "Some Documents Concerning the 'Bradač Affair'," *Analecta
OSBM*, Series II, Section 2, X (XVI) 1-4 (Rome, 1979), pp.
221-228.

218 "The Tenth Anniversary of the Byzantine Metropolitan Province
(1969-1979)," *BCW*, June 3, 1979, pp. 6-7.

219 "Tribute to a Confessor of the Faith, Most Rev. Basil Hopko,
S.T.D.," *BCW*, May 6, 1979, pp. 4 and 13.

220 "U 30-tu richnytsiu nasylnoï likvidatsiï hreko-katolytskoï tserkvy na
Zakarpatt'i," *Shliakh*, October 14, 1979, pp. 2-3.

221 "Zhytt'evyi shliakh sviatoho Vasyliia Velykoho," *Svitlo*, XLII, 12
(Toronto, 1979), pp. 425-426.

1980

222 *Apostol Khrystovoho Sertsia—zhyttiepys ierom. Khrystofora Mys'kova, ChSVV. Rome: Basilian Press, 1980, 95pp.

223 Bishop Paul P.Gojdich, OSBM: Confessor for Our Times. Pittsburgh: Byzantine Seminary Press, 1980, 39pp.

224 "From the Life of Bishop Gojdich, O.S.B.M., 1888-1960," BCW, June 22, 1980, p. 5
(2) "Bishop Gojdich Continued to Live as a Monk ," BCW, June 29, 1980, p. 5.
(3) "The Charitable Heart of Bishop Gojdich," BCW, July 6, 1980, p. 5.
(4) "Prisoner of Jesus Christ," BCW, July 13, 1980, p. 5.
(5) "An Eyewitness to the Trial of Bishop Gojdich," BCW, July 20, 1980, p. 2.
(6) "The Prison Life of Bishop Gojdich," BCW, August 10, 1980, p. 5.
(7) "Finale of a Great Life," BCW, August 17, 1980, p. 3.
(8) "Finally Buried in His Cathedral Church," BCW, August 24, 1980, pp. 6-7.

225 "Thirtieth Anniversary of Action 'P' in Czechoslovakia," BCW, June 8, 1980, pp. 6-7.

226 *"V 30-ti rokovyny nasyl'stva nad nashoiu tserkvoiu na Priashivshchyni," Shliakh, June 8, 1980, pp. 2-3.

227 *"Vladyky-Ispovidnyky Sribnoï zemli," in Kalendar Svitla na 1980 rik. Toronto: Basilian Fathers, 1979, pp. 75-85.

1981

228 "Archbishop Kociscko's Silver Jubilee of Episcopal Service," BCW, October 25, 1981, pp. 6-8.

229 "Heroic Faith of Our Three Bishops in Subcarpathia," BCW, July 12, 1981, pp. 5 and 7.

230 "In Search of St. Methodius' Tomb," *BCW*, May 31, June 7 and 14, 1981, p. 9, p. 8 and p. 8.

231 "Msgr. Dunda, A True Champion of Christ," *BCW*, October 18, 1981, p. 2.

232 "On the Sixtieth Anniversary of the Basilian Sisters," *BCW*, August 9, 1981, pp. 5 and 8-9.

233 *"Ostanni dni Vladyky-muchennyka T.Romzhi," *Shliakh*, August 12, 1981, pp. 4 and 6-7.

234 "Our Three Modern Bishop-Confessors of the Carpatho-Ruthenian People," *BCW*, February 15, 1981, pp. 6-7.

235 "Recalling the Ordination of the Most Rev. Stephen J. Kocisko, D.D. (1941—March 30—1981)," *BCW*, April 5, 1981, p. 2.

236 "SS. Cyril and Methodius—Co-Patrons of Europe," *BCW*, May 17 and 24, 1981, pp. 6-7 and pp. 6-7.

237 "Spomyny pro Khrystovo viaznia Vladyku Goidycha," *Ameryka*, February 24, 25 and 26, 1981, pp. 2 and 4, pp. 2 and 4.

238 *"335-richchia Uzhhorods'koï uniï," *Shliakh*, May 31, 1981, pp. 4 and 7.

239 *"Vladyka Romzha—nepokhytnyi svidok sv. Iednosty," *Shliakh*, May 24, 1981, pp. 3 and 6.

1982

240 "In Commemoration of Bishop Dudas," *BCW*, October 10, 1982, pp. 6-7.

241 *Ispovidnyky viry nashoï suchasnosty (prychynok do martyroloha UKTserkvy pid Sovitamy).* Ukraïns'ka dukhovna biblioteka, no. 60. Toronto and Rome: Basilian Fathers, 1982, 332pp.

242 "Last Day of Our Martyred Bishop Theodore Romzha," *BCW*, November 7, 1982, pp. 5 and 8.

243 "Na vichnu pam'iat' Vladyky Muchennyka Preosv. Teodora Romzhi," *Svitlo*, XLV, 6, 7-8, 9, 10, 11, 12 (Toronto, 1982), pp. 222-224, 261-262, 301-302, 339-341, 374-380 and 374-380.

244 *"Storichchia narodyn o. Kyryla Fedelesha (1881-1950)," *Shliakh*, February 21, 1982, p. 7.

245 *"Storichchia obnovlennia Vasiliians'koho Chynu," *Ameryka*, June 23, 24, 25, 29, 30 and July 1, 1982, pp. 2 and 3, p. 2, pp. 2 and 4, p. 2, and pp. 2-3.

246 "35th Anniversary of the Martyrdom of Bishop Theodore G. Romzha, D.D., Martyred Bishop of Uzhorod, November 1, 1947," *BCW*, November 7, 1982, pp. 3-4.

247 "Tribute to a Great Son of the Ruthenian People—Canon John Kizak," *BCW*, September 26, 1982, p. 3.

248 "Vasyliians'ka Provintsiia sv. Mykolaia na Zakarpatti," *Analecta OSBM*, XI XVII, 1-4 (Rome, 1982), pp. 131-164.

249 *"85-richchia Khrystovoho Ispovidnyka Oleksandra Khiry," *Shliakh*, February 28, 1982, pp. 7-8.

250 *"85-richchia Khrystovoho Ispovidnyka Oleksandra Khiry," *Svitlo*, XLV, 5 (Toronto, 1982), pp. 183-185.

1983

251 "Bishop A. Stojka—Father of the Poor," *P-E*, May-June, 1983, p. 3.

252 "Bishop Alexander Chira Dead (1897-1983)," *ECL*, June 19, 1983, p. 6; *P-E*, June 1983, p. 3.

253 "Bishop Alexander Chira Dies for the Faith," *BCW*, June 19, 1983, pp. 5 and 8.

254 "Bishop John Bradač: The Last Basilian in the Mukachevo Episcopal See (1732-1772)," *Orientalia Christiana Periodica*, XLIX, 1 (Rome, 1983), pp. 130-152.

255 "First Carpatho-Ruthenian Printed Primer—('*Bukvar*')," *ECL*, May 22, 1983, p. 3.

256 *"Na zaslanni upokoïvsia taiemno imenovannyi Mukachivs'kym Vladykoiu Iepyskop Oleksander Khira," *Ameryka*, June 9, 1983, pp. 1-2; *Shliakh*, June 26, 1983, pp. 5-6; *Svitlo*, XLVI, 10 (Toronto, 1983), pp. 336-338.

257 "Our Martyred Bishop Gojdich: Lest we Forget—July 19, 1960," *BCW*, July 17, 1983, p. 1.

258 "Soviet Prisoner Remembers Our Confessor Alexander Chira," *BCW*, June 19, 1983, pp. 6-7.

259 "Vasyliany pid bil'shovykamy," *Svitlo*, XLVI, 3, 4, 5, 6, 7-8, 9, 11 and 12 (Toronto, 1983), pp. 107-108, pp. 145-146, pp. 181-182, pp. 221-222, pp. 258-259, pp. 289-299, pp. 378-380 and pp. 419-420.

1984

260 "Church in Silence Raises its Voice," *BCW*, March 25, 1984, pp. 6-8.

261 "The First Byzantine Rite Priest in the USA [Rev. E. Burik] 1883," *BCW*, December 30, 1984, pp. 13-14.

262 "Joseph Terelya—Our Most Recent Confessor of the Faith," *BCW*, April 8, 1984, pp. 6-9.

263 "The Last Days of the Unforgettable Bishop Alexander Chira," *BCW*, June 3, 1984, pp. 6-8.

264 "Remembering the Death of Father John J. Satmarij, OSBM," *BCW*, November 4 and 18, 1984, pp. 6-7 and pp. 6-7.

265 "Uzhorod—The Cradle of Subcarpathian Choral Music," *BCW*, April 22, 1984, pp. 7-10.

266 *"V pershu richnytsiu smerty o. Vasylia Laria (1892-1983)," *Ameryka*, January 6 and 10, 1984, pp. 2-3 and pp. 2-3.

267 *"Vasliiany pid bil'shovikamy," *Svitlo*, XLVII, 1, 2 and 3 (Toronto, 1984), pp. 18-19, pp. 61-62, and pp. 103-104.

268 *"Vladyka A. Bachyns'kyi—kandydat na Halyts'koho Mytropolyta (1732-1809)," *Shliakh*, December 23, 1984, pp. 5 and 7.

1985

269 "Ieromonakh Anatolii Kralyts'kyi, ChSVV," *Shliakh*, May 19, 1985, p. 4.

270 "Father Joseph Huha—An Underground Priest," *ECL*, December 15, 1985, p. 6.

271 "A Fitting Tribute to Bishop Alexander Chira," *BCW*, December 29, 1985, p. 5.

272 "In Commemoration of Bishop Paul P.Gojdich, OSBM: On the 25th Anniversary of his Death," *BCW*, July 14, 1985, pp. 6-7.

273 "Otets' M. Vavryk, ChSVV, iak istoryk Vasyliians'koho Chynu (1908-1984)," *Analecta OSBM*, Series II, Section 2, XII (XVIII), 1-4 (Rome, 1985), pp. 171-187.

274 "Otets' P. Bulyk, ChSVV—ispovidnyk viry," *Shliakh*, February 17, 1985, p. 6.

275 "The Martyrs and Confessors of the Byzantine (Greek) Catholic Church in Review," *BCW*, February 10 and 24, 1985, pp. 6-7 and pp. 6-8.

276 "Pys'mennyts'ka diial'nist' o. H. Kinakha, ChSVV," *Analecta OSBM*, Series II, Section 2, XII (XVIII), 1-4 (Rome, 1985), pp. 103-116.

277 "1100 lit vid smerty Sv. Metodiia," *Shliakh*, April 21, 1985, p. 3.

278 "You Shall Be Witnesses Unto Me," *Contribution to the Martyrology of the Byzantine Catholic Church in Subcarpathian Ruthenia*. Pittsburgh: Byzantine Seminary Press, 1985, 112pp.

279 "Zapysnyk o. H. Kinakha pro pochatky reformy na Zakarpatti,"
    Analecta OSBM, Series II, Section 2, XII (XVIII), 1-4 (Rome,
    1985), pp. 117-164.

280 "Zhadaimo Bat'ka Avhustyna Voloshyna," *Shliakh*, July 7, 1985,
    pp. 1 and 6.

281 "Zhyttevyi shliakh o. H. Kinakha, ChSVV (1888-1980)," *Analecta
    OSBM*, Series II, Section 2, XII (XVIII), 1-4 (Rome, 1985), pp.
    85-99.

1986

282 "In Remembrance of Msgr. A. Voloshin (1874-1945)," *P-E*,
    February 1986, p. 3.

283 "Joseph Terelya—Prisoner of Christ," *BCW*, January 12, 1986, pp.
    6-7.
    2. "Carpatho-Ruthenian Terelya's Letters from Communist Prison,"
    BCW, January 26, 1986, pp. 6-7.
    3. "Carpatho-Ruthenian Terelya's Sufferings for his Greek Catholic
    Faith," *BCW*, February 9, 1986, pp. 6-7.

284 "The Most Reverend Bishop Theodore Romzha, Martyr (April 24,
    1911—November 1, 1947)," *BCW*, September 7, 1986, pp. 6-7.

285 "Na spomyn Ep. S. Ortyns'koho," *Shliakh*, March 16, 1986, p. 1.

286 "Professor Augustine Stefan Dies," *P-E*, October 1986, p. 8.

287 "Testimony to Bishop Alexander Chira," *BCW*, September 7, 1986,
    p. 8.

1987

288 "Fortieth Anniversary of the Martyrdom of Bishop Romzha,"
    BCW, November 1, 1987, pp. 6-7.

289 "Joseph Terelya Finally Free," *BCW*, November 29 and December
    12, 1987, p. 6 and p. 6.

290 *"Tserkovna polityka madiariv na Zakarpatti," in *Zbirnyk na poshanu M. Chubatoho, Zapysky NTSh, CCD* (New York and Toronto, 1987), pp. 297-306.

291 "The Youth of Bishop Romzha," *P-E*, November 1987, p. 3.

1988

292 "Bishop Alexander Chira (1897-1983)," *BCW*, January 24, 1988, pp. 6-7.

293 *Bishop Alexander Chira: Prisoner of Christ*. Pittsburgh: Byzantine Seminary Press, 1988, vi and 30pp.

294 "Centennial of Bishop Paul J. Gojdich's Birth," *BCW*, July 10, 1988, pp. 6-7.

295 *"Cherneche zhyttia Kyïvs'koï Rusy v domonhols'kyi dobi," *Analecta OSBM*, Series II, Section 2, XIII (XIX), 1-4 (Rome, 1988), pp. 15-65.

296 *"Doba zanepadu ukraïns'koho chernetstva (pol. 13-ho do kintsa 16-ho stolittia)," *Analecta OSBM*, Series II, Section 2, XIII (XIX), 1-4 (Rome, 1988), pp. 66-91.

297 *"Documents Concerning the Visitation of the Basilian Fathers in Transcarpathia (1856-1858)," *Analecta OSBM*, Series II, Section 2, XIII (XIX), 1-4 (Rome, 1988), pp. 306-356.

298 "The Fifth Anniversary of Bishop Chira's Death," *BCW*, May 29, 1988, pp. 4-5.

299 *"Monasticism in the Ukrainian Church," *Analecta OSBM*, Series II, Section 2, XIII (XIX), 1-4 (Rome, 1988), pp. 378-404.

300 "The Origin of Monastic Life in Rus'-Ukraine," *Analecta OSBM*, Series II, Section 2, XIII (XIX), 1-4 (Rome, 1988), pp. 357-370.

301 "Storichchia narodzhennia Iep. P. Goidycha, ChSVV," *Shliakh*, August 14, 1988, p. 6.

1989

302 "Church Liquidated Forty Years Ago," *BCW*, August 6, 1989, pp. 6-8.

303 "The Church of Silence in Subcarpathia is Finally Heard," *BCW*, December 10, 1989, pp. 6-7.

304 "Sheptyts'kyi and the Carpatho-Ruthenians in the United States," in Paul R. Magocsi, ed. *Morality and Reality: The Life and Times of Andrei Sheptyts'kyi*. Edmonton, Alberta: Canadian Institute of Ukrainian Studies, 1989, pp. 363-374.

305 "Two Carpathian Greek Catholic Bishops Come Out into the Open," *BCW*, April 16, 1989, pp. 6-7.

306 "U sorokovu richnytsiu likvidatsiï Greko-Katolyts'koï Tserkvy na Zakarpatti," *Shliakh*, August 13, 1989, pp. 1 and 4.

307 "U sorokovu richnytsiu likvidatsiï Tserkvy na Zakarpatti," *Svitlo*, LII, 7-8 (Toronto, 1989), pp. 205-207.

1990

308 "Bishop Alexander Chira Fully Rehabilitated," *BCW*, September 16, 1990, p. 5.

309 "The Consecration of Bishop John Hirka," *BCW*, June 24, 1990, pp. 6-7.

310 "Ending Our Historic Pilgrimage in Prague," *BCW*, August 5, 1990, pp. 5-8.

311 "Father Stephen Papp, 1917-1990, Necrology," *BCW*, April 1, 1990, pp. 6-7.

312 "Historic Visit of the Graves of Our Confessors," *BCW*, June 10, 1990, pp. 6-7.

313 "Our Pilgrimage to the Carpathian Land," *BCW*, July 8 and 22, 1990, pp. 5-8 and pp. 6-7.

314 "Tribute to Father Michael Luchkay—Bicentennial of his Birth (1789-1843)," *BCW*, February 4, 1990, pp. 6-7.

315 "U 30-tu richnytsiu muchenyt'skoï smerty priashivs'koho iepys-kopa-ispovidnyka Pavla Goidycha, ChSVV," *Svitlo*, LIII, 10 (Toronto, 1990), pp. 353-354.

316 "Visti z Zakarpattia," *Shliakh*, March 25, 1990, pp. 4-5.

Maps

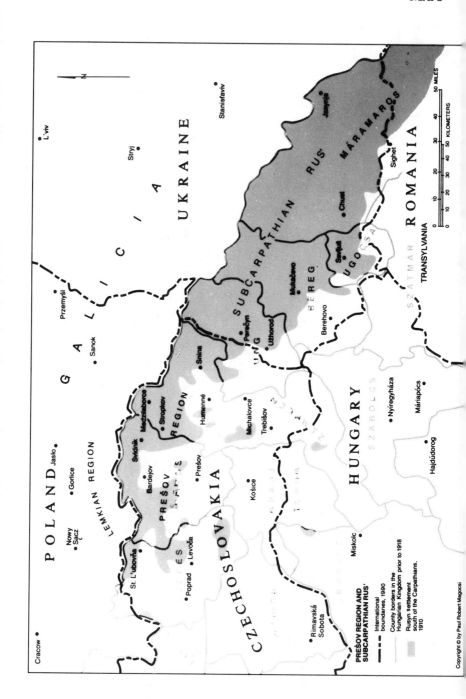

PREŠOV REGION AND
SUBCARPATHIAN RUS'

International
boundaries, 1990

County borders in the
Hungarian Kingdom prior to 1918

Rusyn settlement
south of the Carpathians,
1910

Copyright © by Paul Robert Magocsi

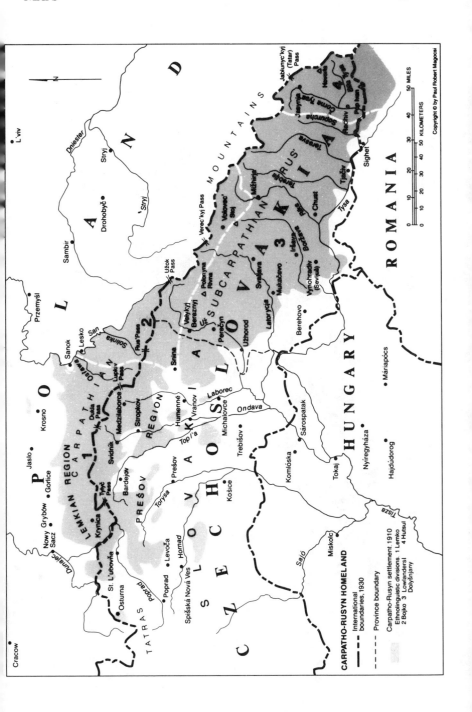

CARPATHO-RUSYN HOMELAND

— ▬ International
boundaries, 1930

— — — Province boundary

Carpatho-Rusyn settlement 1910
Ethnolinguistic divisions   1 Lemko
2 Bojko   3 Lowlanders(4 Hutsul
Dolyšnjany

Copyright © by Paul Robert Magocsi

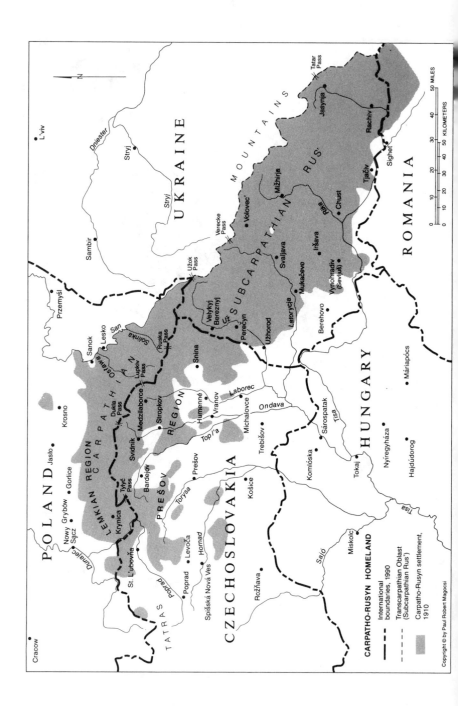

CARPATHO-RUSYN HOMELAND

International
boundaries, 1990

Transcarpathian Oblast
(Subcarpathian Rus')

Carpatho-Rusyn settlement,
1910

Copyright © by Paul Robert Magocsi

The History of the Church
in Carpathian Rus'

I love You, O Lord, my strength;
The Lord is my rock and my refuge.

—Motto of Bishop Romža

1947-1967

To the Lasting Memory of

Teodor Jurij Romža

Martyred Bishop of Mukačevo

on the Twentieth Anniversary of His Heroic Death

The Author

A Former Student

Dedicates this Book

Preface

Carpathian Rus' endured more than a thousand years of Hungarian rule. In spite of this, the Carpatho-Rusyns preserved their national and religious identity and retained their distinctiveness. Indeed, the centuries-long struggle only served to temper the spirit of this people and enable it to survive harsh persecutions and numerous attempts at denationalization.

Refusing to countenance a national and religious self-awareness on the part of the Carpatho-Rusyns, the Hungarians endeavored to deprive them of their history and deny their national individuality, as is evident from the assertion of Hungary's representative, Count S. Csáky, at the Paris Peace Conference in 1920: "The Ruthenian people of Hungary have no distinct history, no historical basis, because they lack a national consciousness."[1] Small wonder that under Hungarian rule, Carpathian Rus' remained an "unknown land" and the Carpatho-Rusyns a "forgotten brother" even to their countrymen in the Ukraine.

For the reasons mentioned above, the Hungarians saw to it that all their archives dealing with Carpathian Rus' remained inaccessible, that the population of this region remained shrouded in the forgotten past, and that its history was presented in such a manner in order to propound among the common people the misleading and historically unfounded epithet: *gens fidelissima*—people most loyal [to Hungary].

Under the pressure of magyarization at the end of the nineteenth century, there emerged a few Carpatho-Rusyn historians who wished to write at least an objective history of the Church in what has been called the "Silver Land"—Subcarpathian Rus'. But they were not permitted to go beyond the eighteenth century. Thus, for example, I. Duliškovyč had to break off his history with the death of Bishop Ivan Bradač (1772), because on instructions from the Hungarian authorities the magyarized bishop of Mukačevo I. Pankovyč "forbade him to proceed further." Professor A. Hodinka was able to take his account only as far as the era of bishop Andrij Bačyns'kyj (d. 1809), because archives containing materials on subsequent periods "were closed to him." Analogously, after publishing a long article on the struggle with the bishops of Eger in [the Hungarian journal] *Századok* (1884), the Reverend Jurij Žatkovyč was "silenced." He was able to publish articles in the Galician press, but only clandestinely. Even the Russian scholar, Professor Aleksej L. Petrov, who worked in the Budapest archives on grants from the Hungarian government, was unable to venture beyond the eighteenth century. At the request of his "patrons," he was to destroy "the historical basis" of Carpathian Rus' and consequently he attempted to date the historical beginnings of this region only from the fourteenth century.

After World War I, it seemed essential to write the history of Carpathian Rus' from the very beginning. This interest in the past grew, prompting the search for historical data in archives, but the principal archives remained in Hungarian hands. Thus, historians began to turn to local county and district archives. The Reverend Vasyl' Hadžega managed to gain access to the eparchial archive in Užhorod. Some materials from the archives of the Mukačevo monastery were also published. Still, no historian emerged to write the complete history of the Church in Carpathian Rus'.

Finally, after World War II, I was able to work in the Vatican archives in Rome. There, I was fortunate to discover a number of documents from the eighteenth century, which enabled me to write my study of the canonical erection of the Mukačevo eparchy (1956). My example inspired two other Carpatho-Rusyns who were then studying in Rome—the Reverend Julius Kubinyi and the Reverend Alexander Baran. They were joined by the Slovak Jesuit, the Reverend Professor Michael Lacko, a native of Slovakia. Unfortunately, the Reverend Kubinyi's study on the education of the clergy in Carpathian Rus' (which he defended at the Urban University in Rome in 1953) has not yet appeared in print. He is now working on the history of the canonical erection of the Prešov eparchy and hopefully this work will soon be published.[2]

A number of valuable studies by the Reverend Baran have already appeared. These include his investigation of relations between the Mukačevo eparchy and the Kiev metropolitanate (1960) and of the Máramaros eparchy (1962), a monograph on bishop Andrij Bačyns'kyj (1963), and numerous archival studies that appeared in the journals *Zapysky ČSVV (Analecta OSBM)* and *Orientalia Christiana Periodica* in Rome.[3] Also of major importance to the history of the Church in Carpathian Rus' is Professor Lacko's study on the Union of Užhorod (1955) and some of his archival publications in *Orientalia Christiana Periodica* and *Slovak Studies.*[4]

Unfortunately, Professor Lacko attempts to slovakize the church history of Carpathian Rus', especially that of the Prešov eparchy. Hence, I was also fortunate enough to interest the Reverend Basil Boysak, a fellow Carpatho-Rusyn, to study the history of the union. His work on the fate of the union in Carpathian Rus' appeared in English in 1963. His work on the unity of the Holy Church in the writings of Bishop Manuil Ol'šavs'kyj is also expected to appear.[5] Another study by the Reverend Kubinyi on the creation of the Prešov eparchy will also help to refute certain claims put forward by contemporary "slovakizers."[6]

In the course of writing biographies of Bishops Gojdyč (1961), Romža (1962), and Gebej (1963) and while preparing historical articles for *Svitlo* and *Ameryka*, I gathered many materials on the modern church history of Carpathian Rus', even though I did not have access to all existing archival sources. I also found helpful the works of such Soviet [and East European Marxist] historians as Ivan Kolomiec (1953, 1959), József Perényi (1957), L'udovít Haraksim (1961), Oleksa Myšanyč (1964), and Mychajlo Mol'nar (1965).[7] Thus, at last I felt able to publish this history of the church in Carpathian Rus'. My purpose is to enable the reader to obtain a true picture of the church and of religious life in the Silver Land, even if only in general terms. It is my hope that this work will fill, at least in part, a serious lacuna in Carpatho-Rusyn church historiography.

I dedicate this work to a great son of Carpathian Rus', Bishop Teodor Romža, on the occasion of the twentieth anniversary of his martyrdom. Like a bright meteor, he lighted the horizon of the Silver Land for a short time and then was abruptly extinguished. His unvanquished spirit, however, will continue to inspire all Carpatho-Rusyns with a sacred love of their people and their suffering Church.

Introduction

The purpose of this study is to examine the more important stages in the *external* history of the Church and of religious life in Carpathian Rus'. Hence, this is not a complete history of the Church in the region known as the Silver Land, but rather a history of the development of the Church's organizational structure.

The term Carpathian Rus' as used here does not refer only to that territory which was granted autonomy at the Peace Conference of Saint Germain in 1919 and was incorporated into Czechoslovakia as Subcarpathian Rus' (Podkarpatská Rus). Our use of the term embraces all Carpatho-Rusyn lands south of the Carpathians which until 1818 constituted a single ecclesiastical unit known as the Mukačevo eparchy. In this sense, Carpathian Rus' includes: (1) the former Czechoslovak province of Subcarpathian Rus', or Carpatho-Ukraine, which existed as an independent state in 1938-1939, and then in 1945 was annexed to the Ukrainian S.S.R. as the Transcarpathian (*Zakarpats'ka*) oblast; (2) the "Trans-Tisza region" (*Zatyssja*)—territory on the left bank of the Tisza (Tysa) river which was ceded to Romania after World War I; (3) the "Cis-Tisza region" (*Potyssja*)—territory west of the Tisza river, which became intensely magyarized at the end of the nineteenth century and remained part of post-Trianon Hungary; and (4) the Prešov Region (Prjašivščyna)—which, against the desire of the Carpatho-Rusyns, was placed under Slovak administration in 1919 and is today undergoing intense slovakization.[1]

In ecclesiastical-hierarchical terms, the Rusyn population of Carpathian Rus' has been organized as follows: (1) Subcarpathian Rus' and the southern portion of Zemplén county (in the Prešov Region) constituted the Mukačevo eparchy; (2) the Trans-Tisza region, originally part of the Mukačevo eparchy, became after 1919 a separate vicariate and in 1930 was incorporated into the Romanian Maramureş

(Máramaros) eparchy; (3) the larger portion of the Cis-Tizsa region was incorporated in 1912 into the Hungarian Hajdúdorog eparchy, while a smaller portion has since 1923 constituted the Miskolc apostolic exarchate; (4) the Prešov Region has since 1818 constituted the Prešov eparchy.

The Rusyn population of Carpathian Rus' is autochthonous. Antedating the arrival of the Magyars in Central Europe by a whole century, this population was constantly strengthened by the influx of settlers from territories north of the Carpathians. Despite the difficult national and cultural conditions in which the Carpatho-Rusyns lived during a whole millenium in the Hungarian Kingdom, the Hungarians were not able to divest this people of its distinct national character.[2] Carpathian Rus' has never comprised a single administrative unit within the borders of Hungary.[3] Between 1280 and 1321, the larger portion of the Silver Land belonged to the Galician-Volhynian state ruled by the Romanovyč dynasty.

The beginnings of Christianity in this region date to the times of SS. Cyril and Methodius (ninth century). The life of the Church was centered around the Basilian monastery of St. Nicholas on Černeča Hora near Mukačevo, from which the name of the Mukačevo eparchy is derived. For the Carpatho-Rusyns, the bishop was not only their archpastor, he was also their leader and the champion of the people's rights. The Holy Union aided the Carpatho-Rusyns in their unequal contest with the Hungarians by safeguarding the rights and privileges of the Catholic Church and providing the protection of the Holy See.

When the Hungarians became aware that union not only assisted the Carpatho-Rusyns in the religious sphere, but also supported their national and cultural aspirations, they did everything in their power to limit the rights and privileges of the Mukačevo bishops. Citing "the good of the Union" as a pretext, the Hungarians attempted to hinder the religious and cultural development of Carpathian Rus'. This ultimately led to a struggle for the independence of the Mukačevo eparchy which lasted until 1771, when the Holy See granted canonical confirmation to the eparchy. At that time, the territory under the jurisdiction of the Mukačevo eparchy included all Carpatho-Rusyn Catholics who lived in compact settlements or who were dispersed in the thirteen counties of what then comprised northern Hungary.[4]

The creation of an independent eparchy gave rise to a golden age in the region's religious and cultural life, initiated by Bishop Andrij Bačyns'kyj (1773-1809). This religious and cultural flowering of the Carpatho-Rusyn people profoundly disturbed the Hungarians. Resorting to the ancient Roman policy of "divide and conquer," they prevented the Mukačevo eparchy from becoming part of the Galician metropolitanate, which had been restored by the Apostolic See in 1807. Instead, the Mukačevo eparchy was gradually partitioned into smaller units. In 1818, a portion of the Mukačevo eparchy was formed into the Prešov eparchy;[5] in 1823, 72 of the Mukačevo eparchy's parishes were incorporated into the Oradea[6] eparchy in Romania; in 1853, 94 more parishes were attached to the Gherla eparchy;[7] and finally, in 1912, 76 parishes became the Hajdúdorog[8] eparchy in Hungary.

Despite the existence of four separate Greek Catholic eparchies on the territory of the Hungarian Kingdom by the beginning of this century, the Hungarians did not allow the Carpatho-Rusyns to unite into one metropolitanate. The Mukačevo, Prešov, and Hajdúdorog eparchies were subordinated to the Hungarian primate, the archbishop of Esztergom, as their metropolitan, while the Križevci eparchy was placed under the jurisdiction of the Roman Catholic archbishop of Zagreb. The aim of Hungary's political and ecclesiastical authorities was to divide the Carpatho-Rusyns, thereby preventing their full development in the religious and cultural spheres.

In the aftermath of World War I, the Carpatho-Rusyns were also divided by political borders. As a result, the threat of denationalization became very real in some Rusyn territories. Thus, for example, the 76 parishes incorporated into the Hajdúdorog eparchy and the 22 Rusyn parishes of the Miskolc exarchate which remained in Hungary are today completely magyarized. The Rusyns living in the Trans-Tisza region, that is, in the former Hungarian counties of Szatmár and part of Máramaros, which are now part of Romania, have become romanianized. A planned policy of slovakization has been under way for decades in the Prešov Region, which was ceded to Slovakia. Some authors already deny the existence of Carpatho-Rusyns in the Prešov Region, calling them instead Greek Catholic Slovaks.

During the interwar period, the Apostolic See attempted to implement the hierarchical unification of the Carpatho-Rusyn church in a single metropolitanate, at least on the territory of Czechoslovakia. There were plans to partition the Mukačevo eparchy into the Užhorod and Mármaros (or Chust) eparchies. The bishop of Užhorod was to become the metropolitan with suffragan bishops in Prešov and Chust to assist him. Unfortunately, the activity of various political interests and the outbreak of World War II put an end to these plans, and instead of the creation of a metropolitanate, both Carpatho-Rusyn eparchies were [after the war] forcibly liquidated by the Communists.

During the reign of Maria Theresa (1740-1780), many Carpatho-Rusyns from the Prešov Region settled in what was then lower Hungary—the Vojvodina (Bačka) that today is part of Yugoslavia. Their parishes were placed under the jurisdiction of the Križevci eparchy, which the Apostolic See established in 1777.

[After the 1880s], the large Carpatho-Rusyn emigration to the United States prompted the creation in 1924 of the Pittsburgh apostolic exarchate. Today, the Carpatho-Rusyns in the United States have a metropolitan province in Pittsburgh with three eparchies in Passaic, Parma, and Van Nuys. We will give a short history of the eparchies in the emigration at the end of this study.

CHAPTER ONE

The Beginnings of Religious Life

The beginnings of Christianity in Carpathian Rus' date back to the second half of the ninth century, being introduced there by the Slavonic apostles SS. Cyril and Methodius and their disciples. When the Magyars migrated across the Carpathians in 896, they already found evidence of Christian faith among the East Slavs inhabiting the territory of Carpathian Rus'. The steady influx of settlers from Galicia, Kievan Rus', and Podolia continued to strengthen the population of the region both in the ethnic and religious spheres. The newcomers from the northeast brought with them priests and monks who completed the Christianization of Carpathian Rus' in the eleventh and twelfth centuries.

From the very beginning, the Basilian monastery of St. Nicholas on Černeča Hora near Mukačevo served as the religious center of Carpathian Rus'. It is likely that the monks settled there as early as the reign of Hungary's king András I (reigned 1046-1061), who married Anastasia, the daughter of prince Jaroslav the Wise of Kiev (reigned 1019-1054). The new queen brought with her to Hungary many of her countrymen from Kievan Rus', including missionary monks, who settled on Černeča Hora. It was from here that the monks soon began spreading Christianity and organizing the religious life of Carpathian Rus'. Such were the origins of the Mukačevo eparchy.

As in the case of other dioceses of that period,[1] it is impossible to provide any precise data about the historical beginnings of the Mukačevo eparchy, since the first documented mention of a bishop of Mukačevo does not occur until the fifteenth century. However, there has survived among the people "an ancient and sacred oral tradition"[2] that the origins of the eparchy reach back to pre-Mongol times (before 1242). Moreover, "local traditions are usually reliable evidence of facts of the past about which there exist no written

13

records. It is frequently the case that subsequently discovered historical monuments corroborate popular tradition."[3]

The Mongol invasions devastated Carpathian Rus', and it was to be some time before life returned to normal. The monastery of St. Nicholas in Mukačevo also suffered, and it was not until the fourteenth century that it began to regain its original importance as a religious and cultural center. The revival occurred under prince Fedir Korjatovyč of Podolia (d. 1415), whom the Hungarian king appointed lord of Mukačevo and governor of Bereg county in central Carpathian Rus'. Prince Korjatovyč rebuilt the monastery and church on Černeča Hora and endowed the monastery with estates and some tithes.

In the second half of the fourteenth century, the Basilian monastery of St. Michael near Hruševo in eastern Carpathian Rus' began to increase its importance. It soon became the religious and cultural center for the entire Máramaros county. The monastery's patrons, the Romanian nobles Balica and Drag, endowed it generously and obtained for it the right of stauropegion—the privilege of being under direct authority of the ecumenical patriarch of Constantinople and not the local bishop. A patriarchal charter of 1391 exempted the Hruševo monastery from the jurisdiction of the bishop, and the monastery's *hegumen* (from the Greek *hegumenos*—abbot), Pachomij, became the exarch for the surrounding parishes. Soon the *hegumen*-exarch extended his authority over the entire Máramaros region, administering it "in the name of the patriarch."[4]

The first mention in historical documents of the bishop of Mukačevo occurs in 1491, when the Hungarian king UláSzló II (reigned 1490-1516) ordered all "Ruthenian parish priests under the jurisdiction of the church of St. Nicholas the Confessor in Mukačevo" to acknowledge Ivan as their bishop "in accordance with ancient custom."[5] Ivan, who is mentioned in documents from 1491 to 1498, tried to secure for himself as bishop of Mukačevo the monastery's revenues and to unify under his jursidiction all Carpatho-Rusyns, including those of the Hruševo exarchate in the Máramaros region. In the absence of later documents, the outcome of bishop Ivan's endeavors cannot be established. However, a 1551 decree issued by emperor Ferdinand I (reigned 1527-1564) recognizing the authority of bishop Vasylij I of Mukačevo over Máramaros suggests that by the beginning of the sixteenth century the Hruševo exarchate had ceased to exist.[6] In 1556, the Hruševo monastery also lost the right of stauropegion and was placed under the control of bishop Ilarion of Mukačevo.[7] Thus, at last, the whole of Carpathian Rus' was united hierarchically under the jurisdiction of the Mukačevo bishop.

The great political changes that took place in Hungary during the first half of the sixteenth century also affected the religious and cultural life of the Carpatho-Rusyns. In 1526, the Ottoman sultan Suleiman I the Magnificent (reigned 1520-1566) defeated the Hungarian army at Mohács. The Hungarian king Lájos II (reigned 1516-1526) also died in the battle, leaving no heir to the throne. The fate of the country was now in the hands of the Hungarian nobles, who split into two hostile camps. The so-called court party invited the Habsburgs of Austria to ascend the throne, while the opposing camp proclaimed as their king the courageous commander János Zápolyai. During the internecine struggle that ensued, the only ones to profit were the Turks, who in 1541 occupied Buda. Consequently, Hungary was divided into three parts: the Habsburgs took western Hungary; the central part of the country was occupied by the Turks; while the eastern regions formed the autonomous principality of Transylvania and proclaimed the son of Zápolyai, János Zsigmund, their ruler. Thereafter, the Transylvanian princes continually put forward their claim to the Hungarian throne and frequently fought against the Habsburgs.

It was the fate of Carpathian Rus' to become a corridor between the Habsburg and Transylvanian domains. As a result, until 1711, when the Habsburgs finally triumphed over the Transylvanian princes, Carpathian Rus' served as a battlefield between the two warring sides. Protestantism became firmly entrenched in the Transylvanian principality as an expression of Hungarian patriotism in the struggle against the Catholic Habsburgs. Following Protestant custom, the Transylvanian magnates meddled in church affairs in Carpathian Rus', which was then part of Transylvania.

Unfortunately, the residence of the bishop of Mukačevo and the monastery of St. Nicholas with all its holdings were in the hands of Protestant nobles. The latter seized the monastery's possessions for themselves and restricted the authority of the Mukačevo bishop. Confusion, abuses, and often violence became part of religious life in Carpathian Rus'. The fate of the bishop depended wholly on the will of the landlord of Mukačevo.[8]

With the western portion of their eparchy under Habsburg rule, the Mukačevo bishops sought a way out of their difficult situation by supporting whichever party was stronger. Thus, bishop Vasylij I supported the Habsburgs and in return was confirmed bishop by emperor Ferdinand I in 1551 and given control over all of the monastery's revenues.[9] As a supporter of the Transylvanian ruler, Vasylij's successor, bishop Ilarion, was forced to flee before the Habsburg imperial army to Hruševo. Thus, in 1556, Hruševo was placed under the jurisdiction of the bishop of Mukačevo,[10] and in 1558, princess Isabella, the wife of János Zápolyai, exempted the Mukačevo prelate and the monastery from paying taxes and from serfdom.[11] In order to win the support of the bishop of Mukačevo, who wielded great influence among the Carpatho-Rusyns, prince János Zsigmund granted him the right "to appoint his own successor."[12]

When in 1567 the imperial army retook the Mukačevo castle, and with it the monastery of St. Nicholas on Černeča Hora, bishop Vasylij II succeeded in regaining the favor of the Habsburgs. He was now able to visit the western counties of his eparchy, most of which were owned by the Catholic Drugeth family, which had supported the emperor.[13] Emperor Maximilian II (reigned 1564-1576) restored the ancient privileges of the Mukačevo monastery and offered his protection to both the bishop and the clergy.[14]

During the years of war and political turmoil, the Basilian monastery was plundered and destroyed several times. The princes of Transylvania, especially Zsigmund Rákóczi (reigned 1606-1608), persecuted the bishops of Mukačevo by confiscating all their possessions, including the right of the tithe. During this period, the Protestant rulers of Transylvania also destroyed all the founding charters and privileges. The bishop and the monks were left without any protection and support.

In 1597, bishop Vasylij II[15] went to Prague to inform the Habsburg emperor of his difficult circumstances. The bishop accused prince Zsigmund Rákóczi of having seized the villages of Bobovyšče and Lavky from the monastery, of plundering the monastery's possessions, and of continually meddling in the bishop's administration of his eparchy. The emperor summoned Rákóczi to answer the charges at a trial. Rákóczi won the case and threw Vasylij II into prison for "slander and wrongful accusations." He released the bishop only after the latter had paid him 700 gold florins in damages. Unappeased, Rákóczi dismissed Vasylij and in his stead named Havryjil as bishop.[16]

The monastery of St. Nicholas and the bishop of Mukačevo were thus stripped of their possessions for ever. Almost all their privileges were abrogated and the Mukačevo bishop became wholly dependent on the arbitrary will of the lord of Mukačevo, who arrogated to himself the right to appoint and dismiss bishops in accordance with Protestant custom. All this occurred during the years after the Union of Brest (1595) [in neighboring Poland]. Hence, failing to secure the protection of the Habsburg emperor, the bishops of Mukačevo were inclined to seek the protection of Rome.

CHAPTER TWO

The Movement for Union with Rome

April 24, 1646 marks the beginning of a new era in the history of the Church in Carpathian Rus'. That day, in the chapel of the Užhorod castle, 63 Carpatho-Rusyn priests returned to the belief of their ancestors and declared their confession of Catholic faith. This small seed gave birth to the mighty tree of the union in the shade of which all of Carpathian Rus' found refuge.

In accepting union with Rome, the Carpatho-Rusyns did not renounce their Eastern rite nor their age-old traditions. On the contrary, owing to the union, they were able to preserve their religious and ethnic distinctiveness for centuries to come. As a result, the union was opposed both by those who rejected it as well as by Hungarian Roman Catholics. As in Poland, the opponents of the union regarded it as a "betrayal" of the Rusyn national and religious heritage.

The Hungarian Roman Catholics who supported magyarization soon saw that the union served as a bulwark of the cultural and religious patrimony of the Carpatho-Rusyn people, and that instead of fostering it hindered the process of assimilation. Consequently, as elsewhere, the movement for union in Carpathian Rus' encountered difficulties, forcing the Uniate clergy to wage a persistent struggle not only against the dissidents, but also against the Roman Catholic Hungarians.

1. The First Attempts to Implement the Union with Rome

Towards the end of the sixteenth century, the famous Hungarian Jesuit missionary, Péter Pázmány,[1] initiated the Counter-Reformation in Hungary. Under his influence, many of Hungary's noble families were converted to the Catholic faith. Faced by the loss of the majority of the magnates, the Protestants began to propagate the Reformation among the common people. Since the Mukačevo do-

18

main had been in the hands of Protestant lords after 1588, strong Protestant influences were also evident in Carpathian Rus'. At that time, "Protestant ministers began to administer the entire Mukačevo eparchy. The local bishop could do nothing without their permission. These ministers even decided who would be chosen bishop of Mukačevo."[2]

The attempts of the Protestants to spread their ideas among the populace of Carpathian Rus' evoked strong opposition from the Hungarian Catholic nobility. With the help of Roman Catholic missionary monks (e.g., Franciscans, Conventuals, Paulites, and Jesuits), they endeavored to convert all of Carpathian Rus' to Catholicism. However, neither side was successful in its mission.[3]

Sensing the threat from both Protestantism and Roman Catholicism, the Carpatho-Rusyns grew even more strongly attached to their Eastern rite and their customs, thereby hoping to preserve not only their faith, but also their national identity. A great transformation occurred in the spiritual life of the Carpatho-Rusyns. Their rite became for them not only "the external expression of their faith," but also the vehicle of their national identity and the bulwark of their cultural and religious heritage. The Carpatho-Rusyns thus began to identify their rite with their faith and their faith with their nationality. Their Church became for them the Rusyn Church and their faith, the Rusyn faith.[4]

Under the dual pressure of Protestants and Roman Catholics, the Carpatho-Rusyns saw their only hope in union with Rome. Abiding by the decision of the Council of Florence (1439), Pope Clement VIII had assured the Ruthenians (Ukrainians and Belorussians) of Poland-Lithuania when they accepted the Union of Brest in 1596: "We will permit you to retain your rite and ceremonies, which in no manner contradict the wholeness of the Catholic faith and bilateral union."[5] As a result, the Union of Brest rapidly found a favorable response in Carpathian Rus'.

The movement for union with Rome in Carpathian Rus' was initiated by count György Drugeth III, a large landowner in the western part (Prešov Region) of Carpathian Rus'[6] who also owned estates in Poland. Count Drugeth had converted to Catholicism under the influence of Pázmány, and he fervently desired that his subjects should follow his example. Since the Jesuits, whom he had brought to his residence at Humenné, were not of great assistance to him insofar as the majority of his subjects were Carpatho-Rusyns, he decided instead to invite Uniate missionaries from Poland.

Drugeth appealed for assistance to the Roman Catholic bishop S. Sieczyński in Przemyśl, where the Ukrainian Uniate bishop Atanasij Krupec'kyj (1610-1652) was residing at the time. At the request of Siećiński, Krupec'kyj agreed to go to Carpathian Rus' to initiate a movement for union there. Thus, in 1613, bishop Krupec'kyj arrived in Humenné, where he was warmly welcomed by count Drugeth and given freedom to act as he deemed best.[7]

Krupec'kyj began his activity on behalf of the union among the Basilian monks and secular clergy in the domain of count Drugeth. The Protestant magnates did not permit him to extend his mission into eastern Carpathian Rus'. Moreover, in order to counteract the work of Krupec'kyj, the lord of Mukačevo, M. Eszterházy, appointed as bishop of Mukačevo the priest Sofronij Rečko, a bitter opponent of the union about whom little is known.

Bishop Krupec'kyj soon gained the support of the monks at the Monastery of the Holy Spirit in Krásny Brod (Krasnyj Brid)[8] and made this his base for work among the clergy. He assumed that the people would follow their pastors. Over a period of several months, Krupec'kyj won over more than 50 priests to the cause of union. His success was due largely to the fact that he was able to promise the priests of Carpathian Rus' the same conditions as those on which union had been accepted in Brest.

Count Drugeth had just built a new church at the Krásny Brod monastery. A miraculous icon of the Blessed Virgin was installed in the new house of worship. The icon, which had earlier been housed in a small chapel, drew thousands of pilgrims each year, including many from beyond the Carpathians. Drugeth, who was the patron of both the church and the monastery, took advantage of the presence of bishop Krupec'kyj to have the new church consecrated. And so on Pentecost, in 1614, the monastery's principal pilgrimage day when indulgences were granted and which drew as many as ten thousand pilgrims, Krupec'kyj resolved to proclaim the act of union with the Roman See.

This haste proved fatal to the cause. Although most of the clergy were ready to accept union, the people were completely unprepared to take this step. It required only one or two opponents to turn the populace against the union, and that is precisely what happened.

More than 13,000 pilgrims had gathered in Krásny Brod on the eve of Pentecost. They had come to pray to the miraculous icon of the Blessed Virgin and to see the new church. Late in the evening, bishop Krupec'kyj visited the church in order to make certain that everything was ready for the consecration the following day. Pilgrims crowded around the icon, making it impossible to decorate or clean the church. The bishop ordered the people to exit into the courtyard and locked the church doors. Enemies of the union took advantage of this situation to stir up the people by telling them that if they accepted the union they would no longer be able to worship at will.

The people began shouting curses and threatening the bishop. They shattered the windows of the church, broke down the doors, and attacked the bishop and his companions with canes. Had it not been for the count's guard, the angry mob would almost certainly have killed Krupec'kyj and his assistants. The proclamation of union had to be postponed until a later date.[9]

After the incident at Krásny Brod, bishop Krupec'kyj returned to Przemyśl, but continued to maintain contacts with those priests in Carpathian Rus' who supported union. He also served as an intermediary between the bishop of Mukačevo Vasyl' Tarasovyč (1634-1651) and the Kievan metropolitan Josyf Ruts'kyj (1613-1637) and became Tarasovyč's principal advisor in laying the groundwork for the act of union, which was proclaimed in Užhorod in 1646.

2. The Basilians as the Propagators of Pro-Union Ideas

The incident at Krásny Brod convinced the apostles of the union that it could not be imposed on the people from above until a proper "pro-union atmosphere" had been created. Metropolitan Ruts'kyj decided to use the Basilian order for this purpose. The opportunity came in 1623 when Petronij, a great advocate of the union, once again became bishop of Mukačevo.[10]

Petronij had been dismissed in 1600 from his bishopric by the lord of Mukačevo and had found refuge among the Basilians in Poland. He was accompanied into exile by a young Basilian monk named Ivan Hryhorovyč, who later completed his theological studies in Vilnius (Wilno). In Poland, the two met with Josyf Ruts'kyj and Josafat Kuncevyč and became converts to the idea of union. When bishop Petronij and Ivan Hryhorovyč were at last able to return to Carpathian Rus', metropolitan Ruts'kyj sent with them a young Basilian from Galicia, Vasylij Tarasovyč. Together they formed the first so-called "union triumvirate" in Carpathian Rus' and all three were eventually elevated to the episcopate: Petronij in 1623-1627 (for the second time); Ivan Hryhorovyč in 1627-1633; and Vasylij Tarasovyč in 1634-1651.

Bishop Petronij was not able to fulfill metropolitan Ruts'kyj's plan for the union with Rome. Physically and mentally exhausted, he died soon after returning to his eparchy. With the assistance of Hryhorovyč and Tarasovyč, he did, however, succeed in creating an atmosphere conducive to the union at the Mukačevo monastery. He also played a role in ensuring that his collaborator and former fellow exile, Ivan Hryhorovyč, OSBM, succeeded him as bishop on January 12, 1627.[11]

Hryhorovyč, too, had to exercise caution. On the one hand, prince Gábor Bethlén, the ruler of Transylvania and an ardent Calvinist, was adamantly opposed to the union. On the other hand, the poorly educated Carpatho-Rusyn clergy was slow to accept the notion of submission to Rome. After reaching an understanding with metropolitan Ruts'kyj,[12] Ivan Hryhorovyč travelled to Iaşi (Jassy) to be consecrated bishop by the Moldavian Orthodox metropolitan. He was accompanied by Vasylij Tarasovyč.

On their return voyage from Iaşi, bishop Ivan Hryhorovyč and Vasylij Tarasovyč visited Galicia, where at the beginning of February 1628, they met with metropolitan Ruts'kyj. Ruts'kyj described his meeting with Hryhorovyč in a report to Rome dated June 28, 1628:

> The Greek-rite bishop of Mukačevo from Hungary, whom the metropolitan of Walachia at the beginning of this year consecrated bishop of those areas of Hungary and Transylvania where numerous Rusyn settlements have existed since ancient times, passed through these parts at the beginning of February. The bishop is himself a Rusyn and is well known to me. He, too, is with us, although not yet perfectly so. With God's help, we will win him completely, maintaining our relations with him through our emissaries. Moreover, with his help, we will also be able to establish relations with the metropolitan and bishops of Walachia and Moldavia. Like our Meletij [Smotryc'kyj], he has also written a letter to the patriarch of Constantinople, which will serve as a pretext for breaking off relations with the latter. I am enclosing a copy of his letter [to the patriarch].[13]

There can be no doubt that during their meeting Ruts'kyj and Hryhorovyč discussed detailed plans for promoting the union in Carpathian Rus'. Ruts'kyj's expression that Hryhorovyč "is with us, although not yet perfectly so" clearly indicates that Hryhorovyč was already a Uniate in his heart, but needed to wait for the right moment to proclaim publicly the union with Rome.

From the letter cited above, we also learn of the plan to break off relations with the ecumenical patriarch of Constantinople, whom the Carpatho-Rusyns regarded as the formal head of their church. The patriarchal see of Constantinople was then occupied by the famous Cyril Lucaris (Kyrillos Loukaris),[14] who was intent on Calvinizing the Orthodox Church. On Ruts'kyj's advice, Hryhorovyč wrote a letter to the ecumenical patriarch Lucaris,[15] asking him to send his catechism. This would have served Hryhorovyč as a pretext to issue a public condemnation of Lucaris's Protestant teachings, to break off relations with him, and to proclaim the union with Rome. Lucaris, however, suspected Hryhorovyč of links with Ruts'kyj and ignored his request. Thus, the plan to proclaim the union in Carpathian Rus' on this occasion failed.

Unfortunately, the time that Hryhorovyč was able to spend working for the union in Carpathian Rus' was also brief, since he died in 1633. Before his death, however, he ensured the succession to the Mukačevo see for his colleague, the hieromonk Vasylij Tarasovyč.[16] With respect to Tarasovyč, I unreservedly agree with M. Lacko, who writes: "Although he did not publicly proclaim the union in his eparchy, he nevertheless sowed the seeds which God soon allowed to take root and grow."[17]

Immediately after his consecration, bishop Vasylij Tarasovyč (1634-1651) established relations with bishop Atanasij Krupec'kyj of Przemyśl, who had not ceased to work on behalf of the union in the western part of Carpathian Rus'.[18] There can be no doubt that the principal subject of their consultations was the question of the union with Rome. They both reached the conclusion that before anything could be done to further the cause of the union, bishop Tarasovyč would have to consolidate his authority over all the faithful in Carpathian Rus' by uniting them under the Mukačevo eparchy,[19] by gaining the support and trust of the clergy, and by securing his independence from the ruling princes who were opposed to the union.

In a short period of time, Tarasovyč won over the clergy and established his jursidiction over the whole of Carpathian Rus', including the Máramaros region. He then began collecting the necessary documents to enable him to prove his right to the possessions of the Monastery of St. Nicholas, which the ruler of the Mukačevo domain, prince György Rákóczi I, had seized in 1633. However, Tarasovyč was not in a position to oppose the "omnipotent" prince on his own; he therefore had to obtain the support of the emperor and the Catholic hierarchy. Towards this end, he decided to make a personal profession of Catholic faith.

But on December 13, 1640, before Tarasovyč was able to leave Mukačevo, he was arrested in the middle of the Divine Liturgy by the military commander of the Mukačevo castle, János Ballingh, and charged with attempting "to remove himself from under the control of the prince." All Catholic circles, including the emperor, rallied to Tarasovyč's defense. But Rákóczi was then already prepared to begin an uprising against the emperor and therefore ignored all appeals on Tarasovyč's behalf. He released the bishop only after the latter had signed a statement promising "to obey the will of the prince in all matters."[20]

Upon his release, Tarasovyč tried to establish contacts with the papal nuncio in Vienna, but his letters were intercepted. Ballingh once again imprisoned the bishop for "breaching his promise" and placed him on trial. The proceedings took place in February 1642. The court deprived bishop Tarasovyč of the right to administer the Mukačevo eparchy, stripped him of all his possessions, and banished him from the domains of prince Rákóczi.[21]

Dispossessed of his residence and the larger portion of his eparchy, Tarasovyč travelled to Vienna to seek the protection of the papal nuncio and the emperor. The nuncio's correspondence with Rome yielded no results and brought only the brief reply that the Apostolic See could not provide any material assistance to Tarasovyč and that he was to return to his eparchy and continue working on behalf of the union.[22]

Tarasovyč did not allow his misfortune to dissuade him from his mission. At the beginning of May 1642, in the presence of the emperor and his family, he submitted his profession of Catholic faith to the papal nuncio. Emperor Ferdinand III (reigned 1637-1657) assigned Tarasovyč a residence in the town of Nagykálló and 200 gold florins for his needs.[23] At the same time, the emperor sent his peace negotiator György Jakusics to Rákóczi to try to recover for Tarasovyč his residence in Mukačevo. Rákóczi disregarded the emperor's appeal[24] and named Ivan Jus'ko, an opponent of the union who had fallen under the influence of Calvinism, to head the Mukačevo see.[25] In the spring of 1643, Rákóczi began a new campaign against the emperor.

While residing in Nagykálló, bishop Tarasovyč administered the western portion of his eparchy which was under the control of Catholic magnates, and he continued his zealous campaign for the union among the clergy and the faithful. In a suprise attack on

Nagykálló, Rákóczi's rebels seized Tarasovyč and took him back to Mukačevo in chains. Once again a captive of prince Rákóczi, bishop Tarasovyč was compelled to sign a new statement renouncing the union and recognizing the authority of the prince in all matters. In exchange, Rákóczi reinstalled Tarasovyč as bishop of Mukačevo and returned part of the eparchial possessions to him.[26]

In absence of adequate information, it is impossible to determine Tarasovyč's intentions at the time he renounced the union. But one conclusion is certain: had Tarasovyč allowed the Mukačevo eparchy to pass out of his control at this time into the hands of Jus'ko, the cause of the union in Carpathian Rus' would have been delayed for another century. Through his "external apostasy," as the Carpatho-Rusyn historian Antal Hodinka calls it, Tarasovyč wanted to secure the Mukačevo see for his successor, bishop Partenij P. Petrovyč, OSBM.[27]

3. The Union of Užhorod of 1646

Upon his return to Mukačevo, Tarasovyč tried to regain control over the eastern portion of his eparchy, the major part of which lay within the domains of the Transylvanian Protestant magnates. For the western portion of his eparchy, he assigned the Basilian hieromonk Partenij Petrovyč, who had shared exile with him in Nagykálló and who was an ardent supporter of the union. It was in Užhorod where Petrovyč concentrated his work for the union. He was joined there by Havryjil Kosovyc'kyj, a Basilian from Galicia who had just completed his studies in Rome and had come to Užhorod from Vienna to assist Petrovyč. The two monks soon won the support of the clergy, primarily that of the monks at Krásny Brod, who helped them in spreading union ideas.

Finally, on April 24, 1646,[28] in the castle chapel of the Drugeth family in Užhorod, 63 priests from Carpathian Rus' made the Catholic profession of faith in the presence of the Roman Catholic bishop of Eger, György Jakusics (1642-1647). This solemn proclamation of union with Rome has come to be known in history as the Union of Užhorod.[29]. Thus, bishop Tarasovyč lived to see his dream at least partly fulfilled.

The act of union proclaimed in Užhorod was confirmed on May 14, 1648 by the primate of Hungary, archbishop György Lippay (1642-1666),[30] and in the fall of the same year by the national synod of Hungarian bishops in Trnava (Nagyszombat).[31] Finally, the cause of union received the necessary support of the Latin hierarchy and the Catholic magnates.

Sensing the approach of death, bishop Vasylij Tarasovyč—"by living word and in writing which he signed with his own hand"—appointed the Basilian monk Partenij Petrovyč his successor.[32] Without delay, Petrovyč went to Alba Iulia in Transylvania, where the Romanian Orthodox Metropolitan Stefan Simonovici (1643-1651) ordained him bishop.[33]

Carrying the charter of his chirotony, bishop Partenij hastened to Mukačevo, where the monastic community welcomed him with great joy. But princess Zsuzsanna Lorántffy[34] rejected Partenij's claim to the Mukačevo see and instead appointed Joannykij Zejkan'[35] to head the eparchy. The emperor's efforts on Partenij's behalf were to no avail and the new bishop was forced to return to Užhorod.[36] Thus, in effect, the Mukačevo eparchy was divided into two parts.

In 1660, princess Zsuzsanna and her successor, the reigning prince György Rákóczi II, both died, and the territories under Rákóczi's control passed to the young widow of György, princess Zsófia of the Catholic Báthory family. At last the Mukačevo domain, the seat of the Mukačevo eparchy, had a Catholic overlord. Partenij, whom Pope Alexander VII (1655-1667) had confirmed on June 8, 1655 as bishop of Mukačevo, expected that he would finally be able to recover his historic residence on Černeča Hora. But new complications arose.

Under the pretext of building a new church at the Černeča Hora monastery, princess Zsófia ousted the Orthodox bishop Joannykij Zejkan' from Mukačevo. Nonetheless, she refused to appoint bishop Partenij to the see. Partenij was a protégé of the emperor and Zsófia did not wish to relinquish to the emperor her right to nominate the bishop of Mukačevo. Instead, she asked the Kiev metropolitan to put forward a suitable candidate. The question of the Mukačevo episcopate was considered by Ruthenian bishops at a synod held in Žyrovyci in 1663. The synod agreed to appoint a bishop to the Mukačevo eparchy, but on condition that it would be placed under the jurisdiction of the metropolitan of Kiev.

Princess Zsófia, heeding the advice of her Latin clergy, refused to subordinate the Mukačevo see to the Ruthenian metropolitan of Kiev. It was her wish that the bishop of Mukačevo be subject to the Hungarian archbishop of Esztergom. When she heard, however, that the emissary of the Ruthenian episcopate in Rome, bishop Jakiv Suša, was seeking to have the Mukačevo eparchy incorporated into the Kiev metropolitanate, Zsófia hastily summoned bishop Partenij to Mukačevo in 1664 and placed the Monastery of St. Nicholas and its new church under his authority. This step assured the success of the Union of Užhorod.[37]

4. Obstacles on the Path toward the Union

Although it appeared at first that the installation of bishop Partenij in Mukačevo would assure the general acceptance of the union in Carpathian Rus', this was not the case. I have already mentioned that the principal opposition to union had come from the Protestant nobles. Once this obstacle had been removed, the union would be rapidly accepted throughout almost all of Carpathian Rus'. But then there ensued a struggle with the Latin hierarchy and the Catholic magnates for the right of the Uniate Church to implement the principal conditions of the Union of Užhorod. These included the right to retain its Eastern rite, the right to elect its own bishops, and equal privileges with the Latin clergy.

Despite the fact that the Hungarian primate, archbishop György Lippay, had confirmed these conditions and that the whole Hungarian episcopate had agreed to them at the synod of Trnava, the Uniate Church still had to wage a protracted struggle before it was able to implement the conditions of the union. Specifically, these conditions were:

(1) *Preservation of the Eastern rite.* This had always been and continues to be the principal demand of advocates of the union. For the Carpatho-Rusyns, the Eastern rite was a treasured part of their spiritual, cultural, and national heritage. Preserving this rite became for them a sacred duty. The ecumenical council of Florence, the synod of Brest, and the national synod of Trnava had all provided the Uniate Church with inviolable guarantees. Nonetheless, the situation proved different in practice.

The Latin-rite Catholics regarded the Uniates who wished to retain their own rite only as "half-Catholic" and considered the union as no more than a "transitional stage" on the way to Latinization. The principal proponent of these ideas was the Roman Catholic bishop of Eger, who from the outset of union strove to impose his authority over the Mukačevo eparchy. He was determined to effect the gradual incorporation of the Carpatho-Rusyn Catholics into the Latin rite as a means of magyarizing them.

In order to influence bishop Partenij to move in this direction, the bishop of Eger instructed the Jesuit fathers in Užhorod to act as Partenij's "advisors." However, instead of advising the bishop on how best to spread the cause of the union and to secure his return to Mukačevo, the Jesuits exerted pressure on Partenij and his retinue to attend the Latin-rite Divine Liturgy on Roman Catholic holy days, to make confession to them, and "to set an example for the faithful" by receiving Holy Communion in the Latin rite. The Jesuits also began instructing the Carpatho-Rusyn clergy in the "proper," that is, Latin manner of administering the Holy Sacraments.[38]

The Basilian priest Havryjil Kosovyc'kyj was put forward as an example of a "true Uniate." Disappointed at not having been named bishop of Mukačevo, Kosovyc'kyj refused to return to the monastery and, instead, offered his services to the bishop of Eger, Benedek Kisdi (1648-1660). Kisdi appointed him pastor of Humenné, where Kosovyc'kyj began to celebrate the liturgy in Latin. When news of this reached Rome, the Apostolic See forbade Kosovyc'kyj to celebrate the Liturgy in the Latin rite and ordered him to return to the monastery.[39] Backed by the bishop of Eger, Kosovyc'kyj disregarded the orders of Rome and continued to "convert" prominent citizens to the Latin rite.[40]

At first, bishop Partenij tolerated the injudicious zeal of his "advisors," because he needed their help to return to Mukačevo. But after his installation at the Monastery of St. Nicholas on Černeča Hora in 1664, he protested against these encroachments on the Eastern rite and appealed to the Apostolic See to take the necessary measures to ensure that Latin-rite Catholics did not hinder the Carpatho-Rusyns from "living in accordance with their own rite."[41] Even though Rome defended the traditional rite of the Carpatho-Rusyns, in practice it was the bishop of Eger, who was intent on Magyarizing all of Carpathian Rus' with the help of the Church and who always emerged the victor. The controversy over observing Roman Catholic holy days serves as a classic example of the unequal struggle that took place.[42]

Both the Jesuits and the Roman Catholic clergy insisted that in addition to their own, the Uniates also observe Roman Catholic holy days. As a result, believers in some parishes began celebrating both Eastern- and Latin-rite feasts. This was opposed by the landowners, because it left the peasants with fewer days in which to perform their statutory labor. Citing the landowners' complaints, the bishop of Eger, György Fényessy (1687-1699), ordered the Carpatho-Rusyns to observe only the Roman Catholic holy days and allowed them to celebrate just two or three Eastern-rite feasts a year, and only in those communities that were inhabited by a homogenous Rusyn population. In locations with mixed populations, only Roman Catholic holy days were to be observed.[43]

Fortunately, however, the bishop of Mukačevo at that time was the zealous and highly erudite Basilian monk of Greek birth, Josyf de Camillis (1689-1706). He was determined not to allow the Roman Catholic bishop of Eger to interfere in matters pertaining to his flock. Thus, although some magnates exerted pressure on their subjects in an attempt to force them to observe Latin holy days, the people, encouraged by their bishop, did not succumb. Consequently, both the clergy and the people were subjected to considerable persecution by the Roman Catholics.[44]

Realizing that he could not win against bishop de Camillis, the bishop of Eger decided to bide his time. In 1706, on hearing of the death of de Camillis, he nominated the Roman Catholic Jesuit monk Ferencz Ravasz vicar-general of the Greek Catholics of Mukačevo. This angered the people and the clergy, but there was little they could do about it. However, when Ravasz resolved to change the calendar, the Carpatho-Rusyn clergy gathered at a synod in Mukačevo on March 7, 1715, and sent a sharp protest to Rome against the nomination of the Jesuit as their vicar-general. With regard to the calendar issue, the synod informed the Apostolic See that "in view of our ancient rights and traditions and in order to avoid sowing confusion among the people, we absolutely refuse to observe holy days in accordance with the Gregorian calendar until the new style is confirmed by the authority of the Roman Curia among all Greek Catholics, including those who live outside the borders of Hungary."[45]

The calendar issue was referred to the Hungarian diet, which insisted that a single calendar be introduced for all rites. Rome feared handing down a decision lest it harm the cause of the union, especially since the Máramaros region had not yet accepted the union. The newly-appointed bishop of Mukačevo, Jurij H. Bizancij (1715-1733), also appealed to Rome to withdraw the calendar issue at all costs.[46] In response, the Apostolic See charged the papal nuncio in Vienna to attempt "to persuade the bishop of Eger to stop insisting on changes in the calendar, since this was bound to provoke the Rusyns who had only recently accepted the Catholic faith."[47]

The bishop of Eger ignored this instruction, and on the advice of the Hungarian primate he initiated a campaign of intimidation against the Mukačevo prelate, in which he undertook to expose to the

Apostolic See the "terrible abuses" that had allegedly been tolerated in the Mukačevo eparchy.[48] Failing to receive a reply to his appeal from Rome, the intimidated bishop Bizancij finally signed an "agreement" to "observe those holy days which the Latin-rite Catholics celebrate."[49] The bishop of Eger wasted no time informing Rome of this agreement. And so on June 20, 1718, the Congregation for the Propagation of the Faith issued a decree ordering all Carpatho-Rusyns of the Mukačevo eparchy "to observe the holy days of the Latin Church."[50]

In making his demands, the bishop of Eger cited the imperial decree issued in 1692 by emperor Leopold I. In order to circumvent this obstacle, bishop Bizancij explained to emperor Charles VI (reigned 1711-1740) why he could not implement the decision of the Congregation for the Propagation of the Faith. The emperor accepted the bishop's reasons and in 1720 issued a new charter of privileges for the Carpatho-Rusyn clergy, in which he made no mention of the holy days or of the calendar.[51] Rome's instruction thus remained a dead letter and the Carpatho-Rusyns continued to observe their holy days in accordance with the old style.[52]

The issue of the calendar and of the feast days has been mentioned because it is well documented and casts ample light on the manner in which the Hungarian hierarchy did its best to latinize the Eastern rite in order to facilitate the magyarization of Carpathian Rus'. Even as late as 1770, the bishop of Eger accused the Carpatho-Rusyn bishop Ivan Bradač of adding the doxology, *Jako Tvoje jest' carstvo* (For Thine is the Kingdom), to the Lord's Prayer and of deleting the short prayer, *Presvjataja Marije, Maty Boža* (Holy Mary, Mother of God), from the "Hail Mary," arguing that the latter indicated that Bradač ostensibly "did not believe that Mary was the Mother of God."[53]

Nonetheless, the Carpatho-Rusyns did not succumb. They preserved their traditions and their rite as best they could. Nonetheless, under the influence of fellow Uniate Ukrainians and Belorussians, they still incorporated certain Latin practices into their rite. But this is another problem.[54]

(2) *The election of bishops.* The right of the Uniates to elect their own bishops was the second condition on which the Union of Užhorod had been accepted. As mentioned earlier, for the Carpatho-Rusyns the bishop was much more than just their hierarch in the strict sense of the word. He was also their leader, that is, their lord in the broadest sense. Precisely because this was so, the [Hungarian] bishops of Eger attempted to oust the Carpatho-Rusyn bishop from

Mukačevo and to place Rusyn Catholics directly under their own jurisdiction from the very outset of the union. This century-long struggle and the canonical erection of the Mukačevo eparchy will be discussed in the following chapter, but it should be noted here that as a result of this struggle the Carpatho-Rusyn clergy lost the privilege of electing its own bishop. The cause of the union also suffered, because the clergy of the Máramaros region refused to relinquish this privilege and continued to elect its own Orthodox bishop until 1721.

In his struggle with the bishop of Eger, the Mukačevo prelate had the support of the imperial court. Generally speaking, the Habsburgs were well disposed toward both the Uniate and non-Uniate Christians of the Eastern rite. Thus, while the Uniates were being forced to accept the jurisdiction of the Latin archbishop as their metropolitan, the Habsburgs established a separate metropolitanate in Karlovci (Carlowitz) for the Orthodox.

In his comprehensive study of Habsburg church policy during the Enlightenment, Professor W. Ploechl concluded:

> Although the Austrian rulers were decidedly Catholic in their policy and favored the return of the separated Orientals to the Church of Rome, they respected the will of those who wanted to remain Orthodox. In a similar way they protected and supported the specific needs and interests of the tradition and ecclesiastical customs of both the Catholic and Orthodox Orientals. The establishment of Catholic bishoprics for the needs of the Ruthenian and Romanian faithful was chiefly due to the initiative and persistent policy of the Austrian rulers. The fact, on the other hand, that the metropolitan see of Karlowitz [Karlovci] eventually became the spiritual and ecclesiastical head of eight eparchies proves that this policy was also applied to the benefit of the Orthodox Orientals. Finally it must be stressed once more that this legislation was of pre-eminent importance in the social progress and emancipation of the peoples concerned.[55]

The Holy Union, which by the middle of the eighteenth century encompassed the whole of Carpathian Rus', gave rise to a "golden age" in the spiritual and cultural development of Carpathian Rus'. An important role in this belongs to empress Maria Theresa (reigned 1740-1780), who argued vigorously before the Apostolic See that the Carpatho-Rusyns deserved to have "their own bishop."[56] Nonetheless, she invoked her "right of patronage" and thereby reserved for herself the privilege of nominating candidates for the

Mukačevo eparchy which were then submitted to the Apostolic See for confirmation. This meant the eparchy lost the privilege to elect its own bishop.

(3) *Privileges for the clergy.* These were guaranteed by the third provision of the Union of Užhorod, but their implementation entailed as protracted a struggle and as many sacrifices as the other conditions of the un. on, despite the recognition by the Apostolic See of all privileges for the Uniate clergy as early as 1624.[57]

In 1633, prince György Rákóczi I had seized the possessions of the bishop of Mukačevo and of the Monastery of St. Nicholas on Černeča Hora and stripped them of all their privileges. The subsequent acceptance of the union with Rome should have resulted in the restoration to the Mukačevo prelate of his holdings and privileges. Yet, although princess Zsófia Báthory permitted bishop Partenij to return to the Černeča Hora monastery in 1664, she did not return the monastery's possessions to him. The bishop of Mukačevo thus remained without material security and was dependent on the good-will of the monastic community. In 1751, the Basilians evicted bishop M. Ol'šavs'kyj from the monastery and he was forced to move his official residence to the Mukačevo parish house.[58]

The clergy also suffered materially as a result of the union. Before the union, the faithful paid their offerings and tithes to their own pastors. After the union, the Roman Catholic pastors regarded the Uniate priests merely as their "ritual assistants" and thus collected tithes from the Carpatho-Rusyns as well as from their own parishioners. Their example was followed by Protestant ministers, who also tithed the Carpatho-Rusyns. As a result, the social conditions of the Uniate clergy deteriorated.[59] I stress this fact because some authors still attribute the success of the union in Carpathian Rus' to the "social improvements" of the clergy. This, however, did not occur until some 150 years later.

In 1690, bishop Josyf de Camillis started a campaign for the right to receive the tithes and stole fees from his faithful. Finally, he succeeded in obtaining from emperor Leopold I a decree that the Carpatho-Rusyns were to pay the tithes and stole fees to the priests of their own rite. It was in this same decree of 1692 that the emperor also insisted on the observance of Roman Catholic holy days.[60] The bishop of Eger took advantage of the opposition of the Carpatho-Rusyns regarding the observance of the Latin feasts. He interpreted the emperor's decree to mean that the right of the Rusyn clergy to receive the tithes was conditioned on the observance of Latin holy days. Since the

Carpatho-Rusyns continued to celebrate their own holy days, the bishop of Eger continued to collect from them tithes and frequently as well stole fees given to their priests. The struggle over the right of the tithe between the Uniates and the Latin clergy thus continued. The Roman Catholic clergy had the support of the landowners, who showed no desire to allocate church lands from their estates or to exempt the Uniate clergy from serfdom.

It was not until 1756 that an imperial decree finally established that the tithes and stole fees of the Carpatho-Rusyn faithful rightfully belonged to their clergy.[61] And only in 1776 did Maria Theresa provide material security for the bishop of Mukačevo by granting him estates and an annual income.[62] On the other hand, the Monastery of St. Nicholas still had to wage a legal battle before its possessions were finally restored in 1794.[63] It took until 1806 for the granting of privileges to the Uniate clergy and of endowments to Carpatho-Rusyn parishes to be completed owing to the persistent efforts of bishop Andrij Bačyns'kyj (1773-1809). Thus it was not until the beginning of the nineteenth century that the Carpatho-Rusyn clergy saw the fulfillment of the third condition of the union agreement, that is, full equality with the Latin clergy.

This is a sad page in the history of the union in Carpathian Rus'. The Uniates spent more than a century engaged in struggle with their brothers in faith, the Latin clergy, and the ambitions of the bishops of Eger. Despite this unequal contest, the Carpatho-Rusyns retained their rite and traditions, attained the right to have their own bishop, and finally won equal privileges for their clergy.

5. The Triumph of the Union with Rome

The deceitful approach of Roman Catholics to the union almost brought to nought the cause of unity with Rome in Carpathian Rus'. The Hungarians supported the union only because they saw in it an instrument for magyarizing the Carpatho-Rusyns. But they encountered a heroic people who united around their bishop and clergy. The Holy Union—the cause of God—triumphed because the people sought the truth. The words of the Saviour came true: "And you will know the truth and the truth will set you free" (John 8:32).

In the middle of the eighteenth century, when the union had been accepted throughout Carpathian Rus', the plight of the Mukačevo eparchy was unenviable. Before the union, the Carpatho-Rusyns had had their own bishop, who governed the eparchy with relative freedom. After entering into union with Rome, the eparchy lost its independence and was incorporated into the Latin diocese of Eger. The bishop of Mukačevo was made subject to the Eger prelate as his "ritual vicar." The Mukačevo bishop could not ordain priests or consecrate a new church without the permission of the Eger ordinary. Before the union, the Carpatho-Rusyns were able to observe their rite and traditions freely, whereas after the union the diocese of Eger tried to impose on them Latin customs and holy days. Even though prior to the union the Carpatho-Rusyn clergy did not possess so-called "clerical privileges," they were able to collect tithes and stole fees from their parishioners without hindrance. After the union, not only did the Latin authorities refuse to grant the Uniate clergy equal privileges, they also stripped them of their meagre tithes and stole fees.

Understandably, this situation fostered great discontent among both the Rusyn clergy and the faithful, provoking clashes, protests, and demands for their own rights. What at times seemed a hopeless struggle quite naturally caused some to revert to Orthodoxy. Thus, at the end of the eighteenth century, Mychajlo Andrella, a priest from Orosvyhovo, openly opposed the union and condemned it as evil.[64] Only the zeal of bishop Josyf de Camillis assured the survival of the union through these critical times. Through the convocation of synods,[65] de Camillis consolidated the shaken union and even attempted to spread it to Máramaros county and among the Romanians.

A second, more serious threat to the Holy Union came in 1760-1761 from Serbia in the person of the hieromonk Sofronij.[66] Sofronij already had some success in persuading Romanian Uniates in Transylvania to abandon the union after the Hungarian diet had refused to grant them equal privileges. His task was facilitated by the fact that Maria Theresa had just granted privileges to Orthodox Serbs on the territory of Austria.[67]

Exploiting the downtrodden status of the Uniates in Transylvania and Carpathian Rus', Sofronij and his followers began to preach schism, promising that the [Orthodox] Serbian patriarch in Karlovci would offer the Uniates his protection and would grant the clergy religious privileges and safeguard the people's religious and national freedom. Sofronij also promised that in place of bishop-vicar M. Ol'šavs'kyj, the patriarch would appoint a "real bishop" for Mukačevo, one that would be independent of the Eger ordinary who was bent on imposing the "Roman faith" and the "Latin rite" on Uniates. Sofronij's partisans assured the populace that by returning to the "old faith," that is, Orthodoxy, they would also gain their freedom from the despotism of the nobles and would enjoy a better life.[68]

In fact, disturbances occurred in certain parts of Szatmár county. In some cases, parishioners locked their churches, expelled the Uniate priests, and refused to receive the Holy Sacraments from the hands of Uniate pastors. In other places, Uniate clergymen were not even permitted to bury the dead.

The bishop of Mukačevo, Mychajil Ol'šavs'kyj, took immediate action. In the winter of 1761, he set out on a long pastoral tour of his eparchy for the purpose of restoring peace and strengthening the Holy Union. Ol'šavs'kyj convoked synods in the larger towns, consulted with the local clergy and with prominent members of the community, and preached to the people. He based his preachings on his famous "Sermon on the Holy Union," which has survived to our day.[69]

Bishop Ol'šavs'kyj's labors were rewarded and he succeeded in restoring peace to the eparchy. This experience led him to conclude that the survival of the union in Carpathian Rus' required complete independence from the bishop of Eger. With this end in view, he began a campaign for the canonical erection of the Mukačevo eparchy. After 1771, when the Mukačevo eparchy gained its independence, many of the earlier obstacles and misunderstandings disappeared, and cultural and religious life began to flourish in Carpathian Rus'.

CHAPTER THREE

The Canonical Erection of the Mukačevo Eparchy[1]

The union with Rome contributed in great measure to the strengthening and enrichment of religious life in Carpathian Rus'. At the same time, it gave rise to a protracted struggle which the Carpatho-Rusyn Church was forced to wage for its independence from the Hungarian Roman Catholic hierarchy. The reasons for this 125-year-long struggle were numerous, but principal among them were: (1) the lack of a written record of the establishment of the Mukačevo eparchy; (2) the fact that the union had been entered upon only with the Hungarian episcopate and not with the Apostolic See; (3) the absence of a formal act of the Union of Užhorod; (4) disputes surrounding the right of patronage over the Mukačevo eparchy; and (5) the harsh treatment of the Uniates in Poland, which, in turn, affected the treatment of Eastern-rite Catholics in Carpathian Rus'.[2]

The Roman Catholic bishop of Eger, whose jurisdiction also extended over the Roman Catholics of Carpathian Rus', did everything in his power to assume control over the region's Greek Catholics as well. Influential both at the imperial court and in the Roman Curia, the bishop of Eger tried to undermine the existence of the Mukačevo eparchy in order to subordinate the Uniates to a ritual vicar under his own authority. The bishops of Mukačevo, on the other hand, were intent on securing their eparchy's complete independence from Eger, a goal they ultimately attained in 1771.

1. The Legal Status of the Eparchy at the Time of the Union

The first documented mention of a bishop of Mukačevo occurs in 1491. Henceforth, the historical record contains a list of Mukačevo prelates who were elected by the clergy and confirmed by the Holy Roman emperor as king of Hungary. The Mukačevo eparchy derived its name from the location of the bishop's residence at the Basilian monastery of St. Nicholas on Černeča Hora (Monk's Hill) near the city of Mukačevo. In accordance with the canonical requirements of the Eastern Church, the bishop of Mukačevo had always to be a monk-archimandrite. This meant that he was also the superior of the Basilian Order in Carpathian Rus' and that he had at his disposal the revenues of the monastery of St. Nicholas, which had been endowed by prince Fedir Korjatovyč at the end of the fourteenth century.[3]

In 1622, as one of the provisions of his peace settlement with the Transylvanian prince Gábor Bethlén, emperor Ferdinand II gave Bethlen the Mukačevo domain in return for the latter's renunciation of his claim to the throne of Hungary. Along with the Mukačevo domain, the Transylvanian princes assumed control as well over the seat of the Mukačevo bishops. On the basis of his right of ownership, prince Bethlen claimed the right of patronage over the Mukačevo eparchy, and thus already in 1623 he named Petronij bishop of Mukačevo "by his princely grace."[4] From then on, the lords of the Mukačevo domain regarded themselves as patrons and protectors of the Mukačevo see.

But the lords of Mukačevo soon turned an avaricious eye on the holdings and income of the Monastery of St. Nicholas. Taking advantage of the death of bishop Ivan Hryhorovyč in 1633, prince György Rákóczi I seized the monastery's possessions for himself. The Mukačevo bishops thus became wholly dependent on the good-will of the Transylvanian princes and their appointed regents of the Mukačevo domain.

In an attempt to secure independence from his Calvinist overlords and to recover the monastery's possessions, bishop Vasylij Tarasovyč turned to the emperor for assistance. In retaliation, the Transylvanian ruler imprisoned Tarasovyč and released him only on condition that he leave the territory of the principality. In his place, the prince appointed Ivan Jus'ko, a parish priest from Dorobratovo, as bishop of Mukačevo (1643-1645).[5]

Once outside the borders of Rákóczi's domain, bishop Tarasovyč converted to Catholicism and thus secured the protection of the emperor on the basis of the latter's right of patronage as "Apostolic King."[6] The emperor gave Tarasovyč a small house in the city of Nagykálló to serve as his residence and granted him an annual allowance of 200 gold florins from the religious fund.

In the spring of 1643, György Rákóczi led an uprising against the emperor. The rebels attacked Nagykálló, seized bishop Tarasovyč, and brought him back to Mukačevo in chains. After holding

Tarasovyč prisoner for two years, the prince compelled him to renounce the union with Rome and, in return, re-installed him as bishop
of Mukačevo, restoring a portion of the monastery's holdings to him.
Hence, the bishop of Mukačevo once again became totally dependent
on the rulers of Transylvania.

In order to free themselves from the arbitrary rule of the Transylvanian princes, in the Union of Užhorod the Carpatho-Rusyn clergy retained for itself the right to elect their own bishop to be confirmed by
the Apostolic See and not by the prince.[7] Unfortunately, the original
document of the Union of Užhorod (assuming that one existed) has
yet to be found. The "act of union" of January 15, 1652, which is
cited by historians, is in fact only a request from the Carpatho-Rusyn
clergy for confirmation of their bishop-elect Partenij Petrovyč. There
is no reference in the document to the Mukačevo eparchy. The priests
did not foresee the possibility that the Apostolic See could confirm a
bishop without an eparchy, as the Eger bishops later attempted to
prove had been the case.

Meanwhile, Partenij, although himself a Uniate, asked the Orthodox metropolitan of Transylvania to ordain him bishop in the hope
that this tactic would make possible his return to Mukačevo.
However, Rákóczi's widow Zsuzsanna Lorántffy, a staunch Calvinist,
appointed instead Joannykij Zejkan' (1651-1686), a priest-widower
from Imstyčevo, to replace Tarasovyč.[8]

The primate of Hungary, archbishop György Lippay, took personal
charge of bishop Partenij Petrovyč's case and named him temporary
visitator for the Uniate Carpatho-Rusyns.[9] At the same time, he appealed to Pope Innocent X to lift "all censures" from Partenij and to
confirm him as "the true and lawful bishop of Mukačevo."[10] The
Congregation for the Propagation of the Faith, which at the time
regulated the affairs of the Eastern Churches, advised the pope to admit Partenij into the Catholic Church and to confirm him "bishop of
the people in question."[11] But the case was forwarded to the Holy Office of the Apostolic See for investigation of the validity of Partenij's
episcopal ordination.[12]

The validity of Partenij's consecration was confirmed, and the pope
was prepared to clear him of all censures. What did emerge, however,
was the question of whether "the city of Mukačevo holds episcopal title, be it only in the Ruthenian rite."[13] Archbishop Lippay was
charged with exploring the matter of the existence of the Mukačevo
eparchy.

On July 2, 1654, the Hungarian primate sent a long report to Rome, in which he argued that the Mukačevo eparchy had existed "from time immemorial." Citing the Apostolic See's traditional practice in matters relating to the union, Lippay asked that "the Mukačevo eparchy be canonically recognized as independent and that it be placed under the jurisdiction of the Esztergom archbishop as its metropolitan."[14]

Without further delay, on June 8, 1655, Pope Alexander VII cleared Partenij of all censures and irregularities and gave him jurisdiction "to perform all episcopal duties among the Carpatho-Rusyns in Mukačevo and other localities in the kingdom of Hungary."[15] Since the pope had not bestowed on Partenij any titular episcopal see,[16] the Hungarian primate Lippay proclaimed Partenij to be "the true and lawful Catholic bishop of Mukačevo confirmed by the Apostolic See," granting to him full episcopal jurisdiction over all Carpatho-Rusyns who "have customarily been subject to the bishop of Mukačevo."[17]

It seemed that with this act the Apostolic See had *de facto* recognized the existence of the Mukačevo eparchy. The primate of Hungary promulgated the decision of the Apostolic See and emperor Leopold I confirmed it on November 10, 1659.[18] Subsequent events, however, took a different turn.

2. The Transformation of the Eparchy into an Apostolic Vicariate

Archbishop Lippay believed that the royal confirmation of Partenij would make the position of the bishop of Mukačevo secure. He failed to take into account, however, the intentions of the Transylvanian princes who still ruled over Mukačevo and the eastern part of the eparchy. From the middle of the seventeenth century, the Transylvanian princes embodied Hungarian aspirations for independence from the Habsburgs and they opposed the emperor's will in everything. On this occasion, too, they ignored the emperor's confirmation of Partenij to the Mukačevo see and, under the pretext of "the good of the cause of the union," began a search for their own candidate for the episcopal office.[19]

Through her Jesuit confessor, S. Milley, the widow of György Rákóczi, princess Zsófia Báthory asked the Kiev metropolitan to nominate a candidate for the episcopal see of Mukačevo. Since the office of the metropolitan was vacant at the time, the question of the Mukačevo appointment was taken up at the episcopal synod in Žyrovyci, which took place in 1663. The synod resolved to seek the canonical incorporation of the Mukačevo eparchy into the Kiev metropolitanate.[20]

The decision of the Žyrovyci synod greatly disturbed the princess and her advisors. In 1664, in order to prevent the subjection of the Mukačevo eparchy to the Kiev metropolitan, Zsófia agreed to re-install bishop Partenij.

However, Partenij died in 1665, and the nomination of a Mukačevo bishop was once again raised in Rome. Bishop Jakiv Suša of Chełm (Cholm), the representative of the Kiev metropolitanate in Rome, made a detailed report to the Apostolic See on the circumstances of the Church in Carpathian Rus', and he requested that the eparchy of Mukačevo be placed under the jurisdiction of the Kiev metropolitan. Both the emperor and the Transylvanian prince claimed the right to nominate the Mukačevo bishop by right of patronage. In his report to Rome, the new Hungarian primate, archbishop György Szelepcsényi (1666-1685), who was much less favorably disposed toward the Carpatho-Rusyns than his predecessor Lippay, went so far as to deny the existence of the Mukačevo eparchy on the ground that only "missionary bishops" resided there. Thus, he demanded that the Carpatho-Rusyns be subordinated to the Eger ordinary.[21]

In order to weaken the influence of the emperor and to strengthen the recently converted princess Zsófia in her Catholic faith,[22] the Apostolic See granted the right of nominating the Mukačevo bishop to the Transylvanian rulers.[23] Thereupon, archbishop Szelepscényi, with the consent of Zsófia, moved to prevent the incorporation of the Mukačevo diocese into the Kiev metropolitanate, as had been re-quested by bishop Suša. With the help of the Jesuits, Szelepcsényj found Josyf Vološynovs'kyj, a Basilian from Galicia who had not ac-cepted union with Rome. In 1667, emperor Leopold I named Vološynovs'kyi bishop of Mukačevo (1667-1675) on condition that he convert to Catholicism and place himself under the jurisdiction of the Esztergom archbishop as metropolitan. Vološynovs'kyj agreed and as bishop did much harm to the Mukačevo eparchy.[24]

Shortly thereafter, great political turmoil ensued in Carpathian Rus' as a result of the conspiracy of Ferenc Wesselényi and the upris-ing of Imre Thököly. Each new occupier of the Mukačevo castle ap-pointed his own supporter as bishop. For a number of years, it was difficult to determine who was in fact the rightful bishop of Mukačevo. This situation lasted until 1689, when the Mukačevo see was assumed by Josyf de Camillis, a Basilian monk of Greek birth.

In 1686, the grand chancellor of Hungary, bishop Leopold

Kollonits, was elevated to the dignity of cardinal. He was a great supporter of the union, and it was in fact his doing that on November 5, 1689, Pope Alexander VIII appointed de Camillis apostolic vicar "of the Greek Catholics of the Mukačevo eparchy and other acquired territories in Hungary."[25] In order to gain favor with the Transylvanian magnates, Kollonits prevailed upon emperor Leopold I to subordinate de Camillis to the bishop of Eger as his suffragan.[26] Although this constituted a legal anomaly, for years to come it served the bishops of Eger as grounds for laying claim to the Mukačevo eparchy and for attempting to make the Mukačevo bishops subject to their jurisdiction.

For example, in March 1692, bishop György Fényessy demanded direct jurisdiction over the Carpatho-Rusyns and their apostolic vicar, bishop de Camillis. As secretary to the Hungarian primate, Fénessy had familiarized himself with the situation of the Mukačevo eparchy, and on the basis of certain acts issued by Rome regarded it as part of his diocese.[27]

However, Fénessy encountered in the person of de Camillis a learned legal mind who was able to defend his rights: "In accordance with the holy canons, a bishop cannot be a suffragan of another bishop, only of an archbishop. He [i.e., Fénessy] is a bishop of the Latin rite and I am a bishop of the Greek rite. Such is the custom of the Catholic Church, even if a Latin and a Greek bishop should live on the same territory, or even in the same city, as is the case, for example, in L'viv, Vilnius, Chelm, etc."[28] Bishop de Camillis never allowed the bishop of Eger to meddle in the affairs of the Mukačevo eparchy, which he administered as fully independent of Eger.

3. The Struggle for the Right to Elect Bishops

In 1703, prince Ferenc Rákóczi II began a new rebellion against the Habsburgs. Seeing in Rákóczi a "champion of the poor and downtrodden," the impoverished population of Carpathian Rus' eagerly rallied under his rebel flag. Rákóczi's concern was hardly the liberation of the masses, but he was able to exploit their support to fulfill his own political ambitions—to expel the hated Habsburgs from Hungary and himself ascend the Hungarian throne.[29]

Rákóczi, who had taken refuge in neighboring Poland, crossed into Carpathian Rus' in the late spring of 1703 and took control of his former lands in the Mukačevo domain, which the Habsburgs had confiscated during the rising of Imre Thököly. Immediately upon occupying the eastern portion of Carpathian Rus', Rákóczi dismissed all the emperor's protégés from key posts. Considering bishop de Camillis to be a supporter of the emperor, Rákóczi compelled him to resign. Rome, however, did not accept de Camillis's resignation and ordered him to remain in Mukačevo.[30]

Rákóczi did everything in his power to make de Camillis leave Mukačevo, and in fact on March 30, 1706, he ordered him "to leave the territory of Hungary immediately."[31] Bishop de Camillis hurriedly moved to Prešov, which was still under the protection of the emperor's troops, and he entrusted the governing of the eastern sections of his eparchy to his vicar-general Ivan Hodermars'kyj. On August 22, 1706, while still in exile, bishop de Camillis suddenly died. With his death, the Mukačevo eparchy lost one of its staunchest defenders and one of its greatest prelates, who had been largely responsible for reviving the Holy Union and safeguarding its future in Carpathian Rus'.

Before Hodermars'kyj was able to reach Rome to ask the Apostolic See to name a successor to de Camillis,[32] prince Rákóczi requested that the Kiev metropolitan Lev Zalens'kyj (1694-1708) "once again incorporate the Mukačevo eparchy under the jurisdiction of the Kiev metropolitanate" and consecrate as bishop of Mukačevo "the very deserving monk Petronij Kamins'kyj."[33] Without waiting for metropolitan Zalens'kyj's reply, on February 28, 1707, Rákóczi named Kamins'kyj, who was very favorably disposed towards him, to head the Mukačevo eparchy.[34]

Metropolitan Zalens'kyj found himself in a difficult situation. He could not extend his authority over the Mukačevo eparchy and appoint a bishop to head it without the permission of the Apostolic See, nor did he consider Kamins'kyj worthy of the office of bishop.[35] At the same time, he feared that J. Stojka, the Orthodox bishop of Máramaros, might try to occupy the Mukačevo bishopric.

Rome was unaware of Rákóczi's dealings with the Kiev metropolitan. On the basis of reports from Hodermars'kyj and the Basilian procurator in Rome, Syl'vester Peškevyč, the Congregation for the Propagation of the Faith at its meeting on March 28, 1707 decided "to nominate bishop Ju. Vynnyc'kyj the temporary administrator of the apostolic vicariate of Mukačevo in Hungary, and in the meantime to request the necessary information from the internuncio, asking him to put forward with the consent of His Eminence the archbishop of Esztergom worthy and suitable candidates for the vicariate in question."[36] Thus, on April 7, 1707, Pope Clement XI named bishop Ju. Vynnyc'kyj of Przemyśl the apostolic administrator of the "Mukačevo eparchy."[37]

Surprised by his nomination, bishop Vynnyc'kyj turned for advice to the Kiev metropolitan Zalens'kyj. The metropolitan saw that the question of the Mukačevo bishopric had to be resolved without further delay and so he wrote to Rome.[38] He advised Vynnyc'kyj to appoint Kamins'kyj his vicar-general, fearing that otherwise the latter would interfere with bishop Vynnyc'kyj's return to Mukačevo. In this manner they blocked the consecration of Kamins'kyj by the Orthodox bishop J. Stojka of Máramaros (1690-1711), who had already begun ordaining priests for the Mukačevo eparchy.[39]

Having appointed bishop Vynnyc'kyj apostolic administrator, Rome did not hasten to name a new bishop. These were revolutionary times and good sense dictated caution. In the meantime, Rome instructed metropolitan Zalens'kyj to submit a detailed report on Kamins'kyj's qualifications for the office of bishop.[40]

When Hodermars'kyj heard of Kamins'kyj's prospects for being elevated to the episcopate, he mobilized his supporters. But Rome ignored their demand that vicar-general Hodermars'kyj be named bishop of Mukačevo.[41] Therefore, the clergy asked the emperor that he, "as apostolic king," appoint by right of patronage Hodermars'kyj to the Mukačevo see.[42] This served the emperor's interests, since it won him the support of the clergy in Rákóczi's domain. Hence, on September 27, 1707, emperor Joseph I (reigned 1705-1711) named Hodermars'kyj bishop of Mukačevo on the basis of ancient custom and his royal privilege of patronage.[43] The emperor's appointment of Hodermars'kyj was also confirmed by the Hungarian primate.[44]

Relations between Rome and Austria deteriorated badly at the beginning of the eighteenth century because of the War of the Spanish Succession (1701-1714). The pope supported Louis XIV of France, who was a supporter of Rákóczi. In retaliation, emperor Joseph I occupied a portion of the Papal States in northern Italy.[45] Under these circumstances, the Roman Curia automatically rejected all of the emperor's requests with regard to the appointment of bishops.

Meanwhile, the Rákóczi rebellion was gaining wider support.[46] The Apostolic See was still having difficulties with Rákóczi's candidate Kamins'kyj, who was determined not to allow bishop Vynnyc'kyj to take up his post in Mukačevo as apostolic administrator.[47] Still, on the basis of detailed reports, Rome could not confirm Kamins'kyj's appointment to the Mukačevo see.[48] Consequently, the question of the Mukačevo bishopric was postponed for a time.[49]

Prince Rákóczi suspected that Kamins'kyj's confirmation in Rome was being delayed because of the emperor's nomination of Hodermars'kyj. He therefore began an action against Hodermars'kyj among the Hungarian clergy. Rákóczi's supporters did not hesitate to use any means in their determination to compromise Hodermars'kyj in the eyes of the Apostolic See. The campaign against Hodermars'kyj was headed by the bishop of Eger, because "he was displeased that Hodermars'kyj had been nominated without consultation with him."[50] The leading supporter of Hodermars'kyj was the Hungarian primate himself.[51]

In order to circumvent the nominations of both the emperor and the prince, Hodermars'kyj's supporters took the primate's advice and denied the existence of the Mukačevo eparchy, claiming that there existed only an apostolic vicariate as in the times of bishop Josyf de Camillis. Apostolic vicars could be appointed only by the Apostolic See without regard for the right of patronage. Thus they insisted that Rome appoint Hodermars'kyj apostolic administrator of Mukačevo and bestow on him the title of titular bishop.[52] This proved to be a costly mistake.

Rome was relieved to find a way out of a complex situation. Rákóczi's rising was disintegrating and the Apostolic See felt free to reject the candidacy of Kamins'kyj. But in order not to recognize the emperor's right to nominate the bishop, Rome also rejected the candidacy of Hodermars'kyj. Instead, the Apostolic See named Polykarp Fylypovyč, a Basilian from Galicia, to the office of the apostolic vicar.[53]

The defeat of Rákóczi and the death of Kamins'kyj on June 17, 1710 put an end to the conflict over the right to name the bishops of Mukačevo. At the same time, the Kiev metropolitan lost his supporter in the person of Prince Rákóczi for the plan to incorporate the Mukačevo eparchy into the Kiev metropolitanate. The struggle, however, continued between the Apostolic See and the imperial court.

At the suggestion of Hodermars'kyj's supporters, Rome took the position that the Mukačevo eparchy did not exist in view of the lack of valid evidence of its establishment and canonical erection.[54] It was clear from the Roman Curia's style that by then it recognized only the existence of an apostolic vicariate in Mukačevo. The nomination of apostolic vicars did not fall under the right of patronage of even an "apostolic king." The Apostolic See thus had the right to appoint its candidate to Mukačevo without regard for any claims that the emperor in Vienna might have.

The imperial court, however, continued to assert the *de facto* existence of the Mukačevo eparchy and to insist that Rome uphold the royal right of patronage over it. In order to eliminate all difficulties for the future, the Viennese chancery requested that the Mukačevo eparchy "be recognized and canonized once and for all," and that only those candidates be confirmed bishops whom "the Hungarian kings nominate."[55] In a letter to his ambassador in Rome, emperor Joseph I wrote that he would never permit the episcopal see of Mukačevo to be headed by a "foreign and unknown candidate." He was referring to Polykarp Fylypovyč.[56]

Neither the intervention of the apostolic nuncio, nor the appeals of the Hungarian primate who was prepared to maintain Fylypovyč at his own expense, were of any avail.[57] The emperor refused to yield. Hodermars'kyj, too, demanded a hearing in ecclesiastical court concerning the slanderous charges that had been made against him in Rome. He was prepared to resign if the court could prove the "canonical obstacles" that supposedly prevented him from becoming a bishop.[58] The emperor continued to support Hodermars'kyj,[59] despite Rome's unequivocal rejection of his candidacy on the grounds that "someone else had already been nominated," meaning Fylypovyč.[60]

Rome expected that after the death of Joseph I in 1711, his successor Charles VI (reigned 1711-1740) would accept the Apostolic See's proposal. But the new emperor persisted in maintaining his right of patronage over the Mukačevo eparchy and claimed that by confirming Partenij Petrovyč bishop of Mukačevo, Rome had in fact canonized the Mukačevo eparchy.[61] Moreover, the Carpatho-Rusyn clergy had clearly reserved for itself the right to elect bishops in the act of union. Therefore, since the clergy had elected Hodermars'kyj and the emperor as king of Hungary had approved the choice, the emperor now insisted upon the acceptance of Hodermars'kyj by the Apostolic See.[62]

Hodermars'kyj was losing patience. His injudicious opposition to Fylypovyč's nomination had provoked even greater hostility towards him in Rome.[63] But perhaps Hodermars'kyj's greatest lack of judgment was revealed in his conduct towards the newly-appointed vicar-general Jurij Bizancij, who was one of the most prominent priests of the Mukačevo eparchy.

Bizancij had been made archdeacon of Szabolcs by bishop Josyf de Camillis in 1703.[64] Two years later, de Camillis had sent him on a pastoral visit to Bihár county.[65] Because he was a supporter of Rákóczi, the prince named him vicar-general of the bishop-elect Petronij Kamins'kyj.[66] After the death of Kamins'kyj, Bizancij became Rákóczi's candidate for the episcopate of Mukačevo,[67] which also brought him the support of the Eger ordinary, who had taken the side of the rebels.[68] Bizancij thus became Hodermars'kyj's new rival for the Mukačevo bishopric.

After the death of emperor Joseph I, the Hungarian primate, Cardinal Ágost Keresztélyi (1707-1725), instructed the bishop of Eger to remove Hodermars'kyj from his position as administrator of the Mukačevo eparchy.[69] The Carpatho-Rusyn clergy, however, strongly opposed this measure and meeting at a diocesan synod in Mukačevo declared their continued support of Hodermars'kyj's candidacy.[70] The bishop of Eger was at a loss for what to do. But upon learning that Rome had definitively rejected Hodermars'kyj's nomination, on April 9, 1713, he named Jurij Bizancij vicar-general of the Mukačevo eparchy with full subordination to Eger.[71]

Hodermars'kyj retaliated by abrogating all of Bizancij's acts and by summoning him to stand trial.[72] The Hungarian primate suspended both Hodermars'kyj and Bizancij and convoked a new synod to elect a vicar-general. The primate also informed the Carpatho-Rusyn clergy that "there was no hope that Hodermars'kyj would ever obtain confirmation from the Apostolic See for the episcopate."[73]

The bishop of Eger, István Telekesy (1702-1715), hoped to take advantage of this opportunity to establish complete control over the eparchy of Mukačevo. Towards the end he took the necessary steps to ensure that a Roman Catholic parish priest from Mukačevo, the Jesuit Ferenc Ravasz was elected vicar. Ravasz's election roused the entire Carpatho-Rusyn ecclesiastical body. On March 7, 1715, the Rusyn clergy met at a diocesan synod in Mukačevo, headed by both vicars Hodermars'kyj and Bizancij, and sent a protest to the Apostolic See stating that:

(1) They would not tolerate a Roman Catholic priest as their vicar-general and therefore rejected the Eger ordinary's candidate, Ferenc Ravasz, S.J.;

(2) There had been ample proof in both Vienna and Rome of the existence of the Mukačevo eparchy;

(3) They maintained their right to elect the bishop of Mukačevo as well as the emperor's right to nominate and the Apostolic See's right to confirm their choice;

(4) They could prove that all charges against Hodermars'kyj, and even more so against Bizancij, were false and malicious;

(5) They would respect the bishop of Eger as befitted his office, but would not pledge him "obedience or subordination" since they

recognized the metropolitan jurisdiction of the Hungarian primate; and

(6) They appealed to the Apostolic See to confirm Hodermars'kyj to the episcopate, because "the clergy as a whole could testify to his worthy life and exemplary behavior," and, if needed, they could "prove his complete innocence."[74]

Had the Carpatho-Rusyn clergy not insisted on Hodermars'kyj's appointment to the bishopric, they might have saved the existence of the Mukačevo eparchy. But as things stood, on May 7, 1715, the Congregation for the Propagation of the Faith replied: (1) that the establishment of the Mukačevo eparchy, and in particular its endowment, had not been proven; (2) that given these circumstances, the clergy did not have the right to choose, nor the emperor the right to nominate, the bishop of Mukačevo; (3) that as before, the Apostolic See had the sole right to appoint an apostolic vicar; and (4) that the candidacy of Hodermars'kyj for apostolic vicar of Mukačevo was rejected once and for all and that Rome would find its own candidate for the office.[75]

On April 17, 1715, the bishop of Eger with the consent of the Hungarian primate appointed Jurij Bizancij "the episcopal vicar of the Greek-Catholics" but stipulated that he had to pledge that he and the Carpatho-Rusyn clergy would submit to the jurisdiction of Eger.[76] At the time, Hodermars'kyj was in Galicia taking his monastic vows in order to ensure for himself the position of superior of the Mukačevo monastery. During his absence, a new synod met in Užhorod on May 4, 1715 on the instructions of the Eger ordinary and named Jurij Bizancij as their new candidate for bishop. Returning from Galicia as a Basilian monk, Hodermars'kyj attempted to protest this measure, but, intimidated by the threats of the bishop of Eger,[77] on November 14, 1715, he resigned from the episcopate, retaining only the title of the archimandrite of St. Nicholas' Monastery on Černeča Hora, near Mukačevo.[78] Bizancij thus became the sole candidate for the Mukačevo bishopric.

The process of Bizancij's nomination and confirmation now began to take on a faster pace. Although Bizancij was the Eger prelate's candidate, he had been elected by the Carpatho-Rusyn clergy at the Užhorod synod and emperor Charles VI had forwarded his nomination for confirmation "in place of Hodermars'kyj, who had voluntarily submitted his resignation to His Majesty."[79] Both the Hungarian primate and the Eger ordinary recommended Bizancij to the Apostolic See. It looked as if all parties involved were satisfied with the solution.

But Rome once again rejected the "right of patronage," which the emperor had invoked with regard to the Mukačevo eparchy. Still, in order not to delay matters further, on January 14, 1716, the Congregation for the Propagation of the Faith resolved: "Although the emperor's nomination for the see of Mukačevo cannot be accepted, nonetheless, without making mention of this nomination, to appoint to the apostolic vicariate of Mukačevo Jurij Bizancij, who was recommended by the papal nuncio in Vienna and His Eminence of Saxony [i.e., A. Keresztély, the primate of Hungary]. At the same time, His Holiness must be asked to bestow on the above-named Jurij Bizancij a titular bishopric among non-believers."[80]

On February 5, 1716, Pope Clement XI (1700-1721) named Jurij Bizancij "apostolic vicar of the Mukačevo eparchy and other conquered territories in Hungary," and two months later bestowed on him the title of bishop of Sebaste.[81] Bizancij was consecrated bishop by the Kiev metropolitan Lev Kiška (1714-1728) on December 9, 1716.[82] Finally, after ten years of struggle, the Carpatho-Rusyns had their own bishop. However, during this unequal contest, they lost the title "Bishop of Mukačevo" and were made subject to the jurisdiction of the Eger ordinary, who soon began exercising his authority over the Carpatho-Rusyns with increasing ruthlessness.

4. The Machinations of the Bishops of Eger

Because the Latin-rite Eger diocese encompassed the territory of Carpathian-Rus' and all union matters were conducted through that see, the Eger prelates began to appropriate for themselves jurisdiction over the Uniates in the Mukačevo eparchy as well.

This trend was already initiated in 1688 by Petronij Kamins'kyj who wished to oust bishop Metodij Rakovec'kyj (1688-1689) from the Mukačevo monastery so that he himself could become its archimandrite. Kamins'kyj wrote to the bishop of Eger asking him to summon bishop Rakovec'kyj to Eger as his "vicar" on the grounds that the Monastery of St. Nicholas should be occupied "not by bishops, but by the superiors of monks."[83] Although this notion appealed to the Eger ordinary, he was unable to do anything at the time, because bishop de Camillis soon assumed the Mukačevo see. The new bishop was successful in defending his rights and forced the return of Kamins'kyj to Galicia.

At the insistence of the bishop of Eger, the emperor confirmed bishop de Camillis only as suffragan of Eger,[84] even though the papal bull had made no mention of his subordination to the Eger ordinary.[85] De Camillis cited canon law to prove the illegality of such subordination and did not permit the bishop of Eger to interfere in the affairs of the Mukačevo eparchy. But the Eger prelates did not cease in their schemes to take control over the Carpatho-Rusyn eparchy.

An opportunity presented itself, as mentioned earlier, after the death of bishop de Camillis in 1706, when a dispute arose between the imperial court, the Transylvanian prince, and Rome regarding the right to nominate the bishop of Mukačevo. In the ensuing confusion, the bishop of Eger, I. Telekesy, citing as a pretext "the preservation of the union," named Jurij Bizancij as his vicar in Mukačevo,[86] even though Rome had already appointed the hieromonk Polykarp Fylypovyč to that office.[87] Because Rome had rejected the emperor's candidate Ivan Hodermars'kyj for the Mukačevo see, the emperor refused to accept the papal candidate. Consequently, Bizancij, the candidate of the Eger ordinary, emerged the victor. He, however, had to pledge "obedience, respect and submission" to the Eger ordinary before his appointment.[88]

The pope appointed Bizancij apostolic vicar "for all Greek Catholics of the *Mukačevo eparchy* with all rights bestowed by the Apostolic See,"[89] making no mention of any subordination to Eger. Disregarding the papal decree, the bishop of Eger "named" bishop Bizancij his "ritual vicar," specifying, moreover, that he was assigned only to "the Mukačevo region," thereby denying, contrary to the papal charter, the very existence of the Mukačevo eparchy.[90] Since bishop Bizancij regarded the bishop of Eger as "his particular patron,"[91] he did not dare oppose this anti-canonical designation. This gave the bishop of Eger complete control over the religious life of the Carpatho-Rusyns.

It soon became obvious that the Eger ordinary's goal was the complete latinization and magyarization of the Mukačevo eparchy. But when he attempted to replace the Julian calendar with the Gregorian one, bishop Bizancij protested to the Apostolic See. Rome ordered the bishop of Eger, Gábor Erdődy, "not to introduce anything new" without the approval of the Apostolic See.[92] In order to discredit bishop Bizancij in the eyes of the Apostolic See, Erdődy sent a list of charges to Rome against him. He described "terrible abuses" that had taken root among the clergy owing to Bizancij's "shortcomings," and he accused the apostolic vicar of being a rebel who wanted to remove himself from the supervision of the Eger ordinary to the "scandal of the heretics."[93]

Disturbed by the charges of "abuses" and "scandals," on June 20, 1718, the Congregation for the Propagation of the Faith sent Bizancij its so-called "Secret Instructions," ordering him to eliminate all abuses in his eparchy as soon as possible in consultation with the bishop of Eger.[94] The Eger prelate interpreted this act of the Apostolic See as Rome's recognition of his authority over the apostolic vicar of Mukačevo. Rome's view was different, however: "in accordance with the document by which the Mukačevo apostolic vicar was appointed, he is not obliged to submit to the authority of the bishop of Eger." The claims of the Eger bishops were based exclusively on "the decree of the emperor"[95] and on the fact that the "above-named vicariate [i.e., the Mukačevo eparchy] lies within the boundaries of Eger territory."[96] However, because bishop Bizancij had opponents to his appointment among his clergy, especially in the person of his vicar-general Hodermars'kyj, he submitted to the jurisdiction of the Eger ordinary and executed his instructions conscientiously.[97]

Bizancij's successors, bishop Symeon Ol'šavs'kyj (1734-1737) and bishop Havryjil Blažovs'kyj (1738-1742), followed the same course. Not only did they accept the authority of the Eger bishops, they also renounced the title of "apostolic vicar" and acted only as "ritual vicars" of the Eger ordinary. During this period, the very concept of the "Mukačevo eparchy" disappeared from official documents and was described only as the "Mukačevo region."[98] Carpathian Rus' thus lost its ecclesiastical independence and was made subject to the jurisdiction of the Roman Catholic ordinary of Eger.

5. Bishop M. Ol'šavs'kyj's Attempts to Attain Independence

The Apostolic See continued to appoint apostolic vicars to Mukačevo. But the candidates were nominated by the emperor on the recommendation of the bishop of Eger. In order to assure their supremacy over the Carpatho-Rusyns, the Eger prelates put forward only those candidates who pledged them loyalty and obedience.

The claims of the Eger bishops were unlawful, since the very institution of *apostolic vicar*—the office held by Mukačevo bishops after Josyf de Camillis—required that a bishop with this title govern the given territory in the name of the Apostolic See and be subject only to it. Had Rome wished to appoint only a "ritual vicar" to Mukačevo to assist the bishop of Eger, it would have bestowed the title of "auxiliary bishop" on the Mukačevo prelate and not that of apostolic vicar. The fact that the Eger ordinary demanded a pledge of loyalty from the bishops of Mukačevo indicates that the issue at stake was one of power and not of right.

Having to endure the "subjugation to Eger," the Carpatho-Rusyn clergy began to demand the implementation of the rights that the union had guaranteed them. The struggle came to be headed by bishop Mychajil Manujil Ol'šavs'kyj (1743-1767), who dared to speak out in defense of his rights.

Before his nomination, Ol'šavs'kyj like his predecessors had had to swear an oath of loyalty to the bishop of Eger.[99] But neither the imperial decree[100] nor the papal brief[101] had made any mention of Ol'šavs'kyj's subordination to the bishop of Eger. This permitted Ol'šavs'kyj to initiate a struggle for his eparchy's independence from the Eger ordinary, who hoped to denationalize all of Carpathian Rus' with the help of the church.[102]

The treatment of bishop Ol'šavs'kyj by the new Eger ordinary, Ferenc Barkóczy (1744-1760) was rude and heavyhanded. Barkóczy also instructed the Roman Catholic pastors to collect the tithes and stole fees from the Carpatho-Rusyn faithful. The latter rebelled against this unlawful directive, because they were already paying these dues to their own pastors. The Roman Catholic clergy began resorting to force and calling in the civil authorities to assist them. Ol'šavs'kyj personally visited Eger in an attempt to resolve the question of the tithes and stole fees.

An agreement was signed on May 8, 1747, which specified that the tithes and stole fees were to be collected by Carpatho-Rusyn priests and that Roman Catholics were forbidden "to treat Greek-Catholic priests inhumanely."[104] In return, Ol'šavs'kyj was forced to renew his oath of loyalty to Eger, because, as Barkóczy put it, he "had failed to show proper obedience and submission to his ordinary."[105] Upon receiving the renewed pledge, Barkóczy granted Ol'šavs'kyj "jurisdiction," but only for a period of three years.[106]

The following year, Barkóczy came to Mukačevo on a canonical visitation of the bishop's residence and the cathedral church. This constituted a gross breach of the rights of an apostolic vicar. In protest against this unprecedented disregard for canon law, bishop Ol'šavs'kyj did not come to greet the bishop of Eger. Only under the threat of military intervention was Ol'šavs'kyj ultimately compelled to yield and to permit Barkóczy to make the canonical visitation to the Mukačevo cathedral.[107]

The visitation took place on July 16, 1748, resulting in great resentment among the Rusyn clergy and the faithful. Soon after, Ol'šavs'kyj convoked a diocesan synod at Mukačevo, which sent a strong protest to Rome concerning the unlawful conduct of the Eger ordinary and demanded that Rome make the Mukačevo see independent. Ol'šavs'kyj personally gave a copy of the synod's letter to empress Maria Theresa and to the papal nuncio in Vienna, asking them to grant canonical status to the eparchy.[108]

Maria Theresa was anxious to settle the conflict between the Eger and Mukačevo prelates.[109] As had been the custom of his predecessors, Barkóczy defended himself by enumerating various "possible and impossible" abuses among the Carpatho-Rusyn clergy and faithful.[110] Ol'šavs'kyj would not allow himself to be intimidated by these charges and, instead, embarked on a canonical visitation of all the Rusyn parishes of his eparchy in order to underscore his authority and prove Barkóczy's accusations unfounded.

Ol'šavs'kyj's visitation of his far-flung eparchy lasted from 1750 to 1752. Upon its completion, he submitted a detailed report to the imperial court.[111] Ol'šavs'kyj's account shows that in the majority of cases Barkóczy's charges had been exaggerated. Ol'šavs'kyj concluded that the shortcomings among the Carpatho-Rusyn clergy stemmed from their difficult material condition and their oppression by the Roman Catholic clergy. As for the religious decline among the faithful, this was the result of an insufficient number of priests and churches, a situation brought about by the Eger bishops who posed obstacles in this sphere in order to compel the Carpatho-Rusyn population to attend Roman Catholic churches.[112]

On March 16, 1752, the imperial court issued a decree recognizing the right of bishop Ol'šavs'kyj to govern the faithful of the Eastern rite and forbidding the Roman Catholic clergy and Protestant ministers "to hinder the Rusyn pastors in administering the Holy Sacraments and collecting the stole fees of their people."[113] But the bishop of Eger had no intention of yielding. He now put forward "canonical arguments" against Ol'šavs'kyj, who once again visited Vienna and successfully defended his rights as apostolic vicar to administer his flock independently of the Eger ordinary.[114]

On September 16, 1756, Maria Theresa issued a decree designed to reconcile the differences between the Eger and Mukačevo bishops. The bishop of Mukačevo, as the "ritual vicar" of Eger, was to acknowledge the supremacy of the Eger ordinary. However, the bishop of Eger was forbidden to meddle in the administration of the Greek Catholic faithful. Should the need arise, the bishop of Mukačevo had the right to build churches for his faithful and establish new parishes. The Rusyn parishioners were to pay the tithes and church offerings to pastors of their own rite and the Roman Catholic pastors were not permitted to hinder the Greek Catholics in administering the Holy Sacraments to their flocks. All abuses in the designated spheres were to be reported to the imperial court.[115]

The court expected this decision to normalize relations between the two bishops, but new disputes soon arose when count Károly Esterházy replaced Barkóczy as bishop of Eger (1762-1799). Bishop Esterházy's brother was chancellor at the emperor's court in Vienna, and so he resolved to ensure Ol'šavs'kyj's submission once and for all. At the beginning of 1763, he demanded a new oath of "loyalty to the Eger ordinary" from Ol'šavs'kyj, after which he granted him the right to perform his episcopal duties for a period of only five years. He also renewed his predecessor's instructions of 1747 regarding the collection of the tithes and stole fees, while describing the Carpatho-Rusyn priests as merely "ritual assistants to Roman Catholic pastors." When bishop Ol'šavs'kyj protested to the Hungarian primate, citing the orders of the Austrian imperial court, the primate called upon the Rusyns "to render respect and filial trust to the Eger bishop."[116] This act, as Professor Edward Winter points out, was to have ultimately "sealed the complete dependence" of the Carpatho-Rusyn church on the bishop of Eger.[117]

A diocesan synod was held in Mukačevo on January 30-February 1, 1764. It resolved "to break once and forever its dependence on the bishop of Eger." With this end in view, the synod sent a delegation to Vienna, headed by archdeacon Ivan Bradač, which opened the way for the canonical erection of the Mukačevo eparchy.[118]

An incident in Hajdúdorog added weight to the demands of the Carpatho-Rusyns. In 1765, the faithful there asked that they be assigned an Orthodox pastor because the Protestants constantly harassed them with the argument that "their bishop is nothing more than the servant of the bishop of Eger and the Uniate priests are but the assistants of the Latin-rite priests."[119] This demonstrated that Ol'šavs'kyj's fears that dependence on Eger would become the primary obstacle to union had been justified.[120]

Bishop Esterházy still failed to see the threat posed by his treatment of the Uniates. He continued to maintain that bishop Ol'šavs'kyj's only reason for wanting to become independent was to enable him "to return to the [Orthodox] schism more easily."[121] In the end, violence erupted between the members of the clergy of the two rites, and this persuaded the imperial court of the need for action for the good of the union. Thus, in 1766, empress Maria Theresa asked the Apostolic See "to make the Mukačevo eparchy independent."[122] The Carpatho-Rusyns were overjoyed at the thought of finally becoming free of their "captivity to Eger."

6. The Austrian Imperial Court in Defense of the Rights of the Carpatho-Rusyns

Maria Theresa's request was very favorably received in Rome. In his response, Pope Clement XIII announced his readiness to create an independent Mukačevo eparchy, but stated that he first needed to have more information.[123]

The papal nuncio in Vienna was certain that the Eger ordinary would protest the planned erection,[124] but for his part supported the demand of the Carpatho-Rusyns, describing them as "deserving of this grace from the Holy Father."[125] The matter was submitted for review to the Congregation for the Propagation of the Faith, which at the time governed the affairs of the Eastern-rite churches.[126]

Bishop Esterházy of Eger was well informed about the matter by his brother in Vienna and his procurator G. Merenda in Rome.[127] Esterházy had the support of the Hungarian primate, the former bishop of Eger, Ferenc Barkóczy, and the newly appointed papal nuncio, A. Visconti (1767-1774), who had recently been transferred from Warsaw to Vienna. Experiencing some initial difficulties at the imperial court, the new nuncio took the side of the Eger ordinary, who was determined to block the creation of a Mukačevo eparchy.[128]

On March 31, 1767, bishop Esterházy sent a detailed report to Rome about the creation of an independent eparchy for the Rusyn population of Carpathian Rus'. He argued that the creation of a Mukačevo eparchy would prove "a great detriment to the Holy Union," that it would become the cause of "continual misunderstandings and disputes" between the two bishops, and that it would constitute "a great loss for the Eger diocese." Esterházy supported his contentions with appropriate documents.[129]

Upon receipt of Esterházy's account, the Pope immediately changed his mind about establishing a Mukačevo eparchy. On the pope's instructions, his Secretary of State, Cardinal L. Torrigiani, asked the papal nuncio to persuade Maria Theresa that "for the good of the Holy Faith" she abandon the idea of creating an independent Mukačevo eparchy.[130] In turn, the pope praised Esterházy's "zeal and concern for the Holy Union" and asked him to visit Vienna to relate the whole issue to the empress in person.[131]

It was at this point that bishop Ol'šavs'kyj died on November 5, 1767. In his place, empress Maria Theresa proposed as a successor Ol'šavs'kyj's chief advisor and assistant, archdeacon Ivan Bradač. However, the bishop of Eger opposed Bradač's candidacy, claiming that "he [Bradač] had tried at all costs to free himself of dependence on the Latin ordinary."[132] In order to facilitate matters for his nuncio, on January 27, 1768, the pope named Ivan Bradač apostolic vicar and postponed the question of the eparchy's independence.[133]

It appears that the Apostolic See was not informed about the Orthodox disturbances that were occurring at the time in Máramaros, Szatmár, and Hajdú counties. Relying on Esterházy's assurance that only the bishops of Eger could guarantee the success of the union, the Apostolic See decided to uphold the dependence of "the unreliable Greeks" on Eger.[134] Maria Theresa, however, continued to press the Apostolic See on the matter through her ambassador in Rome, baron Nenni, who personally described to the papal secretary of state "the abuses and inhumane treatment of the Carpatho-Rusyns by bishop Esterházy of Eger."[135] The imperial protector in Rome, Cardinal A. Albani, submitted the so-called "Motives" to the secretariat, demanding the restoration of the "ancient Mukačevo eparchy" on the grounds: (1) that a large number of faithful of the Greek rite demanded it; (2) that there existed a difference in language and customs between the faithful of the two rites; (3) that this was provided for in the 65th and 66th canons of the Third Synod of Carthage (419); and (4) that the bishop of Mukačevo had a guaranteed income.[136]

The papal nuncio in Vienna delayed informing the empress that Pope Clement XIII had changed his mind. Finally, on April 21, 1768, he handed Maria Theresa the pope's "Memorandum" (dated November 14, 1767), in which the Holy Father regretted that he could not agree to the establishment of an independent eparchy for the "Mukačevo Uniates," informing the empress that "the old manner of administration" would be retained.[137] The pope's refusal angered the imperial court, which regarded this measure of the Apostolic See to be "a violation of the right of patronage" enjoyed by the empress. The Austrian imperial State Council (Staatsrat) pointed out that the reasons put foward by Rome for its refusal were "negligible" in comparison "with the abuses of the Eger bishops" and "the persecution and degradation of the Rusyn Catholics." The imperial council, therefore, insisted that Maria Theresa "invoke her right of supreme patronage" and "make the Mukačevo eparchy independent."[138]

By then, the papal nuncio had also realized that "the good of the

Catholic faith'' and the preservation of the Holy Union dictated the creation of the Mukačevo eparchy. But it was too late. He was compelled to defend the position of the Apostolic See and set about persuading the archbishop of Vienna, Cardinal Migazzi, to support Rome's stand.[139] At the request of the pope and the papal nuncio, bishop Esterházy of Eger came to Vienna in the summer of 1768 to attempt to gain the support of state ministers and court advisors. At the same time, Pope Clement XIII elaborated upon the "canonical" obstacles (Fourth Lateran Council, the decision of Pope Benedict XIV) that prevented him from granting independence to the Mukačevo eparchy.[140]

On August 15, 1768, the first plenary session of the Austrian State Council was held in the presence of Maria Theresa. It was also attended by the bishop of Eger. Only the bishop of Mukačevo was not represented at the meeting. After hearing the opinions of her ministers, Maria Theresa did not dare to oppose the pope's decision and decided to wait and see if the bishop of Eger could not be persuaded to treat the Uniates of Carpathian Rus' "more favorably and less despotically." Thus, the establishment of the Mukačevo eparchy was once again postponed.[141]

The bishop of Eger regarded this turn of events as a sign of victory. He was certain that the question of the Mukačevo eparchy had finally been resolved to his advantage. For bishop Bradač, too, securing the independence of his eparchy seemed a hopeless cause. Nevertheless, the pope did express concern that Maria Theresa "would change her mind.''[142]

7. Renewed Attempts to Attain Independence

Throughout the eighteenth century, the Eger see was occupied by bishops from such prominent Hungarian noble families as Erdődy (1715-1744), Barkóczy (1745-1761), and Esterházy (1762-1799). Their pride did not allow them to make concessions to the Mukačevo bishops, who were of common birth. This was the reason for the contempt, arrogance, and "inhumane conduct" of the Eger prelates towards the Mukačevo bishops. Upon winning his case in Rome and Vienna, bishop Esterházy became even more arrogant and hostile towards bishop Ivan Bradač, despite the latter's great erudition.[143]

In order to improve relations between the two bishops, Maria Theresa issued a new order on August 24, 1768, which stipulated the Mukačevo prelate's continued subordination to the Eger ordinary as the latter's "ritual vicar" for the Rusyn Catholics of northern

Hungary. In turn, bishop Esterházy was to show respect to bishop Bradač "as the leader of the Uniate clergy and faithful" and "to treat him with the dignity befitting his office," honoring "all the privileges and rights" that had been granted the Carpatho-Rusyn Catholics. The Rusyn parish priests were "true pastors" and not merely the "chaplains of Latin pastors" and were therefore entitled to both the tithes and stole fees of their faithful. In order to resolve the conflict, Bradač was to go to Eger to settle all matters under dispute with Esterházy "in a peaceful manner."[144]

This decision of the Viennese court was a heavy blow to the Carpatho-Rusyns. Numerous protests were sent to Rome and Vienna, all to no avail. They had no choice but to submit to the order of the empress. On September, 15, 1769, bishop Bradač finally arrived in Eger accompanied by his archdeacons Ju. Sabadoš, A. Žetkej, A. Bačyns'kyj, and I. Bokšaj.[145]

The bishop of Eger received them with great disdain. Before allowing bishop Bradač to speak, Esterházy demanded that he swear an oath of loyalty and submission to him. Bradač refused to make such an oath, since neither Rome nor Vienna had imposed it upon him. Esterházy then assailed Bradač, calling him a "malicious man," a "cheat," a "man of bad conscience," an "enemy of Rome," a "Pharisee," and much more. Bradač left the conference room, but before leaving he stated: "I realize that the famous family of Esterházy is influential and powerful. But I can say in good conscience that even such famous a family is powerless to amend the great harm and injustice that Your Excellency has done to the Uniate clergy, the faithful, and the Holy Union."

To this the bishop of Eger replied indignantly: "I am doing these things not as count Esterházy, but as the ordinary of Eger. The king himself allotted me the tithes and stole fees from the Carpatho-Rusyns and Romanians and I exercise jurisdiction over 1,000 parishes. Bradač responded: "Your Excellency is powerful in both respects [i.e., as count and as bishop] and can therefore persecute and slander me. But I still have hope that the Good Lord will not abandon me and my faithful, and that Her Majesty [i.e., Maria Theresa] will not permit the persecution of my flock to continue forever."[146]

This atmosphere was hardly conducive for any agreement between the two prelates. Subsequently, bishop Bradač collected all the pertinent facts and necessary documents, and at the beginning of 1770 he sent his vicar-general, archdeacon Andrij Bačyns'kyj, to Vienna with instructions to endeavor once again to secure the independence of the

Mukačevo eparchy. At first, no one in Vienna would speak with Bačyns'kyj. Finally, after two months, he managed to win the support of two advisors to the court, K. Plümegen and F. Höller. Through them, Bačyns'kyj submitted bishop Bradač's memorandum to Empress Maria Theresa.[147]

On April 1, 1770, with the help of minister Plümegen, Bačyns'kyj "by chance" was admitted to an audience with the empress. To Bradač's report, Bačyns'kyj also added his own description of the relations between the Eger and Mukačevo bishops. The audience had a decisive effect on the creation of the Mukačevo eparchy. After consulting with her ministers, Maria Theresa on May 12, 1770 asked Pope Clement XIV (1769-1774) to grant independence to the Mukačevo eparchy. In order to lift all suspicion from the Mukačevo prelate, she proposed that he be placed under the jurisdiction of the archbishop of Esztergom as his metropolitan.[148] This time Maria Theresa's request was backed by the papal nuncio.[149]

The imperial office summoned both bishops to Vienna. Esterházy preceded Bradač to the capital by a whole month. By the time Bradač arrived in the middle of July,[150] Esterházy had managed to obtain the support of several influential advisors at the imperial court. Realizing at last that he could no longer disregard Bradač, Esterházy granted him wide powers to govern his faithful. During his audience with Maria Theresa, Esterházy assured the empress that in the future he would treat the Carpatho-Rusyn clergy and faithful kindly and with respect. Maria Theresa, however, announced that the final decision rested with Rome.[151]

Without the slightest hesitation, Esterházy wrote a letter to the pope, in which he informed the Apostolic See: (1) that the reasons the empress had given for making the Mukačevo eparchy independent were unfounded; (2) that the full responsibility for the conflict was with Bradač, because he "behaves improperly" and then accuses Esterházy of abuses at court; (3) that the Carpatho-Rusyns were not concerned with the good of the union, but merely wanted to "humiliate the bishop of Eger"; (4) that the establishment of the Mukačevo eparchy would "enable the Greek Catholics to triumph over the Roman Catholics" and then return to the [Orthodox] schism; and (5) that Maria Theresa had assured him at his audience with her that she would submit to the pontiff's decision because of the great respect she felt for him.[152]

At the same time that Rome received Esterházy's letter it also received a report from the papal nuncio, who informed the pope of the unyielding determination of the empress in the matter of the Mukačevo eparchy, of which the nuncio knew from Maria Theresa herself. The nuncio wrote that the empress was convinced that the Mukačevo eparchy had to be made independent or else "both the Holy Union and public peace would suffer." For his part, the nuncio added: "Here in Vienna, the bishop of Eger does not have the support of a single influential person."[153]

Rome, however, chose to believe the bishop of Eger rather than the nuncio. The pope once again tried to persuade Maria Theresa that the creation of a Mukačevo eparchy could cause a great deal of harm for which the empress would be held responsible.[154] But Maria Theresa was prepared to take the responsibility for all "the unfortunate consequences" which Rome feared, and she continued to press for the erection of the Mukačevo eparchy.[155] In the meantime, the imperial council of ministers decided that Maria Theresa should herself establish the Mukačevo eparchy in accordance with her "supreme right of patronage as the apostolic king of Hungary." The nuncio immediately informed Rome of this decision.[156]

The Apostolic See realized that it was time to take action. In a letter dated November 17, 1770, Pope Clement XIV hastened to inform Maria Theresa about his decision to appoint a "Greek Catholic bishop subject to the jurisdiction of the archbishop of Esztergom" for the Carpatho-Rusyns, and that all that was now required was the completion of the necessary formalities for the erection.[157]

8. The Proclamation of an Independent Eparchy

The pope's decision to create an independent Mukačevo eparchy caused great discontent in Hungarian circles. The Hungarian nobility had not expected that a common Carpatho-Rusyn bishop like Ivan Bradač would triumph over count Esterházy. As a concession to the Hungarians, the empress agreed to place the Mukačevo bishop under the supervision of the Hungarian primate of Esztergom as the metropolitan.

The matter of the erection of the Mukačevo eparchy was examined at a meeting of the Consistorial Congregation in Rome on March 20, 1771. Since there were no obstacles to the proposal, the Congregation issued a decree on March 23, canonically establishing the Mukačevo eparchy.[158] However, some of the expressions used in the text did not meet with the approval of the imperial chancery and had to be emended.[159] The final text of the bull of erection and the details of the erection were approved on July 20, 1771.[160]

Still, the bishop of Eger refused to yield. Although he could no longer block the creation of the Mukačevo eparchy, he was determined to take personal revenge against Bradač by not permitting him to become the first bishop of the newly established eparchy. He therefore accused Bradač before the nuncio of "possible heresy and schism." Bradač did not wish to enter into another conflict with Esterházy and submitted to the judgment of the Apostolic See. The Papal Commission, which reviewed the charges against Bradač, cleared him of all suspicion and moved to complete the erection formalities.[161]

On September 19, 1771, Pope Clement XIV promulgated the bull "Eximia Regalium Principum" by which he created the Mukačevo eparchy on the following conditions: (1) the bishop of Mukačevo was to submit his profession of faith every year to his chapter of canons, which was then to forward it in writing to the papal nuncio in Vienna[162] and (2) the bishop of Mukačevo was subject to the authority of the archbishop of Esztergom as his metropolitan.[163]

The ancient city of Mukačevo was made the seat of the eparchy, and the parish church of the Dormition of the Blessed Mother became the cathedral. Because the residence and cathedral of Mukačevo were in a state of disrepair and there were no suitable premises in the city for the diocesan seminary and members of the chapter, in 1780, the successor of bishop Bradač, Andrij Bačyns'kyj (1773-1809), transferred the seat of the eparchy to Užhorod. Despite the transfer of the seat, the name of the eparchy remained that of Mukačevo.[164]

Bishop Bačyns'kyj also succeeded in obtaining the necessary endowments for the eparchy and its institutions from the imperial court. The bull of erection had allotted the bishop 3,000 gold florins in annual income. Bačyns'kyj was able to have this sum raised to 12,000 annually, and in 1776 this payment was exchanged for the estates of the extinct Monastery of Sts. Peter and Paul in Tapolcza near Miskolc in Hungary.[165] Through the efforts of Bačyns'kyj, a cathedral chapter consisting of seven canons was established in Užhorod and installed in 1777.[166]

The erection of the Mukačevo eparchy was thus complete. Its creation was the work of three bishops: M. Ol'šavs'kyj, I. Bradač, and A. Bačyns'kyj, whose names are inscribed in gold letters in the history of Carpathian Rus'. The formation of an independent eparchy of Mukačevo initiated rapid progress in the religious and cultural life of Carpathian Rus'. The Carpatho-Rusyns were now about to enter into

a "golden age," the architect of which was the great bishop Andrij
Bačyns'kyj.[167]

CHAPTER FOUR

The Fate of the Máramaros Eparchy

One of the thirteen counties that the Mukačevo eparchy encompassed was Máramaros. In terms of ethnic composition, half the population of this region comprised Carpatho-Rusyns, one quarter Romanians, and the remainder Hungarians, Germans, and Jews. The Carpatho-Rusyn and Romanian inhabitants were Orthodox, while the Hungarians and Germans were Roman Catholics. At the end of the sixteenth century, the majority of Hungarians [in neighboring Transylvania] converted to Calvinism as a form of protest against the Catholic Habsburgs. As the dominant class, the Hungarians hoped to convert both the Carpatho-Rusyns and the Romanians to Protestantism, and therefore they posed the main obstacle to the union with Rome in Máramaros county. After the union with Rome was accepted, the Orthodox bishops of Mukačevo sought to gain a foothold in the Máramaros region and adopted the title "bishop of Máramaros."

1. The Origins of an Independent Eparchy

The history of the Máramaros region is closely linked with that of Carpathian Rus'. In the fourteenth century, the center of religious and cultural life in Máramaros was the Monastery of St. Michael in Hruševo, which had been granted the right of stauropegion by patriarch Antony IV of Constantinople in 1391. Consequently, the Hruševo monastery was exempt from the jurisdiction of the local bishop.[1] In addition, the patriarch bestowed on the monastery's hegumen the title of "exarch" and placed the surrounding parishes under his control. Under the protection of his patrons, during the fifteenth century, the archimandrite-exarch of Hruševo extended his authority over most of the Máramaros region, and it was this development that later gave rise to the idea of establishing a separate

62

Máramaros eparchy.

The bishops of Mukačevo were unwilling to tolerate the spread of the Hruševo exarch's jurisdiction. Thus, at the end of the fifteenth century, bishop Ivan of Mukačevo made an attempt to extend his control over the Hruševo exarchate. The exarch of Hruševo, Ilarij, citing the charters of his patrons and the patriarch, appealed to king Ulászló II (reigned 1490-1516), who acknowledged the exarchal rights of Hruševo and placed it under the jurisdiction of the Transylvanian metropolitan. However, Ilarij was instructed to respect the bishop of Mukačevo and pay the homage due him.[2]

Failing to gain control over the Hruševo exarchate, bishop Ivan tried to limit the exarch's authority to the original seven parishes designated in the patriarchal charter. The king, however, upheld the rights of the Hruševo exarchate.[3] The Mukačevo prelates persisted in their efforts, and in 1551 we find the first reference to the fact that all of Máramaros county had been placed under the jurisdiction of bishop Vasylij of Mukačevo, even though there were still individual priests who refused to recognize the authority of "their bishop" and to pay tithes to him.[4] Finally, in 1556, the Transylvanian count György Báthory, to whose domain Hruševo and Mukačevo then belonged, invested the bishop of Mukačevo Ilarion (1556-1567?) with the Hruševo monastery and all its possessions.[5]

During the seventeenth century, the bishops of Mukačevo began adding to their title other regions which lay outside the boundaries of the Mukačevo domain. Thus, for example, in 1623, prince Gábor Bethlén of Transylvania (1613-1629) confirmed bishop Partenij as the hierarch of Bereg, Ung, Szabolcs, Zemplén, Sáros, and Máramaros counties.[6] When the Romanian bishops later tried to extend their authority over the Máramaros region, prince Bethlen in 1627 named Ivan Hryhorovyč "bishop of Mukačevo and Máramaros of the Greek rite."[7] At the same time, Bethlen expelled the Romanian Orthodox bishop Dositej from Alba Iulia.[8] The Máramaros magnates, who opposed Bethlen's rule, took Dositej under their protection and named him "bishop of Máramaros."

After the death of Dositej, the Romanian clergy elected the Romanian priest Dimitrie Pap as their bishop. The new Transylvanian ruler, prince György Rákóczi I (1630-1648), did not allow Pap to be consecrated bishop and exerted pressure on the Máramaros diet to accept the jurisdiction of the bishop of Mukačevo over the region. In 1634, prince Rákóczi, who was also lord of the Mukačevo domain, named Vasylij Tarasovyč "bishop of Mukačevo and Máramaros."[9]

Rákóczi's action made it appear that he recognized the existence of a separate Máramaros eparchy, which gave rise to the notion of an independent diocese in the region.

2. The Máramaros Region as the Stronghold of Orthodoxy

At the end of the sixteenth century, the majority of the ruling class of the Máramaros region converted to Calvinism. As in the other counties, the Protestant lords were hostile to the Holy Union. When at the end of 1640 bishop Tarasovyč proposed the idea of union with Rome and was imprisoned, the Máramaros diet demanded that prince Rákóczi name a separate Orthodox bishop for the Máramaros region. In order not to lose control over the church there, Rákóczi placed Máramaros under the jurisdiction of the Romanian Orthodox archbishop of Alba Iulia, Stefan Simonovici (1643-1651).

Simonovici paid relatively little attention to the Máramaros region, and this enabled Tarasovyč after his return to Orthodoxy to regain control over the area. This time, however, Rákóczi returned only the Carpatho-Rusyn parishes to Tarasovyč while appointing an administrator, the hieromonk Sylvester (adm. 1645-1650) and later the priest Simeon Petraško (mentioned in 1652), for the Romanian parishes. From 1653-1662, the bishop of Máramaros was Mychajil Molodec', most likely an itinerant Orthodox bishop who had come to the region from abroad. He had no appointment, but as an ordained bishop he administered all the parishes of the Máramaros region.

In 1662, the Orthodox faithful of Máramaros split into two separate national groups. The Romanian parishes acknowledged the authority of the metropolitan of Alba Iulia, while the Carpatho-Rusyns recognized the Orthodox bishop of Mukačevo, Joannykij Zejkan', as their prelate. There was already a Uniate bishop of Mukačevo at the time, but he still resided in Užhorod. In 1664, when the Uniate bishop Partenij Petrovyč was permitted to make Mukačevo his seat, the Orthodox prelate, Zejkan', moved temporarily to Imstyčevo,[10] and later to the Uhlja monastery from where he administered the Orthodox Rusyn parishes in the Máramaros region. From then on, the Máramaros Orthodox bishops had their seat in Uhlja.

During this period, the union in Carpathian Rus' was still in a very precarious state. This was the period of struggle for the right to appoint the bishop of Mukačevo. Moreover, all of Carpathian Rus' was then in turmoil as a result of the uprising of Imre Thököly, who wanted to liberate Hungary from the Habsburgs with the help of the Turks. In 1686, Thököly's forces occupied the Mukačevo domain and installed at the monastery on Černeča Hora the hieromonk Metodij Rakovec'kyj, who was then consecrated bishop in Moldavia.

After putting down Thököly's uprising, the Austrian emperor appointed the Uniate bishop Josyf de Camillis (1689-1706), a great advocate of the union, to the Mukačevo episcopate. Rakovec'kyj then converted to Catholicism and was named superior of the Mukačevo monastery by de Camillis. However, when in an alliance with Mychajil Andrella, the pastor of Orosvyhovo, Rakovec'kyj began working against the union, bishop de Camillis expelled him from Mukačevo.[11] Rakovec'kyj spent a short time in the Imstyčevo monastery and then tried his luck in the Máramaros region. But the prince of Transylvania had already installed another bishop there—Josyf I. Stojka (1690-1711).

Bishop de Camillis's work to implement the union roused the Máramaros magnates. Under pressure from them, Rákóczi named Stojka bishop of Máramaros. After his episcopal ordination in Moldavia, Stojka settled at the Uhlja monastery and used the title: "By the Grace of God, Orthodox bishop of Máramaros, exarch of the patriarchal stauropegion of Constantinople, administrator of the Bilhorod [Alba Iulia] and Počajiv metropolitanates, etc. etc."[12]

Bishop de Camillis intended to bring about the union with Rome in the Máramaros region as well, and therefore he asked the Austrian imperial court to place this county under his jurisdiction, arguing that "the Máramaros region has recognized the bishop of Mukačevo as its rightful hierarch from the earliest times."[13] However, determined to avoid new civil disturbances, the emperor left the Máramaros region under the control of the Orthodox bishop Stojka.

The Máramaros clergy accepted Stojka as their bishop on condition that he would govern the eparchy with the assistance of an eparchial synod. Stojka dispensed with the synod and began to move closer to the Protestants, while the clergy increasingly favored union with Rome. Not surprisingly, regular conflicts and disputes soon broke out between the clergy and their bishop. In order to retain his control, bishop Stojka finally placed himself under the jurisdiction of the Calvinist Church in Transylvania, which had promised him equal privileges with the Catholics and the Protestants.[14]

However, when it became obvious that the promised privileges were not forthcoming, in 1705, the Orthodox eparchial synod ousted Stojka from the bishopric and imprisoned him pending an investigation. The trial concluded the following year with the dismissal of Stojka from the eparchy and the confiscation of his property by the county authorities.[15]

In 1708, a Romanian priest named Job Czirka, also a sympathizer of Calvinism and an inveterate foe of the union, was chosen to take Stojka's place. Czirka's free-thinking soon alienated the clergy, which saw union with Rome as their only solution. Because of his drunkenness and scandalous conduct, Czirka also lost favor with the magnates, who had appointed him administrator of the Máramaros region. In 1710, the court dismissed him from the episcopate and entrusted the administration of the Máramaros eparchy once again to bishop Stojka. The clergy accepted Stojka but only on condition that prince Rákóczi would confirm him as bishop.

Rákóczi had just led a rebellion against the Habsburgs, but in 1711, the rising ended in defeat. The emperor's troops occupied the whole of Transylvania, including the Máramaros region. Bishop Stojka died the same year, leaving behind great disorder and decadence in the eparchy.[16]

3. Attempts at Implementing the Union in Máramaros

Fear of the union was the main reason why the Máramaros region split away from the Mukačevo see in 1690 and elected its own Orthodox bishop.[17] Unfortunately, the Máramaros bishops were unable to govern their eparchy independently and became subject to a Protestant administration. The local clergy became divided into three groups. One group wanted to remain under the jurisdiction of the Protestant superintendent; a second group wished to secure independence as an Orthodox entity; a third group favored union with Rome.

After the failure of Rákóczi's rebellion, sympathy for Protestantism diminished. On the other hand, the struggle between the Orthodox and pro-union groups intensified. Unfortunately, until 1716, the Mukačevo see also was deprived of a bishop who could have taken an interest in the ecclesiastical affairs of the Máramaros region after the death of bishop Stojka.[18] As a result, the anti-union group succeeded in electing the hieromonk Dosytej Teodorovyč, hegumen of the Uhlja monastery, as their bishop. Advocates of the union put forward the candidacy of the Romanian priest Stefan Petrovan, who took the religious name Serafim. The pro-union group won at the diocesan synod and Petrovan became bishop (1711-1717).

Petrovan wasted no time. Immediately after his episcopal consecration, he asked the Uniate archbishop Athanasius Anhelu of Alba Iulia

to extend his guardianship over the Máramaros eparchy.[19] In retaliation, his opponents took measures to oust him from the bishopric.
They initiated legal proceedings which lasted three years. Finally, on
April 9, 1717, the Máramaros county court sentenced Petrovan to imprisonment "for various abuses" and stripped him of his office. The
bishop died in prison that same year, his only crime being that he had
wanted union with Rome.

However, Petrovan's work and sacrifice were not in vain. He sustained the union movement among the Máramaros clergy until
assistance could come from the Mukačevo eparchy in the person of
the hieromonk Prokopij Hodermars'kyj, OSBM. In order to
strengthen the union movement, Hodermars'kyj convoked a synod of
clergy who favored union with Rome in Sighetul, but the Protestants
disbanded the synod. This prompted the Military Council of Transylvania to intervene in the religious affairs of Máramaros in an attempt to re-establish peace in the region. The council decided that
parishes that did not wish to enter into union with Rome should remain under the jurisdiction of their Orthodox bishop,[20] while the
magnates were ordered to allow Hodermars'kyj to govern those
parishes which favored the union. In 1716, Hodermars'kyj again convoked a synod in Sighetul, which was attended by 60 Carpatho-Rusyn
priests from the Máramaros region. They all accepted the union and
placed themselves under the jurisdiction of the bishop of Mukačevo.
Thus, the foundation of the union in the Máramaros region was laid.

Nonetheless, Transylvania's magnates were determined to keep
Máramaros Orthodox. After the death of Petrovan, they named
Dosytej Teodorovyč bishop of the Orthodox eparchy (1718-1733) and
endeavored to make the Uniates of the region also subject to his
authority. But emperor Charles VI blocked these attempts. In 1719, he
issued a charter which guaranteed the rights and privileges of the
Uniate parishes of the Máramaros region.

Having brought order to the Mukačevo eparchy, bishop Jurij H.
Bizancij (1716-1733) turned his attention to Máramaros. He began by
obtaining jurisdiction from emperor Charles VI over the entire
Máramaros region, as had been the case earlier. The emperor then
suspended bishop Dosytej Teodorovyč and forbade him to interfere in
the administration of parishes in Máramaros.[21]

In August 1721, bishop Bizancij began a tour of the Máramaros
region for the purpose of bringing about the union. Individual
parishes gladly accepted the union because Bizancij had secured for
them all the benefits and privileges of the so-called "accepted"

religions. Bizancij concluded his tour in December 1721, by which time the union had been consolidated throughout all of Carpathian Rus'.[22]

Bizancij also tried to persuade bishop Teodorovyč to accept the union, but the latter refused the conditions offered. Consequently, in accordance with the emperor's decree, Bizancij stripped Teodorovyč of all episcopal functions, although he provided him with the revenues of the Uhlja monastery. Despite the ban, Teodorovyč continued to ordain priests in secret and to grant various dispensations, which created serious problems for Bizancij.[23] Teodorovyč died in 1733 at the Uhlja monastery. With his death, the so-called Máramaros eparchy ceased to exist and all the parishes in Carpathian Rus' were finally united under the jurisdiction of the Mukačevo hierarch.

4. The Struggle for Control over the Máramaros Region

As part of Transylvania, the Máramaros region was together with that principality incorporated in 1733 into the Hungarian kingdom. After accepting the union, the Carpatho-Rusyn clergy of Máramaros gladly accepted the jurisdiction of the Mukačevo bishop. The Romanian clergy, on the other hand, wanted to join the Transylvanian Romanians, who had also entered into the union with Rome in 1698. It was for this reason that bishop Bizancij had asked the emperor for a charter to allow him to extend his authority over the entire Mármaros county "according to ancient custom."[24]

When the Greek Catholic Romanian eparchy of Făgăraş was created in 1721, bishop J. Giurgiu de Pataky (1723-1727) established relations with the Romanian clergy of the Máramaros region, in order to place them under his own jurisdiction.[25] Through the efforts of bishop Pataky, in 1723 the Transylvanian governor recognized the authority of the Făgăraş prelate over the Máramaros region, but bishop Bizancij opposed this decision, citing the imperial charter of 1720. This gave rise to a struggle for jurisdiction over the Máramaros region between the Mukačevo and Făgăraş bishops.

The matter ultimately ended up in Rome. At its meeting on May 7, 1725, the Congregation for the Propagation of the Faith was unable to reach any decision and had to wait for the opinion of the papal nuncio in Vienna.[26] While Bizancij responded to the nuncio's inquiry,[27] Pataky ignored it. Thus, on June 24, 1727, Bizancij once again raised in Rome the issue of jurisdiction over Máramaros.[28] Just then bishop Pataki died and the Vatican appointed bishop Bizancij the temporary administrator of the Făgăraş eparchy.[29] This helped Bizancij to consolidate his jurisdiction over Máramaros.

In 1731, the new bishop of Făgăraş, Giurgiu Micu-Klein revived the struggle for ecclesiastical jurisdiction over Máramaros. For its part, Rome waited for a decision from the Austrian imperial court. On November 15, 1732, the papal nuncio in Vienna advised Rome to wait before making a decision, because the imperial court, too, was unable to determine whether Máramaros should belong administratively to Transylvania or to the kingdom of Hungary.[30]

Finally, in 1733, the Transylvanian principality was abolished, and the bishop of Făgăraş no longer had a basis for his claim to episcopal authority over the Máramaros region. Thus, after the death of bishop Bizancij, emperor Charles VI named S. Ol'šavs'kyj (1733-1737) "bishop of Mukačevo and Máramaros." The Apostolic See concurred with the emperor's decision. Thus, jurisdiction over the Máramaros region passed into the hands of the Mukačevo hierarch.[31]

5. The Establishment of the Máramaros Vicariate

Bishop Jurij Bizancij found the Máramaros clergy to be in a deplorable condition. As earlier in other parts of Carpathian Rus', very little distinguished this clergy from the rest of the serfs. Priests had to perform all the duties of serfdom, including statute labor. In addition to lacking education, the priests had fallen under Protestant influence. Superstition and drunkenness were also widespread. It was essential that the clergy be liberated from the control of the secular lords and that the dignity of their office be raised to the same level as that of the Catholic clergy.

Both Hodermars'kyj and Bizancij were convinced that the only way in which to improve the lot of the Carpatho-Rusyn clergy was through union with Rome. With the authority of the emperor and the Military Council of Transylvania behind him, Bizancij set about ordering the affairs of individual parishes immediately after his arrival in Máramaros county. His principal problem was to find appointments for priests, whose number had uncontrollably swelled. In larger localities he appointed assistant pastors, but in other places he had to appoint some priests as cantors or sextons in order to secure for them the exemptions. This forced the landowners to exempt all these priests from serfdom and to provide them with church lands. In this manner, bishop Bizancij elevated the prestige of the Máramaros clergy and won their trust.

In order to placate the Romanians and preserve the Máramaros region as a traditionally independent unit, Bizancij in 1723 established the "Máramaros vicariate" together with its own consistory. As the first vicar in Sighetul, Bizancij appointed the Basilian monk Prokopij Hodermars'kyj (1723-1726) who had worked hard to bring about the union in the Máramaros region.

Because of the struggle for control over the Máramaros region, Hodermars'kyj's successor, vicar S. Ol'šavs'kyj (1729-1733), was forced to return to Mukačevo, where he was appointed bishop after the death of Bizancij in 1733.

The Mukačevo bishops also encountered difficulties with the Transylvanian princes, because the Máramaros clergy had not paid them taxes since the seventeenth century. In order to resolve the problem, bishop Havryjil Blažovs'kyj (1738-1742) called a synod in 1739, at which it was decided to pay prince M. Apafi at least a "nominal tax."[32] In return, the prince exempted the Máramaros clergy from taxes and statute labor.

The synod also resolved to revive the Máramaros vicariate, which had ceased to exist when S. Ol'šavs'kyj was elected bishop. Acting on a proposal of the synod, on September 6, 1740, bishop Blažovs'kyj appointed the proto-hegumen Hryhorij Bulko, OSBM,[33] vicar of Máramaros. Bulko held the position briefly because he died two years later.

The principal city of the county, Sighetul (Marmației),[34] was designated the seat of the vicariate, even though there was no Carpatho-Rusyn parish there at the time. A building to serve as the vicar's residence and land for a church were donated by the nobleman, Rudolf A. Eldbeck, who was well disposed towards the Carpatho-Rusyns. The first vicar, P. Hodermars'kyj, took up residence in the new building. At first, the faithful held religious services in the Roman Catholic church, but in 1748 vicar Andrej Bačyns'kyj (1746-1754) built a wooden church in Sighetul for the Greek Catholics. These were difficult times for the Máramaros vicars. They had no income and had to rely on the bishop of Mukačevo for material assistance. The bishop thus preferred to name Basilian monks to head the vicariate, since they received aid from their monasteries.

The conditions of the Máramaros vicariate improved during the tenure of bishop Andrej Bačyns'kyj, who managed to obtain an annual income of 400 florins for the vicar from the religious fund. Bačyns'kyj also succeeded in securing grants of land for the parish priest, his assistant, the cantor, and the sexton, since the Sighetul parish had grown significantly during the eighteenth century.

Through the efforts of bishop Bačyns'kyj, in 1778 an attractive residence was built for the vicar in Sighetul and in 1800 work began on the erection of a new stone church. The Máramaros vicar thus gained respect and prestige, and was able to perform his high office with dignity.[35]

After the death of bishop Bačyns'kyj in 1809, there were attempts to attach the Máramaros vicariate to the Romanian Greek Catholic eparchy of Oradea, but the Mukačevo consistory, headed by the capitulary vicar Ivan Kutka, vigorously opposed this. When a new Romanian Greek Catholic eparchy was established in Gherla in 1853, almost all the Romanian parishes of the Máramaros vicariate were attached to it.[36]

A dispute also arose at the time about the fate of the Sighetul parish, which included both Carpatho-Rusyns and Romanians. The vicar Peter Anderko (1815-1869), of Romanian descent, wanted to incorporate the Sighetul parish into the Gherla eparchy. After a protracted debate, on August 29, 1865, the Supervisory Council of Hungary recognized the Sighetul parish as Carpatho-Rusyn and left it under the jurisdiction of the bishop of Mukačevo.

The Romanians were not satisfied with the decision, and so, supported by the vicar Anderko himself, they built a separate church. In order to bring the matter to a close, the Mukačevo bishop granted separate status to the Romanian parish in Sighetul, but did not relinquish his jurisdiction over it.

After World War I, Sighetul and eleven Carpatho-Rusyn parishes became part of Romania. At first, these parishes constituted a separate administrative unit, but in 1930, they were incorporated into the newly-established Romanian Greek Catholic eparchy of Maramureş with a seat in Baia Mare.[37] This marked the end of the historic Máramaros vicariate. In its place, the parishes that after World War I remained in the Mukačevo eparchy were formed into the so-called Maramoroš archdiaconate with a seat in Chust.[38]

Shortly before the outbreak of World War II, there were plans to create a metropolitanate in Carpathian Rus'. Then, it was proposed to transform the Maramoroš archdiaconate into a new Chust eparchy, but the war put an end to these plans.

CHAPTER FIVE

The Creation of the Prešov Eparchy

Religious and cultural life in Carpathian Rus' experienced a golden age during the episcopate of bishop Andrij Bačyns'kyj (1773-1809). Even though the people did not enjoy full political freedom, they were united under one spiritual leader, the bishop of Mukačevo. As a member [ex officio] of the upper house of the Hungarian parliament, the Mukačevo prelate was able to defend the interests of his people in the political arena. Consequently, the Carpatho-Rusyns regarded their hierarch as their father and leader.

This unity of the Carpatho-Rusyns, albeit only in the religious sphere, ran counter to Hungarian policy. In order to hold in check Hungarian aspirations to "independence," at the beginning of the nineteenth century Austria began to support the interests of the national minorities. For their part, the Hungarians endeavored to weaken the non-Magyar nationalities by dividing them administratively, politically, economically, and even culturally.

The canonical erection of the Mukačevo eparchy in Carpathian Rus' brought strong spiritual and cultural unity to the Carpatho-Rusyns, who had the support of the Austrian Habsburgs. In order to cripple the religious and cultural aspirations of the Carpatho-Rusyns, the Hungarians decided to divide the Mukačevo eparchy. This gave rise to the notion of establishing the Prešov eparchy.

1. A Vicariate as the Nucleus of the Prešov Eparchy

On July 26, 1776, the Hungarian court chancery issued a directive creating two episcopal vicariates in order to facilitate the administration of the vast Mukačevo eparchy: (1) the Máramaros vicariate in the eastern part of Carpathian Rus'; and (2) the Satu Mare vicariate in the Trans-Tisza region, where the majority of the parishes were Romanian.[1] Practical considerations dictated the need for a separate

72

vicariate in the western portion of the Mukačevo eparchy, that is, in the Prešov Region, as well. Thus, at the request of bishop A. Bačyns'kyj, on July 27, 1787, the Hungarian chancery established the Košice vicariate. Canon Ivan Pastelij was appointed the first vicar of Košice.[2]

The founding charter stipulated that the Košice vicar always had to be chosen from among the canons of the Mukačevo cathedral chapter and that his appointment had to be confirmed by the Austrian emperor. The Košice vicar was given the Dominican monastery as his residence and a yearly allowance of 1,200 florins. Since at that time the Dominican monastery was occupied by state institutions, the vicar's residence was moved to the Franciscan monastery in Košice.

The Košice municipal council objected to a Carpatho-Rusyn vicar. The bishop of Eger also interfered by hastening to house his Minor Seminary in the Franciscan monastery. Discouraged by the intrigues of the Košice city authorities and the Eger ordinary, Pastelij resigned from the vicariate, and on January 13, 1790, canon Mychajil Bradač was named to replace him.[3]

Bradač resolved to fight the city council of Košice. In the meantime, in order not to neglect the administration of the vicariate, he settled on his family estate in Kamienka in Szepes (Spiš) County.[4] To keep the Carpatho-Rusyn vicar out of Košice, the city council assigned the Benedictine monastery for the army's use and returned the Franciscan monastery to the Franciscan order. Bradač was forced to seek a residence elsewhere. He finally found an abandoned monastery and church belonging to the Minorite Friars in Prešov. On December 20, 1792, the Hungarian court chancery transferred the seat of the vicariate to Prešov (Hungarian: Eperjes) and accorded Bradač the holdings he requested.[5]

In Prešov, Bradač encountered new difficulties. As Aleksander Duchnovyč writes, opposition to Carpatho-Rusyns in the Prešov Region was so great that there was reason to fear for the very existence of the vicariate.[6] But Bradač did not become discouraged and continued his efforts on behalf of the vicariate. In 1802, when he became a deputy to the Hungarian parliament from the Mukačevo chapter, Bradač appealed directly to the Habsburg imperial court to settle once and for all the matter of the vicar's residence and church in Prešov.

The seat of the vicariate was officially transferred to Prešov by an imperial decree dated September 2, 1806. The monastery of the Minorite Friars was to serve as the vicar's residence. Bradač obtained funds from the religious fund to restore the monastery and to adapt the church to the requirements of the Eastern rite. The church was to serve as the parish church for Prešov's Carpatho-Rusyn congregation, which until then had had no house of worship of its own. A three-member consistory was created to assist the vicar. Thus, Bradač's endeavors, in which he was supported by bishop Andrij Bačyns'kyj, ended in success and the Prešov vicariate was finally established.

In 1808, the emperor appointed Mychajil Bradač auxiliary to Bačyns'kyj.[7] The pope named Bradač titular bishop of Dorylaeum, but without the right of succession.[8] After his episcopal consecration by the Romanian bishop Samuel Vulcan in Oradea on January 8, 1809, Bradač returned to Prešov to supervise the restoration of the church and vicar's residence.

Bishop Bačyns'kyj died that same year, and the Mukačevo chapter elected canon Ivan Kutka as capitular vicar to administer the eparchy. Bishop Bradač took this election as a personal insult and tried to li-quidate the Prešov vicariate in order to make himself eligible to suc-ceed to the Mukačevo see. But his plans encountered difficulties. When Ivan Kutka died in 1812, the Mukačevo episcopate was still va-cant. Finally, in December of that year, the chapter elected bishop Bradač vicar, and he took over the administration of the Mukačevo eparchy.

The Prešov city council attempted to take advantage of this oppor-tunity to rid itself of a Carpatho-Rusyn vicar. But the Austrian im-perial court did not agree to this and appointed canon Hryhorij Tarkovyč as the new vicar. After the death of Bradač (1815), Tarkovyč became the capitular vicar of the Mukačevo eparchy, and the office of the Prešov vicariate was assumed by canon Ivan Ol'šavs'kyj. Ol'šavs'kyj, who served from 1815 to 1821, was the last vicar of Prešov.

2. Overcoming Obstacles to the Creation of the Prešov Eparchy

The Greek Catholic bishops of Križevci and Oradea hoped to turn the difficulties involved in the establishment of the Košice, later Prešov vicariate to their own advantage. At the same time, the Austrian imperial court was considering the liquidation of the Križevci eparchy because of its small number of faithful. In order to prevent this, the Križevci prelates, Jozafat Bastašić (1790-1793) and Silvestar Bubanović (1795-1810), made repeated demands that the Carpatho-Rusyn parishes located in the Prešov Region be incorporated into the Križevci eparchy. This would have obviated the need for the Košice vicariate.

A similar fate awaited the Oradea Greek Catholic eparchy, where in the eighteenth century the majority of Romanians reverted to Orthodoxy. The bishop of Oradea wanted to incorporate into his eparchy the Carpatho-Rusyn parishes in the Szabolcs and Szatmár counties of the Mukačevo eparchy, thereby eliminating the need for the Szatmár vicariate. These proposals were vigorously opposed by bishop Andrij Bačyns'kyj,[9] even though they had the backing of the Hungarian government.

Fortunately, the Austrian imperial court entrusted the review of these proposals to persons who were well disposed towards Bačyns'kyj and the Carpatho-Rusyns. Both the crown's advisor bishop Mitterpracher and councillor P. Rozzos supported Bačyns'kyj's attempts to establish the Košice vicariate. In order to circumvent the objections of the bishop of Eger and the Košice municipal authorities, they proposed on the advice of Bradač that the seat of the vicariate be moved to Prešov. They firmly opposed the proposals of the Križevci and Oradea prelates.

The Napoleonic wars had engendered a strong national movement among the Hungarians.[10] In order to strengthen the country's ethnic Magyar element, the government in Budapest decided to magyarize the Slavic population throughout the kingdom. The Carpatho-Rusyns, as the smallest national minority, were to serve as a test of the new Hungarian policy. It was this development that gave rise to the idea of dividing the Mukačevo eparchy.

Bishop Andrij Bačyns'kyj unequivocally opposed the division. He understood that the Carpatho-Rusyns would find support at the Austrian imperial court only as long as they remained united under the authority of one bishop. However, the papal nuncio in Vienna favored the Hungarian proposal, regarding the creation of a Prešov eparchy to be "imperative." Nonetheless, he recommended that the matter be postponed until after "the death of the incumbent old bishop, who opposes the division."[11]

The Hungarians succeeded in sowing dissension among the Carpatho-Rusyns when bishop Bačyns'kyj asked in 1808 that his supporter, canon Ivan Kutka, be made his auxiliary. The Hungarian chancery saw to it that Kutka's adversary, Mychajil Bradač, became the auxiliary bishop. Insulted, Bačyns'kyj left Bradač in Prešov and retained Kutka as his vicar-general.

As long as Bačyns'kyj lived, things seemed calm, if only on the surface. But a quiet struggle was already under way between Bradač and Kutka for the succession to the episcopate. After Bačyns'kyj's death, when Kutka became the capitulary vicar, the struggle became public. This was the opportunity for which the Hungarians had been waiting and they used it to advance the idea to partition the Mukačevo eparchy.

The division suited both Kutka and Bradač. Through the formation of a Prešov eparchy, Kutka hoped to rid himself of Bradač as a rival for the Mukačevo see. For his part, Bradač hoped to be rewarded for supporting the Hungarian proposal by being appointed bishop of Mukačevo. Kutka could then become the bishop of Prešov. Thus "both consistories, in Mukačevo and Prešov, began to consider seriously how to divide the large Mukačevo eparchy into more sees."[12]

The Hungarian supervisory council on March 27, 1810 formally asked the Mukačevo consistory whether the eparchy could be divided. The meeting of the consistory, chaired by the capitulary vicar Ivan Kutka, was also attended by bishop Bradač as a canon of the chapter. A lively dispute broke out between Kutka and Bradač, which was joined by the Romanians, who put forward the candidacy of their own canon, Alexis Pócsy, from the Oradea eparchy.

During the discussions, there was also talk of the Galician metropolitanate, which pope Pius VII had restored in 1807, but without incorporating the Mukačevo eparchy in it. This gave rise to the notion of establishing a separate metropolitanate in Carpathian Rus' and dividing the Mukačevo eparchy into three parts: (1) a Prešov eparchy to include 189 parishes and 145,730 faithful; (2) a Máramaros eparchy with 240 parishes (130 Romanian, 110 Carpatho-Rusyn) and 185,717 faithful; and (3) a Mukačevo eparchy, which was to become a seat of the metropolitan, with 262 parishes and 193,552 faithful.

In making this proposal, Kutka hoped to rid himself of both his rivals, Bradač and Pócsy, and at the same time gain the support of the Austrian court chancery, without which there could be no hope of creating a metropolitanate in Carpathian Rus'. In this manner, Kutka also wanted to preserve the national unity of the Carpatho-Rusyns under the leadership of their own metropolitan.

Bradač, however, opposed Kutka's proposal, citing the position of bishop Bačyns'kyj. He still expected to be appointed bishop of Mukačevo and wanted to block Kutka's elevation to the episcopate.

The Hungarian supervisory council summoned the two rivals to Budapest in order to achieve some form of consensus. Hryhorij Tarkovyč, who was then the official censor of Carpatho-Rusyn publications in Budapest, was appointed arbitrator. The inability of Bradač and Kutka to reach an agreement resulted in the postponement of the appointment of a Mukačevo bishop for several more years.

Ivan Kutka died on October 7, 1812, not living to see his plans realized. The administration of the Mukačevo eparchy was taken over by bishop Mychajil Bradač, but only in the capacity of capitulary vicar. Bradač now openly opposed the division of the eparchy, still hoping to become its bishop. With the same goal in mind, he attempted to block the appointment of a new Prešov vicar. However, on the advice of the Hungarian primate, Hungary's ruling circles had already resolved to divide the eparchy. On July 30, 1813, canon Hryhorij Tarkovyč, whom the supervisory council was grooming for the episcopate, was named the new vicar of Prešov.

Bishop Mychajil Bradač did not live to be elevated to the office of bishop of Mukačevo. Broken by the persistent struggle in which he was engaged, he died on December 20, 1815, at the age of 66. Hungary's ruling circles were now in control. In order to prevent the creation of a metropolitanate in Carpathian Rus', they were firmly opposed to establishing three Carpatho-Rusyn eparchies as proposed by Ivan Kutka. This would have meant a loss of control by the Hungarian primate over the Carpatho-Rusyns, who would thus have remained united in a single ecclesiastical province headed by their own metropolitan.

On August 3, 1823, on the proposal of the Hungarian council, the Apostolic See incorporated the Szatmár vicariate with 72 parishes into the Oradea eparchy.[13] In order to obtain the consent for the separation of these parishes, the Hungarians nominated the Romanian canon Alexis Pócsy to the Mukačevo episcopate.[14]

Thus, on August 11, 1816, the Mukačevo see was occupied by a bishop of Romanian nationality, who had no interest in the welfare of the Carpatho-Rusyns and allowed himself to become the instrument of Hungarian policy. It goes without saying that Pócsy agreed to the creation of the Prešov eparchy,[15] thereby ridding himself of his principal rival, Hryhorij Tarkovyč, whom the Hungarian government named to the Prešov bishopric in return for "his loyalty." Naturally, the Prešov eparchy, too, was to be subordinated to the archbishop of Esztergom as its metropolitan. The Hungarians thus attained their goal. They succeeded in dividing the Carpatho-Rusyns without losing control over them.

3. The Canonical Erection of the Prešov Eparchy

Contrary to what the Austrian court chancery wrote to Rome, it was neither "the common good" nor the "good of the Church" that dictated the division of the Mukačevo eparchy.[16] The decision to establish the Prešov eparchy in order to divide the Carpatho-Rusyns was made in the Hungarian parliament on the proposal of the primate of Hungary. He insisted, moreover, that the Prešov eparchy also be made subject to his metropolitan jurisdiction.[17]

Owing to the imprisonment of Pope Pius VII by Napoleon in the years 1809-1814 and opposition within the Mukačevo eparchy, the erection of the Prešov eparchy was delayed. Finally, on November 3, 1815, emperor Francis I (reigned 1792-1835), invoking his "supreme right of patronage," established the Prešov eparchy within the boundaries of the former Košice vicariate without the knowledge of Rome. The newly-created eparchy was composed of 194 parishes and some 150,000 faithful who lived dispersed within seven counties: Abaúj (Abovo-Novhorod), Borsod (Boršod'), Gömör (Gemer), Sáros (Šaryš), Szepes (Spiš), Torna (Turnja), and northern Zemplén (Zemplyn). Administratively, these parishes were organized into five archdiaconates.[18] At the same time, as mentioned before, 72 parishes were transferred to the jurisdiction of the Oradea eparchy. Thus, the Mukačevo eparchy was left with only 464 parishes.

On May 17, 1816, the emperor sent his decision regarding the creation of the Prešov eparchy to the Apostolic See for confirmation. Rome was thus presented with a *fait accompli.*[19] Even earlier, the emperor had named Hryhorij Tarkovyč the first bishop of Prešov.[20] Tarkovyč, fearing canonical consequences because the Apostolic See had not yet confirmed the erection of the Prešov eparchy, turned down the nomination "because of old age."[21] However, when he learned that the emperor had sent a request to Rome to confirm the Prešov eparchy, he gladly accepted the appointment.

The canonical confirmation of the diocese took longer than everyone had expected. In the process of confirmation, it was revealed that in 1775 Maria Theresa had transferred the seat of the Mukačevo eparchy to Užhorod without the knowledge of the Apostolic See.[22] A new papal nuncio had also been appointed to Vienna at this time and it was necessary to wait for his arrival. The nuncio, archbishop Paolo Leardi, did not assume his post until the summer of 1817. What is more, 10 Carpatho-Rusyn parishes in the Nyír district (Szatmár county) protested against their inclusion in the Romanian eparchy of Oradea.[23]

To begin with, while Pope Pius VII confirmed the transfer of the Mukačevo eparchial seat to Užhorod, he resolved to retain the eparchy's ancient name.[24] The nuncio was encountering difficulties in obtaining the necessary information regarding the Nyír parishes, whereas the imperial court was pressing for the confirmation of the new Prešov eparchy.[25] The nuncio therefore asked that the question of the Nyír parishes be postponed and that the decision regarding the Prešov eparchy be expedited instead. The Consistorial Congregation in Rome charged the nuncio with completing the canonical process required for the erection of the Prešov eparchy.[26]

The nuncio already had all the necessary information and documents, which had been brought to Vienna by the bishop-elect Hryhorij Tarkovyč. Hence, after hearing the testimony of two witnesses, he immediately recommended the creation of the Prešov eparchy.[27] On September 1, 1818, the Consistorial Congregation prepared the bull of erection.[28] But the pope ordered that the bull first be examined by the Congregation for the Propagation of the Faith, which at the time governed the affairs of the Eastern-rite churches. Upon receipt of the opinion of the prefect of this congregation, Cardinal Lorenzo Litta,[29] the Consistorial Congregation began to complete the necessary formalities. On September 22, 1818, in the bull entitled "Relata Semper", the Apostolic See announced the canonical erection of the Prešov eparchy.[30]

The costs of creating a new eparchy were usually covered by the Austrian imperial court. But on this occasion, the Hungarian court chancery demanded that the costs be paid instead by the bishop-elect Hryhorij Tarkovyč. Tarkovyč had had to spend the entire year in Vienna in order to expedite the erection of the eparchy and was in debt. Lacking funds to cover the costs, he was prepared to resign the appointment. But the papal nuncio intervened, and in the end the Austrian court chancery agreed to pay the costs, which amounted to 1,055 florins.[31] Tarkovyč still had to wait for the bull of erection and was not able to return to Prešov until the end of 1820.

4. The Organization of the Prešov Eparchy

Although the Prešov eparchy was formally established on September 22, 1818, considerable time passed before it was finally organized and able to function properly. Bishop-elect Tarkovyč had gone to Vienna in the summer of 1817 to take care of the necessary formalities. There he encountered so many problems and difficulties that he had had to summon to Vienna his secretary, the Reverend Andrij Chira, whom he later elevated to the office of canon.

Tarkovyč was determined to obtain the necessary revenues for the bishop, the chapter, and the episcopal curia. Aware of the instability of the Austrian currency, he tried to obtain an endowment in the form of property. He also had to ensure the establishment and necessary revenue for the chapter of canons, arrange to obtain a residence for the bishop, and to secure funds for restoring the cathedral and adequate revenues for eparchial officials. The Hungarians were anxious to create the new eparchy, but when it came to endowing it they posed endless obstacles. It took Tarkovyč an additional three years to complete the financial arrangements. Finally, on November 17, 1820, Tarkovyč returned to Prešov exhausted and seriously ill.

The episcopal consecration took place on June 17, 1821 at the Basilian monastery of the Holy Spirit in Krásny Brod (Rusyn: Krasnyj Brid). The principal consecrator was bishop Alexis Pócsy of Mukačevo. That same day the ceremony of the installation of the new bishop took place in the Prešov cathedral. It was then that Tarkovyč officially assumed the administration of the newly created eparchy as its first bishop.

As mentioned above, the Prešov eparchy consisted of 194 parishes, which earlier comprised the so-called Košice (Prešov) vicariate.[32] The imperial court chancery allocated to the new eparchy from the Mukačevo eparchy: 1,203 florins from the fund for the sick and crippled; 1,517 florins from the seminary fund; 7,903 florins from the fund for assistance to priests; and 15,387 florins from the widows' and orphans' fund. All acts that pertained to the parishes of the new eparchy were transferred from the Mukačevo eparchial archive to Prešov.

The city of Prešov was designated the seat of the eparchy and the see was named after that location. The monastery of the Minorite Friars, which had served as the vicar's residence, became also the bishop's residence, and the vicarial church was elevated to cathedral status. Although both the residence and the church were in dilapidated condition, no funds were allotted for repairs and restoration. The bishop, his curia, and servants were able to occupy only five rooms which had been restored by the vicar Bradač. The remaining rooms lacked doors and windows. Bishop Tarkovyč was thus forced to live in a single room "like an ordinary monk," while the people considered the episcopal residence in Prešov to be "a political scandal."[33] Obviously, Tarkovyč had not supported the Hungarians' denationalization policy to their satisfaction.

It was Tarkovyč's successor, bishop Josyf Gaganec' (1843-1875), who was able to secure the necessary funds to enable him to build a new episcopal residence in 1848. Gaganec' also restored the cathedral and adapted it to the Eastern rite. At the consecration of the restored cathedral the bishop renamed it after St. John the Baptist.[34]

The Austrian imperial chancery granted the bishop of Presŏv an annual income of 6,000 florins. Tarkovyč, however, had insisted that the eparchy be endowed with estates, which could provide the bishop with revenues independent of the government. Moreover, this would help to provide financial security against the progressively falling value of the Austrian currency.

The Hungarian royal chancery offered Tarkovyč the former estates of the Camaldolese order, known as the Red Monastery, located near Lechnica in Szepes county. But these properties were some distance from Prešov. Moreover, the land was rocky and for the most part forested. Tarkovyč preferred instead the property formerly belonging to the Jesuits in Nižná Myšl'a in Abaúj county. For his chapter of canons he asked for additional property in Brestov in Sáros county.

No Roman Catholic bishop was willing to accept the estates of the Red Monastery, and in order to compel the Prešov prelate to do so, the Hungarian court chancery gave the property in Nižná Myšl'a to the Esztergom seminary in the form of an endowment as "the primate had requested." In addition to the Red Monastery, Tarkovyč was given smaller holdings in Vranov (Zemplén county) and Krajná Porúbka (Sáros county). Thus, on December 10, 1820, the Hungarian royal council finalized the endowment for the Prešov eparchy.

The bishop of Prešov had to divide the revenues from the Red Monastery and estates in Vranov and Krajná Porúbka into 13 portions. Of these, 6 portions went to the bishop, 5 to the chapter of canons, and the remaining 2 for the maintenance of the cathedral. It soon became obvious that this income was insufficient for the upkeep of the bishop and the chapter, and so they continued to remain dependent on the court chancery, which assigned them an additional 3,000 florins (guldens) annually as supplementary income from the religious fund.

In 1857, emperor Franz Joseph I (reigned 1848-1916) visited Prešov and saw for himself the deplorable material conditions of the bishop. He then ordered that the annual supplement be increased to 10,000 guldens.

The Prešov see's holdings were significantly augmented by bishop Ivan Valij (1882-1911). Using his own funds, he acquired a large orchard and vineyard for the eparchy. From then on, the Prešov prelate and his canons were able to live comfortably as befitted their office.

Along with the eparchy a chapter with five canons was established in Prešov.[35] The first canons were Ivan Mejhaj (d. 1835), Mychajil

Kanjuk (d. 1832), Vasyl' Hodobaj (d. 1840), Andrij Chira (d. 1840), and Ivan Habyna (d. 1823). Their installation took place on August 6, 1820, without the participation of bishop-elect Hryhorij Tarkovyč, who did not return from Vienna until September of that year.

The bull of erection placed the Prešov eparchy under the metropolitan jurisdiction of the archbishop of Esztergom, who was the primate of Hungary. The Apostolic See acknowledged the nomination of the bishop as the right of the Austrian emperor in accordance with his right of patronage over Hungary as its "apostolic king." But the emperor's nominee had to be confirmed by Rome before he could be consecrated or take over the administration of the eparchy. The bishop of Prešov also had to make an annual profession of faith before two of his canons. They were to sign a copy of the profession and submit it to the papal nuncio in Vienna.

Bishop Hryhorij Tarkovyč was not able to organize his eparchy to any great extent. Discouraged by the obstacles posed by government officials, he gradually removed himself from public life and sought refuge in books. His love of books led him to establish the Kovács diocesan library. János Kovács, who was a close friend of Tarkovyč's from Budapest, donated in 1819 his valuable library to the Prešov eparchy and in 1826 provided an endowment which made possible the regular acquisition of books. Kovács also saw to it that funds were secured to employ a librarian.

It was Tarkovyč's successor, bishop Josyf Gaganec' (1843-1875), who took it upon himself to organize the eparchy and put the church administration in order. Initiating some reforms among the clergy, Gaganec' also attempted to raise the level of the spiritual life of his faithful. Owing to his solicitude, in 1846 the clergy began receiving a monthly supplement—the so-called *congrua*—from the religious fund.[36]

Bishop Gaganec' was a man of the European mold. In order to adapt the clergy to the new circumstances,[37] in June 1848, the bishop convoked the first eparchial synod, which initiated the religious and cultural renaissance not only of the Prešov eparchy but of Carpathian Rus' as a whole. Gaganec' had great love for his people and the traditions of the Eastern rite. He inspired this same love in his secretary, canon Aleksander Duchnovyč (1803-1865), who later distinguished himself as the "national awakener of Carpathian Rus'." Gaganec' also supported the endeavors of Adol'f Dobrjans'kyj, who tried to achieve political autonomy for Carpathian Rus'.

Not surprisingly Hungarian political and ecclesiastical circles initiated a campaign to oust Gaganec' from the episcopate. The bishop disregarded these attempts and continued to support both Duchnovyč and Dobrjans'kyj. In retaliation, the Hungarian cardinal, János Scitovszky (1849-1866), extended to Gaganec' a public "canonical reprimand." This resulted also in the loss of the emperor's favor, which Gaganec' had previously enjoyed. But soon his name was cleared and in 1854 the emperor knighted him with the Order of Francis Joseph. Subsequently, Pope Pius IX (1846-1878) awarded him the title of the "Assistant to the Papal Throne and Count of Rome."

A major contribution to the cultural and material improvement of the Prešov eparchy was made by bishop Nikolaj Tovt (1876-1882), one of the most learned bishops of his time. Although he was brought up as a Magyar, Tovt always remembered that he was "bishop of the Carpatho-Rusyns and not of the Magyars." Bishop Tovt vigorously opposed the use of Hungarian in the liturgy; he introduced the Rusyn language in parish schools; and he organized an eparchial theological seminary which was opened in 1880. The construction of the Prešov seminary was completed during the tenure of his successor, bishop Ivan Valij (1882-1911), who, like Tovt, was a professor at the theological faculty in Budapest.

Following in the footsteps of his predecessor, bishop Valij invested large amounts of money in various eparchial institutions and the education of youth. The Hungarians hoped to exploit Valij for their own purposes, but upon becoming bishop he moved away from politics, devoting all his time and energies to religious and cultural activities. He greatly advanced the public education program initiated by bishop Tovt and ensured its continued growth. All diocesan institutions and schools owe their existence and prosperity to bishop Valij, who did not hesitate to support them even with his own money.

At the beginning of the twentieth century, under the moral pressure of the ruling authorities who threatened to compromise him before the Apostolic See, bishop Valij unfortunately submitted to the policy of magyarization of Carpathian Rus', an orientation that was deliberately pursued by his successor, bishop Stefan Novak (1913-1920). The magyarization of the church and schools of Carpathian Rus' will be discussed in the following chapter.

CHAPTER SIX

Attempts to Magyarize the Church

There exists not the slightest doubt that the goal of Hungarian policy was to use the union as a means of magyarizing Carpathian Rus'. The outcome, however, was quite different. The union in Carpathian Rus' served as a bulwark not only of the religious, but also of the national and cultural life of the small Carpatho-Rusyn community by not allowing it to drown in the Hungarian sea.

In 1867, when the so-called Austro-Hungarian Compromise[1] gave the Hungarians full political power in their kingdom, they initiated a policy of magyarizing the non-Magyar nationalities. Since the Carpatho-Rusyns constituted the smallest minority in Hungary, they became the first target of this policy. Economic oppression quickly broke the Carpatho-Rusyn population both in the social and economic spheres, and national decline soon followed. By the end of the nineteenth century, the sole bastion of national life left to the Carpatho-Rusyns was their Church, a veritable beacon in the midst of a period of national oppression that has been called the "dark age." This is what ultimately prompted the Hungarians to mount an offensive against the Carpatho-Rusyn Church.

1. The Struggle for an Independent Metropolitanate

From the very beginning of the movement for the union, the Carpatho-Rusyns had turned with their problems to the primate of Hungary, the archbishop of Esztergom, who by right of ancient privilege was also the papal legate. At first, the Esztergom prelates were well disposed towards the Carpatho-Rusyns, and much of the credit for the acceptance of the union in Carpathian Rus' belongs to them. Later, however, when the Esztergom see was often occupied by former bishops of Eger, the Esztergom hierarchs supported the attempts of the Eger ordinaries to impose their control over the

Mukačevo eparchy.

With the creation of their own eparchy in 1771, the Carpatho-Rusyns did finally manage to secure independence from Eger, but they nonetheless remained under the jurisdiction of the archbishop of Esztergom as their metropolitan.[2] The Hungarian primate thus retained control over the religious and cultural life of Carpathian Rus'.

Bishop Andrij Bačyns'kyj was well aware of the implications of this circumstance. With the help of his great influence at the Austrian imperial court, as early as 1773 he began taking steps to create a separate metropolitanate for Hungary's Greek Catholics. From the outset, the Hungarians opposed Bačyns'kyj's plans, although he was promised [by Vienna] that the Mukačevo eparchy would be incorporated into the Galician metropolitanate, which Austria was then planning to restore. It was even proposed that Bačyns'kyj should be appointed the first metropolitan of the restored ecclesiastical province.[3]

The restoration of the Galician metropolitanate was already being discussed in 1779, and it was to have included both the Carpatho-Rusyns and the Romanians of Transylvania.[4] But the Hungarians, backed by their primate, the archbishop of Esztergom, protested against this plan on the grounds: (1) that the Greek Catholics already had a metropolitan in the person of the primate of Hungary; (2) that subordination to a foreign (i.e., non-Hungarian) metropolitan could have "unfortunate consequences" for the union; (3) that subordination of Hungarian bishops to a metropolitanate outside the borders of the kingdom constituted "a violation of the Hungarian constitution"; and (4) that the cultural and religious life of the Carpatho-Rusyns and Romanians required "careful supervision and control" by the Esztergom archbishop.[5]

There was a great irony in this, since the argument clearly implied that for Carpatho-Rusyns the Galicians were "foreign," while the Magyars were "their own people." In other words, Hungarian culture was supposedly "native" to the Rusyns, while Ukrainian culture was "alien." According to this reasoning, the Roman Catholic metropolitan of Esztergom had a "better understanding" of the needs of the religious life of the Carpatho-Rusyns than did a metropolitan [in neighboring Galicia] of their own rite and nationality.

The Hungarian authorities succeeded in gaining the support of the governor of Galicia, count J. von Gaisruk. "The Hungarians knew," wrote Julian Pelesz, "that placing the Carpatho-Rusyns and Romanians under the jurisdiction of a metropolitan of their own rite would have fostered their national awakening, something the Hungarians did not want."[6] The candidacy of Andrij Bačyns'kyj was also opposed by the L'viv chapter in Galicia. Hence, when the Galician metropolitanate was finally restored in 1807, the Austrian emperor issued a separate decree stipulating that the bishop of Mukačevo would remain under the "authority of the Esztergom archbishop."[7] Any hopes that the Carpatho-Rusyns would, in ecclesiastical terms, unite with Galicia were thus brought to nought.

Having isolated Carpathian Rus' from Galicia, the Hungarians set out to divide and thereby weaken the Carpatho-Rusyns. Thus, in 1818, they created the Prešov eparchy, which was also placed under the jurisdiction of the "archbishop of Esztergom as its metropolitan." The fact that the two eparchies continued to cooperate with each other did not please the Hungarians, and they began to seek a means by which to drive a wedge between them.

The question of ecclesiastical unification with Galicia rose once again in 1843, when Pope Gregory XVI (1831-1846) considered establishing a Greek Catholic patriarchate within the borders of Austria-Hungary, or at least appointing a single primate for all Greek Catholics in the Habsburg Empire. To forestall opposition from the Hungarian side, the pope proposed a third alternative: to appoint two Greek Catholic primates, one for Austria and one for Hungary. But the Hungarians rejected all three proposals, because they did not want to permit the exemption of any Carpatho-Rusyn eparchies from under their control. They would not permit even the creation of a Greek Catholic metropolitanate within the borders of Hungary alone.[8]

Subordination to the archbishop of Esztergom meant the imposition of a Latin mentality on the clergy and the injection of the same spirit into the training of young seminarians. This had a negative effect on the union. To counter this, Pope Leo XIII (1878-1903), a great friend of the Slavic peoples, sought to raise the prestige of the Eastern rite. Towards this end, he proposed in 1888 to attach the Mukačevo and Prešov eparchies to the Galician metropolitanate. In response, the Hungarian press launched a fierce campaign against the pope's "illegal" and "anti-constitutional" plans. The campaign was headed by no less a personage than the Hungarian primate, cardinal János Simor. As grounds for their opposition, the Hungarians cited three reasons: (1) this measure would violate the constitution and canonical privileges of the Hungarian kingdom; (2) it would lead to a conflict of authority between the Hungarian primate and the Galician metropolitan; and (3) the implementation of the plan would constitute "a grave insult to the national feelings of the Hungarians." The

Hungarian press asserted unequivocally that "all attempts, regardless of their origin, to undermine the rights of the Hungarian Church or state will be resolutely rejected."[9]

Under the pressure of the press campaign and the public protests of the Hungarians, Pope Leo XIII abandoned his plan. It was clear that the Hungarian authorities had their own agenda for the Church in Carpathian Rus'. There was no doubt that the Hungarian hierarchy, led by the Hungarian primate, was working hand in hand with the Hungarian government in order to impose complete control over the Church and religious life of the Carpathian Rusyns.

In order to conclude the question of the metropolitanate, it should be mentioned that after World War I, when Carpathian Rus' became part of Czechoslovakia, the creation of a metropolitan see in the region was raised once again as prescribed by the "Modus Vivendi" reached between the Czechoslovak Republic and the Vatican in 1928.[10] In compliance with this agreement, the Apostolic See was to reorganize the Catholic dioceses throughout the Czechoslovak republic in such a way as to ensure that no bishop or metropolitan found himself outside the borders of the country. Consequently, the Mukačevo and Prešov eparchies were removed from the jurisdiction of the Esztergom archbishop and subordinated directly to the Apostolic See until such time as an independent metropolitanate was erected in Carpathian Rus'.

However, the creation of a metropolitanate in Carpathian Rus' made very slow progress. The Hungarians were determined not to relinquish their only remaining link with Carpathian Rus', and in their attempts to regain the territory for Hungary, they also took advantage of those Greek Catholic priests "devoted to the Hungarian cause."[11]

Finally, all obstacles were overcome, and on September 2, 1937, the Apostolic See issued a charter which removed both Carpatho-Rusyn eparchies from the jurisdiction of the archbishop of Esztergom and promised "to establish a metropolitanate of the Eastern rite in Subcarpathian Rus'."[12] Unfortunately, World War II put an end to these plans, and Carpathian Rus' never did see the formation of its own metropolitanate.

2. The Attitude of the State Toward the Church

The Hungarian government's only interest in the affairs of the Church in Carpathian Rus' was to use the clergy to break the opposition of the people. To justify its meddling in ecclesiastical matters, the government cited the unwritten privilege of Hungarian kings, that is, their supreme right of patronage. On the basis of this privilege, the Hungarian government arrogated to itself the right to nominate bishops and other high church officials as well as to control the education of the Carpatho-Rusyn clergy.[13]

Thus, the Apostolic See was able to appoint to the episcopate only such candidates as had been proposed to Rome by the Hungarian authorities. After 1867, the Hungarian ministry of religion and education put forward only those candidates who supported the magyarization of the Church and of parochial schools. Small wonder that in this "dark age" the Mukačevo and Prešov sees were occupied by bishops, who, at the very best, did not oppose the policy of magyarization.

One such "bishop-patriot" was Stefan Pankovyč of Mukačevo (1867-1874), who on his own authority initiated liturgical reforms that were alien to the Eastern rite. He was the first to begin delivering sermons in his cathedral in Hungarian and the first to give "unofficial" permission to some priests to celebrate the liturgy in Hungarian. For us, who live in a time when the vernacular has been introduced into the liturgy, this does not appear very significant. However, in bishop Pankovyč's time, this constituted a serious breach of ecclesiastical discipline as well as a violation of canon law. Anything that reflected a distinct Rusyn ethnic spirit was condemned by Pankovyč as "Russophilism" and "Orthodoxy." For bishop Pankovyč, only that which was imbued with a Hungarian spirit was considered genuinely "Catholic." The Hungarian language, Hungarian culture, and Hungarian organizations were deemed by him the only bearers of the "true Catholic spirit" in Carpathian Rus'.[14]

A similar role in the Prešov eparchy was played at the end of his episcopate by bishop Ivan Valij (1883-1911). Faced with the threat of having his reputation compromised, he chose to serve the Hungarian cause. The Hungarians exploited Valij as a tool for introducing Hungarian into the Divine Liturgy. For advocating this measure before Pope Leo XIII, the Hungarian press praised bishop Valij as the "Cyril and Methodius of the Hungarians" and "the apostle of the Hungarian liturgy."[15] An even more egregious example was set by the bishop of Prešov, Stefan Novak (1913-1920). Not only was he ashamed of the Carpatho-Rusyn language, but after the war he abandoned his eparchy and moved to Budapest.

A similar attitude pervaded the higher ecclesiastical ranks, the canons, archdeacons, professors of theology, and eparchial officials. Through them, the Hungarian authorities controlled the training of seminarians and the younger clergy. Thus the Užhorod seminary, which until the middle of the nineteenth century served as the bulwark of a Carpatho-Rusyn identity and culture, was transformed during the tenure of bishop Pankovyč into an agent of denationalization. The Prešov seminary was imbued with the same spirit. In their Hungarian patriotism, the Prešov professors tried to outdo even the patriotism of their Užhorod colleagues. As a result, by the end of the nineteenth century, the Carpatho-Rusyn theological seminaries were producing a completely magyarized clergy—priests who were ashamed of their nationality and who preferred to call themselves "Hungarian Greek Catholics" rather than Carpatho-Rusyns.[16]

Fortunately, however, there were also priests who did not renounce their national identity and who loved their people. In the 1860s, they initiated a struggle for autonomy of the Carpatho-Rusyn Church within the framework of the guarantees provided by the 20th statute of the Hungarian constitution of 1848. In accordance with this law, all religions in Hungary were regarded as equal and all were to receive material assistance from the state's religious fund.[17] However, each religious group was to be organized in an autonomous unit with its own charter approved by the ministry of religion. When approving a religious group's charter, the ministry granted it autonomous administrative and organizational rights and allocated it an annual sum in financial assistance. An ecclesiastical denomination recognized by the government thus enjoyed full religious, educational, and cultural rights.

The Protestants and the Orthodox immediately organized into such autonomous groups. They were therefore able to establish their own religious and cultural associations as well as schools and institutions for which they received government funds. More important, they had the right to elect and confirm their own church officials with the approval of the Hungarian authorities.

For the Carpatho-Rusyns, church autonomy would have brought independence of the control of the Hungarian primate, the opportunity to set up their own religious and cultural organizations and to reestablish their own parish schools, and more freedom in electing church officials. In accordance with the Hungarian constitution, the Greek Catholic Church had the right to unrestrained development. The Hungarians were well aware of this and for that very reason both state and church circles refused to grant ecclesiastical autonomy to the Mukačevo and Prešov eparchies.

In order to prevent the Carpatho-Rusyns from enjoying relative freedom in the religious and cultural spheres, they were included at the request of the archbishop of Esztergom into the Catholic group as a whole for the purposes of autonomy. This meant that the Carpatho-Rusyns were part of a Hungarian Roman Catholic autonomous group, which differed from them in terms of nationality and religious practices, but to whom they were subordinate by virtue of their smaller numbers. In short, the Carpatho-Rusyns were forced to continue maintaining their organizations and schools in the Hungarian spirit as required by the Hungarian Catholic "majority." Consequently, religious autonomy, which was to have guaranteed the free development of religious denominations in Hungary, brought the Carpatho-Rusyns only total magyarization and even firmer control over their religious and cultural life.

In 1868-1869, a Preparatory Committee for the Autonomy of the Catholics of Hungary met in Budapest. Adol'f Dobrjans'kyj, the delegate from the Prešov eparchy, fought hard to obtain for Carpathian Rus' separate autonomous status from the Roman Catholic Church. At the committee's second session in 1871, he delivered his well-known address, "The Autonomy of the Carpatho-Rusyn Church," which he based on the Hungarian constitution and the guarantees provided by the Florentine and Užhorod unions. Dobrjans'kyj's courageous defense of the rights of his Church and people evoked great indignation in Hungarian circles. Similar demands were put forward by the Transylvanian Romanians, who also wished to obtain independent autonomous status for their church.

In order to block the autonomy of the Carpatho-Rusyn and Romanian Churches, the committee put its demands to a vote at a plenary session. The session, at which Hungarian delegates of the Latin rite constituted a large majority, rejected the request of the Carpatho-Rusyns and Romanians. Moreover, neither group was even allowed to take the floor before the vote.[18]

The Hungarians, however, did not achieve their end. Other national minorities, even though Roman Catholic, also demanded autonomous status for their Churches, but the Hungarian delegates were determined not to allow this. As a result, the question of church autonomy for Catholics remained unresolved for years, even though "autonomy congresses" were held regularly. The congress of 1899 proved fatal for the Carpatho-Rusyns. It was then that both Carpatho-Rusyn eparchies were placed under the direct jurisdiction of the Central Autonomous Committee of the Catholic Church in Hungary. The Reverend Avhustyn Vološyn described the proposed status at the time as follows:

This proposal does not meet our demands, in particular in terms of eparchial autonomy. We do not need the kind of autonomy that does not take into account the differences between our own and the Latin rite and, without offering any eparchial autonomy whatsoever, makes us subject to the central organs. We have, after all, a great number of matters that only we ourselves can resolve, such as pensions for the widows of priests, the schooling of orphans, of priests, etc. Moreover, the conditions on which we accepted the union provide us with these rights which we cannot relinquish merely for autonomy.[. . .] Our best interests require that we be united with other Greek Catholic eparchies of our rite and, if this is impossible, that we at least be granted eparchial autonomy. This is the minimum that we expect from the autonomy system.[19]

But no decision on this issue was ever reached. Debating endlessly the various proposals for autonomy, the Catholics of Hungary never saw the matter resolved. In the meantime, the government took complete control over church life in Carpathian Rus'.

3. The Introduction of Hungarian into the Liturgy

As mentioned earlier, the bulwark of religious and cultural life of the Carpatho-Rusyns was their Church with its national traditions—the Slavonic language and the Cyrillic alphabet. For this reason, in their determination to magyarize all of Carpathian Rus', the Hungarians did not hesitate to undermine these bastions of Carpatho-Rusyn identity. In short, they decided to liquidate the Slavonic alphabet and to introduce Hungarian into the liturgy.

Attempts to introduce Hungarian as the language of the liturgy date from the 1860s. In 1863, a group of so-called Hungarian Greek Catholics gathered in Hajdúdorog under the leadership of the magyarized army lieutenant, Lajos Farkas. They sent a memorandum to bishop Vasylij Popovyč (1837-1864) demanding that Hungarian be used in the liturgy.[20] Bishop Popovyč had been persecuted earlier by the government for his "populist convictions," and in order to avoid new difficulties with the authorities, he sent this memorandum on to Rome.[21] In the meantime, on November 11, 1863, he strictly forbade the use of the Hungarian language in the liturgy until such time as the Apostolic See gave its unequivocal approval.[22]

The Hungarian patriots were not satisfied with the bishop's decision. They were well aware that under the circumstances the Apostolic See would never agree to the magyarization of the Church, despite the vigorous support this measure had from the Hungarian government and press. But even though Hungary's ruling circles paid little heed to Carpatho-Rusyn feelings, Rome could not allow the Hungarians to use the Church for their purely political ends. And so, on December 7, 1866, the Apostolic See issued a resolution "strictly forbidding the Hungarian liturgy."[23]

The Hungarian patriots then launched a new campaign. This was aimed at the establishment of a separate eparchy for "Greek Catholic Hungarians."[24] The Hungarian government did not support this action at the outset, fearing that it would hinder the magyarization of the remaining Carpatho-Rusyn parishes.[25] But it agreed to the formation of a separate Hajdúdorog vicariate in which Hungarian would be the official language. The creation of the Hungarian vicariate was announced on September 20, 1873. It was made up of 33 parishes numbering 49,922 faithful. The ministry of religion appointed canon Ivan Danylovyč the first vicar of Hajdúdorog.[26]

Some "patriot-priests" in the newly established Hungarian vicariate began to celebrate parts of the Divine Liturgy in Hungarian. This group was headed by the Reverend Emilijan Melleš (Emil Melles), who became the leading advocate of the use of Hungarian in the liturgy. As a reward for his "patriotism," Melleš was named a privy councillor and appointed pastor of the coveted Carpatho-Rusyn parish in Budapest.

When the magyarization of the liturgy did not cease and some priests began to celebrate on their own initiative the entire Divine Liturgy in Hungarian, the Holy Office of the Apostolic See in Rome issued a decree on September 2, 1896. The decree prohibited the use of Hungarian liturgical books and ordered the clergy in the Hajdúdorog vicariate to celebrate the Divine Liturgy in Church Slavonic.[27] However, the Apostolic See's decision was strongly opposed by the "patriots." Hence, on June 20, 1898, they formed a "National Committee" for the magyarization of the liturgy in Budapest, headed by the pro-Hungarian Carpatho-Rusyn representative to the Hungarian diet, Jevhen Sabov (Jenő Szabó). But the real force behind the movement was the Reverend Melleš.[28]

The committee launched a vigorous campaign in the press for the right to celebrate the liturgy in Hungarian. Any priest who defended the canonical grounds of the Slavonic rite was attacked as being a "Russophile" or a "Pan-Slavist." Bishop Fircak was even accused of working "against the interests of the state."[29] In the tense situation that developed, both Carpatho-Rusyn bishops often lost their bearings. The Apostolic See repeatedly banned the use of Hungarian in the liturgy "once and for all." However, despite Rome's ordinances to back them, neither the Mukačevo nor the Prešov bishops dared to take resolute measures against magyarization.[30]

In conjunction with the Holy Year of 1900, a Carpatho-Rusyn pilgrimage set out to Rome under the leadership of bishop Ivan Valij. The Central Committee of Greek Catholic Hungarians took advantage of this opportunity to submit a memorandum to Pope Leo XIII concerning the introduction of Hungarian into the liturgy. The bishop himself was to hand the memorandum to the pope. But when bishop Valij at a public audience intended to deliver a speech on behalf of the use of Hungarian in the liturgy, the papal chamberlain advised him not to broach the subject. Disconcerted, Valij was able only to submit a copy of the document to the chamberlain. The Hungarian patriots realized that Pope Leo XIII would not give in to their demands and so resolved to wait for his successor.[31]

The campaign for the introduction of Hungarian into the liturgy did not cease. Deputy Sabov even raised this issue in the Hungarian parliament. Meanwhile, magyarized priests continued to use Hungarian in the liturgy. This they did despite the protests of their parishioners, knowing that their conduct had the support of the Hungarian government and press. Thus, contrary to the strict prohibition of the Apostolic See, the magyarization of the Church in Carpathian Rus' continued.[32]

4. The Creation of the Hajdúdorog Eparchy

On the advice of the papal nuncio in Vienna, the Apostolic See did not respond to the Central Committee's memorandum of 1900. At the same time, the nuncio informed the confused bishops that although the Apostolic See continued to prohibit the use of Hungarian in the liturgy, it would "not insist" on strict adherence to this ban.[33]

Knowing that Rome was willing to tolerate the use of Hungarian in the liturgy the Hungarians began a campaign to magyarize the rite as well. The Carpatho-Rusyns, citing the resolution of Rome, decided to fight: "We will die before we give up our Slavonic liturgy," they wrote in their protest.[34] However, both Carpatho-Rusyn bishops remained on the sidelines of this struggle. It was the faithful who protested to the Hungarian primate, to the government, to Rome, and they even appealed to the Greek Catholic metropolitan Andrej Šeptyc'kyj of Galicia.[35] Finally, in 1909, Rome ordered Hungary's primate, Kolos Vaszary (1891-1912), "to respect the earlier decrees" of the Apostolic See concerning the Hungarian liturgy. However, not only did the primate fail to put a stop to the magyarization of the liturgy, he actually encouraged the use of Hungarian in the liturgy.[36]

The new ban by the Apostolic See helped the Hungarian Greek Catholic patriots to persuade the government to create a separate Hungarian eparchy, which would lend itself better to magyarization than to attempt to magyarize at once the whole of Carpathian Rus'. On September 12, 1911, the Central Committee appealed to Rome for permission to establish a separate "Greek-rite" eparchy for Hungarians with Greek as the liturgical language. They had no intention of introducing Greek, but used this as a lure to win the Vatican's approval. This new action was once again supported by the Hungarian hierarchy with the primate of Esztergom in the lead.[37]

For its part, the Hungarian government "guaranteed" the Apostolic See that Greek would serve as the liturgical language in the new diocese and that Hungarian would be permitted only in non-liturgical services. As proof of their gratitude, the Hungarian authorities promised Pope Pius X (1903-1914) that they would use their influence to persuade emperor Franz Joseph I "to assume the supreme patronage of the International Eucharistic Congress," which could then take place in Vienna.[38]

On June 8, 1912, Pius X published the bull "Christifideles Graeci Ritus," with which he established a separate Hajdúdorog eparchy for Greek Catholic Hungarians for the following reasons: (1) a great "increase" of Greek Catholic Hungarians; (2) hope for "peace and unity" among the faithful of the same rite who use different languages; (3) hope for closer cooperation between Hungary and the Apostolic See; and (4) the desire of the Holy Father to avert "the danger of the shameful abuses that the Roman Pontiffs have condemned on several occasions, that is, the introduction of the vernacular into the Divine Liturgy."[39]

The Hajdúdorog eparchy comprised 160 parishes and 215,498 faithful. To create the new eparchy, 68 parishes were separated from the Mukačevo eparchy, 8 from Prešov, the Budapest parish from Esztergom, and 83 Romanian parishes. Hajdúdorog was designated the seat of the new eparchy, but the bishop and his chapter took up residence in Nyíregyháza. The Hungarian government undertook the endowment of the Hajdúdorog eparchy.[40]

The pope, however, was determined to eliminate Hungarian from the liturgy. He stressed this clearly in the papal bull:

As regards the liturgical language of this newly established eparchy, we order that it must be ancient Greek; the vernacular will be tolerated only in non-liturgical services in the same manner as it is used in Latin-rite churches in compliance with the disposition of the Apostolic See.

In order to provide priests of the given eparchy with sufficient time to learn ancient Greek, the liturgical language used until now may be used in certain parishes, but only for a three-year period (from the day of the erection of the eparchy). *However, this language may not be Hungarian, which is prohibited because it is not a liturgical language* and as such it may never be used in the Divine Liturgy.[41]

This was the principal condition on which Rome agreed to allow the erection of the Hajdúdorog eparchy. The Hungarian government had to agree on paper that by the end of the three-year period Greek would be used as the language of the liturgy. This, too, was mentioned by Pius X in the bull: "We firmly believe that the Hungarian government will assist the incumbent bishops, as they have taken upon themselves to do in our agreement, to ensure that Our order is strictly adhered to."[42]

But the Hungarian authorities had no intention of introducing Greek into the liturgy. This was, as the Reverend C. Korolevskyj calls it, nothing more than "a politician's trap," insofar as politicians played the "key role" in the establishment of the new eparchy.[43] Not surprisingly, the Greek Catholic press [in neighboring Galicia] called Hajdúdorog "a political eparchy."[44] The reason for creating it was to intergrate the Carpatho-Rusyn and Romanian populations with the Hungarian and to appoint only so-called "bishop-patriots" to this episcopate, thereby accelerating the magyarization of the national minorities.[45] This the Hungarian authorities achieved by creating the Hajdúdorog eparchy.

Owing to canonical abuses, the Hajdúdorog eparchy has now been completely magyarized. Some faithful have even forgotten their Carpatho-Rusyn or Romanian origins. Thus, the prohibition and disposition of the Apostolic See regarding the Hungarian language in the liturgy remained no more than a "dead letter."[46]

5. Efforts Toward Church Reform

The creation of the Hajdúdorog eparchy did not bring the kind of "peace and unity" among the faithful hoped for by Pope Pius X. Having obtained a Hungarian eparchy, the Central Committee of

Greek Catholic Hungarians continued to campaign for the use of Magyar in the liturgy in both the Mukačevo and Prešov eparchies, where some "patriotic" priests demanded that their parishes be incorporated into the Hajdúdorog eparchy. Unrest, confusion, and protests proliferated in the parishes.

To support their campaign, the committee organized the so-called Society of Greek Catholic Hungarians, which demanded that the government create Hungarian parishes in the Mukačevo and Prešov eparchies. During these critical times, the Mukačevo eparchy was headed by the "bishop-patriot" Antonij Papp, while the Prešov eparchy had no bishop for a period of four years (1911-1914), after which another "patriotic bishop," Stefan Novak, was appointed. And though Greek was supposed to become the liturgical language in the Hajdúdorog eparchy, in Carpathian Rus' it was Hungarian that was used in some parishes "in order to preserve peace and unity."

A government-supported National Congress of Greek Catholic Hungarians was formed before the war to facilitate the magyarization of the Carpatho-Rusyn eparchies. This congress made the most of the turmoil of the war years. Under the leadership of the Reverend E. Melleš, it began a concerted attack on the Julian calendar and the Cyrillic alphabet and demanded a reform of liturgical books. This action was conducted under the guise of countering a "Russophile threat" and "a danger posed by Orthodoxy." It was argued that the Cyrillic alphabet and Julian calendar made possible "dangerous relations" with Galicia and Russia, thereby fostering "an anti-government spirit" and "Ukrainianism" in Carpathian Rus'. This, according to Hungarian propagandists, could lead to "treason" given that the war was going on.[47]

The Reverend Melleš compiled a long list of charges against liturgical books used by Carpatho-Rusyns and sent it on behalf of the National Committee to the Hungarian ministry of religion. The committee demanded that the importation of liturgical books from L'viv be banned, that the word *soborna* (universal) in the "Creed" to be changed to *katoličeskaja* (catholic); that the word *tsar* (emperor) be changed to "apostolic king"; that the feast of the Patronage and the commemoration of some other saints (e.g., St. Paraskeva, SS. Borys and Hlib, SS. Cyril and Methodius, St. Volodymyr, SS. Theodosij and Antonij Pečers'kyj, St. Josaphat, and others) be eliminated from the liturgical calendar because they had "no connection with Carpathian Rus'," and that they be replaced by Hungarian saints (e.g., St. István, St. László, St. Erzsébet, St. Imre, and others).[48]

With the consent of the Hungarian primate, cardinal János Csernoch (1912-1927), the ministry of religion established the so-called "Central Commission of Greek Catholic Eparchies within the Esztergom Metropolitanate," for which it prepared the necessary charter.[49] At the time, the Mukačevo, Prešov, and Hajdúdorog eparchies were under the jurisdiction of Esztergom. The Romanian Greek Catholics had been permitted to establish their own metropolitanate in 1853.

The Central Commission was headed by the Hungarian primate himself, with the secretary of the ministry of religion as his vice-chairman. The bishops of the three eparchies in question were all deputy chairmen. Each eparchy was represented on the commission by four delegates to be approved by the chairman.

The charter contained the following agenda:

(1) the determination of the correct text of liturgical books and their publication;

(2) the introduction of the Gregorian calendar;

(3) reform of the education and training of seminarians;

(4) reform of the Basilian Order on the territory of Hungary;[50]

(5) changing the alphabet and orthography; and

(6) the discussion of other important matters should the need arise.

The Reverend Avhustyn Vološyn later commented that "the agenda concealed an ingenious attack on the Slavonic and Rusyn character of our rite and its results could have provoked terrible resentment among our faithful."[51]

The Central Commission's only meeting took place on August 9, 1915 in Budapest. It was chaired by the primate, cardinal János Csernoch. The bishop of Hajdúdorog did not attend the meeting because "the proposed changes" did not affect him. In addition to its bishop, A. Papp, the Mukačevo eparchy was represented by the Reverend Professors Petro Gebej, Symeon Sabov, Jurij Šuba, and Avhustyn Vološyn. They all opposed the reforms from the very outset. The Reverend Sabov spoke for the delegates and said: "Who is demanding these reforms? The clergy is afraid of them and the people vigorously oppose them. The forcible imposition of such changes would mean a violation of the freedom of religion, thereby undermining the dignity of our state."[52]

After the Mukačevo delegates had spoken, bishop Papp took the floor. He publicly condemned the insincerity of the bishop of Prešov,

Stefan Novak, who first agreed to oppose the proposed reforms together with Papp, but then had behind his back assured the Hungarian authorities that he was wholly in favor of the changes.[53] The discussion at the meeting grew heated. The Reverend Šuba then announced that the Mukačevo delegation had sent a memorandum regarding these issues to Rome and that he had personally handed the document to the papal nuncio in Vienna on June 22, 1915. Šuba reported that when he had explained the matter to the papal nuncio, the latter stated indignantly: "I shall impose total silence on the question of church reforms!"[54]

Hearing this, cardinal Csernoch immediately adjourned the meeting and the commission never met again. In any case, the Hungarians did not require further conferences. Instead, they began putting pressure on the individual bishops to eliminate the Cyrillic alphabet from the parish schools and to change over to the Gregorian calendar in their eparchies. The bishop of Prešov, Stefan Novak, needed no convincing. By the fall of 1915, he introduced the new calendar in his eparchy and the Hungarian alphabet in the church schools. The Hungarian press then attacked the consistory of the Mukačevo eparchy, which bishop Papp had used as a shield in resisting the proposed reforms, describing the Cyrillic alphabet and the Julian calendar as "two bridges leading to Moscow."[55]

Finally the question of the alphabet and the calendar was raised in the Hungarian parliament. Citing the decision of parliament, on July 28, 1916 the ministry of education and religion ordered bishop Papp to replace the Cyrillic alphabet with the Hungarian one and to introduce the Gregorian calendar also in the Mukačevo eparchy. Protests and opposition by the people were of no avail. The war and terror made open rebellion impossible. But anti-Hungarian feelings and resentment against the magyarized clergy began to increase among the people.[56]

6. The Unfortunate Consequences of Magyarization

The Hungarians were well aware that they would not succeed in denationalizing Carpathian Rus' as long as the region's population maintained contacts with other Rus' (Ukrainian) territories. Thus, they completely isolated Carpathian Rus' politically, administratively, and economically from neighboring Galicia and Bukovina. They also largely succeeded in breaking off cultural links with those provinces. Still, the circumstances were such that some ties between Carpathian Rus' and Galicia remained, especially in the religious sphere. In the end, Carpatho-Rusyns did not succumb to total Magyarization, even though they barely managed to survive.[57]

The more the Hungarians oppressed the people, the more they rallied round their Church, where they at least felt at home, in a native atmosphere. This is what engendered the close ties of the Carpatho-Rusyns to their churches. It was their church that preserved them from complete magyarization and assured them some protection from the Apostolic See.

The assault of the Hungarians on the Church convinced the Carpatho-Rusyns that the final struggle for their very existence had begun. The deceitful fashion in which the Hungarian language had been imposed on their liturgy, the establishment of a Hungarian "political eparchy," the decisive vote that the Hungarians had in appointing Church leaders, the assumption of control by the authorities over parish schools—all this and more convinced the Carpatho-Rusyns that even Rome was not able to prevent the magyarization of their Church. Consequently, the people began to look to Russia for assistance.

Sympathies for Russia in Carpathian Rus' took root already in the middle of the nineteenth century, when the Russian army put down the Kossuth rebellion.[58] This historical fact was now resurrected by the Hungarian press in order to cast a suspicion of "Russophilism" on the Carpatho-Rusyns and to warn of the threat of "Orthodoxy." This had the unforseen effect of persuading the Carpatho-Rusyns that the only power that the Hungarians feared was tsarist Russia. The "Russian tsar" and "Orthodoxy" were thus perceived as the only forces capable of preventing the total magyarization of the Carpatho-Rusyn people.

Great tensions rose between Austria-Hungary and Russia over the Balkans at the beginning of the twentieth century. Russia began to send its agents into Austria-Hungary in order to provoke discontent and unrest among the Habsburg empire's Slavic minorities. Moscow's agents exploited the religious ferment among the people in Carpathian Rus', promising them the protection of the tsar if they converted to Orthodoxy.[59] This anti-Hungarian agitation, which in practice boiled down to an anti-Catholic action, was also encouraged by Rusyn immigrants in the United States, where an Orthodox movement had begun in 1891 under the leadership of the Reverend Aleksei Toth.[60] A new slogan spread across Carpathian Rus': "All Carpatho-Rusyns must convert to Orthodoxy, the true Rusyn faith! Then the Russian tsar will come and oust the Hungarian lords and Jews!"[61]

This religious ferment, which rose in full force only after the war, will be discussed in the following chapter. But it should be noted here that the principal cause for the Orthodox movement in Carpathian Rus' was the forcible magyarization of the Church and schools. This consistent Hungarian policy alienated the clergy from the people, undermined the prestige of the Apostolic See, reawakened sympathies towards Moscow, and, subsequently, made it possible for the postwar Czechoslovak government to initiate a religious struggle.

CHAPTER SEVEN

The Orthodox Movement

The revolutionary years after World War I ushered in a religious struggle in Carpathian Rus' which shook the foundations of church life in the region. Although this struggle was waged under the banner of Orthodoxy, its true origins lay in the pre-war policy of magyarization.

1. The First Manifestations of Orthodoxy in Carpathian Rus'

In seeking the origins of the Orthodox movement in Carpathian Rus' after World War I, it is necessary to turn back to the first half of the nineteenth century when writings by Russian scholars such as Michail Pogodin (1835) and Izmail Sreznevskij (1842) endeavored to sow the ideas of Russian "Messianism" in this region. The "spring of nations" in Europe galvanized national sentiments among the Slavs, especially in the wake of the first congress of Slavic nationalities held in Prague in 1848. It was then that the Slavic nationalities of Austria-Hungary turned to Moscow as the only "protector" of the Slavs.

The spread of Russian Messianism was also bolstered by the triumphal advance of the tsarist army in 1849 under general I. Paskevič, who put down the Kossuth rebellion in Hungary. The impact of this event was summed up by Stepan Baran:

The march of the Russian armies through Galicia, Bukovina, and Carpathian Rus' and the suppression of the Hungarian rising made a strong impression on the Ukrainian peasantry and intelligentsia as well as on Dobrjans'kyj. This gave rise in large measure to the spread and strengthening of Russophile currents in our midst and of pro-Moscow sympathies in general. Especially because Austria [. . .] made peace rather quickly with the Hungarian and Polish magnates and subjected the Ukrainians [Rusyns] in Carpathian Rus' to Hungarian rule and in Galicia to Polish domination.[1]

The leading proponents of Russian messianism in Carpathian Rus' were Adol'f Dobrjans'kyj (1817-1901) in the national and political spheres and the Reverend Ivan Rakovs'kyj (1815-1885) in the religious sphere. They both maintained links with the Russian embassy in Vienna, then the center for the propagation of pan-Russian and Orthodox ideas throughout Austria-Hungary. The Russian chaplains at the Viennese embassy, especially the archpriest K.L. Kustodiev and the archpriest M.F. Raevskij, brought together Slavic university students in Vienna into various "cultural circles" through which they later exercised influence on all Slavs.[2] They provided the students with material assistance and supplied them with Russian literature, which propagated the "Messianic mission of Holy Russia" under the leadership of the tsar as the "sole" defender of Orthodoxy.[3] Although Dobrjans'kyj formally never left the Catholic Church, there is little doubt that he regarded Orthodoxy as the principal means of preserving the "Rusyn Church and people" in Galicia and Carpathian Rus'.[4] When Dobrjans'kyj travelled to Russia in 1875, he met in St. Petersburg with the procurator of the Holy Synod of the Russian Orthodox Church, Konstantin P. Pobedonostsev, to discuss the Uniate Church.[5] Failing in his campaign at home "to purify the rite," after his return from the tsarist empire, Dobrjans'kyj looked to Russian Orthodoxy as the salvation of the Slavs: "At last, all the Slavs will unite in their own Slavic, national, holy Orthodox Church, which the enlighteners of the Slavs, the equal-to-the-apostles SS. Cyril and Methodius, bequeathed to us in their testament."[6] At the well publicized trial that took place in L'viv in 1882, Dobrjans'kyj openly admitted his sympathies for "the Greek-Eastern, or rather Orthodox Church."[7]

Dobrjans'kyj's relative, the Reverend Ivan Rakovs'kyj, conducted himself with greater caution. In 1850, in Budapest, at the recommendation of Dobrjans'kyj, Rakovs'kyj became the editor for the translation of Hungarian laws into Rusyn. There he met the Russian priest M. Vojtkovskij, who drew him into Raevskij's circle. Vojtkovskij taught Rakovs'kyj the Russian language and Russian literature and became his principal adviser. Under Vojtkovskij's influence, Rakovs'kyj began publishing the Russophile *Cerkovnaja gazeta* for the Carpatho-Rusyns (1856-1858).[8]

Dobrjans'kyj and Rakovs'kyj also imbued the only cultural society in Carpathian Rus', the Society of St. Basil the Great (Obščestvo Sv. Vasylija Velykaho), with the same spirit.[9] In 1871, Rakovs'kyj was expelled from the society (he had been its chairman) because of his Russophilism, and he became the parish priest of the village of Iza, near Chust. As pastor, Rakovs'kyj never openly opposed the Catholic Church, but in his cultural and educational work he propagated the ideas of Russian Messianism. He maintained contacts with Raevskij and leading Russophiles in Austria-Hungary. Long after Rakovs'kyj's death, the people still used to say: "He dreamed only about the Russians and supported only the Russians."[10] Rakovs'kyj tried to flee to Russia, but was turned back at the border by the gendarmerie. The Iza cantor and teacher, Andrij Vladymyr, was strongly influenced by Rakovs'kyj, and after the latter's death (1885) continued to spread Russophilism and Orthodox Messianism.[11]

In the cultural sphere, Russophilism gained no foothold because the Russian language and literature were completely alien to the Carpatho-Rusyn masses and intelligentsia.[12] However, Russophile Messianism had a ruinous effect on the religious life of the people, undermining the prestige of the Apostolic See and sowing the seeds of Orthodoxy among them. This gave the Hungarians further grounds for persecuting the Rusyn population with increasing harshness and for interfering in their religious affairs. Thus, Russophilism was also responsible for intensifying the magyarization of Carpathian Rus'.

In their struggle against the forcible magyarization of schools and the Church, the Carpatho-Rusyns appealed for help first to Vienna and then to Rome. But neither Vienna nor Rome were able to help. Vienna was powerless because the Hungarians had equal political rights, and Rome "did not insist on compliance" with its decress. Vienna was in mortal fear of "Russophilism," while Rome was sensitive to the threat of "Orthodoxy." And so, under the guise of combatting Russophilism and Orthodoxy, the Hungarians pursued their policy of denationalization in Carpathian Rus' with impunity. By accusing the Carpatho-Rusyn leaders of contacts with Russia, they ultimately succeeded in convincing at least some of the Rusyn population that Russia, as the protector of the Slavic heritage and Orthodoxy, offered the only hope of salvation in the face of the Hungarian threat.

Some Carpatho-Rusyn emigrants took this conviction to the United States, where they were free to develop their cultural and religious institutions and where they formed fraternal associations, founded their own parishes, and built churches. In the United States, however, they encountered the hostility of the Roman Catholic hierarchy. Instead of assisting their brothers in faith, the Roman Catholics thwarted the establishment of the Greek Catholic Church in the United States. Rome's protests were of no avail. And so, the Carpatho-Rusyn immigrants in the United States came to believe that the Apostolic See was "hostile" to the Greek Catholic Church. They thus began to seek help from Russia in the New World as well.

The leader of this movement was the Reverend Aleksei Toth, to whom the Latin-rite ordinary of St. Paul, Minnesota, archbishop John Ireland (1884-1918), refused jurisdiction just before Christmas of 1889. An immigrant from the Prešov eparchy, Toth was a sympathizer of Dobrjans'kyj's and Rakovs'kyj's circle. Failing to obtain the necessary help from both his bishop Ivan Valij and from Rome, in 1891 Toth and his entire parish in Minneapolis joined the Orthodox church. With the help of his brochure *Hde hljadaty pravdu?* (Where to Seek the Truth) and of Russian "missionaries," Toth initiated a movement toward Orthodoxy among the Carpatho-Rusyn immigration under the slogan: "Let us preserve our Rusyn faith and our Rusyn rite!" Over a period of four years, Toth managed to convert some 20,000 faithful to the Orthodox faith. These converts laid the foundation for the Russian Orthodox Greek Catholic Church in America.[13]

The immigrants who returned temporarily or permanently from the United States brought back these new ideas of Russian Orthodoxy to Carpathian Rus'. The Hungarians were determined to put an end to the spread of these ideas, even by force if necessary. The result was the Máramaros trial, which is regarded as the beginning of the Orthodox movement in Carpathian Rus'.[14]

2. The Máramaros Trial

The first converts to Orthodoxy in Carpathian Rus' appeared at the beginning of this century in the village of Iza among a small group of peasants led by the cantor-teacher Andrij Vladymyr. They all disliked their magyarized pastor, the Reverend Andrij Azarij Jr., who was ashamed of his Carpatho-Rusyn origins and of the Rusyn language. The group drew inspiration from the anti-Uniate brochures and letters they received from their fellow villagers who had emigrated to the United States. Very soon, the Vladymyr circle began to grow.[15]

In 1902, the group asked the Serbian patriarch to send them an Orthodox priest to serve as their pastor. The patriarch appointed the

Reverend Harasim Petrović to Iza, which evoked a strong protest from the bishop of Mukačevo, Julij Fircak. The Hungarian ministry of religion ordered that Petrović be recalled from Iza, and it launched a harsh assault on "Orthodox believers." Thus, Iza produced the first champions of Orthodoxy to be persecuted for their "Rusyn faith."

In late 1903, the Hungarian authorities arrested all the Iza proselytizers of Orthodoxy along with their leader A. Vladymyr. At the beginning of the following year, they were put on trial in Sighetul (Máramarossziget) "for their ties with Russia." In fact, this movement arose because of the villagers' dissatisfaction with their pastor A. Azarij, since he had changed the language of instruction in the parish school where Vladymyr had taught from Rusyn to Hungarian. All that needed to be done to liquidate the so-called "Orthodox movement" in Iza was to appoint a new village pastor and reopen the Rusyn parish school. But the Hungarians were not concerned with maintaining peace among the people. They wanted to demonstrate to the world that their magyarization policy was essential to the security of Hungary, and they therefore found the simple peasants guilty of "treason."[16]

As a result of the Máramaros trial, Iza was joined by the village of Velyki Lučky, to which some immigrants had returned from the United States. The people began to view conversion to Orthodoxy as a means of retaliating against the Hungarians. This drew the attention to Carpathian Rus' of Russophile agents, who were just then organizing the second pan-Slavic congress to be held in 1908 in Prague. The president of the Galician-Russian Society [Galicko-Russkoe Obščestvo] and chief of propaganda, count Vladimir A. Bobrinskoj, resolved to exploit the religious strife in Carpathian Rus' for his own ends. To head the Orthodox movement in Carpathian Rus', he sent two Bukovinian Russophiles who were the grandsons of Adol'f Dobrjans'kyj. The older of the two brothers, Dr. Aleksander Gerovskij, became the leader of the movement in Iza, where he persuaded the peasants that "Orthodoxy meant a return to their old faith, the faith of their ancestors."[17]

The Máramaros trial also made a strong impression on Aleksander Kabaljuk, a woodcutter from Jasinja, who had just been demobilized from the army, where he had been persecuted by Hungarian officers. Under the influence of the Gerovskij brothers' Russophile newspaper, he became so taken by Orthodoxy and Russia that he made a pilgrimage to Russian monasteries in 1905. Monastic life held a strong attraction for Kabaljuk. After he returned home, he fashioned a chapel in his house, adorned it with Russian icons and gathered people in the chapel for prayers. In 1908, Kabaljuk made a pilgrimage to the Orthodox monastery in Jabloczyn, in the Chełm region [then in the Russian Empire], and from there to the Holy Land. On his return, Kabaljuk stopped off at Mount Athos, where he was formally received into Orthodoxy at the Russian monastery of St. Pantelejmon. After his return home, he became an intermediary between Iza and the Gerovskij brothers.[18]

Through the efforts of count Bobrinskoj, Kabaljuk was allowed to take his monastic vows in Jabloczyn, where he was given the religious name of Aleksej. A few months later, on August 15, 1910, bishop Evlogij of Chełm ordained him to the priesthood.[19] Kabaljuk appealed for jurisdiction to Constantinople, but was directed instead to the Serbian patriarch in Karlovci (Karlowitz) [then in Hungary], who had jurisdiction over all "Orthodox in Austria-Hungary." The Serbian patriarch had been unequivocally forbidden by the Hungarian ministry of religion to interfere in the religious affairs of Carpathian Rus'. In order to circumvent the prohibition, the Serbian patriarch of Karlovci appointed Kabaljuk assistant pastor to the Orthodox parish in Miskolc and gave him oral permission to remain in Carpathian Rus'. Thus, in 1911, the hieromonk Aleksej Kabaljuk arrived in Iza, where a large portion of the village had already converted to the "old faith." He assumed the spiritual ministry to them.

The Hungarian authorities learned nothing from the first Máramaros trial of 1904. At the end of 1913, they began preparing another trial, known as the second Máramaros trial, at which they hoped to expose the Russophile agitation and activities of count Bobrinskoj and the Gerovskij brothers, thereby to set European public opinion against Moscow. The defendants were 94 peasants from Iza led by the hieromonk Aleksej Kabaljuk. All were charged with "violating public order," "treason," and "conspiring to bring down the lawful authorities."

Instead, the trial revealed that the sole reason for the rise of the Orthodox movement had been forcible magyarization and the dissatisfaction of the faithful with their local pastor Azarij. Nonetheless, the court sentenced Kabaljuk to a four-and-one-half-year term of imprisonment and another 32 defendants to an average of one or two years of imprisonment and fines. The remainder were released for lack of evidence. This trial seriously compromised the Hungarian government in the eyes of Europe and it provided the Orthodox community with "heroes" and "champions" of the faith.[20]

When Russian troops reached the Carpathians in 1915, the Hungarians panicked. They began to persecute everyone who had any connection with Orthodoxy, so that Carpathian Rus' experienced a reign of terror. In this political climate, the Hungarian authorities abolished the Old Slavonic alphabet and imposed the Gregorian calendar. All who dared to protest, even priests, were imprisoned and sent to concentration camps.[21] In order to escape deportation, the majority of the clergy sided with the government. Thus, a chasm of mistrust opened between the faithful and their pastors, prompting more and more people to turn to Orthodoxy.

3. The Outbreak of Religious Struggle

For a while, the presence of a harsh military regime contained any outburst of anti-Magyar feelings. But as soon as Austria-Hungary began to collapse, Carpathian Rus' resounded with the call: "Away from the Magyars!" Although the Hungarian revolutionary government promised the Carpatho-Rusyns the moon, the populace would have nothing more to do with Hungarians. All three national councils—in Stará L'ubovňa (in the Prešov Region), in Užhorod, and in Chust—declared themselves for union with the Ukraine. Unfortunately, the Ukrainian army was unable to come to the assistance of the Carpatho-Rusyns against the Hungarians and Romanians. Hence, the Central National Council, which met without advance preparation on May 8, 1919 in Užhorod, proclaimed the union of Carpathian Rus' with Czechoslovakia on the basis of guaranteed autonomy. It should be noted here that the national councils named above, as well as the Central National Council, were organized largely by the Carpatho-Rusyn clergy and that, with only a few exceptions, these devoted priests did not betray the common people to the Hungarians, but led them to national revival and freedom.[22]

When the Czechoslovak army occupied Carpathian Rus', the imprisoned Orthodox believers from Iza were released. Galician and Bukovinian Russophiles also found refuge here and launched a new campaign for conversion to Orthodoxy under the leadership of deputy Dr. Andrej Gagatko. With the help of the Czechs, Gagatko formed the Russian Labor Party (Russkaja Trudovaja Partija), which began publishing *Russkaja zemlja* as its official organ.[23] Velyki Lučky became the center of Russophilism, while Iza, where Kabaljuk founded an Orthodox monastery, became the center of Orthodoxy.[24] Heeding the call, "Away from Rome!," pronounced by the first president of the country, Tomáš G. Masaryk, the Czechoslovak authorities supported both Russophilism and Orthodoxy in order to weaken the Catholic Church in the new Czechoslovak Republic.[25]

Very soon, the Orthodox movement in Carpathian Rus' led to a full-scale religious war. The Czech minister František Němec had this to say about the situation that developed at the time:

> It seemed to some Russophile politicians, both in Prague and in Ruthenia [Subcarpathian Rus'], that the right time had come to convert the Ruthenian peasant back to the Greek Orthodox religion. This opinion was shared by many Russian émigrés who flocked to Czechoslovakia, including Ruthenia, after 1919. A drive for 'Orthodoxy' was started in Ruthenia. . . . It is a question how much of this movement was spontaneous and due to the pro-Russian feelings of the population and to its dislike for the partly magyarized Uniate clergy, and how much of its strength it owed to the propaganda and preaching of the Russian Orthodox émigrés and clergy and to the support of some Czech political circles. However, it certainly added one more element to the confusion reigning in Ruthenia and led to animosities which, in the end, turned against the Prague Government itself.[26]

The hostile attitude of the government to the Greek Catholic Church alienated the Carpatho-Rusyn clergy. It induced the magyarized priests to boycott the orders of the new authorities and to speak out in favor of the Hungarians. Many refused to take an oath of loyalty to the state. In response, the Czechoslovak authorities denied them permission to teach catechism in schools, branded such priests "magyarones" in the press,[27] and limited to a minimum their income.[28] At the same time, the government allowed the Orthodox complete freedom of action and even the use of force. The Reverend Vološyn described this deplorable situation in Carpathian Rus' in a speech in Prague in 1929 at the so-called "Oriental Day":

> The agitation usually began in the local tavern, where the agitator met the most notorious brawlers of the village. After a short talk, emboldened by 'noisy' arguments and whisky, the peasants would begin to shout abuse against the village pastor. In a matter of two or three days, a 'committee' made up of the pastor's 'opponents' would be formed. The committee did not immediately begin advocating Orthodoxy; instead, it showered the bishop with complaints and delegations, demanding that there be an investigation against the pastor or that he be re-

moved outright. Then followed other forms of harrassment, demonstrations, threats against the pastor, intimidation of church curators, and such. The committee would send the pastor letters demanding him to leave the village. As time went on, the committee made increasingly bolder threats that the pastor get out 'or else!' Meanwhile, members of the committee went around telling the peasants not to pay the pastor the *koblyna* and not to perform the *rokovyna*, promising to distribute church lands among the villagers. The parish priest would thus be left without assistance and the necessary income.

If, despite such harrassment, the pastor remained in his parish, the threats escalated. Someone would break his windows, shoot into his windows, poison his well, set fire to his grain or stables, and in some cases even the parish house, assault and beat the priest, etc. The government remained indifferent to all this under the pretext of 'Freedom of conscience! Freedom of religion!'[29]

The local gendarmes frequently refused to defend the priest. On such occasions, the more upstanding and solid members of the community would take it upon themselves to protect their pastor. This would result in bloody clashes in the villages, which gradually swept across the entire Máramaros region, the eastern part of Carpathian Rus'. The people divided into two hostile camps, fighting, retaliating, and inflicting injuries on one another. Lawlessness, violence, and great hatred held sway in Carpathian Rus', sometimes even between members of the same family.[30]

The champion of the Orthodox movement in the Prešov Region was senator Jurij Lažo from Vyšní Svidník. Even before the war, Lažo had vowed to avenge himself on his parish priest, the Reverend M. Dan'ko. After the war, Lažo became an Orthodox proselytizer supported by the authorities. But the first conversions to the Orthodox faith in the Prešov Region actually occurred in the village of Becherov, where the idea of a Russian Orthodox Church had been introduced by villagers who had returned from the United States. Thus, upon his return to Becherov in 1920, the Orthodox priest Hryhorij Varchol, who had been a follower of Aleksei Toth in the United States, converted 84 families to Orthodoxy and built a church and a parish house for them.

In 1922, senator Lažo brought in the Russified archimandrite of the monastery of Počajiv [then in Polish Volhynia], Vitalij Maksimenko, to assist Varchol. Maksimenko made Vyšní Svidník, and later the nearby village of Ladomirová, his "missionary headquarters." Thus Becherov, Vyšní Svidník, and Ladomirová became the centers of Orthodox propaganda in the Prešov Region.[31]

Orthodoxy, however, did not become deeply entrenched in the Prešov Region owing to the zealous work of the Greek Catholic eparchy's bishop-administrator, Dionysij Njaradij, and to the assistance of the local Slovak authorities, who were for the most part loyal Catholics. On the other hand, in the Mukačevo eparchy, the movement spread, reaching its peak in 1925, when the Vatican broke off diplomatic relations with Czechoslovakia. By then, however, the Catholics had managed to consolidate their forces to the degree that they were able to defend their own rights. (See below, Chapter 8).

Government statistics for 1930, which must be taken with some reservations, put the number of Orthodox believers in the Prešov Region at 6,885 and at 112,034 in Carpathian Rus'. This was a great increase over 1900, when those professing the Orthodox faith in both eparchies numbered a total of only 440.[32]

4. Dissension among Orthodox Believers

From the very beginning, the Orthodox movement in Carpathian Rus' developed in a very chaotic fashion, without any real spiritual leadership. To provide this movement with a modicum of canonical order, the hieromonk Aleksej Kabaljuk appealed in 1920 to the Holy Synod of the Serbian Orthodox Church [in the new state of Yugoslavia] to take the Carpatho-Rusyn Orthodox under its jurisdiction. At the very same time, a Czechoslovak National Church was in the process of formation, and it too asked the Serbian Synod for assistance.[33]

In the summer of 1921, the Serbian Synod sent to Czechoslovakia bishop Dositej of Niš [in Yugoslavia] to investigate conditions in both churches. Dositej also visited all the Orthodox congregations in Carpathian Rus'. He subsequently convoked the first Orthodox congress, which took place on August 19, 1921. The congress adopted a temporary charter and the church assumed its official name: the Carpatho-Russian Eastern Orthodox Church (Karpato-russkaja Vostočnaja Pravoslavnaja Cerkov). The congress placed the Orthodox believers of Carpathian Rus' under the authority of a Central Orthodox Committee headed by bishop Dositej himself.

On September 25, 1921, the Serbian patriarch Dmitrij consecrated in Belgrade Matej Pavlik and, after renaming him Gorazd, appointed him bishop of Prague.[34] As head of the Czechoslovak National Church, Gorazd wanted to preserve Orthodox traditions in his new church. But this was opposed by the majority of the faithful, who had adopted a Protestant mentality under the influence of the Hussites. Gorazd was left with only a handful of followers (some 10,000) and, as a result, in 1924 he joined the Czech Orthodox Church.

The origins of the Czech Orthodox Church reach back to the pan-Slavic sympathies of the Czechs, a small group of whom formed an Orthodox congregation in Prague in 1863. After the war, a lawyer named Miloš Červinka re-organized the group into the Orthodox Czech religious community. Its charter was approved by the Czechoslovak government on March 31, 1922. The congregation chose as its spiritual leader the archimandrite Savvatij, expecting that he would be elevated to the episcopate.[35]

Having already ordained bishop Gorazd for the Czechs, the Serbian patriarch was opposed to the establishment of a second eparchy in the Czechoslovak Republic and therefore ignored Savvatij's request. The Czech Orthodox congregation then turned to the Moscow metropolitan in exile Antonij with the same request.[36] Metropolitan Antonij also refused to consecrate Savvatij. The Czechs then appealed to Constantinople.

On March 4, 1923, the patriarch of Constantinople consecrated Savvatij to the episcopate and named him "archbishop of Prague and all Czechoslovakia."[37] Basing his action as the restoration of the Great Moravian metropolitan see from the times of St. Methodius, the patriarch of Constantinople canonically erected an Orthodox ecclesiastical province in Czechoslovakia. In addition to the Prague archepiscopate, he also erected the Moravian and Carpatho-Rusyn Orthodox eparchies. In fact, the new Orthodox metropolitan province existed only on paper in the hopes that the Orthodox movment would spread throughout Czechoslovakia.[38]

Bishop Savvatij's attempts to assume the leadership of Orthodox believers in Czechoslovakia were opposed by bishop Gorazd. The result was a fierce struggle for control of the Orthodox Church in Czechoslovakia between the two prelates, each of whom recognized a different jurisdiction. The issue was decided at the diplomatic table during a meeting of the Little Entente[39] in Belgrade in 1924. At the request of Yugoslavia, the Czechoslovak government agreed to remove bishop Savvatij and to recognize only bishop Gorazd and the authority of the Serbian patriarch. Subsequently, on November 22, 1925, a synod of the Czech Orthodox Church was held in Česká Třebová, which invalidated the election of bishop Savvatij and transferred authority over the Orthodox Church to bishop Gorazd. Thus, owing to "political considerations," the Serbian patriarch won jurisdiction over the Orthodox in Czechoslovakia.

Even though the Serbian bishop Dositej headed the Orthodox parishes in Carpathian Rus', the Czechoslovak authorities did not approve their charter and thus did not recognize the Carpatho-Russian Eastern Orthodox Church. In 1923, bishop Savvatij, whom the government had supported at the beginning, sent the former bishop of Sevastopil', Venjamin (Fedčenko), to Carpathian Rus' to establish his jurisdiction there. While bishop Venjamin tried to win over the Orthodox clergy to recognize the jurisdiction of Savvatij, bishop Dositej launched a campaign in favor of Serbian jurisdiction over Carpathian Rus'. On behalf of the Serbian Holy Synod, Dositej rejected the authority of the patriarch of Constantinople over Czechoslovakia and warned the Carpatho-Rusyn Orthodox faithful that bishop Savvatij planned to Czechize the Orthodox Church in Carpathian Rus' with the support of the government. Thus, a fierce conflict over jurisdiction erupted among the Orthodox of Carpathian Rus' lasting until 1930, when the Serbian side finally triumphed.[40]

The battle over jurisdiction among the Orthodox frequently led to violence and lawlessness. Archimandrite Aleksej Kabaljuk headed the supporters of the Serbian jurisdiction, while those in favor of the Constantinople solution were headed first by the archpriest A. Černjavin and later by archimandrite Bogol'ep.[41] In order to increase the ranks of clergy who supported him, bishop Savvatij ordained many uneducated and untrained priests, who later caused many problems for both sides. Thus, in its attempt to rid itself of "Magyarones," the confused Carpatho-Rusyn populace became a puppet in Czech and Serbian politics. Small wonder that as a result many of the better and more upstanding families returned to the Greek Catholic Church. Those who were weaker or ashamed of their earlier conduct embraced Protestantism, while a large number fell victim to Godless communism.

5. The Formal Establishment of the Orthodox Church

Dissension among the Orthodox was the principal obstacle to the legalization of their church in Carpathian Rus'. Although bishop Savvatij had the majority of the Orthodox clergy behind him, the authorities had agreed to support the jurisdiction of the Serbian patriarch. The Czechoslovak government, however, was displeased with bishop Dositej's anti-Czech agitation and he therefore became *persona non grata*. Consequently, at the end of 1926, the Serbian Holy Synod recalled bishop Dositej and sent bishop Irinej of Novi Sad to head the Orthodox Church in Carpathian Rus'.

Both bishop Irinej and the government refused to recognize the elevation to clerical office of 30 uneducated peasants hastily ordained to the priesthood by bishop Savvatij. Angered by this development, these "priests" attacked Irinej and his followers, calling them "Iza heretics." Despite the government's generous support of Irinej's work in Carpathian Rus', he was unable to deal with the clergy and admitted that "the problems of the Orthodox Church in Carpathian Rus' are internal rather than external."[42] Disheartened by the situation, bishop Irinej left Carpathian Rus' that same year.[43]

The Serbian Synod then sent bishop Serafim of Prizren-Zlatar to Carpathian Rus'. Serafim took up residence in Iza (1928-1930). For its part, the Czechoslovak government took it upon itself to impose order and to organize the Orthodox Church in Carpathian Rus', modelling its charter on that of the Czech-Moravian Orthodox eparchy headed by bishop Gorazd. The Central Orthodox Commmittee in Iza accepted the charter and submitted it to the Czechoslovak ministry of religion for approval. The ministry's approval of the charter in March 1929 formally established the Orthodox Church in Carpathian Rus'.

The charter gave what was called the Subcarpathian Russian Orthodox eparchy (Podkarpato-russkaja Pravoslavnaja Eparchija) broad self-administrative powers as the Serbian Synod had requested. But the Czechoslovak ministry of religion retained for itself the right of "supreme supervision over the administration of the eparchy." In practice, this meant that a candidate for the episcopate was put forward by the Orthodox eparchial synod of Carpathian Rus' to the Serbian Holy Synod, which, in turn, had to inquire through diplomatic channels whether the Czechoslovak government had any objections to the appointment of a candidate before naming him bishop. The bishop-elect then had to swear an oath of loyalty to Czechoslovakia at the ministry of religion in Prague, and only then was the Serbian patriarch able to ordain him bishop.

Czechoslovak government approval was also required for all appointments to higher clerical ranks and to administrative posts in the eparchy. The more important decisions in the eparchial synod also had to be approved by the state authorities. All eparchial officials, from bishop to parish administrator, had to be Czechoslovak citizens. However, since the Orthodox congregation of Carpathian Rus' was at the time unable to propose a qualified candidate for the episcopate, the government "temporarily" allowed the Serbian Patriarchal Synod to send a bishop from Yugoslavia.[44]

On December 2, 1930, the Serbian Holy Synod named bishop Serafim to head the Orthodox eparchy in Carpathian Rus', but he refused the appointment. Thus, the first Orthodox bishop of Carpathian Rus' was Josif, the bishop of Bitola, who was charged with organizing the Orthodox Mukačevo-Prešov eparchy. The official erection of the eparchy took place on July 20, 1931.

When bishop Josif set about organizing the newly established Orthodox eparchy, he encountered considerable opposition from the clergy. The Russian immigrant priests refused to recognize his jurisdiction. The supporters of Savvatij, who by that time had been removed, refused to accept the new charters, while the so-called Missionary Center in Ladomirová was determined not to relinquish control over the Orthodox parishes of the Prešov Region. As a result, bishop Josif resigned that same year, and in his stead the Serbian patriarch ordained on October 2, 1931, bishop Damaskin.

The installation of bishop Damaskin took place in December 1931 in a small wooden church in Mukačevo.[45] This ceremony marked the canonical erection of the Orthodox Church in Carpathian Rus'. The Orthodox bishop made Mukačevo his seat, but he acted under the jurisdiction of the Holy Synod of the Orthodox Church of Serbia. Under bishop Damaskin (1931-1938), internal consolidation within Orthodox ranks was finally achieved. Thus, an Orthodox eparchy came into being in Carpathian Rus' as an unfortunate consequence of forcible magyarization.

CHAPTER EIGHT

The Religious Revival

The Orthodox movement demonstrated that the union with Rome had not been "artificially imposed" on Carpathian Rus' and that it had become an organic part of the life of the people. The inability of Orthodoxy to uproot the union is the best proof of the fact that the Holy Union was God's will. The religious struggle did, however, clear the unhealthy atmosphere which had alienated people from their clergy. By their readiness "to give their lives for their sheep" (John, 10:11), the best Uniate priests regained the trust of the faithful and thus initiated a religious revival in Carpathian Rus'.

1. New Political Conditions

Hungarian policies in Carpathian Rus' drove a wedge between the clergy and the faithful. Since the priests were the only educated stratum of the population, it paralyzed all development of cultural and religious life. Backed by the Hungarian government, the Carpatho-Rusyn clergy felt secure and showed little interest in the common people and their life. Fortunately, however, there still remained a small group of dedicated clerics who sympathized with the hardships and misfortunes of their people and who wanted to help them.

When in the wake of World War I the Austro-Hungarian empire disintegrated, an opportunity arose for Carpatho-Rusyns to break with the Hungarians. Led by their clergy, the people abandoned Hungary and united with Czechoslovakia.[1] On May 8, 1919, the Central National Council, headed by the Reverend Avhustyn Vološyn, proclaimed the autonomy of Carpathian Rus' and its unification with the recently established Czechoslovak republic. Unfortunately, there existed from the very outset misunderstandings between the new "overlords" and the leaders of the Carpatho-Rusyns.

First of all, the Czech army occupied the Prešov Region and part of the Mukačevo eparchy up to the river Už. The Slovaks coveted this strip of Rusyn territory and took more than 200,000 Carpatho-Rusyns under their "protection" without guaranteeing them autonomy. Protests, negotiations, and conferences were of little avail. The Slovaks wanted to augment their population, while the Czechs wanted to weaken their eastern province, now called Subcarpathian Rus', in order to transform it into a colony that would serve as a bridge to the east. The next step taken by the occupational authorities was to sow dissension among the people in order to avoid granting the autonomous status that had been guaranteed Carpatho-Rusyns by the Treaty of St. Germain. In fact, the Czechs occupied all the more important positions in the province and thus took control of all aspects of life in Subcarpathian Rus'.

One means of sowing dissension among the people was through the Orthodox movement, and so the Czech authorities supported it from the outset. The basis of the anti-Catholic policy pursued by the Czechoslovak government derived from the prewar anti-Austrian views of president Tomáš G. Masaryk. Because Austria's ruling class had been supported by the Catholic Church, Masaryk based his struggle for Czech liberation on Hussite ideology.[2] He therefore joined the liberal movement in Europe, which at the time had adopted the slogan "Away from Rome!"[3] When he became president of Czechoslovakia, Masaryk resolved "to liberate democracy from the influence of the Church."[4] Consequently, he supported the anti-Catholic, anti-clerical, sectarian, and anti-religious movements through which he hoped to build his new democracy.

Hussite ideology, founded on Czech nationalism, did not spread to Slovakia and Carpathian Rus'. But it was possible to put forward the slogan "Away from Rome!" in Subcarpathian Rus' as a form of protest against magyarization. This, then, was what prompted the government to support the Orthodox movement.

The anti-Catholic policy of the Czechoslovak government greatly disturbed the ranks of the Catholic Church in the new republic. Still, the government was not able to topple the Church. The 1921 census showed that Czechoslovakia remained a predominantly Catholic country, even though the government was in the hands of free-thinkers. The authorities soon realized that they would not be able to build a state and democracy simply on revolution and religious struggle, and that they had to abide by constitutional law. The first Czechoslovak constitution, which was adopted by the parliament in

1922, guaranteed all citizens freedom of religion and recognized the equality of all religions in the eyes of the state.

The Catholics were wholly in favor of this law. They only wanted protection from violence by other religious groups and to be free to practice their own religion. They therefore welcomed the news of the establishment of diplomatic relations between Czechoslovakia and the Vatican. Already in 1923, the Apostolic See sent Archbishop Francesco Marmaggi as its papal nuncio to Prague.

But before the law was implemented and order was established, the Orthodox movement managed to wreak great havoc in the religious life of Carpathian Rus', especially since the authorities took the side of the Orthodox, leaving the Greek Catholic Church without legal protection. Not surprisingly, in a short time the government lost control over the Orthodox movement, which began resorting to violence and terror.

It would be incorrect, however, to claim that the government alone was responsible for the religious struggle. It broke out in large measure because of the passive resistance to the Czechoslovak state by a great number of Greek Catholic clergy, which openly proclaimed their sympathies for Hungary. Thus, for example, the bishop of Prešov, Stefan Novak, as early as the fall of 1918 abandoned his eparchy to his vicar-general and left for Hungary, where he remained until his death in 1932.[5] While the bishop of Mukačevo, Antonij Papp, remained in Užhorod, he refused to swear an oath of loyalty to the new state, even though all the Roman Catholic prelates had already done so. Papp's example was followed by a large number of Greek Catholic clergy, who thus earned the name "magyarones." Small wonder that the Czech authorities did not trust bishop Papp and left the Greek Catholic Church without legal protection at a time when Orthodox believers began to use force to oust pastors from their parishes and to seize Greek Catholic churches.[5a]

At first the eparchial consistory in Užhorod did not take a serious view of the religious unrest. In some parishes it would have been enough to replace the parish priest; in others, order could have been restored by settling local conflicts. But the consistory did not listen to the demands and complaints of the faithful and waited for "more peaceful times." In the meantime, anti-Catholic agitation and discontent among the people grew. In effect, a full-scale religious revolt broke out in Carpathian Rus', and the Greek Catholic episcopal curia had no concrete plans for mounting a defense.[6]

It was not until September, 1921 that bishop A. Papp convoked an eparchial synod in Užhorod, which decided to establish some sort of relations with the government. A delegation of clergy, headed by canon Petro Gebej, went to see the province's Czech vice-governor, P. Ehrenfeld. The delegation declared the clergy's loyalty to the new republic and protested against the Orthodox terror and forcible expropriation of Greek Catholic churches.[7] The bishop began visiting those parishes in greatest danger, but it was too late. By then, neither the bishop, nor the authorities had the power to put an end to the religious unrest and violence.

In the Prešov Region, where Orthodoxy did not have the support of the state authorities, the movement was not very strong. Owing to the tireless efforts of the eparchy's administrator, bishop Dionysij Njaradij (1922-1927), the religious strife in Prešov soon ended, having never reached the level of violence and terror that was occurring in the Mukačevo eparchy. It became obvious that the only means of successfully defending the Greek Catholic Church against Orthodox attacks in Carpathian Rus' was to appoint a new bishop. The Apostolic See therefore transferred bishop Antonij Papp of Mukačevo to Hungary and on July 16, 1924 named canon Petro Gebej to replace him. Gebej, along with the Reverend Avhustyn Vološyn, took up the defense of the Greek Catholic Church.

Just at that time, the Czechoslovak Catholic hierarchy began consolidating its forces in the wake of President Masaryk's assurances that "the Catholics will get as many rights as they win." Velehrad, the ancient seat of St. Methodius, became the center of the Catholic revival. The Catholic political parties and organizations, which the Carpatho-Rusyns had joined, were able to be victorious in the elections of 1925. The central authorities at last realized that the Greek Catholics and their Church had to be reckoned with. This compelled the government to enforce the constitutional provision on the equality and freedom of all religions. Finally, the Greek Catholic Church was assured the protection of the law against violence and lawlessness.

In compliance with these laws, the Czechoslovak government was obliged to return to the Greek Catholics the churches and church property forcibly seized earlier by the Orthodox. Furthermore, the government paid priests a monthly supplement known as the *congrua*, and all violence and abuses by the Orthodox became subject to prosecution. The clergy, too, began to show greater zeal in working for the people and started to cooperate with the authorities. Following the example of their prelate, bishop Gebej, they began to draw closer to the people.[8] This gradually led to a normalization of relations between church and state and, on February 2, 1928, to the signing of the "Modus Vivendi" with the Vatican.[9]

According to the provisions of this agreement, two commissions were established: one by the Church, the other by the state. Their task was to settle all conflicts between church and state and to restore peaceful relations between the two. The call "Away from Rome!" was no longer heard; anti-Catholic propaganda also ceased. In this manner, the Czechoslovak government was compelled to recognize the existence of the Catholic Church in the republic.

The boundaries of dioceses and eparchies in Czechoslovakia were not to extend beyond the borders of the state. Also, with the exception of the Apostolic See, no ecclesiastical official living outside the country was permitted to exercise authority on the territory of the Czechoslovak republic.

This provision of the Modus Vivendi was not implemented until 1937, when the Vatican finally announced changes in the boundaries of Czechoslovakia's dioceses. Both Carpatho-Rusyn eparchies, that of Mukačevo and of Prešov, were removed from the jurisdiction of the archbishop of Esztergom in Hungary and subordinated directly to the Apostolic See until such time as "a separate metropolitanate for Catholics of the Eastern rite in Czechoslovakia" would be established. Rome planned to divide the Mukačevo eparchy into two smaller sees: Užhorod and Chust. The Užhorod eparchy was to be headed by a metropolitan who was to have jurisdiction over the Prešov and Chust bishops. The Carpatho-Rusyns were thus to be united once again in a single ecclesiastical province.[10]

But the fall of Czechoslovakia and the Hungarian occupation of Subcarpathian Rus' in March 1939 put an end to the Vatican's far-reaching plan, and the Mukačevo eparchy returned once again under the jurisdiction of the archbishop of Esztergom.

2. The Zealous Work of Bishop Petro Gebej

Bishop Petro Gebej was one of those clergymen who did not remain on the sidelines of the religious struggle. He was of the group that was prepared to make the ultimate sacrifice should the good of the people require it. Not suprisingly, therefore, his appointment to the episcopate was welcomed by the Greek Catholic press as "the beginning of the new era."[11] On becoming bishop, he immediately began working to correct "the mistakes of earlier years."[12]

Even before his nomination, Gebej had not approved of the episcopal curia's attitude towards the Czech authorities. He had also condemned the "passive resistance" of the clergy. Therefore, after his elevation to the episcopate, he immediately set about establishing relations with government circles. After swearing an oath of loyalty to the Czechoslovak state, he paid a visit to president Masaryk and met with key ministers. In order to underscore his Slavic orientation, he arranged that his episcopal ordination be held on August 3, 1924 in Velehrad during an ecumenical congress. He established relations with Catholic political parties as well as with the republic's Catholic hierarchy. His installation took place in Užhorod on August 31, 1924 and was attended by representatives of both the Czechoslovak and provincial Subcarpathian governments.

By establishing ties with the government, bishop Gebej hoped to improve the material status of his clergy and assure legal protection for his eparchy. The "Law on relations between various religions," promulgated on April 23, 1925, prohibited all religious agitation and violence. The bishop saw to it that this law was expeditiously enforced, and as a result religious strife in Carpathian Rus' soon ended.[13]

During the period of religious unrest, the Orthodox had seized 80 Greek Catholic churches and an equal number of parish properties. Now with the law behind him, bishop Gebej restored all these churches to the eparchy on the grounds that the Orthodox had taken them illegally and by force. At a meeting of the consistory on April 25, 1931, the prelate joyfully announced to his consultors: "With the help of God and with the consent of the vice-governor of the province [Antonín] Rozsypal, we have successfully attained through legal channels the restitution of Greek Catholic property in the last and most tenacious stronghold of Orthodoxy—the village of Iza in the Máramaros region."[14] This was truly a major achievement by a dedicated bishop.

Another urgent issue on Gebej's agenda was to ensure the material well-being of the clergy. Under the feudal system in effect in Hungary since the seventeenth century, the maintenance of the pastor was the responsibility of the congregation. Each year every family had to donate one measure of grain (called a koblyk, whence the term koblyna is derived) and perform each year one day's labor (known as the rokovyna) as its contribution to the support of their pastor.[15]

The koblyna was the cause of constant conflicts between the clergy and the faithful in Carpathian Rus' as well as throughout Hungary. Consequently, at the request of the clergy, the law of 1848 abolished the koblyna and replaced it with a monthly supplement for priests called the congrua, which was disbursed from the religious fund.

However, the payment of the *congrua* was contingent upon the establishment of a religious group's autonomous status, discussed above in Chapter 6, part 2. Since Hungary's Catholics never did obtain autonomous status, parishioners were compelled to continue contributing the hated *koblyna* to their clergy.

The population of Carpathian Rus' was for the most part poor and unable to furnish the *koblyna* to the pastor. In wealthier villages, owing to the influence of Orthodox propaganda, the people refused to meet this obligation. This led to conflicts, clashes, and even legal suits. In order to compel the clergy to cooperate with the authorities, the temporary administrator of Subcarpathian Rus', Dr. Jan Brejcha, abolished the *koblyna* in 1920, but refused to pay priests the *congrua* in its stead. As a result, many priests were reduced to poverty and were unable to provide for their families.

Bishop Gebej, with the assistance of Monsignor Avhustyn Vološyn, established good relations with the central Catholic party headed by Monsignor Jan Šrámek. On the latter's advice, the Reverend Vološyn prepared a "Memorandum Concerning Governmental Aid to Priests to Replace the Abolished *Koblyna*," which bishop Gebej personally submitted to the ministry of religion in Prague in November 1924.[16] By the summer of the following year, parliament opened debates on the draft of a law on the payment of the *congrua* to clergy of all faiths. This news was enthusiastically welcomed by bishop Gebej:

> After my nomination to the episcopate, I immediately began to work for the abolition of the *koblyna* in the belief that this would put an end to the conflicts between the faithful and the clergy and our priests would be able to work in peace for the good of the people and the state. [...] It is my deep conviction that our clergy must be loyal to the state. Now, when poverty among the clergy is about to be eliminated, I will be able to ensure the realization of this conviction with much greater success.[17]

The decision on government assistance to the clergy became law on June 25, 1926. Each priest was to receive annually 9,000 Czech crowns from the government. In addition, priests were to be paid for teaching religion in state schools. The law also provided a pension for priests and their widows. The *koblyna* for preceding years was partly refunded. Thus, the 1926 law on the *congrua* eliminated the principal cause of conflict between the clergy and the government and led to a rapprochement between the two.[18]

Bishop J. Gebej was also determined to raise the level of the clergy's spiritual life and to restore its apostolic spirit. In words and through the example of his deeds, he called upon the clergy to perform their pastoral duties conscientiously. This was the main thrust of his New Year's pastoral letter of 1926, entitled "Let us renew everything in Christ!" Describing the deplorable state of pastoral work in the eparchy, the bishop reminded his priests:

> The time has passed when it was possible to administer the congregation from the parish office. It is not enough today for the priest to confine himself merely to performing his duty. In our day, intensive pastoral work requires sacrifices of the priest, meaning that he must be a teacher to young people, an advisor to adults, a guardian against the spread of immorality, and a knowledgeable leader of his congregation.
>
> Today, it is not enough to sermonize in churches and to teach in schools. Today, a pastor must also take an interest in the economic and social needs of his flock. Today, in addition to leading church organizations, a priest must tackle economic problems and take part in the cooperative movement. Today, a priest's best sermon is his life, the sum of his activities through which he tries to become, in the words of the Apostle of the Nations: *everything to everyone.*[19]

To raise the spiritual level of the clergy, bishop Gebej initiated annual retreats. He insisted that priests celebrate the Divine Liturgy every day, even if there were no intentions. He reminded priests of their duty to recite at least a portion of the office prayers each day. He held conferences with the eparchial clergy during which he discussed with them the most urgent problems of their pastoral duties. He attempted to bring the clergy closer to the people, reminded them to speak Rusyn, and supplied those who no longer spoke the native tongue fluently with short sermons in Rusyn.

The bishop tried to involve his clergy in work on behalf of the union. Towards that end, he established ties with Velehrad and founded the Apostolate of SS. Cyril and Methodius in Subcarpathian Rus'. With the help of the Basilian Fathers, he founded the Society of St. Josaphat, which was to head a missionary movement among priests. The bishop also wanted to re-educate the clergy politically and to involve some in the Christian movement. In this he was assisted by Monsignor Avhustyn Vološyn, who initiated the movement with the blessing of bishop Gebej.[20]

Bishop Gebej saw to it that Rusyn school manuals were prepared for the study of catechism and of the Bible. He urged his clergy to cultivate their native language, but unfortunately, many priests ignored the bishop's instructions.[21] He called upon clergymen to adhere strictly to liturgical prescriptions and rituals. He also tried to revive church organizations and to set up reading rooms and cooperatives in parishes throughout his eparchy.

In his pastoral letter, "On the Preisthood,"[22] bishop Gebej endeavored to restore the prestige of priests among the people. He explained to the faithful that "good priests are the greatest blessing that can be bestowed on a people." He therefore urged the faithful to abandon "the darkness" of hatred for the clergy to which they had been led by the spirit of the times. During his visitations, bishop Gebej went among the people, spoke with them, welcomed their delegations, handed out holy pictures, medallions, and sometimes even money. During these visits, he saw for himself the sorrowful consequences of the religious struggle, which "shattered the people's strength and created a veritable hell in their midst." The bishop often lamented: "There is anger, enmity, strife and inexpressible hatred everywhere. In a word, a fratricidal war is being waged!"[23]

Even though the religious struggle had not led to apostasy among the clergy, it had destroyed the solidarity and spiritual unity among them.[24] Unfortunately, the priests did not follow the instructions of their bishop and, instead, split off into various groups, that fought one another and publicly attacked one another in the press or at meetings. This was harshly criticized by the bishop, who reminded his priests that "the Church and their homeland require that the clergy be *acies bene ordinata*," because enmity and hatred among the clergy helped only "the enemies of the Church, of the people and of the homeland."[25]

Bishop Gebej also launched a planned offensive against Orthodoxy, sectarianism, and communism, directing his campaign in three spheres of activity: missionary-educational; religious-organizational; and legal-apologetic.

(1) The bishop entrusted missionary-educational work to his "zealous assistants," the Basilian Fathers.[26] The chief organizer and initiator of the missionary movement in Subcarpathian Rus' was the Reverend Stepan Rešetylo, OSBM, who with the blessings of bishop Gebej established the Missionary Society of St. Josaphat for the clergy.[27] The first parish missions were held in Čornyj Ardiv in the Máramaros region in May 1924. In addition to Rešetylo, the first mis-

sionaries included the Reverend Polykarp Bulyk, OSBM, and the Reverend Pavlo Gojdyč, OSBM. Gebej always attended the closing of a mission and called upon the people to "remain loyal to the faith of their fathers!"

Such missions revived the villages spiritually. People began to develop greater religious consciousness, a respect for their priests, and love for their church. The bishop never ceased reminding the clergy: "The time has come for every priest to understand the great and priceless value of the holy mission, especially now when hungry wolves stalk us from all sides."[28]

(2) Through religious-organizational work the bishop hoped to revive spiritual values among young people, the intelligentsia, and the faithful in general. He insisted that priests establish in their parishes such religious organziations as the Apostolate of Prayer, Marian Sodality, Rosary Society, Society of the Holy Cross, and others. Religious retreats were introduced for students and the intelligentsia. Higher attendance at religious services, frequent reception of the Sacraments, distribution of the Catholic press, well-prepared meetings of church organizations—all these instilled in believers devotion and loyalty to their church.

Another important means of raising the level of spiritual life was the organization of numerous pilgrimages to Basilian monasteries in Mukačevo, Imstyčevo, Chust-Boronjava, Užhorod, and Malyj Bereznyj. Before World War I, the principal site of pilgrimages had been the Basilian monastery in Máriapócs, which housed a miraculous icon of Our Lady. However, the new frontiers established after World War I left the Máriapócs monastery in Hungary. Bishop Gebej therefore decided to establish a new pilgrimage center on Černeča Hora near Mukačevo. For this purpose he obtained an ancient icon of the Blessed Virgin (dating to 1453) from Pope Pius XI (1922-1939), and he solemnly installed it at the Basilian monastery at Černeča Hora on June 27, 1926.

Informing the consistory of the acquisition of this icon, bishop Gebej recited the following prayer: "Blessed Virgin Mary, as You graciously take up residence among our people, warm their hearts with the fire of God's love. Confirm in holy faith and piety all those who have abandoned Your Son and You. Protect us, the priests, our Rusyn people, and our beloved eparchy with Your Omophorion. O Heavenly Queen, intercede for us in all our troubles."[29] From then on, the Basilian monastery on Černeča Hora became the pilgrimage center for the entire eparchy, and the feast of the Assumption was transformed into a mighty manifestation of faith among a people which had not allowed itself to be drawn away from the true Church of Christ.

(3) The legal defense of the Church and the defense of the faith were carried on by the Central Office for the Defense of the Faith, which bishop Gebej founded at the beginning of 1925.[30] Under the leadership of the energetic Reverend Aleksander Il'nyc'kyj, the Central Office soon coordinated all legal demands for restitution of damages sustained by Greek Catholic parishes. With the help of prominent lawyers, the office conducted its defense in the courts. In the press, the Central Office exposed the hypocrisy of Czechoslovak policy and showed the deplorable consequences of the religious struggle in Carpathian Rus'.

The office also offered legal counsel to parishes that had suffered losses, protested against the lawless conduct of the Orthodox, and monitored compliance with the interfaith law of 1925. With the assistance of the Basilian Fathers, the Central Office issued religious literature in thousands of copies and disseminated it in areas threatened by Orthodoxy.

Bishop Gebej himself oversaw the activity of the Central Office for the Defense of the Faith. He personally defended the rights of his faithful, protested against the unlawful conduct of local authorities, offered encouragement to disheartened priests, visited threatened parishes, and so forth. Gebej also initiated a campaign for the restoration of parochial schools, courageously exposed insiduous attacks against the Greek Catholic Church and, at the same time, did not hesitate to condemn the apathy and magyarophilism of some of his clergy. Wherever possible, the bishop helped his people, not restricting himself to the religious sphere, but providing assistance in their cultural, economic, and political struggle as well.

Bishop Gebej's efforts put an end to the Orthodox movement. During his time in office, a Modus Vivendi was reached between the Vatican and the Czechoslovak Republic. In addition to many other advantages, the Modus Vivendi assured the revival of the Mukačevo eparchy. But the bishop was still left with such difficult tasks as: reorganization of church schools; resolution of the language issue; and improvements in the economic lot of the impoverished population. However, in all these fields, the bishop was unable to win support and understanding even among his former friends, let alone the clergy. Some members of the chapter and higher clergy began to hinder his cultural and educational efforts. Spent by his labors and discouraged by the intrigues of the clerical ranks, bishop Gebej sub-

mitted his resignation. However, the papal nuncio in Prague, archbishop Pietro Ciriaci (1928-1934), refused to accept it, because he was
convinced that bishop Gebej was pursuing the right course by working
with and for the people.[31]

Thus, the faithful champion of Christ, bishop Petro Gebej, continued his difficult task "to unite in a single camp all the forces of the
people and clergy, not only in the religious sphere, but also politically
and culturally, in order to create a single front in the struggle for a better tomorrow." But, to continue the words of the eparchial organ
Dušpastyr', which concluded in its obituary of the bishop: "his plans
foundered on human obstinacy and shortsightedness."[32]

Hard work, constant worries, and the opposition of some of his
clergy undermined the physical and moral strength of this illustrious
prelate. Bishop Gebej died on April 26, 1931, at the age of 66. With
his death, the Mukačevo eparchy lost a great leader and the father of
its spiritual renewal. The faithful called him "the bishop with the
golden heart" and regarded him as a true "saint."[33]

3. The Steadfast Spirit of Bishop Pavlo Gojdyč, OSBM

While the Mukačevo eparchy was the site of a protracted religious
struggle, the Rusyn population of the Prešov eparchy was subjected to
yet another kind of attack—a policy of slovakization pursued by the
regional authorities according to methods already perfected by the
Hungarians. Bishop Njaradij, the administrator of the Prešov eparchy
from 1922 to 1927, did not permit Orthodoxy to take root in the
Prešov Region. However, as a citizen of Yugoslavia, he was powerless
to withstand the pressure of the policy of Slovakization implemented
by the local authorities. Like the Hungarians before them, the Slovaks
set out to take control over Rusyn parochial schools in order to
slovakize young people as the first step toward ultimately assimilating
the Greek Catholic Church. In order to neutralize any possible opposition from bishop Njaradij, they repeatedly depicted him as a
"foreigner" who wanted to lead the Prešov eparchy into the "Ukrainian" camp.[34]

Bishop Njaradij explained the whole matter to the Apostolic See
and asked that the hieromonk Pavlo P. Gojdyč be appointed bishop
of the Prešov eparchy. To avert a new conflict, on September 14,
1926, Rome named Gojdyč apostolic administrator. On March 7,
1927, after Gojdyč had assumed this office, he was named titular
bishop of Harpasa.[35]

Following in the footsteps of his predecessor, bishop Pavlo Gojdyč maintained close contacts with his faithful and clergy. Whenever a threat arose in some locality, the bishop immediately went there, delivered a sermon, gave instruction and encouragement, and spent many hours in prayer during the night. He also did all he could to elevate the spiritual standards of the eparchy. His numerous pastoral letters, imbued with the spirit of God, constitute a priceless heritage. He, too, encouraged the missionary and retreat movement in the eparchy. The eparchial journal, *Blahovîstnyk*, described bishop Gojdyč's efforts in the following terms:

> Our beloved bishop made it his goal to build the greatest number of institutions in our eparchy. So far, he has already founded and built an orphanage, established a Rusyn Catholic gymnasium, enlarged the Alumneum boarding school for boys, and expanded the girls' boarding school. For the needs of the eparchy, he bought a large plot of land with an orchard in Prešov and built a multi-residential building. To administer the orphanage, he brought in the Sisters Servants of Mary Immaculate, who now have a novitiate here. He placed the girls' boarding school in the care of the Sisters of St. Basil the Great. He entrusted the Alumneum to the Basilian Fathers, who, in addition to Prešov, work in nearby Medzilaborce and Trebišov, and in Prague. The Redemptorists of the Eastern rite, who have their center in Michalovce, are also working here. They also have their residences in Sabinov and Stropkov. [...] In short, under the leadership of bishop Pavlo, there is much activity in our eparchy.[36]

Unfortunately, bishop Gojdyč was not able to concentrate exclusively on his pastoral work. Circumstances made it necessary for him to come to the defense of the national rights of the majority of his faithful, who were being threatened by relentless slovakization. This is how the bishop himself described the situation:

> I took this responsibility upon myself only because there was no one else to do it. Other nationalities have their ministers, their political parties, their deputies to parliament; only my [Rusyn] faithful have no one to defend their national rights. When my faithful turn to me with trust, I cannot ignore their appeals, even though as a result I have to suffer much unpleasantness and great injury.[37]

Thus, this humble and genuine monk entered into an unequal but resolute struggle with the Slovak authorities. He was prepared to make any sacrifice to defend the unalienable rights of his faithful. In this struggle, bishop Gojdyč demonstrated that he was a truly "courageous and steadfast leader," who possessed the kind of character traits of which martyrs are made.[38]

The slovakization of the Carpatho-Rusyns in the Prešov Region, no less than magyarization before it, only made the ground more fertile for Orthodox propaganda, a circumstance that bishop Njaradij had already pointed out. Earlier, under Hungarian rule, the Slovaks had urged the Carpatho-Rusyns to preserve their nationality.[39] But the Slovaks soon learned that the magyarization of the Carpatho-Rusyns had advantages, because "as a result of their inability to read the Cyrillic alphabet (only the Latin alphabet was taught in schools), the Rusyns would turn to Slovak books and newspapers. It is to this that we can attribute the great success of slovakization in the past 30 years."[40] After World War I, when more than 200,000 Carpatho-Rusyns were placed under Slovak rule, the Slovaks initiated a planned policy of slovakization throughout the entire Prešov Region. The only bulwark of national identity among the Rusyns was their parochial school system. Consequently, the Greek Catholic bishops insisted that the Rusyn language and the Cyrillic alphabet be taught in these schools.[41]

On August 10, 1929, bishop Pavlo Gojdyč instructed the principals of parish schools in his eparchy "to teach at least three hours a week of the Rusyn language in all church schools."[42] A census was about to be taken and the Slovaks had launched a concerted campaign urging the Carpatho-Rusyns to register as "Slovaks," since "they live in Slovakia."[43] In line with this policy, on January 15, 1930, the ministry of education in Bratislava issued an order that all schools in the Prešov Region, including parochial ones, must provide instruction only in "the official Slovak language."

The bishop vigorously opposed this abuse of guaranteed liberties: "The Carpatho-Rusyns, together with the Czechs and Slovaks, are a nation-building element within the framework of Czechoslovakia; this is why the Peace Conference guaranteed them equal rights with their Slavic brothers, the Czechs and the Slovaks."[44] But Bratislava insisted that their directive was based on a Hungarian law of 1907 that was still in force.[45] Refusing to yield, bishop Gojdyč cited the inherent rights of the Carpatho-Rusyns, thereby forcing the Slovak department of schools ultimately to permit the teaching of Rusyn, but only for "three hours per week" and even then only "until the final resolution of this issue."[46] To this the bishop responded on April 26, 1930:

We regard the directive of the [school] department not only as a violation of fraternal love and of the provisions of the [Paris] Peace Conference, but also as a violation of the most elementary natural law. I stress once again that our appeal concerns children about whose Rusyn nationality there is not the slightest doubt, who speak only Rusyn at home, and who want to study in Rusyn schools, [because our native language] is as dear to our hearts, as Czech is to the Czechs and Slovak to the Slovaks and which neither would abandon at any price![47]

But the Slovaks would not relent. They introduced Slovak as the only language of instruction in all state schools of the Prešov Region, even where the Carpatho-Rusyns constituted a majority. In parochial schools,[48] where instruction was also to be given in Slovak, the school department allowed only three hours of Rusyn a week. Once again citing natural law and the guarantees of the Peace Conference, bishop Gojdyč ordered that Rusyn be used as the language of instruction in 86 purely Rusyn schools and that in these Slovak be taught only for three hours a week. In response, Bratislava nationalized all parochial schools in 1935, thereby also violating the Modus Vivendi agreement with the Vatican.

Bishop Gojdyč refused to submit to this new [Slovak] directive and appealed to the central authorities in Prague. A series of hearings, discussions, and referendums followed. Finally, in 1938, the ministry of education in Prague restored 65 schools to the eparchy and permitted them to use Rusyn as the language of instruction. But the Slovaks had scored at least a partial victory, because they were able to slovakize 15 Rusyn schools legally. In 1936, with Prague's consent, bishop Gojdyč opened the Greek Catholic Rusyn *gymnasium* [high school] in Prešov. The school became the bastion of Carpatho-Rusyn religious and national life and a major contributor to the cultural development of the eparchy.[49]

Because of his defense of Rusyn schools, the Slovaks branded bishop Gojdyč their "enemy." Consequently, when Slovakia became an "independent republic" in 1939, the Slovak authorities set out to oust Gojdyč from the Prešov see in order to replace him with someone who would support the slovakization of the Carpatho-Rusyn minority.

The Slovaks began by attempting to provoke unrest at the eparchial theological seminary in Prešov. A number of slovakized seminarians denounced the bishop for refusing to ordain "Slovak seminarians," claiming that "speaking Slovak" was forbidden in the seminary and reported that "a spirit of opposition to the state" reigned among the

Greek Catholic clergy.[50] The Slovak press and radio launched their own campaign against the bishop, the seminary, and the clergy. The bishop could not remain silent. Upon investigating the unsubstantiated denunciations, he firmly protested to the Slovak ministry in Bratislava "against the false and groundless attacks" of government authorities and the Slovak press, which was "maliciously denigrating the Rusyn Catholic clergy and its bishop."[51]

The bishop's protest had little effect. The press continued its campaign against both him and the clergy, hoping thereby to arouse distrust and unrest in the eparchy. Perceiving "someone's black hand" behind this, on November 12, 1939, bishop Pavlo Gojdyč appealed directly to the president of Slovakia, Monsignor Jozef Tiso, requesting that as a Catholic priest and head of the Catholic state he use his influence with his subordinates to make them desist from attacking the bishop, clergy, and faithful of Carpatho-Rusyn nationality. With a view to putting an end to anarchy in the seminary, the bishop asked for the names of the informers so that they could be punished accordingly. Gojdyč concluded his letter to president Tiso with the following words: "Otherwise, the undersigned [that is, the bishop] will be forced to conclude that the government of the Slovak republic does not desire the consolidation of Greek Catholic Rusyns and Slovaks and does not wish to help the Greek Catholic ordinary to end the anarchy which black forces are attempting to incite in order to widen the gap between the clergy and the faithful and which may have terrible consequences."[52]

The bishop's letter went unanswered. When president Tiso visited Prešov at the end of the same month and bishop Gojdyč came to greet him, the Slovak president ignored the bishop and did not even shake hands with him.[53] In the evening, when the representatives of various national and religious groups in the Prešov Region came to the president with their petitions, bishop Gojdyč publicly protested the liquidation of Rusyn schools. To the bishop's complaint, the Slovak chauvinist Dr. Halan responded in the presence of other delegates by threatening the bishop with imprisonment. The bishop left empty-handed.[54]

The public insult to a Catholic bishop in a Catholic state in the presence of a Catholic president convinced bishop Gojdyč that for the good of the eparchy he should resign. Since he was still only the administrator of the eparchy, resignation was relatively simple. On November 22, 1939, bishop Gojdyč sent a letter of resignation to the Apostolic See, asking the pope to release him from the post of administrator of the Prešov eparchy "for political and personal reasons," and to appoint "a man with a strong hand and one who would enjoy the complete confidence of the government." Bishop Gojdyč also sent a copy of this letter to president Tiso.[55]

At a meeting on January 26, 1940, the Slovak government gladly accepted bishop Gojdyč's resignation and voted him a "generous" annual pension. He was even permitted to go abroad after he had taken "the necessary steps to ensure that the Apostolic See accepted his resignation."[56] The Slovak representative at the Vatican at the time was the moderate Karel Sidor, a great supporter of bishop Gojdyč and his work. Sidor gave the Apostolic See an accurate and true account of the circumstances and the real reasons for the bishop's resignation. As a result, Pope Pius XII (1939-1958) refused to accept bishop Gojdyč's resignation and, instead, issued a decree, dated July 19, 1940, naming him "ordinary of the Prešov eparchy."[57] The bishop was thus completely vindicated.

Slovakia needed the Vatican's good-will, and so Tiso was forced to swallow this bitter pill. However, he did not send official representatives to bishop Gojdyč's installation, which was held in Prešov on August 8, 1940. The Slovak episcopate also boycotted the ceremony and not a single Catholic bishop attended the solemnity.[57a] This, however, had no effect on the bishop's stance.

When preparations began for a new census in Slovakia in 1940, bishop Gojdyč once again appealed to his clergy to inform the people of the importance of censuses, since "as a result of earlier statistical data the Carpatho-Rusyns suffered a great deal of harm and injustice." He urged the faithful to be sure their nationality was listed as they reported it to the census takers: "Rusyns as Rusyns, Slovaks as Slovaks, Germans as Germans, and Hungarians as Hungarians."[58]

The Slovak government branded the bishop's pastoral letter as "Rusyn agitation against Slovaks," but it was reluctant to oppose him openly in order not to incur the Vatican's displeasure. Instead, the authorities began to persecute the clergy. The more courageous priests who "dared" to read the pastoral letter in church to their faithful were imprisoned. To others, who informed the people about the importance of the census privately, the government cut off payment of the monthly supplement (the *congrua*). Slovakia's well-known and youthful minister of propaganda, Aleksander (Šanjo) Mach, came to Prešov on December 1, 1940 to lend support to the "Slovaks." When bishop Gojdyč refused to attend a welcoming reception for him, the municipal authorities threatened that this could have "harmful consequences for all Rusyns of the Prešov Region.'' When Mach did encounter bishop Gojdyč at a concert, he called him ''a traitor and enemy of the Slovak state'' and ''unworthy of the office of bishop.'' In the face of these charges and amidst the general embarrassment of the public, the bishop left the auditorium.[59]

Despite the Slovaks' determination to convince the world that there ''are no Rusyns'' in Slovakia, the 1940 census showed that there were still some 80,000 nationally-conscious Rusyns in the country who were prepared to fight for the preservation of their national identity. This so enraged the Slovaks that they at once liquidated both eparchial Rusyn schools in Prešov—the *gymnasium* and the teachers' college. Their purpose was to put an end to any influx of Rusyn intelligentsia and teachers. In practice, this signified the total slovakization of parochial schools.[60]

Lacking adequate material resources, the bishop was unable to maintain the *gymnasium*. But he was determined to retain the teachers' college, in order to assure a continuing supply of Rusyn teachers and cantors. The maintenance of the Carpatho-Rusyn teachers' college was also supported by the Apostolic See, which even provided some material assistance. Realizing that Rome was interested in preserving the Rusyn parochial school system in the Prešov Region, the Slovak authorities made some concessions and restored state aid to the bishop to be used to meet ''the cultural needs of Rusyns in Prešov.'' Thus, bishop Gojdyč was able to save both the Carpatho-Rusyn teachers' college and *gymnasium* in Prešov.

Powerless to oust bishop Gojdyč from the Prešov see, the Slovaks began to take steps to transfer the episcopal residence from Prešov to some other provincial town and thereby liquidate the religious and cultural center of the Carpatho-Rusyns of the Prešov Region. In fact, there were plans to transfer the bishop—as an ''enemy of the state''—to the Basilian monastery in Medzilaborce, but the turn that the war took in 1943-1944 disrupted this scheme. The Slovak government, fearing the revenge of the people, changed its attitude toward the bishop and the Carpatho-Rusyn clergy and instead began to seek an accomodation with the Rusyn element in the Prešov Region.[61]

4. The Flourishing of Monastic Life

An important role in the revival of the religious and cultural life of Carpathian Rus' was played by the monastic communities which helped the Greek Catholic bishops to implement their plans. Before World War I, only the Basilian Order existed in Carpathian Rus'.

After the war, the Redemptorist Fathers, the Basilian Sisters, and the Sisters Servants of Mary Immaculate also became active.

(1) The Order of St. Basil the Great has existed in Carpathian Rus' since times immemorial. The monastery of St. Nicholas on Černeča Hora near Mukačevo served as the region's religious and cultural center for many centuries. It was only in the second half of the nineteenth century that Basilian monastic life declined as a result of the reforms of emperor Joseph II and the hostility of official Hungarian circles. Bishop Julij Fircak intended to strengthen Basilian monastic life in Carpathian Rus', and consequently a proposal to reform the order was put forward at the eparchial synod in Užhorod in 1903.[62]

In Galicia, Basilian reform had begun in 1882. At that time, Pope Leo XIII had expressed a wish that the reform be extended to include all monasteries of the Basilian Order.[63] The Galician Basilian Fathers were therefore prepared to introduce the reform in Carpathian Rus' as well. The Hungarians were opposed, however. To facilitate matters, bishop Fircak was willing to entrust the reforms to the Hungarian Jesuits, but they refused. The question of reform within the Basilian Order was also to be considered within the framework of the reforms proposed by the Central Commission of Greek Catholic Eparchies in Budapest in 1915, but these were never implemented.

The lack of missionary monks was strongly felt in Carpathian Rus' during the religious struggle that took place after World War I. As the battle raged, bishop Antonij Papp finally agreed to allow the Basilian Fathers from Galicia to initiate the long overdue reform at the Mukačevo monastery. Thus, in the fall of 1920, the Reverends Jeronym Malyc'kyj, Hlib Kinach, and Polykarp Bulyk arrived in Carpathian Rus'. At Rome's request, the reform was to include also the Basilian monasteries in Hungary and Romania, which had belonged to the Carpatho-Rusyn province before the war.[64]

The first reformed Basilian who completed his novitiate in the Mukačevo monastery in the spring of 1924 was Pavlo P. Gojdyč, the future bishop of Prešov. With the help of the Reverend Stefan Rešetylo, OSBM, and the Reverend Polykarp Bulyk, OSBM, Gojdyč initiated a missionary movement in Subcarpathian Rus' which proved very successful in countering Orthodox propaganda in the far eastern Máramaros region.[65] Throughout Subcarpathian Rus', the Basilians soon organized the Missionary Society of St. Josaphat, popularized the Apostolate of Prayer among the faithful, founded Marian Sodalities, and inculcated devotion to Christ, the Lover of Mankind, in their monthly publication, *Blahovîstnyk*. In Užhorod, the Basilians founded a publishing house which issued prayerbooks, calendars, spiritual books, apologetic brochures, and other religious materials.[66]

In addition to missionary work and publishing, the Basilians also provided religious guidance for the intelligentsia and for young boys and girls. In short, they contributed both to the revival of religious life in Subcarpathian Rus' and to the region's cultural and national rebirth. Before long, the reformed monasteries in Mukačevo, Užhorod, Malyj Bereznyj, Imstyčevo, and Chust-Boronjava began to flourish as the number of vocations increased, and in 1932 the St. Nicholas Province of the Basilian Order in Subcarpathian Rus' (reformed) was established with the Reverend P. Bulyk, OSBM, as its first protohegumen.[67] From then on, the Carpatho-Rusyn Basilians "kept pace with their elder brothers on the Galician side of the Carpathians. Theirs was the second strongest branch of the Basilian Order on the eve of World War II."[68]

With the fall of Carpatho-Ukraine in March 1939, the Hungarian occupational authorities expelled all monks who had come from Galicia and the Prešov Region. These monks found refuge in the Prešov eparchy, where the ancient Basilian monasteries in Krásny Brod and Buková Hôrka stood in ruins. Therefore, Bishop Gojdyč gave them an abandoned parish in Medzilaborce, then the center of Russophilism and Orthodox propaganda.

Despite initial difficulties and hostile propaganda, the Basilians quickly put down roots in the Prešov Region. The people began to rally round their missionary monks, the priests received support from them in their struggle against Orthodoxy and against drunkenness, and the bishop relied on them as his devoted assistants. In 1942, the Basilians built a small house on Buková Hôrka and revived the traditional annual pilgrimages to that site. They took over the administration of the boy's boarding school in Prešov and acquired a small monastery in Trebišov, which became the first Basilian center among slovakized Greek Catholics. In 1945, bishop Gojdyč entrusted to the Basilians the administration of the parish in Prague, and from there the monks ministered to the religious needs of Rusyns throughout the Czech lands. In 1947, they founded a monastery in Prešov, which provided spiritual guidance for youth and religious organizations, for the Sisters Servants of Mary Immaculate, and for the Basilian Sisters.

The Prešov monastery, which served as the religious and cultural center for a large territory, became the first seat of the protohegumen of the new province of SS. Cyril and Methodius, established on March 4, 1948 for the territory of Czechoslovakia. Its first protohegumen was a native of Prešov, the Reverend Sevastijan Sabol, OSBM. Thus, at a time when the Prešov eparchy was in greatest peril, bishop Gojdyč received reliable help and support from the Basilian Order.

(2) The Redemptorist Congregation also made an important contribution to the struggle against Orthodoxy and to the improvement of religious life in Carpathian Rus'. Their beginnings were very modest.[69] During the religious struggle, two Czech Redemptorists, the Reverend D. Trčka and the Reverend S. Nekula, decided to devote themselves to the Uniate cause among the Carpatho-Rusyns. Educated in Galicia, the two priests settled in 1922 in Stropkov in the Prešov eparchy. They were helped by other Czech Redemptorists, who found spiritual inspiration in the ecumenical movement. In 1931, the Redemptorist Fathers extended their activities into the Mukačevo eparchy, making Michalovce their center. During World War II, they established a third monastery in Sabinov. On March 26, 1947, a vice-province of the Redemptorists of the Eastern rite was created in the Prešov Region. Its seat was in Michalovce, which at the time was under the jurisdiction of the bishop of Prešov.

From the outset, the Redemptorists engaged in missionary work and giving retreats. They cultivated the veneration of Our Lady of Perpetual Help and took over the leadership of the Rosary and Sacred Heart Societies in the Prešov eparchy. In 1941, they began publishing a monthly, *Misionar*, for slovakized Greek Catholics. The periodical was designed to cultivate the veneration of St. Joseph. The *Misionar* editorial board also published a series of educational brochures entitled *Bližše ko Chrystu* (Closer to Christ). Their prayer books (*Molitvennik Sv. Rožancja* and *Spasi dušu svoju)* in the Latin alphabet became very popular.

(3) The Sisters of St. Basil the Great came to Carpathian Rus' after World War I, at the invitation of the then administrator of the Prešov eparchy, Monsignor Nikolaj Russnak. Five Basilian Sisters arrived in Prešov from Galicia under the leadership of M. Magdalyna ·Humenjuk to take over the administration of the girls' boarding school. Encouraged by the success of the Basilian Sisters in Prešov, bishop Gebej in 1924 invited four nuns to Užhorod, where they were charged with running another girls' boarding school. The following year, the Basilian Sisters opened their novitiate in Užhorod and took under their own care the orphanage and kindergarten. Monsignor Avhustyn Vološyn became a generous patron of the sisters, extending to them both material and moral support.

During World War II, the Basilian Sisters attempted to strengthen their presence in the Prešov eparchy, because the Hungarian authorities closed their novitiate in Užhorod and would not allow them to expand in the Mukačevo eparchy. In 1947, they opened a novitiate in Prešov. In addition to Prešov, the Basilian Sisters had convents in Medzilaborce, Sečovce, Stropkov, and Svidník. In Prague, they took care of Monsignor Vološyn until he was deported by the Soviets and the Sisters themselves were disbanded.[70]

(4) The Sisters Servants of Mary Immaculate settled in Prešov in 1928, when bishop Gojdyč placed the economic affairs of the seminary in their charge. Later they took over the administration of the orphanage and established a novitiate there. They took charge of the Circle of St. Anne, which took care of servant girls in larger cities. From Prešov, the Sisters Servants expanded their activity to Michalovce, L'utina, and Trebišov, and then founded convents among the Carpatho-Rusyn settlers on Czech lands near Uherské Hradiště and Libejovice.[71]

No account of monastic life in Carpathian Rus' would be complete without mention of the work of some Jesuits of the Eastern rite, a leading role among whom was played by the French Jesuit, the Reverend V. Bourgeois. In 1927-1931, he worked among the faithful in the Máramaros region, in the vicinity of Tereblja.[72] In 1933, bishop Stojka announced that the Jesuits would settle in Mukačevo, where they would take charge of *gymnasium* students. But for reasons unknown, the Jesuits never settled permanently in Carpathian Rus' and worked there only temporarily.[73]

5. Between Two Crises

The world depression of the thirties also produced an economic crisis in Czechoslovakia, while Hitler's expansionism brought on a political crisis, which ultimately led to the outbreak of World War II. Both these crises left their mark on the religious and cultural life of Carpathian Rus'.

In the midst of the economic crisis, Subcarpathian Rus' lost its dedicated leader, bishop Petro Gebej (1931), and during the political crisis, the Hungarians once again occupied Subcarpathian Rus' (1939). During this critical and uncertain period, the eparchy of Mukačevo was headed by bishop Aleksander Stojka (1932-1943), whose activity remains in part a mystery as long as the archives containing information about these years remain inaccessible.

Bishop Stojka assumed the office of administrator of the Mukačevo eparchy at a time when famine began to threaten his flock. This was a period of heightened sectarian struggle and intense communist propaganda. The Orthodox struggle, which had undermined the moral strength of the people, was over. But now various sectarian currents and communist atheism spread among the people, who were living in a state of material and spiritual poverty. In addition, Carpatho-Rusyn political leaders drew the people into the so-called "language struggle," to which the bishop himself contributed in some degree.

From the beginning of his episcopate, bishop Stojka showed great concern for poverty and hunger among his faithful. Small wonder that he earned the name "father of the poor."[74] Even earlier, as an official of the episcopal chancery during World War I, Stojka organized an eparchial fund for the care of war orphans. In his articles, he exposed abuses by the Hungarian authorities that had resulted in famine in the winter of 1917 in Carpathian Rus'. He then headed an aid drive under the slogan: "Bread for the poor."

An experienced canonist and economist, Stojka defended the material interests of the clergy and the church communities during the religious struggle after World War I. As chancellor, he represented the eparchy in court suits against the Orthodox. The restoration of Greek Catholic churches and church property seized by the Orthodox during the religious struggle was due in large measure to his efforts. Stojka himself came from a poor peasant family and as the motto of his episcopate he chose the words of Christ: "The Spirit of the Lord is upon me, because he has annointed me to bring glad tidings to the poor." (Luke, 4:18)

While still only a capitular vicar, Stojka drew the clergy's attention to the poverty of the faithful: "Our Carpathians and Beskyds echo with the prayer: *Give us this day our daily bread!*" Stojka obliged each pastor to take an interest in the misfortunes of his parishioners, to represent them before tax collectors, to seek employment for them, and to try to obtain government assistance for those in need.[75] In his Lenten letter of 1932, Stojka wrote:

> Most of all, be careful of dangerous agitators who exploit your current difficult situation for their own ends and incite you against the law and public order. As the temporary administrator of our orphaned eparchy, I have already drawn the government's attention to the poverty and hardship of our people, because there are places in our Carpathians and Beskyds where our brothers are starving.
>
> But we must admit that our state is also undergoing an economic crisis and we therefore cannot expect it to provide us

with all the assistance we need. That is why it is everyone's sacred duty to help his brother by way of self-help![76]

Monsignor Stojka did not confine himself merely to words. He also acted. In the same letter, he announced the launching of an "Easter Action" and opened it with his own contribution. He conducted this action throughout the eparchy, urging those who were better off to make donations so that "every Rusyn would have his own *paska* [Easter bread] at Easter."[77] On Easter Sunday Stojka celebrated the Divine Liturgy for the poor at the cathedral and afterwards shared Easter breakfast with them.

When named to the episcopate, Stojka refused all celebrations in his honor and asked that the money set aside for these festivities be given to the poor. After his episcopal ordination on July 12, 1932, the bishop dined with 300 of the city's poor, thereby demonstrating his evangelical mission: "I was sent to bring glad tidings to the poor!" That same year, bishop Stojka went to Prague and then to Rome, where he personally pleaded for assistance for his starving people.[78]

Bishop Stojka planned his episcopal visits to coincide with the need to console the hungry or those suffering various misfortunes. Thus, for example, in 1933, when a major flood destroyed virtually all of Ugocsa county, the bishop visited the valley of the upper Tisza, where thousands of families were left without food or shelter. He immediately launched a fund-raising campaign to help the victims.[79] When the danger of unemployment arose in the Máramaros region in 1935, bishop Stojka acted as an intermediary between the government and the workers to bring the strike to an end.[80] Wherever a need arose, he hastened to offer help, advice, and encouragement.

Bishop Stojka's fatherly concern for the hungry and impoverished won him great respect and love among the people. Even the Orthodox, whom he never excluded from his aid, rallied round him and took part in his services. The bishop also devoted his attention to the education of young people. He believed that "the renewal of the Church has to begin with our children." He wanted "God's grace to reign" in his eparchy and "God's peace" to endure among the people. He wanted to be "everything to everybody" in order to save the souls of "all the faithful of his eparchy."[81]

Bishop Stojka had a special devotion to the Blessed Mother, who was the patron of the Mukačevo eparchy. During his first pilgrimage to Černeča Hora as bishop, he made the following solemn promise before the icon of Our Lady: "I swear under oath that during my

apostolic tenure the whole eparchy will resound with Your glory!"[82]
The bishop's great love for the Blessed Mother gave rise to an un-
precedented growth of Marian devotion in the Mukačevo eparchy.
When he was still the capitular vicar, Stojka initiated the Congress of
Marian Sodalities, which was to meet every year at the Basilian
monastery on Černeča Hora near Mukačevo.[83]

In 1938, on the occasion of the 900th anniversary of the consecration of Kievan Rus' to the protection of the Blessed Mother of God by
grand prince Jaroslav the Wise (reigned 1019-1054), hieromonk
Chrystofor Mys'kiv, OSBM, organized with the blessing of bishop
Stojka mass celebrations throughout the Mukačevo eparchy in honor
of the *Queen of Rus'*. Unfortunately, the Russophile press branded
these celebrations as pro-Ukrainian demonstrations and succeeded in
forcing bishop Stojka to withdraw his patronage over the festivities,
while the government banned such celebrations in the future.[84]

Bishop Stojka was a leader of the faithful and the beloved father of
the poor. However, in the national and cultural sphere, he professed
magyarophile convictions. He belonged to that segment of the clergy
who tried to negate the national and cultural aspirations of his
predecessor, bishop Gebej, and Monsignor Vološyn. Upon becoming
bishop, Stojka advocated a third national orientation, which favored
what it called "our language" (*tutešnjac'ka*), and which supported the
pro-Hungarian policy of the Autonomous Agricultural Union.

Bishop Gebej had tried to unite the clergy and faithful in the Christian Populist party headed with the bishop's blessing by Monsignor
Vološyn. In the political sphere, bishop Gebej worked for the attainment of full autonomy for Carpathian Rus' as a whole, including the
Prešov Region. But his successor, bishop Stojka, initially supported
the policy of the Czechoslovak government.[85] Then, after he had won
the confidence of Prague, he began to oppose Monsignor Vološyn and
the Christian Populist movement "on personal grounds."[86] Later, he
clashed as well with Professor Stefan Fencyk and the Russophile
movement.[87] This prompted bishop Stojka to initiate a third orientation based on the local Rusyn dialect that was promoted in the official
eparchial weekly, *Nedîlja*, which spoke of a separate "Carpatho-
Rusyn nationality."[88]

The rise of this third orientation coincided with the establishment in
Budapest of the Hungarian League for the Revision of the Treaty of
Trianon, which advocated a common Hungarian-Polish border, that
is, the incorporation of Subcarpathian Rus' into Hungary. With the
blessing of bishop Stojka, the movement attracted several influential

pro-Hungarian priests who received instructions from Budapest through the Polish consulate in Užhorod. Thus once again the policy of Greek Catholic Church circles assumed a magyarophile direction, which in 1939 led to the Hungarian occupation of Subcarpathian Rus'.[89]

6. On The Wings of Independence

The political crisis that overtook central Europe at the end of 1938 transformed the Czechoslovak republic into a "federative state of Czechs, Slovaks and Subcarpathian Rusyns."[90] The first autonomous government of Subcarpathian Rus' was headed by bishop Stojka's protégé, parliamentary deputy Andrij Brodij, who immediately established relations with the Hungarians. After two weeks of such "treasonous" activity, Brodij was imprisoned by the central authorities in Prague and the government of Subcarpathian Rus' passed into the worthy hands of Monsignor Avhustyn Vološyn. On October 26, 1938, when Vološyn became premier of Subcarpathian Rus', bishop Stojka addressed him as "the father of our people" during a religious service of thanksgiving. At last, the populist movement had triumphed and the Carpatho-Rusyns attained self-government.

The joy of the Rusyn population was of short duration, however. The Vienna arbitration of November 2, 1938 gave the richest portion of Subcarpathian Rus' (soon to be renamed Carpatho-Ukraine), along with its largest cities of Užhorod, Mukačevo, and Berehovo, to Hungary.[91] The capital of the province was moved to Chust, so that the Mukačevo eparchy was now divided by new political frontiers.

Bishop Stojka with his cathedral chapter and curia remained in Užhorod, which was now in Hungary, even though only 35 parishes of the Mukačevo eparchy had been ceded to Hungary. The bishop sent the eparchy's youngest canon, Monsignor Ludovik Minja, to Chust to administer as the bishop's vicar the 280 parishes that remained inside the borders of Subcarpathian Rus'.[92]

Learning of the irregular situation that had developed within the Mukačevo eparchy, the Apostolic See, on November 15, 1938, appointed to Chust an apostolic visitator in the person of Dionysij Njaradij, the bishop of the Greek Catholic eparchy of Križevci [in Yugoslavia].[93] The Mukačevo eparchy's monthly, *Blahovisnyk*, described his arrival in Chust in the following words:

> When His Excellency Dionysij received the appointment naming him apostolic visitator with all the rights of an apostolic ad-

ministrator, he went immediately to Križevci, where he received instructions by telegram to set out at once for the Carpatho-Ukraine. He arrived in Chust on the evening of November 29, and on December 4, 1938, during the Divine Liturgy, he took over the administration of that portion of the Mukačevo eparchy that remained outside the borders of Hungary. That day all of Chust, all the religious and political authorities, and all Carpatho-Rusyn corporations enthusiastically welcomed the first and highest prelate of Carpatho-Ukraine.[94]

Bishop Njaradij immediately began to put in order the church affairs of the eparchy. He called conferences of various deaneries to discuss the new agenda of activities in the altered political circumstances, and he insisted that the clergy should get involved in the cultural and educational work within the framework of "Catholic action."[95] He recalled the eparchy's seminarians from Užhorod and assigned them temporarily to Olomouc, appointing the Reverend Myron Kalynec', OSBM, their rector.[96]

Despite the winter season, the bishop, accompanied by his secretary, the Reverend Stepan Rešetylo, OSBM, visited parishes, took stock of the pastoral work of the clergy, tried to revive church organizations, called upon the clergy to remain dedicated to God and to the Church, warned the faithful against enemy agitators, urged everyone to engage in zealous apostolic and cultural work, and brought fatherly words of encouragement and comfort everywhere. For the more active clergy, the bishop founded the Society of Greek Catholic Priests, which elected as its head the pastor of Vonihovo, the Reverend Julij Stanynec'.[97] The bishop maintained close ties with the clergy through the *Visnyk Mukačivs'koji Jeparchiji v Čechoslovac'kij Respublyci*, the first issue of which appeared in Chust on January 1, 1939.

Bishop Njaradij also gave refuge to the Basilian Fathers and the Basilian Sisters, whom the Hungarian authorities had expelled from Užhorod. They engaged in cultural and educational activities at the *gymnasiums* and the teachers' colleges. Since the Hungarians did not permit the Basilians to take their printing shop out of Užhorod, they were allowed to print their materials at the state publishing house in Chust, including the popular monthly *Blahovisnyk*, the first issue of which appeared already at beginning of January 1939. It was edited by the monk and poet, the Reverend Sevastijan Sabol, OSBM. In addition to monasteries on Černeča Hora near Mukačevo, and in Malyj Bereznyj, Imstyčevo, and Boronjava, all of which remained on the territory of the Carpatho-Ukraine, the Basilians founded houses in Velykyj Byčkiv and Rachiv. The Basilian Sisters concentrated their forces at the orphanage in Chust and in Sevljuš (now Vynohradiv), where the teachers' seminary had been transferred.

The majority of the clergy cooperated with bishop Njaradij. But there were also those who tried to frustrate the efforts of the church and civic authorities. To those priests, the bishop addressed his New Year's letter: "I regard it as my archpastoral duty to remind the Very Reverend and Reverend fathers that keeping in mind their priestly duties they refrain from all manner of anti-government agitation. There does not and cannot exist a temporal power on earth which would tolerate anti-government agitation, regardless of who is engaged in it."[98]

Just when religious life was becoming stable once more in Carpatho-Ukraine, the Hungarian authorities decided to return the former bishop of Mukačevo, Antonij Papp, to Užhorod. At the time, archbishop Papp was administrator of the Miskolc exarchate. In order to embarrass bishop Stojka, the Hungarian occupational forces revived the case of former theology professor, Dr. Stefan Fencyk, whom Stojka had suspended for "insubordination" in 1934. Fencyk, who remained loyal to the Hungarians, now brought a suit against bishop Stojka. The trial ended in January 1939, as a result of which the bishop was compelled to restore Fencyk to his "priestly office" and to clear him of all ecclesiastical censures. The Apostolic See subsequently summoned bishop Stojka to Rome in order to discuss with him the return of archbishop Papp to the episcopal residence in Užhorod.[99]

The plans to oust bishop Stojka were prevented by the events of March 1939. As Czechoslovakia fell, on March 16, 1939, Hungarian troops occupied the entire territory of Carpatho-Ukraine. The episcopal residence in Chust was surrounded by soldiers and bishop Njaradij was taken to Budapest, where the papal nuncio advised him to return to Yugoslavia. The administration of the Mukačevo eparchy was once again entrusted to bishop Aleksander Stojka, while archbishop Papp remained in Miskolc.[100]

This double-dealing conduct finally made bishop Stojka see the Hungarians for what they were. After his return to Užhorod, he never again trusted Hungarian politicians and turned to his own people instead. Taking a bold stand, the bishop refused to permit the demotion of Monsignor Aleksander Chira, whom the Hungarian authorities had kept under house arrest at the seminary for a long time. He also ensured that nationally-conscious priests remained in control of the seminary staff, and he made sure that new candidates for the priesthood came from common peasant families. He likewise tried to raise the religious and cultural level of the faithful.

Bishop Stojka revealed a genuine love for his people in 1941-1943, when Hungarian gendarmes rounded up Rusyn youths and imprisoned them in various concentration camps. Owing to his intervention, more than 200 students, among them several seminarians and priests, were released. He obtained permission for them to complete their studies, even though the court had expelled them from all Hungarian schools.

On May 31, 1943, bishop Aleksander Stojka died suddenly of a heart attack. The faithful mourned him as a spiritual leader, as the father of the poor, and as the "champion of the people's rights." By then, a new storm was descending upon Subcarpathian Rus' from the east, and this was to result in an unprecedented religious devastation.

CHAPTER NINE

The Calvary of the Union

In October 1944, Soviet troops occupied Subcarpathian Rus'. Although the Czechoslovak provisional government abroad continued to assure the population that Subcarpathian Rus' would be reunited with the "liberated Czechoslovak republic," the Soviets behaved from the very outset as if this strategically situated piece of Rusyn territory belonged to them. Thus, as early as the beginning of November of that same year, during the festivities marking the anniversary of the October revolution, they launched a propaganda campaign calling for the union of Subcarpathian Rus' with the Ukrainian Soviet Socialist Republic.

On November 26, 1944, the Soviet authorities convened a congress of "people's committees" in Mukačevo, which passed a resolution "to secede from Czechoslovakia" and "to reunite Subcarpathian Rus' with the Ukrainian S.S.R." The implementation of this decision was entrusted to the so-called National Council, headed by the Moscow-educated Carpatho-Rusyn communist Ivan Turjanycja, who later became a deputy to the Supreme Soviet. By June 29, 1945, pursuant to an "agreement" between Czechoslovakia and the U.S.S.R., all Carpatho-Rusyn lands east of the Už river were annexed to the Soviet Ukraine as a separate administrative unit designated the *Zakarpats'ka oblast'* [Transcarpathian province].[1]

Under the provisions of this agreement, almost all the territory comprising the Mukačevo eparchy was ceded to the Soviet Ukraine. The Prešov eparchy and a small portion of the Mukačevo eparchy remained within "liberated" Czechoslovakia. Since the Communists did not seize power in Czechoslovakia until February 1948, the destruction of the Greek Catholic Church that began in the Mukačevo eparchy was extended to the Prešov Region only somewhat later.

1. The Coming of the Soviets

As a propagandistic gesture, the Stalin restored the Moscow Patriarchate in 1943 with metropolitan Sergej (Starogrodskij) as administrator. That same year, the Soviet government established the Council for the Affairs of the Russian Orthodox Church under Ju. Karpov as chairman. The Russian Orthodox Church thus entered into a partnership with the Soviet authorities and in return was allowed to elect a new patriarch. Thus, on February 2, 1945, Aleksei Šimanskij became the patriarch of Moscow.[2]

The new Russian patriarch's principal task was to extend his jurisdiction over the newly acquired territories. The Ukrainian Catholic Church, which was united with Rome, posed a serious obstacle to the attainment of this goal. Consequently, the "union and Uniates" were persecuted from the very beginning of Soviet rule. The Soviet authorities began by setting up in L'viv an "Initiative Group for the Reunion of the Greek Catholic Church with the Russian Orthodox Church," headed by the apostate priest, Dr. Havryjil Kostel'nyk. Following a relentless campaign against the Ukrainian Catholic Church and the imprisonment of its hierarchy, a so-called synod was held in L'viv on March 8-10, 1946. The synod dissolved the Union of Brest and placed the Galician metropolitanate under the jurisdiction of the Moscow patriarch.[3]

The fate of the Mukačevo eparchy, headed by the young and energetic bishop Teodor Ju. Romža,[4] was equally tragic. Since in Transcarpathia the Communists were unable to sponsor an "Initiative Group" similar to the one in Galicia for lack of apostate priests, they chose as their instrument the local Orthodox Church, which from 1928 onward had functioned as the Mukačevo-Prešov Orthodox eparchy under the jurisdiction of the Serbian Holy Synod.

In January 1939, during the brief period of Carpatho-Ukrainian statehood, the leadership of the Orthodox eparchy was assumed by bishop Vladimir L. Rajić, a native of Yugoslavia. Because Rajić had been loyal to the Carpatho-Ukrainian government of premier A. Vološyn, the Hungarians forced him to return to Yugoslavia after they occupied the region in March 1939. Thus, from 1939 to 1944, the Orthodox eparchy in Subcarpathian Rus' had no bishop.[5]

In December 1944, following the arrival of the Red Army, the Carpatho-Rusyn Orthodox Church sent a delegation to Moscow headed by hegumen Teofan Sabov, at the time the admininstrator of the Orthodox eparchy. The delegation requested that the Mukačevo-Prešov Orthodox eparchy be removed from the jurisdiction of the Serbian Holy Synod and placed under that of the Moscow patriarch. At the same time, the deputy for the Affairs of the Russian Orthodox Church in Carpathian Rus', Professor Petro Lintur, asked the administrator of the Moscow patriarchate Aleksei to liquidate the Mukačevo Greek Catholic eparchy as soon as possible. While in Moscow from December 7 to 13, the delegation visited key officials in charge of church affairs and received exact instructions how to go about ensuring the liquidation of the Mukačevo Greek Catholic eparchy in the shortest possible time.[6]

Following the delegation's return, there began a systematic attack against the Greek Catholic Church in Transcarpathia. It was headed by Professor Petro Lintur, a confirmed atheist. From the Orthodox side, the campaign was led by the archpriest Ivan Kopolovyč, who acted as intermediary between the Orthodox eparchial authorities and the National Council. The actual liquidation of the Mukačevo eparchy, however, was coordinated by the Soviet political commissars, General Mechlis and Colonel Tjulpanov.

2. The Assault on the Greek Catholic Church

As the first step in its anti-Uniate campaign, the National Council announced that in compliance with the law on the separation of the church and state the government would discontinue financial assistance to Greek Catholic priests and to their widows and orphans. At the same time, the National Council continued to disburse state aid to Orthodox clergy in a form of "restitution." The Communists did everything in their power to reduce the Greek Catholic clergy to extreme poverty in order to force them to abandon their pastoral duties or to join the Orthodox Church.

Next, the National Council passed a law that facilitated conversion of Greek Catholics to Orthodoxy. The decree of March 24, 1945 made possible "mass conversion to Orthodoxy" and initiated a wave of forcible expropriation of Greek Catholic churches and church property with the assistance of the militia. Invoking the new law, local village councils would call a meeting of villagers, at which one or two agitators demanded that the community convert to Orthodoxy. The National Council then interpreted these demands as the "will of the people" and proceeded to dismiss the Greek Catholic parish priest and appoint instead an Orthodox pastor to the village, officially conveying to him the local church and parish house.

In villages where such "mass conversions to Orthodoxy" were not possible, so-called "land commissions" would suddenly appear and collect signatures from villagers demanding "land grants." The land commission would then send the list of signatures to the Orthodox eparchial administration in Mukačevo, claiming that "the undersigned wish to leave the Greek Catholic Church and are asking to be accepted into the bosom of the Orthodox Church." The Orthodox eparchial administration forwarded these "petitions" to the National Council in Užhorod, whence came a directive to expel the Greek Catholic priest from the village, bring in an Orthodox pastor, and distribute the church lands amongst the villagers. By resorting to such deceitful measures, the Orthodox seized 73 parishes from the Greek Catholics in the course of a single year.

In order not to alienate the Soviet authorities, bishop Teodor Romža at first tried to reach some sort of understanding with them. But he soon learned that there could be no cooperation between the Communists and the Greek Catholic Church. The Soviet press began attacking the bishop and the clergy openly, and the authorities began resorting to acts of violence. Bishop Romža resolved to fight. He countered by protesting the lawlessness and by denouncing publicly incidents of violence, thereby hoping to expose the perfidious activity of the National Council. In January 1945, he lodged a courageous personal protest to the commander of the front, General Petrov, who temporarily put a stop to the anti-Church action, insofar as formally Subcarpathian Rus' was not yet a part of the Ukrainian S.S.R.

To encourage the clergy and faithful, during the lenten season of 1945 bishop Romža set out to visit those villages threatened the most by Communist propaganda. Usually, he gathered the faithful in the church and tried to persuade them that their faith was the greatest good they possessed on this earth. Then he would conclude: "Divine Providence is watching over us at all times. So, let us rejoice that we have to suffer for our faith, because in doing so we are preparing ourselves for martyrdom!" The people welcomed their bishop with enthusiasm and, inspired by his sermons, pledged loyalty to their Church.

Bishop Romža was well aware of the harm done in Galicia by the so-called Initiative Group. He therefore did everything in his power to prevent the apostasy of even a single priest. Through his emissaries, he maintained close ties with his clergy, providing them with guidance in their pastoral work. He kept a close watch on the temper of his clergy. Those priests, whom Soviet police agents had begun to "pacify" with their well-tested methods, he encouraged to go abroad. Others, who were no longer able to endure the persecution, he counselled to leave the priesthood altogether. In some cases it sufficed to transfer a priest to another parish. But for the most part, the Carpatho-Rusyn clergy stood firm. Aware of the great danger, bishop Romža persistently exhorted his clergy: "Do not give in for anything in the world!"

When the Soviet authorities realized that they could not break the will of the people, they focused their attention on youth and the educational system. On April 20, 1945, the National Council separated the schools from the Church and liquidated all parochial schools in the Mukačevo eparchy. On the basis of this decree, all cantors and wives of priests were dismissed from their teaching posts. Teachers were forbidden to attend church on the grounds that this set "a bad example" for young people. Boarding schools that had been operated by the Greek Catholic eparchial administration were closed. The teaching of catechism and prayers was banned in schools.

The Soviet authorities disbanded all youth organizations, even those that were purely religious in nature, and replaced them with a so-called "Youth League," which later became the Young Communist League, or Komsomol. The new teachers brought in by the Soviet authorities tried to remove the children from under the influence of their parents and to set them against the Church and the clergy. In short, the Soviets were determined to demoralize the young generation, which was something that bishop Romža could not allow. He ordered priests to organize clandestine catechism groups. The priests would instruct parents to bring their children to evening church services, and they, instead of delivering their usual sermon, explained the catechism.

By then it was difficult to obtain prayer books and catechisms. The bishop therefore organized a group of typists, who made copies of the principal prayers, the rudiments of faith, and the commandments. A network of messengers disseminated these typed copies to various parishes. When the Soviets tried to ban what they called the "perfidious" teaching of religion to children, the bishop cited the Soviet constitution which guaranteed "freedom of religion." The bishop defended the practice by arguing that not a single law had been passed banning the private religious instruction of children in churches. "And even if there were such a law," declared the bishop to the National Council, "I, as a bishop, could not comply with it, because it would contradict the principal task with which I have been entrusted by Christ: Go and teach!" (Mt. 28:19)

The Soviet occupational authorities then initiated an intimidation campaign in their press, arrested some of the more influential priests, and began to confiscate churches and their property. Although Romža was certain that all this was leading to the complete liquidation of his eparchy, he refused to yield. He ordered the clergy to hold short prayer services even on weekdays and to instruct young people. The parents understood the importance of these lessons and conscientiously brought their children to church. All religious services were crowded with children.

The pilgrimage to Černeča Hora on the Feast of the Assumption in 1945 turned into a demonstration of the strength of Greek Catholic faith in Subcarpathian Rus'. More than 50,000 pilgrims gathered to hear the courageous words of their prelate: "Cling to your faith and your Church. Our Church will continue to exist only as long as we show that we are strong. With our courage and our devotion, we will safeguard our greatest good—the salvation of our immortal souls!"

The bishop became a living example of courage and of complete dedication to the Church. He continued to visit districts that were under the greatest threat, bringing with him words of encouragement and comfort. Whenever the Communist authorities expelled a priest from a parish by force, the bishop found a place for him in a filial church. In those places where the authorities seized church lands, the bishop appealed to parishioners to support their pastor with their own resources. When they took from the peasants their churches, the bishop reminded the faithful that each Christian soul is a living temple of the Holy Spirit and encouraged them to gather for prayer in private homes.

The courage and steadfastness of bishop Romža and the clergy exerted a powerful influence on the people. Even some Orthodox congregations began to return to the Greek Catholic Church. Consequently, the authorities became more determined than ever to put a stop to this and sent an Orthodox bishop to Subcarpathian Rus'. The Moscow patriarch hastened his talks with the Serbian Holy Synod, and on October 22, 1945, the last Orthodox bishop of the Serbian jurisdiction, Vladimir Rajić, resigned from the Mukačevo-Prešov eparchy and asked the Moscow patriarch to appoint his own bishop. That very same day, patriarch Aleksei appointed the bishop of Uman', Nestor Sydoruk, for Transcarpathia.[7]

Following the installation of bishop Nestor in Mukačevo, the Soviet authorities announced that he was the only rightful bishop in Transcarpathia, thereby abrogating the authority of bishop Romža. But bishop Romža had no intention of relinquishing his eparchy and courageously continued his hopeless struggle against the Soviet terror.

3. The Violent Death of Bishop Teodor Romža

In March 1946, the Greek Catholic Church in Galicia was formally disbanded and forced into the catacombs. There was not the slightest doubt that the Communists were now preparing their final assault on the Greek Catholic Church in Transcarpathia. In the spring of the same year, the deputy of the Council for the Affairs of the Russian Orthodox Church in the Ukraine came to Užhorod and summoned bishop Romža to appear before the National Council. When the bishop arrived accompanied by his vicar-general, Monsignor A. Chira, and his secretary, the Reverend A. Pun'ko, the deputy pointed to a stack of documents before him exposing the "anti-people" activity of the Greek Catholic Church in Transcarpathia. He told the bishop "to repent" as soon as possible and to go to Moscow to make his obeisance to the Orthodox patriarch "while there was still time."

There were more talks between the bishop and the deputy from Kiev. The latter tried to "weaken" the bishop, arguing that the "Greek Catholic Church cannot exist in the Soviet Union!" To all his threats, bishop Romža replied: "I would sooner face torture and death than betray the true Church of Christ!"[7a]

In June, 1946, the Soviet authorities held a "people's trial" of Hungarian collaborators.[8] During the trial, the Greek Catholic Church was attacked and the clergy were denounced as "enemies of the people." The communist press then demanded "the liquidation of the union" and confiscation of church property. In places where the people refused to take over church-owned fields, the Communist authorities converted the land into collective farms. These new Soviet attacks did not intimidate the people, and once again they gathered in great numbers on Černeča Hora to celebrate the Feast of the Assumption.

In order to prevent future mass demonstrations by the faithful, on March 24, 1947, the authorities seized the monastery on Černeča Hora and deported the monks.[9] Bishop Romža protested this new act of violence against the Greek Catholic Church to the Supreme Soviet in Moscow. In the sermon he delivered that year on Good Friday in the Užhorod cathedral, he publicly condemned "the lawlessness of the dark forces of hell." On Easter Monday, Romža was already in Mukačevo, where he reminded the faithful that "the kingdom of this world shall pass," and that only "the kingdom of Christ is eternal." He also announced that the Assumption pilgrimage would be held at the Mukačevo parish church because the Soviet authorities had confiscated the Černeča Hora monastery.

The Orthodox bishop Nestor had intended to announce the dissolution of the Užhorod Union at Černeča Hora on the Feast of the Assumption in 1947, because he expected large numbers of people to make the pilgrimage. He invited several Orthodox prelates, archbishop Makarij of L'viv, bishop Varlaam of Luc'k, bishop Serhij of Odessa, and bishop Antonij of Stanyslaviv to Černeča Hora to witness the dissolution of the union in Transcarpathia. But things did not turn out as he had planned.

While only some 10,000 people gathered at Černeča Hora that year to celebrate the Feast of the Assumption,[10] about 80,000 people crowded around the Mukačevo parish church. Bishop Nestor did not abolish the union that year, but the synod of the Orthodox bishops who were present did resolve "to remove bishop Romža as soon as possible."

A strange calm descended upon Transcarpathia after the 1947 Assumption Day pilgrimage. Bishop Romža was not permitted to leave his residence and was kept under surveillance day and night. In the fall of 1947, the bishop decided, contrary to the warning of his friends, to attend the consecration of a restored church in the village of Lavky, near Mukačevo. He did return to Užhorod, but in a casket, having been murdered on the return journey by the Soviet authorities. The following is a description of the tragic death of bishop Romža, as published by an official of the Congregation for the Eastern Churches in Rome, Monsignor Giuseppe Moioli:

> The renown that our bishop-matyr deservedly merited makes it incumbent for us to inform everyone of his death.
>
> On October 27, 1947, he was returning in the company of two priests and two seminarians from the village of Lavky, where he had consecrated a church the day before. On the road between the villages of Čerejivci and Ivanivci, an armored vehicle carrying militiamen and soldiers crashed into them with the intention of killing the bishop and then being able to announce that he had died in an accident. But Providence determined otherwise. Although the cart in which the bishop's party was travelling was broken into splinters and the horses were killed instantly in the accident, the passengers survived. Then several 'soldiers' emerged from the automobile and tried to finish with the butts of their rifles what they had not managed to do by crashing into the bishop's cart. They then quickly left the scene.
>
> At the moment of the accident, the bishop had been reciting the rosary. In the evening, some people brought the martyrs to

the Mukačevo hospital. The bishop's jaw had been broken in two places, almost all of his teeth had been knocked out, and he had been beaten over his entire body. His travelling companions quickly regained their health, but for the bishop came the end.

This is not the place to describe the terrible pain the bishop suffered and his great endurance, because history will tell the world of this. He lay in the hospital for almost a week, and everyone was inspired by his example. Unfortunately, Good Friday was approaching for our Church. On October 29, a new nurse was assigned to the hospital, to the very ward where the bishop lay ill. The nursing nuns were removed from the ward. At the time, the bishop was just beginning to recover. He was still unable to eat and had to be fed through a tube in his mouth. On the last morning of his life, he made his confession, but was not able to receive Holy Communion. He asked that the Blessed Sacrament be brought to him and he prayed, shedding passionate tears. With great difficulty, he spoke a few words, calling on those present to remain steadfast in their faith.

He died at 12:30 a.m. on November 1, 1947. He had been poisoned a few hours earlier, most likely with gas, by the nurse who had been specially brought in with the cooperation of the hospital director who had removed the regular staff and nuns from the ward that night.[10a]

At the terrible moment of death, the bishop's face reflected profound peace. He could say nothing, but everything about him spoke: his eyes, his face, and his smile. A great number of people came to pay their last respects; they kissed his hands and touched devotional objects to his body to obtain a blessing. In these difficult times, we have been orphaned, but we know that we have gained a great Intercessor in heaven.[11]

A medical commission that arrived all the way from Kiev concluded that the bishop had died of a "cerebral hemorrhage." The funeral of bishop Teodor Romža was held in Užhorod on November 4, 1947 and was attended by a great many faithful.[12] He was buried in the crypt of the cathedral church in Užhorod. His death marked the end of the second phase of the persecution by Soviet authorities of the Greek Catholic Church in Transcarpathia.

4. The Dissolution of the Union in Mukačevo

The violent death of bishop Teodor Romža demonstrated that the campaign of the Orthodox bishop Nestor had not been successful. He even lost the confidence of Orthodox believers, who suspected him of

being a "political commissar in episcopal garb." His only achievement was that he had managed with the help of the NKVD to convert
to Orthodoxy the pastor of Jovra, the Reverend Irynej Kondratovyč,
who had collaborated with the Hungarians earlier and feared deportation to Siberia.

In February 1949, the patriarch of Moscow recalled bishop Nestor
from Transcarpathia and replaced him with archbishop Makarij
(Mychajlo Oksijuk) of L'viv, who had already proven his "apostolic
abilities" by uniting the Ukrainian Catholic Church in Galicia with
the Russian Orthodox Church.[13] Archbishop Makarij began his mission immediately. On February 22, 1949, he took over the Užhorod
cathedral and appointed the apostate priest Kondratovyč "archpriest
and superior of the cathedral." He ordered the arrest of all members
of the chapter and the more active members of the clergy, and he had
them deported to Siberia. There were also mass deportations of
religiously-minded peasants. Makarij ordered all eparchial institutions
to be disbanded, closed all Greek Catholic churches, and forbade
Uniate priests to celebrate the Divine Liturgy. He justified these brutal
measures by the fact that the Greek Catholic Church was not
"registered" by the state and was therefore illegal.

In the summer of 1949, the remaining priests who refused to convert
to Orthodoxy were arrested. NKVD agents succeeded in breaking a
few of them. These were immediately sent to archbishop Makarij,
who accepted them into the Orthodox Church. The Feast of the
Assumption in 1949 was proclaimed the "Feast of Orthodoxy." It
took place at Černeča Hora near Mukačevo. In his description of this
"triumph of Orthodoxy," the Reverend N. Pavlosjuk admits that
Makarij had been sent to Transcarpathia specifically because "reunion looked hopeless there."[14] Pavlosjuk also admits that reunion
with the Moscow patriarchate in Transcarpathia was "the result of six
months of persistent efforts and heroic deeds" by archbishop
Makarij, whom "former pastors of the Greek Catholic Church came
to see at night."[15] And Makarij himself called the forcible liquidation
of the Greek Catholic Church in Transcarpathia "a mission of reconciliation."[16]

The celebrations of the triumph of Orthodoxy were attended also by
prelates from Galicia: bishop Antonij of Stanyslaviv, bishop Mychajil
of Drohobyč,[17] and the initiator of reunion, the archpriest Havrijil
Kostel'nyk. During the Pontifical Liturgy officiated by archbishop
Makarij, the apostate priest Kondratovyč "solemnly" announced that
"on August 28, 1949, the ecclesiastical union of the Carpathian clergy

with Rome ceased to exist in Carpatho-Ukraine, because it had been an anti-populist historical act" and an obvious sign of "foreign oppression."[18] By this proclamation, the Soviet authorities "officially" dissolved the Užhorod union, and Transcarpathian Rus' "officially" embraced Orthodoxy under the authority of the Moscow patriarch.

According to the *Journal of the Moscow Patriarchate*, the patriarch added the following words to the report on the "reunion" of Transcarpathia: "I rejoice in the celebration of the triumph of Orthodoxy held at the Mukačevo monastery."[19] He rewarded Makarij "for his difficult labors for the glory of God and Holy Orthodoxy" with the right to wear a golden cross on his cowl, and he presented the faithful with an icon of the Blessed Mother.[20]

It is not difficult to conclude from Orthodox accounts of the "reunion" that the dissolution of the union was achieved by force and without the participation of either the clergy or laity. The Communist authorities were able at first to "convert" only the three priests named in the *Journal of the Moscow Patriarchate*,[21] and thus the "reunification" could not be carried out at a synod, as had been the case in L'viv. Instead, it had to be proclaimed during a pilgrimage as an already accomplished act that allegedly reflected "the will of the people."

This proclamation of "reunion" in August 1949 gave the Soviets a pretext to liquidate the Greek Catholic Church in Transcarpathia. Applying well tested methods, they tried to compel priests to sign declarations of conversion to Orthodoxy, but met with only modest success. The overwhelming majority of the clergy left the priesthood rather than embrace the Orthodox faith. During this period, many priests were arrested and deported, while some fled abroad. A group of younger priests went underground and hid in the forests. Only a small number converted to Russian Orthodoxy.[22]

Once the Greek Catholic Church was destroyed, the Communists turned to persecuting Orthodox believers as well. Where previously they had praised the Orthodox as "patriots," they now began to harass them and call them "parasites." Both the Orthodox and "reunited" former Greek Catholic churches were subjected to heavy taxes and many were closed. As time went on, fewer and fewer Orthodox churches and priests remained in Transcarpathia. In short, here too the aim of the Communists was to instill their atheistic ideology among the people, an endeavor in which they received considerable assistance from the University of Užhorod, founded in 1946.[23] Thus, the fate of Orthodoxy in Soviet Transcarpathia is equally precarious!

5. The Attack of the Orthodox in the Prešov Region

After the fall of Czechoslovakia in 1939, a so-called independent Slovak Republic was established. Within its borders were included all the parishes of the Prešov eparchy, as well as 50 parishes of the Mukačevo eparchy. The latter parishes were formed by the Vatican into a separate apostolic administration and placed under the jurisdiction of the bishop of Prešov, Pavlo Gojdyč, OSBM.[24]

Although after World War II Slovakia was once again included in the Czechoslovak republic, its border with Soviet Transcarpathia (former Subcarpathian Rus') did not change. The composition of the Prešov eparchy therefore remained the same as it had been in 1939. Moreover, many priests and faithful from the newly-formed Transcarpathian province of the Ukrainian S.S.R. moved to the Prešov Region, not wanting to remain under Communist rule. In 1947, the Reverend Vasylij Hopko was appointed auxiliary bishop to bishop Pavlo Gojdyč and the Prešov eparchy began to flourish once again.[25]

At that time there were fewer than 10,000 Orthodox believers in the Prešov Region. From 1939 onward, they had had only an administrator, the archimandrite Vitalij, residing in Ladomirová, near Svidník. Archimandrite Vitalij escaped with his mission from the Bolsheviks in 1944 and ultimately settled in the United States. The administration of the Orthodox Church in the Prešov Region was then assumed by archimandrite Andrij Kolomac'kyj.

In addition to the Carpatho-Rusyns, there were also some 25,000 Orthodox Czechs in postwar Czechoslovakia. After murdering their bishop Gorazd M. Pavlik in 1942, the Germans subordinated the Czech Orthodox Church to the Orthodox bishop in Berlin. After the war, the Orthodox Czechs placed themselves under the jurisdiction of the Moscow patriarch and asked him to appoint a bishop for them. In the spring of 1946, the patriarch sent archbishop Elevterij Voroncov to Prague and named him "patriarchal exarch of Czechoslovakia." Later Elevterij became the "archbishop of Prague and all Czechoslovakia" and was given control over the Orthodox faithful of the Prešov Region as well.[26]

Upon taking control of the Prešov Region, archbishop Elevterij launched a wide propaganda campaign with the support of the Czech authorities, who regarded the Greek Catholics as collaborators with the Hungarians and the Slovak nationalists. The Orthodox were honored as patriots, while the Greek Catholics were branded "traitors" and "fascist sympathizers." Since the Slovaks had persecuted the Carpatho-Rusyns of the Prešov Region in 1939-1944, the Orthodox movement here took on a national dimension as a widespread protest against forcible slovakization. This made it possible to wage a harsh campaign against the bishops, the clergy, and the Greek Catholic Church as a whole.

To counter this campaign, during Lent of 1947, bishop Gojdyč initiated a broad missionary action. He sent monks and the more capable priests to endangered villages in order to enlighten the people and defend their Catholic faith. The bishop had brochures in defense of the faith distributed among the faithful, while his eparchial journal, *Blahovîstnyk*, published articles against atheistic materialism and Orthodoxy. Both Prešov bishops also visited parishes that were threatened by the government supported campaign; they instructed the faithful; and they called upon them to remain steadfast in their faith. In one of his pastoral letters, bishop Gojdyč wrote: "We have proof that various agitators actively circulate among our faithful. Resorting to promises and threats, they are attempting to draw our people away from the Greek Catholic Church. In response to this intimidation, we remind you of the Christians of the first three centuries of our era, who were ready to sacrifice not only their wealth for their faith, but even their life, enduring great suffering. They knew that eternal life is worth any sacrifice."

Archbishop Elevterij had not expected this kind of defense from the Greek Catholics and appealed to Moscow for help. In the summer of 1947, Moscow ordered the Czechoslovak authorities to arrest bishop Gojdyč, but on this occasion the local authorities protected him. One judge in Prague admitted: "The Slovak National Council opposed the arrest of bishop Gojdyč in order to avert an uprising among the Catholic population of Slovakia. The bishop was held in great esteem in Slovakia, because he was the only bishop who had not allowed himself to be politically compromised."[26a]

Moscow did not insist, because the Communists in Czechoslovakia were then already preparing a coup. They seized power in February 1948. Archbishop Elevterij immediately obtained the support of the central authorities against the Greek Catholic Church. The fate of union was thus sealed in the Prešov Region as well.

6. The Dissolution of the Union in Prešov

Following orders from Moscow, the Communist regime of Czechoslovakia resolved to liquidate the Greek Catholic Church in the Prešov Region. As in neighboring Soviet Transcarpathia, the government refused to register the Greek Catholic Church in Czechoslovakia on the grounds that it was allegedly "hostile to the interests of the people." Thus Greek Catholics found themselves outside the law and subject to liquidation through "legal channels."

The first blow fell on the Basilian Fathers in Prešov. During the night of February 22, 1949, the militia made a surprise raid on the Basilian monastery and removed all 11 monks to a concentration camp in Podolínec. They were charged with collaborating with the Organization of Ukrainian Nationalists headed by Stepan Bandera. However, the real reason for their arrest was that the Basilians were regarded as posing the "principal obstacle" to Orthodox propaganda. More searches, arrests, and interrogations followed. Bishop Gojdyč was also interrogated several times and threatened with imprisonment, while the press proclaimed him an "enemy of the people" and an "agent of the Vatican."[27]

During this anti-union campaign, the pernicious consequences of the forced slovakization policy of the 1930s became evident. The Orthodox agents now represented the union to the people as the principal cause of slovakization and thereby as inimical to the cultural and national development of the local Ukrainians [Rusyns]. This agitation fell on receptive ears, especially in the mountainous regions of Prešov, which were inhabited predominantly by Carpatho-Rusyns, upon whom the Slovaks had attempted to impose the Slovak language and Slovak schools by force. The Rusyn population of this region had suffered most from the Slovaks, because it possessed a higher degree of national consciousness.[28]

The dissolution of the union of Mukačevo on August 28, 1949 had a negative effect on the population and clergy of the Prešov Region. Several intimidated priests converted to Orthodoxy and formed an "initiative group" to unite with the Orthodox Church. On December 30, 1949, the Moscow patriarch, certain of an Orthodox victory in the region, named a former officer, Aleksei Dechterev, as bishop of Prešov. His consecration took place in the unfinished Orthodox cathedral in Prešov on February 12, 1950, in the presence of the Orthodox delegation from Moscow.[29]

With the help of the authorities, in March of the same year, bishop Aleksei established a "Central Committee for the Return to Orthodoxy," which included six apostate Greek Catholic priests. The committee immediately launched an attack against the Greek Catholic clergy and in the period of one month succeeded in bringing over to their camp 32 morally unstable priests and several thousand faithful.

This made it possible for them to convoke a synod.

On April 28, 1950, the Central Committee for the Return to Orthodoxy convoked a "peace rally" in Prešov, enjoining each village to send a delegation led by the local pastor. Priests who refused to attend the congress were denounced as warmongers and then imprisoned. According to the *Journal of the Moscow Patriarchate*, the Czechoslovak authorities were "supportive of this movement because its aim was not only to bring about the moral strength and unity of the people, but also the ultimate liquidation of the hostile agitation by supporters of the Vatican. It became clear that continued relations of the Greek Catholic bishops and clergy with the Vatican could lead to intensified anti-government propaganda, because the talks with bishop Gojdyč and his auxiliary Hopko had produced no results. The Czechoslovak government therefore agreed to the return of the Uniates under the spiritual authority of the Orthodox bishops."[30]

The committee prepared the auditorium of the Black Eagle Hotel in Prešov as the site for the alleged "peace rally," which was then shrewdly turned into a demonstration against the union. Portraits of patriarch Aleksei of Moscow and archbishop Elevterij of Prague were hung on each side of a three-barred cross. The walls were decorated with anti-Uniate slogans such as the falsified slogan of St. Methodius: "Slavs, fear Rome!" When the delegates saw these anti-Union slogans, many wanted to leave the auditorium, but were prevented from doing so by the militia. According to the *Journal of the Moscow Patriarchate*, the congress was attended by 820 delegates (of whom "more than one hundred were Greek Catholic priests") and up to 4,000 laymen.

The head of the Central Committee for the Return to Orthodoxy, a layman named Benicky,[30a] opened the "congress" with the statement: "Our people and the overwhelming majority of the clergy[31] want to dissolve the union. The union has ceased to exist here, as it has ceased to exist in Western and Carpathian Ukraine!"[32] On his motion, the congress "unanimously" proclaimed the meeting to constitute a "Church synod" and passed the following resolution:

> The synod of Greek Catholic clergy and laity, which has met on April 28, 1950 in Prešov and through its 820 delegates representing the whole Greek Catholic Church in Czechoslovakia, [...] has passed the following resolutions:
> (1) To abrogate the provisions of the Union of Užhorod of 1646 and 1649;[33]

(2) To dissolve the union and break relations with Rome, and return to the bosom of our ancestral, holy Orthodox faith, to the Russian Orthodox Church;

(3) Guided by the words of Christ, "Let all be one!" and having resolved to return to the Holy Orthodox Church, the synod petitions His Holiness the patriarch of Moscow and all Russia to accept us under his jurisdiction![34]

At the end, the synod appealed to all Greek Catholics of Czechoslovakia to return to the faith of their ancestors—Holy Orthodoxy.[34]

After adopting this resolution and dissolving the union, a delegation of the "synod" went to bishop Gojdyč with the demand that he comply with "the wishes of the people" and hand over the episcopal cathedral to the Orthodox. Since the bishop categorically refused to hand over the keys, he was arrested for opposing "the will of the people." The incited mob then forced its way into the cathedral and sang "religious songs" until the Orthodox prelates, archbishop Elevterij and bishop Aleksei, arrived and celebrated a "service of thanksgiving" on the occasion of the triumph of Orthodoxy. Thus, "officially", the union in the Prešov Region ceased to exist.

On May 27, 1950, the state authorities ratified the decision of the Prešov "synod" and proclaimed the dissolution of union throughout the territory of Czechoslovakia. A ministerial decree automatically handed over all holdings and rights of the Greek Catholic Church to the Orthodox.[35] Then came the systematic liquidation of Greek Catholic parishes and the confiscation of all church property. Soon, auxiliary bishop Vasyl' Hopko was imprisoned, priests were forced to sign declarations that they join the Orthodox Church, while all Greek Catholic eparchial institutions were disbanded. There was no news of the imprisoned bishop Gojdyč, although the Reverend Sabol later provided this account:

"After his arrest, all trace of bishop Gojdyč disappeared. It was rumored among the people that he had been deported to the U.S.S.R., but in reality he was held in Šebeš, Podolínec, the Tatra mountains, and later in prison in Košice. He finally appeared in the prison of the regional district court in Bratislava, where in January 1951 the Communist authorities held a sensational show trial." He was tried by a "people's court" on January 10-15, 1951, and charged with "treason" and "spying for a foreign state," namely, the Vatican.[36]

According to Communist press reports, bishop Gojdyč "admitted all his crimes." On the other hand, the Ukrainian Catholic press in the West wrote the following about the "criminal trial" in Bratislava: "Today, the whole world knows that at Communist trials defendants admit committing every crime with which the prosecution charges them. This is also true in cases in which the defendant has not committed them physically." Continuing his description of bishop Gojdyč, Dr. S. Baran wrote: "He is a true servant of Christ, a man of crystal clear character and noble heart, and thus incapable of any criminal acts."[37]

On January 15, 1951, the "people's court" of Bratislava condemned bishop Pavlo Gojdyč to life imprisonment, ordered the confiscation of all his (namely, eparchial) property, and stripped him of all his civic rights.[38] The Italian press commented:

> It would take too long to describe in detail the contemptible farce staged in the capital of Slovakia, Bratislava. We wish to recall, however, that the real motives behind the Bratislava verdict lay not in political 'crimes', since no such crimes had been committed, but in the bishop's loyalty to Christ and His Holy Church. He was imprisoned because he refused to hand over the keys to the cathedral in Prešov to the Orthodox and to lead his faithful into schism. The alleged 'crimes of treason and espionage' were fabricated only after he had been imprisoned in order to allow the present-day Neros to justify their actions before the world and to camouflage the liquidation of the Prešov eparchy, as well as the violent persecution of the Catholic Church in Czechoslovakia.[39]

After the trial, the Communists shunted bishop Gojdyč from prison to prison in an attempt to prevent public demonstrations by the people who used to gather and pray under the window of the prison cell where the bishop was held. On July 17, 1958, Pope Pius XII sent bishop Gojdyč greetings on his 70th birthday to the prison in Ilava. Although the bishop was then seriously ill with cancer, the world learned that he was still alive. But his sufferings were drawing to an end. He died in Leopoldov prison on July 17, 1960, having offered his holy life for his faith.[40]

Following the "unsuccessful" trial of bishop Gojdyč in Bratislava, the Communists did not dare to put auxiliary bishop Hopko on trial before a "people's court." He was sentenced for the same "crimes" as bishop Gojdyč, but without witnesses. He, too, was moved from prison to prison until he was released in 1963, a physically and psychologically broken man.

The Moscow patriarch divided the Prešov Region into two Orthodox eparchies. The northern part of the region, populated predominantly by Rusyns, retained the name of the Prešov eparchy and was headed by bishop Aleksei Dechterev. In the southern part of the region, the patriarch established the Michalovce eparchy with Slovak as its official language. On October 8, 1950, the apostate canon Viktor Mychalyč became the first bishop of Michalovce, taking the name Aleksander at his consecration.[41] Thus, there were four Orthodox eparchies on the territory of Czechoslovakia: the Prague archeparchy, and the Olomouc-Brno, Prešov, and Michalovce eparchies.

Having achieved the reunion of the Greek Catholic Church with the Russian Orthodox Church in Czechoslovakia, the patriarch of Moscow proclaimed the autocephaly of the Czechoslovak Orthodox Church on November 23, 1951 and named Elevterij its first archbishop-metropolitan.[42] Consequently, the Orthodox Church in Czechoslovakia became an independent, authocephalous metropolitanate, while the Greek Catholic Church, as in neighboring Soviet Transcarpathia, went underground.

CHAPTER TEN

In the Immigration

No history of the Church in Carpathian Rus' would be complete without a brief account of the religious life of the Carpatho-Rusyns in the countries to which they emigrated. The first large emigration of Carpatho-Rusyns occurred in the eighteenth century, when many settled on lands devastated by the Turks in the Vojvodina (Bačka) of what was then southern Hungary and is today Yugoslavia. The "Bačka Rusyns," as they call themselves, have preserved their national and religious consciousness despite having lived two centuries outside their native land. In religious terms, they are organized in a number of parishes that are part of the so-called Križevci Greek Catholic eparchy.

The second mass exodus of Carpatho-Rusyns began in the 1880s and took them to the United States. The "American Rusyns" also have well-organized parishes, their own Metropolitan Province with its archbishop's seat in Pittsburgh, Pennsylvania, and three suffragan sees: Passaic, New Jersey; Parma, Ohio; and Van Nuys, California.

1. The Carpatho-Rusyns in the Križevci Eparchy

The sole Greek Catholic eparchy in Yugoslavia, the Kirževci eparchy, was canonically erected by the Apostolic See in 1777. The origins of this eparchy date back to the first half of the seventeenth century, when the Orthodox bishop Simeon Vratanja, who was the archimandrite of the Marča monastery near Križevci, accepted union with Rome. At that time, many Serbian and Croatian refugees from the Turks, who called themselves *uskoky*, also united with Rome. Because they had settled on the border of what is today Croatia and Slovenia, near the fortress of Žumberak, they were later called *žumberčany*. The *uskoky*, however, called this area Vratanija. Thus, at the beginning of the seventeenth century, the Marča (or Vratanija) eparchy was established by Rome.

The Roman Catholic bishops of Zagreb regarded the bishops of Marča as their suffragans and were determined to exercise control over them. Towards this end, they succeeded in persuading the Austrian imperial court to appoint the bishop of Marča titular bishop of Svidnik.[1] But the Apostolic See opposed this and instead bestowed on the Marča prelate the titular see *in partibus infidelium*, usually of Plataea,[2] without mentioning his submission to the jurisdiction of the Roman Catholic bishop of Zagreb.

After the Marča monastery burned down in 1739, the bishop settled in Pribić, and later in Preseka. Bishop Vasilije Božičković (1759-1785) persuaded Rome to grant the eparchy independence, and on June 17, 1777, Pope Pius VI (1775-1799) published a bull entitled *Charitas Illa* establishing the Križevci eparchy for all the Greek Catholics of Croatia and the Vojvodina (Bačka).[3] After World War I, the Apostolic See extended the authority of the bishop of Križevci to all the Greek Catholics of Yugoslavia. In addition to the *žumberčany* (Croats) mentioned earlier (ca. 12,000), the Križevci eparchy now includes Macedonians (ca. 4,500), Romanians (ca. 1,600), Ukrainians from Galicia (ca. 12,000), and the "Bačka Rusyns" (ca. 30,000), who constitute the largest group.

Carpatho-Rusyns began settling in the Vojvodina (Bačka) in the middle of the eighteenth century. In 1746-1751, migrants from Zemplén county settled in the village of Krstur, which had been destroyed by the Turks, and they renamed it Ruski Krstur (in Rusyn: Rus'kij Kerestur). In 1765-1768, immigrants from Borsod county settled in the Bačka village of Kocur. The new settlers in both villages numbered close to 3,000 people, but they soon began dispersing throughout the Vojvodina, Slavonia, and Syrmia (Srem).

At first, the Bačka Rusyn parishes were placed under the jurisdiction of the Roman Catholic bishop of Kalocsa, but were later placed under the jurisdiction of the Greek Catholic eparchy of Križevci after its canonical erection in 1777. To this day, the Bačka Rusyns comprise the majority of faithful of the Križevci eparchy.

In administrative terms, the Križevci eparchy was initially subordinated to the archbishop of Esztergom, and from 1853 onward to the archbishop of Zagreb as its metropolitans. There were attempts to dissolve the Križevci eparchy at the beginning of the nineteenth century on the grounds that the number of faithful was small, but owing to the efforts of Konstantin Stanić, who became bishop in 1814, the eparchy survived. At the turn of the twentieth century, Slavonia and

Bosnia received an influx of Ukrainian settlers, primarily from Galicia, and the number of parishioners increased once again. At the present time, the Križevci eparchy comprises 50 parishes with about 60,000 faithful.[4]

Almost no Greek Catholics remain today in the eparchial seat of Križevci. In addition to being the site of the episcopal residence and a cathedral remodeled by bishop Julij Drohobec'kyj in 1897, the town also serves as the seat of the chapter, which consists of four members. The Križevci chapter was established in 1846 at the request of bishop Gabriel Smićiklas (1834-1856). A seminary, founded in 1680 by bishop Pavao Zorčić (1671-1685), who endowed it with the revenues of the Pribić property, is located in Zagreb.

The Križevci eparchy underwent its greatest period of growth under bishop Dionysij Njaradij (1920-1940), who did much to raise the level of the cultural and religious life of his flock, in particular that of the Bačka Rusyns. He brought in the Basilian Sisters from Galicia and charged them with the management of the orphanage and the care of young students. The Sisters Servants of Mary Immaculate were put in charge of the sick and of kindergartens. The Basilian Fathers were entrusted with the education of seminarians. Bishop Njaradij founded a cultural society called Prosvitne Družtvo, whose goal was to raise the level of cultural and educational life as well as to publish materials in Rusyn. The Društvo published three newspapers: *Žumberačke novini* for the Croats; *Ridne slovo* for the Ukrainians; and *Ruski novyny* for the Bačka Rusyns. Bishop Njaradij was a true "father and benefactor of the people," and his name is inscribed in gold in the history of the Križevci eparchy.

Bishop Njaradij also devoted attention to the two Carpatho-Rusyn eparchies. As apostolic administrator of the Prešov eparchy from 1922 to 1926, he halted the Orthodox movement and ensured the succession of a worthy candidate to the bishopric in the person of Pavlo Gojdyč, OSBM. Later, during the critical years of 1938-1939 in Carpatho-Ukraine, bishop Njaradij went down in history as a true pastor and church leader. He died as he lived—in the performance of his pastoral duties during a canonical visitation to the parish of Mrzlo Polje on April 14, 1940.[5]

World War II ushered in a new political regime in Yugoslavia, and in its wake the Communist government of Marshal Tito (Josip Broz), which assumed power in 1945, began to persecute the Catholic Church. One of the victims of this persecution was the bishop of Križevci, Janko Šimrak (1942-1946), a distinguished religious leader and scholar.[6] After his death, the greatly admired and loved Havryjil Bukatko took over the helm of the Križevci eparchy (1952-1981). Appointed apostolic administrator by Rome in 1950, he succeeded in winning the confidence of the Yugoslav Communist government and, on April 27, 1952, was consecrated bishop in Zagreb. From then on, the lot of the Križevci eparchy improved.

Bishop Bukatko's intelligent and able conduct abroad broke the ice between Tito and the Vatican. At the request of Tito's government, in 1961 Rome named Bukatko auxiliary bishop to the Roman Catholic archbishop of Belgrade, J. Ujčić, and after the latter's death on March 24, 1964, elevated him to the Belgrade archbishopric. Thus, for the first time in history, a Greek Catholic bishop became simultaneously a Roman Catholic archbishop.[7]

In 1963, the Apostolic See appointed the pastor of Ruski Krstur, the Reverend Joakym Segedi, as auxiliary bishop to archbishop Bukatko.[8] After the death of archbishop Bukatko, the eparchy was administered by bishop Segedi (1981-1985), who transferred his seat to Zagreb. In 1983, the Apostolic See appointed the Reverend Slavomir Miklovš as the ordinary bishop of the Križevci eparchy.

2. Carpatho-Rusyn Religious Life in the United States

The first Carpatho-Rusyns began to arrive in the United States in the 1870s. They were driven overseas by severe economic hardships of the Hungarian authorities designed to impoverish the Rusyn population in order to ensure that, having been reduced to social and material ruin, they would lack the strength to resist the government's forcible denationalization policy.[9] As a result, by the end of the nineteenth century, almost half the Rusyn population had left Carpathian Rus' and settled, for the most part, in the United States.[10] The Carpatho-Rusyn exodus was accompanied by a similar emigration from Galicia.

(1) The beginnings of church life. The first Rusyns[11] to arrive in the United States had neither a Church of their own, nor their own organizations. Hence, they joined Polish or Slovak parishes. It was not until 1885 that the first Greek Catholic priest arrived in the United States from the L'viv archdiocese. This was the Reverend Ivan Voljanskyj, who organized the first Greek Catholic parish in Shenandoah, Pennsylvania, and built the first church there in 1886.[12]

Under Voljanskyj's leadership, the immigrants began to establish their own parishes in other places as well as to bring in priests from Galicia and Carpathian Rus'. Greek Catholic parishes were soon formed in Freeland, Pa. (1886), Hazleton, Pa. (1887), Kingston and Olyphant, Pa. (1888), Jersey City, N.J., Minneapolis, Minn. and Wilkes-Barre, Pa. (1889), Passaic, N.J. (1890), and so forth. By 1894, the number of Greek Catholic congregations in the United States had reached 30.[13]

It seemed at first that in the conditions of complete national and religious freedom that prevailed in the United States, the Galician and Carpatho-Rusyn immigrant communities would unite, at least in the ecclesiastical sphere. But in the absence of proper leadership this did not happen. In the words of the Reverend I. Sochoc'kyj:

> Each priest acted on his own, without any plan or guidance, in accordance with his personal convictions. The clergy who came to the United States were not properly trained for missionary work and knew neither the [English] language nor local conditions. Priests came to the United States at the invitation of so-called 'church councils', and it was the laity that founded church committees, collected funds for the construction of churches, and managed church property. Consequently, church life in our parishes was controlled by 'laymen', or rather by a few influential members of a given church committee, who very often had little concern for the good of the church or the parish. One need only read the minutes of a few parish meetings to see how much harm was done by such 'popular rule' to religious life in the United States.[14]

In addition to these internal problems, there were external circumstances that made the missionary work of the Greek Catholic clergy in the United States very difficult. These included: (1) an unfavorable and in some cases outrightly hostile attitude on the part of the Roman Catholic hierarchy; (2) subversive activities engaged in by the Russian Orthodox mission; and (3) Hungarian political influence which led to strife and ultimately to a split between the Carpatho-Rusyn and the Galician immigrants.

The Latin-rite hierarchy, which at the time was engaged in an effort to "Americanize" the Catholic Church in the United States, was not willing to tolerate the existence of a "Rusyn Catholic Church" based—if only in appearances to outsiders—on a distinctly foreign ethnic foundation. Moreover, the Roman Catholic episcopate was rigidly opposed to married clergy. Such priests were anathemized by the American Catholic authorities and barred from celebrating the Divine Liturgy. The Greek Catholic clergy disregarded the ban imposed on them by the local hiearchy, citing that they had been charged with their duties by their bishops in the homeland. This led to even more serious conflicts.[15]

On October 1, 1890, at the demand of the American hierarchy, the Apostolic See issued a decree concerning newly arriving Greek Catholic clergy, which specified that: (1) before sending one of his priests to the United States, the Greek Catholic bishop in question had to inform the Apostolic See of his intention to do so; (2) upon their arrival in the United States, Greek Catholic priests were obliged to report to the local Roman Catholic bishop under whose jurisdiction they would be working in order to receive jurisdiction; and (3) only *unmarried priests* could be sent to the United States and all married clergy had to be recalled to Europe.[16] With the exception of the Reverend Alexis Toth, who was a widower, all the other nine Greek Catholic priests working in the United States at the time were married. Learning of the Vatican's decree, they met on October 29, 1890 in Wilkes-Barre to hold the first consultation of Greek Catholic clergy.[17]

Those attending the meeting adopted several decisions regarding their life and work in the United States and forwarded to their bishops the following demands: (1) that bishops in the homeland reach an agreement among themselves and appoint one of the local priests as adminstrator in the United States; (2) that bishops in the homeland not remove the priests whom they assigned to the United States from under their own jurisdiction and not place them under the authority of the American hierarchy; (3) that bishops in the homeland continue sending married priests to the United States, since both the faithful and the conditions of union demanded this; and (4) that church property not be registered in the name of the local Roman Catholic bishop, but rather in the name of a board of trustees within each parish, with the board consisting of the local parish priest as administrator, and two members of the church committee.[18]

The decisions of the Wilkes-Barre consultation were never realized, because Rome insisted on compliance with the decree of October 1, 1890. Tensions between the Greek Catholic clergy and the Latin-rite hierarchy grew. Then, just before Christmas of that year, archbishop John Ireland of St. Paul suspended the Reverend Toth from his parish in Minneapolis. On March 25, 1891, Toth and his congregation of 360 faithful formally accepted the jurisdiction of the Russian Orthodox bishop Vladimir, who was then residing in San Francisco.[19] Not content with the conversion of his parish alone, the Reverend Toth engaged in missionary work to spread the Orthodox faith among other

Carpatho-Rusyns as well, primarily in the vicinity of Wilkes-Barre, Pennsylvania. Over a period of a few years, he brought more than 20,000 people into the fold of the Russian Orthodox Church and organized these congregations of converts into 15 parishes.

Just when it seemed that a degree of unity was achieved between the Carpatho-Rusyn and Ukrainian communities in the United States, Pope Leo XIII decided to subordinate the Carpatho-Rusyn eparchies of Mukačevo and Prešov to the Galician Metropolitanate. This was vigorously opposed by the Hungarian government, which wanted to maintain Carpathian Rus' in complete isolation from Galicia.[20] Every possible measure was therefore taken to prevent the unification of the Carpatho-Rusyn and Galician clergy even in the United States. To achieve their purpose, the Hungarians turned to the Carpatho-Rusyn priests themselves, instructing them through the Hungarian embassy in the United States.[21] Small wonder that the Rusyn community in the United States soon split into two hostile camps. In 1892, the Carpatho-Rusyns formed the Greek Catholic Union (Sojedinenije Greko-Kaftoličeskich Russkich Bratstv),[22] while in 1894, the Galicians seceded and established their own Ruthenian National Association (Rus'kyj Narodnyj Sojuz).[23] In their struggle to win members, these two organizations played a deplorable role in the history of the Rusyn community in the United States and they laid the groundwork for opposition to the first Greek Catholic bishop in the United States, Soter Ortynsky, OSBM, which eventually led to the hierarchical split into the Pittsburgh and Philadelphia exarchates.

(2) The first Greek Catholic bishop in the United States. When archbishop Francesco Satolli, the first apostolic delegate to the United States (1893-1896), arrived in Washington, D.C., the Greek Catholic immigrants immediately began to lobby for the appointment of a Greek Catholic bishop for their new country. The threat posed by the Orthodox movement, particularly among the Carpatho-Rusyns, enabled the Hungarians to have their "own" man, canon Andrej Hodobay of the Prešov eparchy, sent to the United States as apostolic visitator. But his mission was doomed to fail from the very beginning. Not only was he boycotted by the Galicians, but some Carpatho-Rusyn priests, who hoped to be named bishop, also launched a vigorous campaign against him, alledging that he was a "Hungarian agent." The latter group also supported by Russian Orthodox propagandists. Not surprisingly, on March 28, 1907, Rome recalled the Reverend Hodobay from the United States[24] and sent the hieromonk Soter S. Ortynsky, OSBM, to serve as the first bishop for all Rusyn

Greek Catholics in America.[25]

However, on June 14, 1907, before bishop Ortynsky had even arrived in the United States, the Apostolic See published a bull, *Ea Semper*,[26] which greatly restricted the authority of the Greek Catholic prelate in the United States and abrogated a number of privileges inherent to the Byzantine rite. Not unsurprisingly, Greek Catholics in America were seriously disturbed by the decree. The Carpatho-Rusyns were further affronted by the fact that their "own man" had not been appointed bishop, since at the time they comprised the overwhelming majority of Greek Catholic immigrants. The Hungarian press also reacted with hostility to the nomination of bishop Ortynsky:

> We are forced to report the unhappy news that Hungarian policy has been unsuccessful in assuring the appointment of Hungary's candidate as bishop in America. The highest Roman curia has recalled from the United States the Reverend A. Hodobay, a true and loyal Hungarian who had until now defended our Rusyns from pan-Slavic pressures, and instead has appointed a Basilian from Galicia as bishop. As a result, the workers and faithful there, who are loyal Hungarian patriots in their hearts, are now exposed to the threat of pan-Slavism.
>
> We hope that the good sense of the competent ecclesiastical and secular authorities will find a way to ensure that the spirit of Hungarian patriotism of our Rusyn emigrants will not suffer any harm even in the United States of America.[27]

As could have been expected, immediately upon his arrival in the United States,[28] bishop Ortynsky became a target for attacks from all sides, and especially from the Carpatho-Rusyns.[29] The fight against the bishop was under the aegis of the Greek Catholic Union (Sojedinenije) led by the former president of this organization John Uhryn who by then headed the so-called Executive Committee, a post to which he had been elected at a public meeting in Braddock, Pennsylvania on May 14, 1908. Informing the bishop of this action by the Carpatho-Rusyns, the apostolic delegate, archbishop Diomede Falconio, OFM (1902-1911), wrote: "These people confuse religion and politics and stubbornly oppose the orders of the Apostolic See, arrogating to themselves rights that were never theirs or that contradict the principles of canon law. . . . What is even more unfortunate is the presence among them of many priests who have forgotten their pastoral duties and are working for the ruin rather than the good of their own people."[30]

On September 23, 1909, a portion of the Carpatho-Rusyn clergy[31] met at a meeting in Harrisburg, Pennsylvania and formed a so-called "Committee of Priests" headed by the Reverend K. Lavryšyn. The committee demanded that bishop Ortynsky release them from his jurisdiction and that he obtain for them a bishop of "Uhro-Rusyn" descent. Towards this end, the priests and executive committees united and called a "public meeting" of Carpatho-Rusyns in Johnstown, Pennsylvania on January 11-12, 1910. The Johnstown assembly proclaimed the "autonomy" of the Carpatho-Rusyn parishes and placed their administration in the hands of a diumvirate made up of the chairman of the Priests Committee, the Reverend Lavryšyn, and the head of the Executive Committee, layman John Uhryn.[32] Naturally, the apostolic delegate could not allow such an anomaly within the Catholic Church.

Credit must be given to that part of the Carpatho-Rusyn immigrant community and its clergy who formed the United Societies of Greek Catholic Religion in the U.S.A. (Sobranije Greko-Katholičeskich Cerkovnych Bratstv v Z.D.A.) for their support of bishop Ortynsky, whom they elected their supreme protector in 1909.[33] In describing this decision, one of the delegates wrote: "All that we have is our faith and our melodious language. Should we lose our faith or our language, we would cease to be Rusyns. The delegates to the United Societies were well aware that our Church and our people can flourish in the United States only if we have a bishop, and as a result we stand behind him as one man!"[34]

(3) The creation of a Greek Catholic eparchy. Despite the great obstacles posed by the faithful and the clergy, as well as by the Roman Catholic hierarchy, bishop Ortynsky did everything in his power to protect his flock from Orthodox propaganda. He visited the areas that were in great danger, delivered inspiring sermons, conducted missions, and exhorted the people to remain steadfast in their faith. He tried to establish order in those parishes that recognized his authority. Peace soon reigned in these communities and religious life blossomed. Filled with admiration for bishop Ortynsky's work, on May 28, 1913 the Apostolic See finally gave the Greek Catholic prelate full episcopal power, creating a separate and independent "Rusyn-rite" eparchy in the United States.[35]

In a pastoral letter dated August 25, 1913, announcing the establishment of an independent eparchy to his flock and clergy, bishop Ortynsky wrote: "I appeal to you all and urge you to put an end to this mutually destructive struggle and waste of our efforts to no purpose.

Let us put all this behind us! Let us rally, instead, under the banner of Christ and the liberated Rusyn Catholic Church and try to free our people of harmful, foreign influences."[35a] By this he meant especially the interference of the Hungarian authorities in the affairs of the Greek Catholic Church in the United States.

The Greek Catholic Union (Sojedinenije) and the Executive Committee were the first to protest the granting of full jurisdiction to bishop Ortynsky, and instead they demanded the appointment of their "own Uhro-Rusyn" bishop.[36] Lay leaders from the Greek Catholic Union met with bishop Ortynsky on October 16, 1913, and presented him with 15 conditions for their cooperation.[37] The bishop received them with great understanding, and he also received their clergy, which on the orders of the apostolic delegate either had to acknowledge the jurisdiction of bishop Ortynsky or enter into schism. Following his reconciliation with the Carpatho-Rusyns, bishop Ortynsky appointed the leader of the opposition, the Reverend Alexander Dzubay, as his vicar-general.[38]

On the occasion of the erection of the Greek Catholic eparchy in the United States, on August 17, 1914 the Apostolic See published a decree, *Cum Episcopo*, in which the canonical principles of the administration of the new eparchy were determined and proclaimed valid for a period of ten years.[39] As the Reverend Sochoc'kyj later commented: "It [the *Cum Episcopo*] was an achievement of great historic significance and, at the same time, perhaps undeserved satisfaction to our immigration. The decree made our bishop independent of the Latin rite ordinaries and granted him complete freedom of action. It also nullified some regulations set forth in the *Ea Semper* bull, which apparently discriminated against our rite, making it now equal in all respects with Latin rite."[40]

No matter how hard bishop Ortynsky tried to accommodate the Carpatho-Rusyns, he always experienced their passive resistance and insincerity. He therefore made every effort to persuade the Apostolic See to appoint a separate bishop for them. But on March 24, 1916, bishop Ortynsky died suddenly. On the recommendation of the apostolic delegate, Rome named two apostolic administrators: the Reverend Peter Poniatyshyn for the Galician and the Reverend Gabriel Martyak for the Carpatho-Rusyn parishes. This set the stage for the estalishment of two separate exarchates, which were formed in 1924.

(4) The establishment of two exarchates. Because of World War I and the events that followed, it was impossible to appoint a successor

to bishop Ortynsky. However, something had to be done in view of the emergence in 1916 of a new movement for conversion to the Orthodox faith, which was headed by the leader of the Carpatho-Rusyn opposition and former vicar-general, the Reverend Alexander Dzubay.

Angered by the fact that not he but the Reverend Martyak had been appointed administrator for Carpatho-Rusyn Greek Catholics after the death of bishop Ortynsky, the Reverend Dzubay joined the Russian Orthodox Church. To enable him to bring the Carpatho-Rusyn parishes with him, the Russians ordained him bishop on August 7, 1916 in Pittsburgh.[41] With the help of tsarist Russian funds, Dzubay launched a widespread Orthodox propaganda campaign among the Carpatho-Rusyns, especially in the Pittsburgh area, where the majority of the Rusyn parishes were located. This movement soon declined, however, as Russian funds, depleted by the outbreak of the Russian Revolution in 1917, ran out. Dzubay was reduced to extreme poverty, and in 1924, he returned to the fold of the Catholic Church. After his repentance, he lived in a monastery at Graymore, New York. He died in Trenton in 1933 while visiting his granddaughter.[42]

On May 8, 1924, the Apostolic See appointed two bishops to the United States: Constantine Bohachevsky to administer the Galician Greek Catholic parishes and Basil Takach for the Carpatho-Rusyn parishes. Bishop Takach, who arrived on September 1, 1924 in the United States, took over the administration of the newly-created Carpatho-Rusyn Pittsburgh Exarchate, which then comprised 129 priests, 155 churches, and 288,390 parishioners.[43]

In his first pastoral letter, published on September 19, 1924, bishop Takach described himself as a "loyal son of Carpathian Rus'" and promised to elevate his faithful "to the level of the most culturally advanced people."[43a] In a subsequent pastoral letter, dated February 7, 1925, Takach described the period of his predecessors: "If we review the history of our Church in this country, we will see that it has witnessed a period of constant personal attacks and partisan struggles. What one group built, another tried to destroy. Consequently, at the present we still find ourselves at the beginning of the beginning."[43b]

Bishop Takach began to work very energetically. Having obtained an extension of the *Cum Episocopo* decree for an additional ten years,[44] he hoped to institute canonical order in the exarchate. But very soon, the "lay leaders" who wanted to dictate to the bishop began to oppose his orders. By the end of 1929, open opposition broke out, as it had in the case of bishop Ortynsky. The pretext for this new struggle was the *Cum Data Fuerit* decree published by the Apostolic See on March 1, 1929. Its purpose was to regulate relations between the Greek and Roman Catholics in the United States.[45]

Following in the spirit of earlier instructions from the Apostolic See, the *Cum Data Fuerit* decree reiterated that Greek Catholic clergy on the territory of the United States must be celibate. Although earlier Rome had tacitly ignored the issue of celibacy, it now insisted that American-born seminarians could be ordained to the priesthood only if they were single. As a result, some priests and lay leaders of the Greek Catholic Union rose in protest against the "latinization" and "destruction" of the Eastern rite. Their press began to carry malicious attacks against the bishop and the Vatican. At its 21st Convention in Detroit in 1932, the Greek Catholic Union formed a Committee for the Defense of the Eastern Rite (Komitet Oborony Vostočnoho Obrjada—KOVO). Once again, as in the case of Ortynsky, the United Societies of Greek Catholic Religion (Sobranije) came to the bishop's defense along with its official organ, *Prosvita*.[46]

The fight over celibacy reached a state where some parishioners and their pastors began to oppose the authority of the bishop and the Apostolic See. Consequently, bishop Takach was forced to suspend several priests for insubordination. Foremost among them were Orestes Chornock and Stefan Varzaly.[47] At the beginning of 1936, they founded an independent "Carpatho-Rusyn Administration" headed by the Reverend Chornock.

The "movement for independence," as it was called, spread rapidly throughout the entire Pittsburgh exarchate. When the First Synod of the Carpatho-Russian Eparchy in the U.S.A. was convened in Pittsburgh on February 23, 1937, the so-called "independents" had the support of some 30 parishes and more than 40,000 faithful. The synod proclaimed itself independent of bishop Basil Takach of Pittsburgh and elected the suspended Orestes Chornock as its new bishop. Patriarch Beniaminos I of Constantinople (1935-1946) consecrated Chornock on September 19, 1938, and canonically erected the so-called Carpatho-Russian Greek Catholic Diocese of the Eastern Rite (later to be known as the American Carpatho-Russian Orthodox Greek Catholic Diocese).[48]

Subsequently, court battles over the ownership of churches were waged, and in many places congregations split into warring factions. Bishop Chornock began ordaining new priests to head the parishes under his jurisdiction. Strife and anarchy rent individual parishes and pitted parishes against each other. Only then did the leaders of the

Greek Catholic Union begin to realize the harm they had caused their Church with their calls for "rule by the people."[49] To his credit, the new president of the Greek Catholic Union, John Sekerak, who was elected in 1936, slowly began to restore peace within the dissentious community and to bring back some branches of the Greek Catholic Union under the bishop Takach's authority. At last, at the beginning of the 1940s, tranquility and religious discipline were established in the Pittsburgh exarchate.

The prolonged strife, press attacks, threats against his person, and vengeful activities seriously sapped bishop Takach's energies. Moreover, cancer of the throat had begun to undermine him physically. On August 30, 1946, the Apostolic See appointed the Reverend Daniel Ivancho coadjutor bishop with the right of succession.[50] But bishop Takach was able to enjoy Ivancho's assistance for only a short time. He died on May 13, 1948, having finally succeeded in clearing—as was said—"the Greek Catholic Church in the United States of weeds."[51]

(5) The theological seminary in Pittsburgh. One of the most pressing needs that plagued the Greek Catholic community in the United States was a shortage of priests. The influx of clergy from the homeland was insufficient to meet local requirements and, moreover, the newly arriving priests were not trained for missionary work in American conditions. The religious life of the faithful suffered great harm as a result. The only solution to this problem was to train priests locally.[52]

The Latin hierarchy also insisted that the Greek Catholics train American-born clergy. Their purpose, however, was not to ensure the well-being of the Greek Catholic Church, but merely to enforce celibacy and Americanize the Church in the United States. It was towards this end that the Roman Catholics had persistently urged that a local seminary be established ever since bishop Soter Ortynsky had first arrived. But, faced with continual discord and strife, bishop Ortynsky had not been able to carry out this plan and was forced to send his seminarians to Latin theological schools, primarily to the one in Baltimore, Maryland.[53]

After World War I, candidates were sent to seminaries in Užhorod and Prešov. When Rome later ordered bishop Takach to ordain only unmarried seminarians, the bishop sent his candidates to the College of St. Josaphat in Rome and to Budapest. When the number of seminarians increased, bishop Takach began to send them to the Benedictine seminary in Lisle, Illinois. Almost all the seminarians trained between 1940 and 1950 were graduates of this institution.

In the spring of 1950, the Benedictines informed bishop Daniel Ivancho (1948-1954) that they would no longer be able to accommodate the Pittsburgh candidates and so the bishop resolved to build his own theological seminary. "After more than 60 years of talking, waiting, hoping, and praying," declared bishop Ivancho, "we are finally beginning to realize our plan of building our own seminary."[54]

Instruction at the SS. Cyril and Methodius Seminary in Pittsburgh began on October 16, 1950 in two old buildings in which 40 seminarians were temporarily housed. But just a year later, on October 18, 1951, bishop Ivancho dedicated a large new structure at a ceremony attended by the clergy and thousands of faithful. This was a major achievement on the part of the Carpatho-Rusyn community in the United States.[55]

In fact, the year 1950 marked a turning point in the life of the Pittsburgh exarchate. It began to flourish once again. A major role in this belonged to the parochial schools that had been started by the Basilian Sisters back in 1925. The Sisters Servants of the Immaculate Conception and the Benedictine Sisters also worked in parochial schools throughout the Carpatho-Rusyn community.

Owing to a large number of vocations and to the zealous work of its clergy, the level of religious life of the Carpatho-Rusyn community in the United States was high. As the Reverend S. Sabol remarked:

Each parish has a Society of the Holy Rosary, almost all have a Society of the Sacred Heart, Marian Sodalities with several chapters, and a Society of the Holy Name for men in most parishes. All the members of these organizations make confession and receive Holy Communion every month. . . .

The flowering of spiritual life in the Pittsburgh exarchate is also evident from the fact that retreats for cantors, for older men and women, and for younger women and girls are held each year at the retreat house of the Basilian Sisters in Uniontown, Pennsylvania. Between 40 and 150 participants from all over the United States take part in each of these retreats.

The mother-house of the Basilian Sisters at Mount Saint Macrina near Uniontown has become the spiritual center for all Carpatho-Rusyn Greek Catholics. There, the annual pilgrimage on the Feast of the Assumption takes place in the beautiful natural surroundings of the convent. It draws up to 50-60 thousand worshippers from all corners of the United States. The pilgrimage is attended by the bishops and at least 100 priests, who hear confessions around the clock. The large crowds of people; the beauty of the services perpetuated as they are by Carpatho-Rusyns with a special fervor; the impressive candlelight processions; the evening illuminations; the singing of religious songs by thousands of faithful throughout the night—all this speaks of the high degree of spirituality among [America's] Carpatho-Rusyns.[56]

(6) The creation of a metropolitan province. After the forcible liquidation of the Greek Catholic Church in Subcarpathian Rus' by the Soviet authorities (1949), the Apostolic See sought to strengthen the religious life of the Carpatho-Rusyn community in the United States by establishing an independent metropolitanate. Thus, in 1963, Pope Paul VI (1963-1978) divided the Apostolic Exarchate of Pittsburgh into two eparchies with seats in Pittsburgh, Pennsylvania and Passaic, New Jersey. Bishop Nicholas T. Elko, then the exarch, was named the ordinary of the Pittsburgh eparchy, and bishop Stephen J. Kocisko, then auxiliary bishop of Pittsburgh, the ordinary of the Passaic eparchy. After the Apostolic See recalled bishop Elko to Rome in 1967, Pope Paul VI transferred bishop Kocisko to Pittsburgh and appointed Michael J. Dudick bishop of Passaic (1968). In 1969, the Holy Father created in Parma, Ohio a third Carpatho-Rusyn eparchy comprising 53 parishes formerly belonging to the Pittsburgh exarchate.

The partition of the original Apostolic Exarchate of Pittsburgh into three eparchies came about in view of the canonical establishment of a Carpatho-Rusyn metropolitanate in the United States. On April 2, 1969, the Apostolic See established the Byzantine Ruthenian Metropolitan Province of Munhall, changing the name of the Pittsburgh eparchy to the Munhall Archdiocese since the cathedral is located in Munhall, Pennsylvania. Bishop Stephen Kocisko was appointed the first archbishop and metropolitan of Munhall. His installation as metropolitan took place on June 11, 1969. The Munhall metropolitan province also included the Passaic and Parma eparchies. On December 3, 1981, Pope John Paul II (1978-) created the Van Nuys (California) eparchy consisting of 18 parishes that had previously belonged to Parma. The Van Nuys eparchy was initially headed by the former auxiliary bishop of Passaic, Thomas V. Dolinay, who was installed as ordinary on March 9, 1982. Eight years later, on March 13, 1990, bishop Dolinay was appointed Coadjutor archbishop of Pittsburgh with the right of succession to metropolitan Kocisko. Within a few months, on October 23, 1990, the auxiliary bishop of Passaic, George M. Kuzma, replaced Dolinay as bishop of the eparchy of Van Nuys.

As mentioned above, the official name of the Carpatho-Rusyn metropolitanate was the Byzantine Ruthenian Province of Munhall, because the cathedral of St. John the Baptist was located in Munhall, Pennsylvania. However, since the metropolitan's residence is in Pittsburgh, metropolitan Kocisko asked the Apostolic See to change its name. Hence, on March 11, 1977, the metropolitanate was officially named the Byzantine Ruthenian Province of Pittsburgh. Thus the Carpatho-Rusyns at last attained their own metropolitan see abroad, even though they had not been fortunate enough to have an ecclesiastical province in their homeland where their bishops had been subordinated to the Hungarian Roman Catholic archbishop of Esztergom. In the United States, the Carpatho-Rusyn Catholic Church is flourishing independently and freely, and in the person of Metropolitan Kocisko has a worthy representative at the Senate of Catholic Bishops in Rome.

Appendix

A Biographical List of the Bishops of Carpathian Rus'
According to ancient tradition, the beginnings of the hierarchical structure of the Church in Carpathian Rus' need to be sought in the ninth-tenth centuries, in the period of the spread of Christianity among the Slavs in central Europe by SS. Cyril and Methodius and their disciples. However, the first documented mention of a bishop of Mukačevo does not appear until the end of the fifteenth century, followed by a new gap of more than fifty years. Thus, at least at the very beginning, this list is incomplete because of a lack of documentary evidence.

A. Bishops of the Mukačevo Eparchy before the Union

1. IVAN—the first bishop of Mukačevo mentioned in documents from 1491 to 1498. Appointed bishop of Mukačevo by the Hungarian king Ulászló II, he attempted to extend his authority over all of Carpathian Rus'.

2. VASYLIJ I—mentioned in the years 1551-1552.

3. ILARION—mentioned in the years 1556-1561. He secured the right of tithes for the bishop of Mukačevo and brought the Hruševo monastery under his own jurisdiction.

4. VASYLIJ II—mentioned in documents from 1568-1597. Some historians claim that these documents in fact refer to two different bishops named Vasylij. He tried to secure the protection of the emperor and as a result was dismissed from the episcopate by prince Zsigmond Rákóczi.

5. HAVRYJIL—mentioned in 1599, when he was imprisoned by prince Zsigmond Rákóczi.

6. PETRONIJ—consecrated bishop of Mukačevo in 1600. Ex-

pelled that same year from Mukačevo by its secular landlord, he spent his years of exile in Galicia and Belorussia. There he established relations with metropolitan Josyf Ruts'kyj of Kiev and became an advocate of the union with Rome. See No. 11 below.

7. SERHIJ—of Romanian birth, occupied the Mukačevo bishopric with several interruptions between 1600 and 1616. He secured a charter of privileges for the Mukačevo monastery which served as the seat of the Mukačevo bishop. During his tenure, in 1612-1614, the bishop of Przemyśl (Peremyšl') A. Krupec'kyj tried to implement the union in Krásny Brod but failed.

8. SOFRONIJ—mentioned in 1614 as the bishop of Mukačevo, when the landlord M. Esterházy imprisoned him and dismissed him from the bishopric.

9. EVTYMIJ—mentioned as bishop in 1618, but his appointment is not certain.

10. SOFRONIJ (REČKO)—mentioned in a document ca. 1620, probably the same person as in No. 8 above, serving a second term.

11. PETRONIJ (1623-1627)—serving a second term after his return from exile (see No. 6 above). He brought the idea of union to Carpathian Rus' which culminated in the Union of Užhorod of 1646.

12. IVAN HRYHOROVYČ (1627-1633)—re-established relations with metropolitan Ruts'kyj of Kiev and sought to raise the prestige of the Eastern Church. He continued his predecessor's efforts on behalf of the union, but its actual implementation was left to his successors. He founded the first school at the Mukačevo monastery.

13. VASYLIJ TARASOVYČ (1634-1651)—a native of Galicia who came to Carpathian Rus', most probably with bishop Petronij, to help propagate the idea of the union. He was a principal collaborator of bishop Ivan Hryhorovyč, who appointed him his successor. In 1634, prince György Rákóczi I appointed Tarasovyč bishop of Mukačevo and Máramaros, but Tarasovyč administered the Máramaros region for only a short time (1639-1640). Because of his pro-union ideas, the protestant prince persecuted Tarasovyč and forced him to flee Mukačevo. In 1642, Tarasovyč made a profession of the Catholic faith and settled in the western portion of the Mukačevo eparchy, in Nagykálló. There, in 1643, he was seized by Rákóczi's rebels and brought back in chains to Mukačevo. To save his eparchy, Tarasovyč was compelled to renounce the union and in return was reinstalled as bishop of Mukačevo. The exact date of his death is not known but it is assumed that he died in 1651.

14. JOANNYKIJ ZEJKAN' (1651-1687)—of a noble family from Imstyčevo, where he served as pastor. After the death of his wife, he founded a monastery in Imstyčevo and lived there with a community of monks. Princess Zsuzsanna Lorántffy, disregarding the will of the clergy, named Zejkan' bishop of Mukačevo in order to prevent bishop Partenij Petrovyč from occupying his seat, since he had accepted union in 1646. In 1661-1664, Zejkan' built a new stone church on Černeča Hora, then the site of the bishop's residence. In 1664, after her conversion to Catholicism, the widow of prince György Rákóczi II, princess Zsófia Báthory, permitted the united bishop Partenij Petrovyč (see No. 1 on list C. United Bishops of the Mukačevo Eparchy) to return to Mukačevo and forced bishop Zejkan' to take up his residence at the Imstyčevo monastery. After a short time, bishop Zejkan' moved to the Uhlja monastery in the Máramaros region and from there administered the Máramaros eparchy until his death (see No. 10 on list B. Bishops of the Máramaros Eparchy before the Union).

B. Bishops of the Máramaros Eparchy before the Union

The origins of the Máramaros eparchy date to the fourteenth century when the patriarch of Constantinople bestowed the title of exarch on the hegumen of the Hruševo monastery and granted the monastery the right of stauropegion. Although the Máramaros region was annexed to the Mukačevo eparchy in 1556, the movement for independence persisted there, especially in the seventeenth century.

1. SPIRIDON—mentioned as bishop of Máramaros in 1608-1609, but had jurisdiction only over the Romanians.

2. SERHIJ—the same person as above, No. 7 in list A. Bishops of the Mukačevo Eparchy before the Union.

3. DOSITEJ (1628-1637)—the archbishop of Alba Iulia in Transylvania, who after his expulsion from Alba Iulia settled in the Máramaros region and performed the duties of the bishop of Máramaros.

4. DIMITRIE PAP (1637-1639)—elected bishop of Máramaros by the clergy, but prince György Rákóczi I of Transylvania did not permit his consecration because he wanted the Máramaros region to remain under the authority of the bishop of Mukačevo. The prince's wishes were fulfilled in 1639 when the Máramaros synod recognized bishop Vasylij Tarasovyč of Mukačevo as its ordinary.

5. VASYLIJ TARASOVYČ (1639-1640)—the same person as the

non-Uniate bishop of Mukačevo (see No. 13 in list A. Bishops of the Mukačevo Eparchy before the Union).

6. STEFAN SIMONOVICI (1641-1650)—after imprisoning bishop Tarasovyč, prince György Rákóczi I entrusted the ecclesiastical government of the Máramaros region to archbishop Simonovici of Alba Iulia, who administered it through his vicar, hegumen Sylvester.

7. SIMEON PETRAŠKO (1652)—bishop-designate, never consecrated.

8. MYCHAJIL MOLODEC' (1653-1664)—an itinerant bishop who came to the region probably from Poland. He pushed aside bishop-designate Petraško and governed the Máramaros eparchy without an appointment.

9. SAVA BRANKOVIĆ (1662-1680)—bore the title of "archbishop of Alba Iulia and Máramaros," but administered only the Romanian parishes in the Máramaros region.

10. JOANNYKIJ ZEJKAN' (1665-1686)—the same person as the Orthodox bishop of Mukačevo (see No. 14 in list A. Bishops of the Mukačevo Eparchy before the Union). After his expulsion from Mukačevo (ca. 1665), he settled in the monastery at Uhlja and governed the Carpatho-Rusyn parishes in the Máramaros region. In 1680, after the death of archbishop Sava Branković, he took control of the Romanian parishes as well. He died on November 8, 1686.

11. JOSYF I. STOJKA (1690-1711)—the first bishop of Máramaros in the full meaning of the term, he was of noble birth from the village of Čumalevo, where he was the parish priest. He later served as pastor in Byčkiv (Máramaros county). When his wife died, he entered the monastery at Uhlja, where he soon rose to become the superior. He was appointed bishop of Máramaros by prince M. Apáffi and was consecrated in 1690 by metropolitan Dositej of Suceava (then a refugee from the Turks). Opposed to the union with Rome, Stojka led his eparchy toward Calvinism. In 1705, the eparchial synod with the approval of the prince ousted him from the episcopate and entrusted the administration of the eparchy to Job I. Czirka (1708-1709). Stojka was rehabilitated in 1710, but he died the following year.

12. SERAFIM S. PETROVAN (1711-1717)—though Romanian by birth, he was a great advocate of union. After his episcopal consecration, he tried to implement the union in the Máramaros eparchy but failed. In 1714, opponents of the union ousted him from the episcopacy and handed over the administration of the eparchy to the

Reverend Ivan Mojseni. Bishop Petrovan was put on trial and the proceedings dragged on until the spring of 1717. He was sentenced to imprisonment and died shortly thereafter. While the trial was still going on, hieromonk Prokopij Hodermars'kyj, OSBM, from the Mukačevo eparchy won over some 60 Máramaros priests to the union cause.

13. DOSYTEJ TEODOROVYČ (1718-1721)—the last bishop of Máramaros. He was the hegumen of the Uhlja monastery and an opponent of the union, but he was unsuccessful in preventing its spread in Máramaros. In 1721, the entire region accepted the union and acknowledged the authority of the bishop of Mukačevo Jurij Bizancij. Left without a flock, bishop Teodorovyč ended his days at the Uhlja monastery, although he continued performing episcopal duties and ordaining priests clandestinely. He died toward the end of October 1733 at the age of 83. His death marked the end of the Máramaros Orthodox eparchy.

C. United Bishops of the Mukačevo Eparchy

1. PARTENIJ PETRO PETROVYČ (1651-1665)—the first Uniate bishop in Carpathian Rus'. While still a Basilian monk, he played a decisive role in the acceptance of Union of Užhorod in 1646. In 1651, he was elected bishop by the clergy at the behest of bishop Vasylij Tarasovyč. Without waiting for confirmation from Rome, he went to Alba Iulia to be consecrated bishop of Mukačevo by the Orthodox metropolitan Stefan Simonovici. On June 8, 1655, Pope Alexander VII finally cleared him of all censures and irregularities and confirmed him bishop of Mukačevo. Emperor Leopold I followed suit only in 1660. Princess Zsófia Báthory did not allow him to assume the Mukačevo seat until 1664, when she removed the Orthodox bishop Joannykij Zejkan' (see No. 14 on list A. Bishops of the Mukačevo Eparchy before the Union) to Imstyčevo. Bishop Partenij died at the beginning of 1665.

2. JOSYF VOLOŠYNOVS'KYJ (1667-1675)—a native of Galicia, who was appointed bishop of Mukačevo on July 16, 1667 by emperor Leopold I at the request of the Hungarian primate György Szelepcsényi, even though he was of the Orthodox faith. After his conversion to Catholicism, he was consecrated in 1668 by the non-Uniate bishop of L'viv, J. Šumljans'kyj. Exempted from all irregularities, Vološynovs'kyj was confirmed by Rome on March 13, 1669. In 1670, princess Zsófia Báthory seized the property of the monastery and expelled Vološynovs'kyj from Mukačevo. After some

time (1675?), he returned to Galicia. The last time we hear of Vološynovs'kyj in Galicia occurs in 1680.

3. IVAN MALACHOVS'KYJ (1671-?)—After expelling the emperor's candidate, bishop Josyf Vološynovs'kyj, from Mukačevo, princess Zsófia Báthory entrusted the government of the Mukačevo eparchy to bishop Malachovs'kyj of Przemyśl. Failing to obtain confirmation, he left Carpathian Rus' in 1672 and administered the Mukačevo eparchy through his vicar. We find mention in 1681-1687 of his vicars, Ivan Lypnyc'kyj and Porfirij Kul'čyc'kyj, as trying to win the Mukačevo bishopric but failing to do so.

4. THEOPHANES MAUROCORDATO (1676-1686)—a Greek by birth and native of Izmir (Smyrna). At the request of the emperor, the pope named him apostolic administrator in 1676. Upon arriving in Carpathian Rus', he immediately set about restoring ecclesiastical order among the clergy and strengthening the union. But in 1678, he fled Imre Thököly's rebels to Vienna. To compel him to return, the emperor in 1680 named him the bishop of Mukačevo. But Maurocordato delayed his return until the Turks made it virtually impossible. After the liberation of Vienna (1683), cardinal Leopold Kollonits sent him to Rome (in 1686), where he probably died in 1688.

5. RAFAJIL A. GAVRILOVIČ (1687-1688)—a Belorussian by birth and a Basilian monk who somehow became the metropolitan of Ancyra (Ankara) in Asia Minor (Galatia). Persecuted by the Greeks and the Turks, he finally reached Rome in 1684, where he converted to Catholicism. At Rome's request, Gavrilovič went to Vienna in 1687, where the emperor named him in place of Maurocordato as administrator of the Mukačevo eparchy. By October 1688, Gavrilovič was dismissed from his post and returned to his homeland, where he was imprisoned as a spy. After his release, he returned to Rome at the end of 1690. He lived in Rome for a number of years, and in 1707, after the death of bishop Josyf de Camillis, he once again tried to obtain the Mukačevo see. The date of his death is not known.

6. METODIJ RAKOVEC'KYJ (1688-1690)—a priest, who after the death of his wife was ordained a bishop in Galicia by Dositej, the exiled Romanian Orthodox metropolitan of Suceava. In the hope of winning the appointment to the Mukačevo eparchy, he converted to Catholicism, but neither the secular nor ecclesiastical authorities were willing to recognize his consecration as bishop. In 1690, bishop de Camillis appointed him hegumen of the Mukačevo monastery, but prohibited him from performing any episcopal functions. He caused a

great deal of trouble for bishop de Camillis because he supported the anti-union faction in Carpathian Rus'. In 1690 he fled to the Perehins'ko monastery in Galicia, where he died in 1693.

7. JOSYF J. DE CAMILLIS (1689-1706)—a Greek from the island of Chios, born in 1641. After completing his theological studies at the Greek College in Rome, he was engaged for a time in missionary work among the Italo-Greeks in Albania. Upon his return to Rome, he took monastic vows as a Basilian and assumed the religious name of Josyf. He was then appointed procurator general of the Basilian Order in Rome and scribe at the Vatican library. In 1689, at the request of cardinal Leopold Kollonits, Pope Alexander VIII named him apostolic administrator of the Mukačevo eparchy. De Camillis was a learned and very zealous bishop. He strengthened the Holy Union in Carpathian Rus', brought order to the ranks of the clergy, and restored the prestige of his eparchy. He obtained a charter of privileges for the clergy, which emperor Leopold I signed in 1692. In 1698, in Trnava, he published a *Katechysys* (Catechism) for religious instruction, and the following year made possible the appearance of a *Boukvar jazŷka slaven'ska (Primer of the Slavonic Language)*. These were the first two books ever published for the Carpatho-Rusyns. In 1704, he secured three scholarships for Mukačevo seminarians at the Jesuit College in Trnava. When prince Ferenc Rákóczi II began his uprising, he persuaded bishop de Camillis to resign, but Rome refused to accept his resignation. Finally, in 1705, Rákóczi forced de Camillis, as a supporter of the emperor, to leave the territory of Hungary and instead named his own supporter, the Galician hieromonk Petronij Kamins'kyj, to head the Mukačevo see. De Camillis settled in Prešov and after a long illness died there on August 22, 1706. He was one of the great bishops of Mukačevo.

8. JURIJ VYNNYC'KYJ (1707-1710)—the bishop of Przemyśl (Peremyšl'), named apostolic administrator of the Mukačevo eparchy by Rome on April 7, 1707, but never took possession of the see. Prince Ferencz Rákóczi II had moved faster than Rome and had named hieromonk Petronij Kamins'kyj the bishop of Mukačevo. On September 27, 1707, emperor Joseph I appointed the eparchy's vicar-general Ivan J. Hodermars'kyj to head the Mukačevo see. This gave rise to a protracted struggle for the right to nominate the bishop of Mukačevo, which resulted in a ten-year long vacancy in the episcopacy.

9. JURIJ GENNADIJ BIZANCIJ (1716-1733)—born in 1656 in

Velykyj Rakovec' (then Ugocsa county, now in the Iršava district of the Transcarpathian oblast), Bizancij completed his theological studies at Trnava with high honors. After his ordination to the priesthood in 1701, he served as parish priest in Nagykálló. In 1703, he was elevated to archdeacon, and after the death of bishop de Camillis he became the vicar-general of the eparchy and the rival of Ivan Hodermars'kyj for the episcopate. On February 5, 1716, Pope Clement XI named Bizancij titular bishop of Sebaste and apostolic vicar of the Mukačevo eparchy. On December 21, 1716, Kievan metropolitan Lev Kiška consecrated him a bishop. Even before his consecration, he had joined the Basilian order and taken the religious name Gennadij. After the death of archimandrite Ivan Hodermars'kyj, OSBM (1729), bishop Bizancij also became the superior of the Mukačevo monastery.

Bishop Bizancij worked very hard to strengthen and spread the union, and he won the entire Máramaros region to this cause. Although he submitted completely to the authority of the Eger bishop in the administrative sphere, he endeavored to raise both the moral and material standards of his priests. He obtained a confirmation of privileges for his clergy (1720) and procured land endowments for individual parishes. In 1727, he published in Trnava the *Kratkoe pripadkov moral'nych ili nravnych sobranie (A Casuistry in Moral Theology)* for the clergy, and he proclaimed the resolutions of the Zamość Synod as binding for the Mukačevo eparchy. He died at Černeča Hora on July 22, 1733 at the age of 76 and was buried in the monastery vault.

10. SYMEON STEFAN OL'ŠAVS'KYJ (1734-1737)—born ca. 1695 in Ol'šavica (Szepes county, now in the Prešov Region of Czechoslovakia). His real family name was Žydyk, but upon becoming bishop he changed it to Ol'šavs'kyj. He studied at Trnava, where in 1717 he obtained a doctorate in philosophy. After his ordination, he became the parish priest of Mukačevo, and from 1728 onward the vicar-general of bishop Jurij Bizancij. Named titular bishop of Pella, he made his monastic vows (taking Stefan as his religious name) and was consecrated in L'viv in 1734. His excessive loyalty to the Eger ordinary disillusioned his clergy. In 1734, Ol'šavs'kyj held a diocesan synod in order to uproot certain abuses among the clergy. Because of a protracted illness, he made his brother Mychajlo his assistant, who in fact governed the eparchy. He died on December 24, 1737, and was buried in the vault of the Mukačevo monastery.

11. JURIJ HAVRYJIL BLAŽOVS'KYJ (1738-1742)—born in

Blažov (Sáros county, now in the Prešov Region of Czechoslovakia). His family name was Mankovyč, but he later changed it to Blažovs'kyj. He obtained a degree in philosophy at Košice and in theology at Trnava. He was ordained into the priesthood in 1729 by bishop Jurij Bizancij and became his secretary. On May 11, 1738, the emperor appointed him bishop of Mukačevo. He therefore took monastic vows and assumed the religious name Havryjil. The pope named him titular bishop of Agnus and appointed him apostolic vicar of Mukačevo. Metropolitan Atanasij Šeptyc'kyj of L'viv consecrated him bishop in Univ on December 22, 1738. He endeavored to obtain material assistance for the clergy and the right to sit in parliament as bishop. Bishop Blažovs'kyj was very ambitious, and the historian Duliškovyč accuses him of latinizing the rite. Fleeing the plague, he fell ill at the monastery in Malyj Bereznyj (Ung county) and died on December 20, 1742.

12. MYCHAJIL MANUJIL OL'ŠAVS'KYJ (1743-1767)—the brother of bishop Symeon S. Ol'šavs'kyj, born in 1697 also in Ol'šavica. He studied philosophy in Levoča and theology in Trnava (doctor of philosophy) and was ordained to the priesthood by bishop Jurij Bizancij in 1725. He was vicar-general during his brother's tenure and parish priest in Mukačevo during the tenure of bishop Jurij Blažovs'kyj. After naming him titular bishop of Rossos, the pope on September 6, 1743 named him apostolic vicar of the Mukačevo eparchy. Upon taking his monastic vows, he assumed the name Manujil. His consecration took place on December 9, 1743 in Máriapócs by the Romanian bishop of Făgăraş, I. Micu-Klein.

M.M. Ol'šavs'kyj was one of the greatest bishops of Mukačevo. He endeavored to raise the standards of the clergy both in the moral and the material spheres. In 1744, he founded a theological school in Mukačevo, which later developed into the eparchial seminary. In 1746, he published the *Načalo pîsmen dîtem k nastavleniju na latinskom jazŷkî* for the study of Latin. In 1756, he completed the construction of the church in Máriapócs, which had been begun by bishop Jurij Bizancij. There he founded a Basilian monastery and school. Because of constant conflicts with the monks at the Černeča Hora monastery, in 1766 bishop Ol'šavs'kyj abandoned this traditional seat of the Mukačevo bishops and built a new episcopal residence at the parish church of Mukačevo.

Bishop Ol'šavs'kyj made a major contribution to the cause of the union. In 1746, he pacified the Romanians in Transylvania who wanted to leave the union and was awarded the title of "imperial counselor" for this service. In 1750-1752 he made a visitation to all his parishes (675 parishes, 839 churches) and, after submitting a report to the imperial court, he demanded that they be adequately endowed. When the anti-union disturbances began in the Szatmár (Satu-Mare) county in 1761, bishop Ol'šavs'kyj restored order there as well. His treatise on the union, *Slovo o svjatom' meždu vostočnoju i zapadnoju cerkvoju soedinenii,* published in Počajiv in 1769, was translated into several languages and appeared in scores of editions.

Bishop Ol'šavs'kyj's greatest attainment was his role in obtaining the decision of the eparchial synod in Mukačevo in 1764 to strive for independence from the Eger ordinary. He took the matter of the eparchy's independence so far that there was no turning back. He died as he lived, a holy death on November 5, 1767 in Mukačevo. At his request, he was buried in the church of Máriapócs.

13. IVAN BRADAČ (1768-1772)—born on February 14, 1732 in Torysky (Szepes county, now in the Prešov Region of Czechoslovakia). He studied at Levoča and Trnava, graduating in 1756. He was ordained while still a student in 1755. He served as parish priest of Orosvyhovo for a brief time and then as professor of theology and the archdeacon of the cathedral. In 1764, bishop Mychajil Ol'šavs'kyj sent him as his delegate to Vienna to take the necessary steps at the imperial court for the eparchy's independence. While in Vienna, Bradač was named auxiliary bishop, but upon his return home he found bishop Ol'šavs'kyj dead. The pope then appointed him apostolic vicar of Mukačevo on January 27, 1768. His consecration took place on May 1, 1768 in Máriapócs and was performed by bishop M. Kovács of Oradea (Nagyvárad). Bishop Bradač spent his entire episcopacy in a struggle with the Eger ordinary in an attempt to win the independence of the Mukačevo eparchy. His efforts met with success when on September 19, 1771, the Apostolic See in its bull *Eximia Regalium Principum* canonically erected the Mukačevo eparchy and appointed Bradač its first bishop on September 23, 1771. Bishop Bradač also prepared the publication of liturgical books, which caused him great difficulties in Rome, because bishop Božičković of Križevci and bishop Esterházy of Eger denounced him for "suspicion of schism." Exhausted by work and worry, Bradač died on July 4, 1772, at the age of 39. He was buried in the vault at the Černeča Hora monastery in Mukačevo.

14. ANDRIJ BAČYNS'KYJ (1773-1809)—the greatest bishop of Mukačevo, born in Beňatina (Ung county, now in the Prešov Region of Czechoslovakia), on November 14, 1732, where his father Teodor

was the parish priest. He attended the *gymnasium* at Užhorod and then studied philosophy and theology at Trnava. After his ordination to the priesthood in 1756, he was sent for further study to Trnava and in 1758 obtained a doctoral degree. He began as assistant pastor, but soon became pastor and archdeacon in Hajdúdorog and in 1769 was appointed pastor and archdeacon of Mukačevo, simultaneously acting as the bishop's vicar-general. He was the right hand of bishop Ol'šavs'kyj and later of bishop Bradač. After the death of Bradač, Bačyns'kyj was elected capitular vicar and on March 8, 1773 appointed bishop of Mukačevo. He was consecrated to the episcopate by bishop Božičković of Križevci at the imperial chapel in Vienna on June 6, 1773. Bishop Bačyns'kyj had the task of organizing the newly established Mukačevo eparchy and he succeeded brilliantly. He moved the eparchial seat to the more central location of Užhorod (1775), established a cathedral chapter with seven members (1777), founded a modern theological seminary (1778), and transformed the former Jesuit college into an episcopal residence and cathedral (1780). He completed the process of endowing the churches in his eparchy, organized an eparchial school system, and initiated a golden age in Carpathian Rus'. By creating the Košice (later called the Prešov) vicariate in 1787, he lay the foundations for the future Prešov eparchy. In 1808, owing to illness, he received an auxiliary bishop in the person of Mychajil Bradač. He died in Užhorod on December 19, 1809 at the age of 76 and was the first bishop to be buried in the crypt under the cathedral.

Auxiliary Bishop MYCHAJIL BRADAČ (1808-1815)—born on April 2, 1748 in Kamienka (Szepes county now in the Prešov Region of Czechoslovakia), he was the younger brother of bishop Ivan Bradač. He completed his theological studies in Trnava. In 1777, bishop Andrij Bačyns'kyj appointed him pastor of the cathedral in Mukačevo, professor of the seminary in Užhorod in 1780, and canon in 1786. In 1790, he became the vicar of Košice and transferred the seat of the vicariate to Prešov. In 1808, he was named titular bishop of Dorylaeum and auxiliary to bishpo Bačyns'kyj. He was consecrated in Oradea on January 8, 1809. After his episcopal ordination, he remained the vicar of Prešov. Following the death of the capitulary vicar I. Kutka in 1812, Bradač was elected to that post and moved to Užhorod, expecting to succeed to the episcopacy. But he died suddenly on December 20, 1815, at the age of 67.

15. ALEXIS PÓCSY (1816-1831)—born in 1753 in Kokod (Bihar county, now in Romania), where his father was the parish priest. He

completed his theological studies at the Barbareum in Vienna. After his ordination to the priesthood in 1778, he administered a parish in Eger, later served as an army chaplain, and in 1794 became the parish priest of Makó. In recognition for his excellent pastoral work, he was elevated to the rank of archdeacon and in 1800 became the rector of the cathedral and a canon in Oradea.

At the emperor's request, Pope Pius VII on August 11, 1816 appointed him bishop of Mukačevo. He was consecrated that same year by his ordinary, bishop Samuel Vulcan of Oradea. Pócsy was an exceptionally hardworking bishop. In 1818, he agreed to the separation of the Prešov eparchy and in 1823 to the inclusion of 72 parishes from the Mukačevo to the Oradea eparchy. During the vacancy of the Mukačevo see, Latin had been introduced as the language of instruction at the Užhorod seminary. But bishop Pócsy ordered that pastoral theology and the catechetics be taught in the Rusyn language. He founded the orphanage of St. Aleksij in Užhorod. He died in Užhorod on July 11, 1831, and was buried in the crypt of the cathedral.

16. VASYLIJ POPOVYČ (1837-1864)—born on September 12, 1796 in Komjaty (Ugocsa county, now in the Transcarpathian oblast), where his father Jurij was the parish priest. He studied at the *gymnasium* in Užhorod and received his education in philosophy and theology in Budapest, graduating with a doctorate in philosophy. After his ordination (1820), he became assistant pastor in Svaljava and later in Sighetul Marmației. In 1822, bishop Tarkovyč of Prešov summoned him to serve as his secretary. In 1835, Popovyč became a canon and rector of the cathedral in Prešov. On the emperor's recommendation, he was appointed bishop of Mukačevo on October 2, 1837, and was consecrated in L'viv by metropolitan M. Levyc'kyj on March 18, 1838.

Popovyč was a very hard-working bishop and he raised considerably the religious, cultural, and material standards of his eparchy. He founded an orphanage for the daughters of priests, built a new teachers' seminary, and provided the theological seminary with a private chapel (1858). He also restored the episcopal residence and obtained the so-called *congrua* for his clergy. He was persecuted by the Hungarians for his love of the Rusyn people, but, nonetheless, he was able to introduce the teaching of the Rusyn language and religion at the Užhorod, Mukačevo, and Sighetul *gymnasiums*. He passionately loved his rite and saw to it that it was strictly observed. In 1853, some 94 Romanian parishes were separated from the Mukačevo see and incorporated into the newly-created Gherla eparchy. He died on October 19, 1864 in Užhorod and was buried in the cathedral crypt.

17. STEFAN PANKOVYČ (1867-1874)—born on October 29, 1820 in Vel'aty (Zemplén county, now in the Prešov Region of Czechoslovakia), where his father was a parish priest. Orphaned as a little boy, he received his secondary education in Satu-Mare (Szatmár) and his priestly formation at the eparchial seminary in Užhorod where he was an excellent student. He postponed priestly ordination and became a tutor for children of the Hungarian aristocracy. In 1851, he decided to receive holy orders, hoping to make a swift career in the episcopal curia. But bishop Popovyč, knowing that Pankovyč lacked pastoral experience, appointed him instead to his native parish. Driven by ambition, Pankovyč soon returned to tutorial work and tried to ingratiate himself into influential Hungarian circles as a "patriot." Indeed, after the death of bishop Popovyč, the Hungarian authorities persuaded Rome to appoint Pankovyč bishop of Mukačevo. He was consecrated bishop in Prešov on May 5, 1867.

Pankovyč devoted a great deal of energy in building new churches, schools and parish homes. He hoped to introduce the Gregorian calendar, but failed because of opposition from the faithful and clergy. At the request of the government, he founded in 1873 the Hungarian vicariate of Hajdúdorog, thereby laying the foundations for a separate Hungarian Greek Catholic eparchy. In contrast to his predecessor, the Eastern rite became alien to him and he latinized it wherever he could. Pankovyč was the first Carpatho-Rusyn bishop to take part in the Ecumenical Council in 1869. He died suddenly on August 29, 1874, at the age of 53.

18. IVAN PASTELIJ (1875-1891)—born on May 8, 1826 in Vel'aty (Zemplén county, now in the Prešov Region of Czechoslovakia). His mother was the sister of bishop Stefan Pankovyč, and because of this Pastelij enjoyed his uncle's patronage. He was educated at the Užhorod seminary, and in 1849 bishop Popovyč ordained him to the priesthood. He served as a catechist in Chust and later as parish priest and archpriest of the Chust district. In 1867, bishop Pankovyč named Pastelij archdeacon and, in 1869, the vicar of Máramaros with a seat in Sighetul. In 1869-1872, Pastelij served as deputy to the Hungarian diet, where he supported Hungarian interests and gained the reputation of a "true Hungarian patriot." In 1871, the Hungarians rewarded his loyalty by awarding him the title of archimandrite.

Rome appointed Pastelij bishop of Mukačevo on March 15, 1875. His episcopal ordination was performed by bishop Josyf Gaganec' of

Prešov on April 18, 1875. Bishop Pastelij devoted special attention to the welfare of the poor and orphans and improved the status of church institutions, but he failed to defend the national interests of his faithful. During his tenure, the magyarization of Carpathian Rus' progressed significantly. He died on March 24, 1891.

19. JULIJ FIRCAK (1891-1912)—born on August 22, 1836 in Chudl'ovo (Ung county, now in the Transcarpathian oblast), where his father Vasylij was the parish priest. He completed his theological studies in Vienna, where he defended a doctoral thesis in the field of dogmatic theology. After his ordination on September 26, 1861, bishop Vasylij Popovyč appointed him a seminary professor in Užhorod. Fircak was exceptionally well-read, well-travelled, and fluent in various European languages. In 1876, he was elevated to the rank of canon and assumed the post of rector at the seminary (1876-1887). In 1887, he was elected a deputy to the Hungarian parliament, where he zealously defended the rights of his people.

On December 17, 1891, the Apostolic See appointed him bishop of Mukačevo. He was consecrated by bishop Ivan Valij of Prešov on April 10, 1892. As bishop, Fircak founded a teacher's college for women in Užhorod, he initiated a campaign to provide social assistance for the poor called the "Verchovyna Action," and he conducted two diocesan synods (in 1897 and 1903), thereby trying to renew the spiritual life and love for the Eastern rite among his flock. With his blessings, the Reverend A. Karcub founded in 1903 the Society of the Holy Rosary, which fostered devotion to the Blessed Virgin. By that time Fircak was quite ill and he requested that an auxiliary bishop be appointed. On June 1, 1912, he died in Užhorod at the age of 75 before the consecration of his auxiliary bishop, A. Papp.

20. ANTONIJ PAPP (1912-1924)—appointed coadjutor to bishop Julij Fircak on April 29, 1912, with the right of succession, assumed the administration of the eparchy on June 1, 1912. Papp was born on November 17, 1867 in Nagykálló (Szabolcs county, now in Hungary), where his father Antonij, a titular archdeacon, was parish priest. He obtained his secondary education in Užhorod and Levoča and his theological formation in Budapest. Even before his ordination to the priesthood (1893), bishop Julij Fircak appointed him to the episcopal chancery, where he served in various capacities, including that of chancellor. Although Papp regarded himself a Hungarian, he sought the assistance of priests to defend the rights of the Rusyn people, such as the canons Ju. Suba, S. Sabov, and A. Mykyta, and professors P. Gebej, A. Vološyn, and others.

After World War I, a religious struggle broke out in Subcarpathian Rus', during which more than 100,000 faithful left the Greek Catholic Church. Bishop Papp proved helpless in the face of the Orthodox movement, and so on July 14, 1924 the Apostolic See transferred him to Hungary to serve there as apostolic administrator of Miskolc, (from 1943 exarch), naming canon Petro Gebej to take his place. Papp died in Miskolc on Christmas Eve 1945.

21. PETRO GEBEJ (1924-1931)—born on July 20, 1864 in Kal'nyk (Bereg county, now in the Transcarpathian oblast). He attended *gymnasium* in Užhorod and completed his theological studies in Budapest. After his ordination (1889), bishop Ivan Pastelij appointed him prefect of the theological seminary and professor of church law and history. In 1892, Gebej also became the spiritual director of the teacher's college for women in Užhorod. In 1906, when Carpatho-Rusyn schools were threatened with total magyarization, bishop Julij Fircak appointed him instructor of religion at the Užhorod *gymnasium* in order to preserve the Rusyn language. At that time, Gebej also became the director of the boys boarding school known as the Alumneum. In 1912, bishop Antonij Papp named him a canon and rector of the cathedral. Gebej loved the Eastern rite and his people and played a leading role in the liberation of Subcarpathian Rus' in 1919. In 1922, at the height of the religious struggle, he became vicar-general of bishop Papp. From then on he headed the defense of the eparchy against the violence of the Orthodox. After transferring bishop Papp to Hungary, the Apostolic See appointed Gebej the bishop of Mukačevo. On August 3, 1924, he was consecrated during an Ecumenical Congress in Velehrad (Moravia) in the presence of the papal nuncio to Czechoslovakia, archbishop F. Marmaggi.

Bishop Gebej's ascendance to the episcopacy ushered in the beginning of a new era in the Mukačevo eparchy. He ended the religious struggle with the Orthodox and brought order to the eparchy. Because he unselfishly served the interests of the Rusyn people, Gebej encountered considerable opposition from some of his magyarized clergy, who sought to bring about his resignation. But the papal nuncio supported bishop Gebej's policy and did not accept his resignation. He died in Užhorod on April 26, 1931, at the age of 66, having earned the reputation among the people of a "saintly bishop."

22. ALEKSANDER STOJKA (1932-1943)—born October 16, 1890 in Karačyn (Ugocsa county, now in the Transcarpathian oblast) into a peasant family. He graduated from the Užhorod *gymnasium* in 1910 and enrolled at the eparchial seminary. After two years, he was sent to

the central seminary in Budapest. Upon completing his theological studies in 1915, Stojka became the archivist at the bishop's chancery. On December 17, 1916, having received a master's degree in moral and pastoral theology, he was ordained into the priesthood by bishop Antonij Papp. As an official of the bishop's chancery, Stojka wrote a great deal on social, ecclesiastical, and legal subjects. He was known as a talented preacher and soloist with the cathedral choir for many years. In 1930, bishop Gebej elevated him to the rank of canon and put him in charge of the bishop's chancery. After bishop Gebej's death, Stojka administered the eparchy for more than a year as capitular vicar until he was appointed bishop of Mukačevo. He was consecrated in Užhorod on July 12, 1932.

Bishop Stojka sought to improve the lot of the poor, initiated an "Easter Action" to help the needy, involved himself in the socioeconomic life of his people, and fostered the Marian movement in his eparchy. Unfortunately, he supported Hungarian interests in Subcarpathian Rus' and contributed to its annexation to Hungary in 1939. During the period of autonomy in Carpatho-Ukraine (October 1938—March 1939), when Užhorod and Mukačevo were ceded to Hungary, he remained with his curia in Užhorod, sending only his vicar, the Reverend Canon L. Minja, to Carpatho-Ukraine. Rome therefore appointed the bishop of Križevci, Dionysij Njaradij (see No. 6 on list D. Bishops of the Prešov Eparchy), as apostolic visitator to Chust. In March 1939, after the Hungarians had occupied all of Carpatho-Ukraine, bishop Stojka once again took over the administration of the Mukačevo eparchy with the exception of 80 parishes in the Zemplén region, which were placed under the jurisdiction of the bishop of Prešov. Bishop Stojka died prematurely on May 31, 1943, at the age of 52. He was buried at the seminary cemetery at the foot of the Užhorod castle.

23. MIKLÓS DUDÁS, OSBM (1944)—apostolic administrator. After the death of bishop Stojka, the eparchy was governed by the capitular vicar Monsignor Aleksander Il'nyc'kyj while Rome held talks with the Hungarian authorities about a successor to the episcopacy. When the two sides failed to reach an understanding, on January 1, 1944 the Apostolic See appointed the bishop of Hajdúdorog, M. Dudás, OSBM, apostolic administrator of the Mukačevo eparchy. Bishop Dudás had been educated at Carpatho-Rusyn and Galician monasteries and studied theology in Rome. He was born in 1902 in Máriapócs in Hungary. After the war, he entered the novitiate of the Basilian Order in Mukačevo. He took his monastic

vows in 1925 and was ordained a priest on September 8, 1927. He was appointed bishop of Hajdúdorog on April 25, 1939.

Bishop Dudás did not govern the Mukačevo eparchy for long because the Red Army drew near. Thus, at the end of 1944, the Apostolic See entrusted the administration of the eparchy to bishop Teodor Romža, whom it appointed as auxiliary bishop to Dudás. Bishop Dudás continued to head the Hajdúdorog eparchy, and from 1945 onward (after the death of bishop A. Papp) he also administered the Miskolc exarchate. He died on July 15, 1972, and was buried in Máriapócs.

24. TEODOR JURIJ ROMŽA (1944-1947)—born on April 14, 1911 in Velykyj Byčkiv (Máramaros county, now in the Transcarpathian oblast). He graduated from the Chust *gymnasium* and completed his theological studies in Rome (at the Russicum), where he was trained to serve as a missionary among the Russians. He was ordained to the priesthood in Rome on Christmas Day, 1936. He returned home during the critical years before World War II and was immediately drafted into the Czechoslovak army. In the fall of 1938, bishop Aleksander Stojka appointed him pastor of Nyžnij Bystryj in the Chust district (with a filial church in Berezovo) and in September 1939, spiritual director and professor of philosophy at the eparchial seminary in Užhorod. He retained these posts (in 1942 receiving the title of Monsignor) until September 8, 1944, when the Apostolic See appointed him titular bishop of Appia and auxiliary to bishop Miklós Dudás. Romža's nomination was accompanied by an instruction that he be consecrated in the shortest possible time and given the administration of the Mukačevo eparchy. His consecration was held in Užhorod on September 24, 1944, while the sound of Red Army bombers filled the air.

In October 1944, Subcarpathian Rus' was occupied by the Red Army. Bishop Romža did everything in his power to defend his flock against attacks from the Communists. Finally, on November 1, 1947, he himself fell victim in this struggle and died a martyr's death. He was buried in Užhorod. Bishop Romža's death brought to an end the long line of prelates of the Mukačevo eparchy which was forcibly dissolved on August 28, 1949 by the Soviet authorities.

Auxiliary Bishop ALEKSANDER CHIRA (1945-1983)—born on January 17, 1897 in Vil'chivci (Máramaros county, now in the Transcarpathian oblast), into the family of a priest. He completed his theological studies in Budapest and was ordained a priest on December 19, 1920. After serving as a parish priest for several years, he was appointed a spiritual director and professor at the eparchial seminary in Užhorod in 1924. In 1930, he became a papal chamberlain and in 1934 a canon and rector of the seminary, where he taught moral and pastoral theology until the Soviets closed the seminary in 1947. In 1943, he was elevated to the rank of papal prelate.

After the Soviets occupied Subcarpathian Rus', Chira became bishop Teodor Romža's closest assistant. In 1945, Romža secretly consecrated him a bishop and appointed him his vicar-general. On February 10, 1949, just before the suppression of the Mukačevo eparchy, bishop Chira was arrested, deported to Siberia, and later to labor camps in Kazakhstan. He was released in 1962, but had to remain in exile. He settled in Karaganda, Kazakh S.S.R., where he performed pastoral duties among German exiles, at first clandestinely and later as a registered Roman Catholic priest. At the same time, he secretly ministered to the spiritual needs of Ukrainian and Carpatho-Rusyn exiles in the vicinity of Karaganda. Bishop Chira died in Karaganda on May 26, 1983, and was buried near the church there that he helped to build.

D. United Bishops of the Prešov Eparchy

The Prešov eparchy was established on September 22, 1818 by the papal bull *Relata Semper*.

1. HRYHORIJ TARKOVYČ (1818-1841)—born on November 20, 1754 in Pasika (Bereg county, now in the Transcarpathian oblast). He graduated from the *gymnasium* in Užhorod and studied philosophy in Oradea and theology at the Barbareum in Vienna. He was ordained at Černeča Hora on January 1, 1779 and later taught at the eparchial seminary. In 1793, Tarkovyč was made pastor of Haj-dúdorog and in 1798 of Užhorod. From 1803 until 1813, he worked in Buda as the censor of Slavonic books. In 1813, he became the vicar of Košice, and in 1815 the capitular vicar of Mukačevo. Although the Austrian emperor Francis I nominated him for the Prešov episcopacy in 1816, Rome did not confirm the appointment until September 26, 1818. Tarkovyč was consecrated bishop in Krásny Brod on June 17, 1821. His task was to organize the newly established Prešov eparchy. He died in Prešov on January 16, 1841.

2. JOSYF GAGANEC' (1843-1875)—the greatest bishop of Prešov, born on April 10, 1793, in Vyšný Tvarožec (Sáros county, now in the Prešov Region of Czechoslovakia). He attended the *gymnasium* at Satoraljújhely and Levoča, and he studied philosophy at

Oradea and theology at Trnava. Because there was no bishop of Prešov or Mukačevo at the time, he was ordained to the priesthood by bishop Samuel Vulcan in Oradea on March 8, 1817. Gaganec' served as pastor in Ruské Pekl'any (1817-1820), then in Viszló (1820-1928) and Hejőkeresztúr (1835) in the Hungarian lowland. In 1835, he was named a canon, and after the death of bishop Tarkovyč was elected capitular vicar. The Apostolic See appointed Gaganec' the bishop of Prešov on January 30, 1843, and his episcopal ordination took place in Vienna on June 25, 1843 in the presence of the imperial court. As bishop, he completed the organization of the Prešov eparchy. Gaganec' dearly loved the Byzantine rite and the Rusyn people and suffered greatly from the Hungarians as a result. In 1848, he and his clergy held the first eparchial synod, which marked the beginning of the national and religious revival of the Prešov eparchy. In these efforts, he was assisted by the prominent "awakener of the Carpatho-Rusyns," canon Aleksander Duchnovyč. Bishop Gaganec' died in Prešov on December 22, 1875, at the age of 81, leaving behind a rich spiritual and cultural heritage.

3. NYKOLAJ TOVT (1876-1882)—born on August 10, 1833 in Mukačevo (now in the Transcarpathian oblast), where his father was a cantor. He graduated from the *gymnasium* at Satu-Mare, where he also completed his philosophical studies. His subsequent theological formation was in Budapest. He was ordained a priest by bishop Vasylij Popovyč at Černeča Hora on the feast of St. Nicholas on December 18, 1857. In 1860, Tovt was awarded the degree of doctor of theology at Vienna, after which he became a spiritual advisor and professor at the Užhorod seminary. He was such a distinguished teacher that by 1872 he became associate professor of theology at Budapest University. In 1875, bishop Pankovyč made him a canon and appointed him rector of the Užhorod seminary. On April 3, 1876, the Apostolic See named him bishop of Prešov. He was consecrated by his protector, bishop Pastelij on May 21, 1876.

After assuming the Prešov episcopacy, bishop Tovt devoted himself first of all to the welfare of young people and orphans. In 1881, he opened a theological seminary in Prešov (until then Prešov candidates for the priesthood studied at the Užhorod, Budapest, and Esztergom seminaries). Tovt built up the parochial school system in the Prešov eparchy and donated large sums of his own money for the education of young people. Bishop Tovt died suddenly in the midst of pastoral work at the age of 47 on May 21, 1882, the sixth anniversary of his episcopacy.

4. IVAN VALIJ (1882-1911)—born on September 22, 1837 in Gávavencsellő (Szabolcs-Szatmar county in present-day Hungary), where his father was parish priest. He completed his secondary education in Debrecen, Užhorod, and Oradea. He studied theology in Užhorod and then in Vienna, where he also obtained a doctorate in theology at the Augustineum in 1869. He was ordained to the priesthood by bishop Josyf Gaganec' on October 26, 1865. After several months of pastoral work, Valij was appointed prefect of the seminary in Užhorod and professor of canon law and history. In 1878, he was named a canon of the Mukačevo eparchy and on October 11, 1882 bishop of Prešov. He was consecrated on May 20, 1883 in Užhorod.

As bishop, Valij improved the parochial education system and did not hesitate to donate his own money for the support of worthy causes. He also completed the construction of the eparchial seminary. Even though he loved his people and the Byzantine rite, the Hungarians, by bestowing various honors on him, were able to exploit his influence and erudition for the purposes of magyarizing the Church in Carpathian Rus'. He died on November 19, 1911, the Hungarian press acclaiming him the "Hungarian Methodius."

5. STEFAN NOVAK (1913-1920)—born on December 4, 1879 in Ubl'a (Zemplén county, now in the Prešov Region of Czechoslovakia). He attended *gymnasium* in Užhorod, studied theology at Esztergom, and obtained his doctoral degree in Vienna. Upon his return from Vienna, in 1906 he was appointed prefect and professor at the theological seminary in Užhorod. From 1908 to 1913, he tutored the children of count M. Pálffy, then in the Hungarian diplomatic service in Rome, who helped secure Novak's appointment to the Prešov episcopate on November 20, 1913. Novak was consecrated in Užhorod on January 11, 1914. Administering the eparchy during World War I, he was unable to broaden the scope of his episcopal duties. In the fall of 1918, Novak abandoned the eparchy and settled in Hungary, where, as bishop Gojdyč wrote: "Providence allotted him a very thorny path." (*Dušpastyr'*, IX, 10, Užhorod, 1932, p. 280). Left alone and in extreme poverty, Bishop Novak died in Budapest on September 16, 1932.

6. DIONYSIJ NJARADIJ (1922-1927)—apostolic administrator. Born on October 10, 1874 in Ruski Krstur (now in the Vojvodina region of Yugoslavia). He completed his studies in Zagreb and graduated with a doctorate in theology. Ordained on January 1, 1899, he served as prefect and later rector of the Križevci eparchial seminary

in Zagreb. On June 3, 1914, Rome appointed him apostolic administrator of the Križevci eparchy. Consecrated to the episcopacy on January 9, 1915 in Rome, bishop Njaradij headed the Križevci eparchy as its administrator, and from 1920 as its ordinary. In 1922-1927, he also administered the Prešov eparchy as apostolic administrator, and was successful in containing the Orthodox movement that at the time was decimating the Mukačevo eparchy. In 1927, bishop Njaradij returned to Yugoslavia as ordinary of the Križevci eparchy. In 1938-1939, he was appointed by Rome apostolic visitator to Carpatho-Ukraine. As a bishop of apostolic stature, he lived and worked for his people. After returning to Yugoslavia, he died during an apostolic visitation to Mrzlo Polje on April 14, 1940.

7. PAVEL PETRO GOJDYČ, OSBM (1927-1960)—born on July 17, 1888 in Rus'ké Pekljany (Sáros county, now in the Prešov Region of Czechoslovakia), where his father was the parish priest. After graduating from the Prešov *gymnasium,* he entered the theological seminary in Prešov, but a year later he was sent to continue his theological studies in Budapest. He was ordained a priest in Prešov on August 27, 1911. After a year of pastoral work, he was assigned instructor of religion and prefect of the boys' boarding school in Prešov. In 1914, bishop Novak appointed him to the episcopal chancery, where he remained until 1922, when he joined the Basilian Order on Černeča Hora near Mukačevo. As a monk, he took an active part in the missionary activity in Subcarpathian Rus'. On September 14, 1926, Rome appointed him apostolic administrator of the Prešov eparchy. Wanting to prepare for his final vows (he made them on November 28, 1926), he did not assume the government of the eparchy until February 20, 1927. He was consecrated titular bishop of Harpasa in Rome on March 25, 1927.

As bishop he significantly raised the standard of spiritual and cultural life in the Prešov Region and he succeeded in saving some Rusyn parochial schools from complete slovakization. He built and expanded eparchial institutions and schools. On July 17, 1940, bishop Gojdyč was confirmed by the Apostolic See as ordinary of the eparchy. In the post-war years, when the eparchy faced great danger, he was assigned the Reverend Dr. Vasylij Hopko as auxiliary bishop. Bishop Gojdyč was imprisoned for his faith on April 28, 1950, and on January 15, 1951 was sentenced by a Slovak "People's Court" in Bratislava to life imprisonment. He died a confessor's death in the prison at Leopoldov (near Bratislava) on July 17, 1960.

Auxiliary Bishop VASYLIJ HOPKO (1947-1976)—born on April

21, 1904 in Hrabské (Sáros county, now in the Prešov Region of
Czechoslovakia) into a peasant family. He completed his secondary
and theological education in Prešov and was ordained to the
priesthood on February 3, 1929 by bishop Pavel Gojdyč. Hopko performed his pastoral duties among Rusyn students and workers living
in Czech lands, and he organized a Greek Catholic parish in Prague.
During this time he also continued his studies and was granted a doctorate in theology by Comenius University in Bratislava in 1937. In the
fall of 1936, bishop Gojdyč appointed him spiritual director and professor at the Prešov theological seminary. At the same time Rome
awarded Hopko the title of papal chamberlain. From 1941 onward, he
was a member of the bishop's chancery.

At the request of bishop Gojdyč, Rome named Hopko titular
bishop of Midila and appointed him auxiliary bishop of Prešov. He
was consecrated in Prešov on May 11, 1947. Together with bishop
Gojdyč, bishop Hopko defended the eparchy against Communist and
Orthodox attacks. After the arrest of bishop Gojdyč, Hopko was
put under house arrest for several months. In October 1950, the Communist authorities arrested him and attempted to brainwash him.
Finally, in 1952, they sentenced him to 15 years of imprisonment. In
1965, because of his illness, he was moved to a rest home in Osek,
western Czechoslovakia, and held there under police surveillance.
After the restoration of the Greek Catholic Church in Czechoslovakia
in 1968, he was released but not permitted to govern the Prešov eparchy. Instead, the Apostolic See appointed the Reverend Ján Hirka administrator of the eparchy. Until his death on July 23, 1976, Vasylij
Hopko remained only an auxiliary bishop.

8. JAN HIRKA (1990-present)—born on November 16, 1923 in
Abramovce (Sáros county, the Prešov Region of Czechoslovakia). He
received his secondary and theological education in Prešov and was
ordained a priest on July 31, 1949. He served for a short time as the
assistant pastor in L'utina, and then at the cathedral in Prešov. With
the liquidation of the Greek Catholic Church in Czechoslovakia in
April 1950, the Reverend Hirka was forced from the active ministry
and became a laborer. For his underground pastoral activity he was
sentenced to three years in prison by the Communist authorities. After
the legal restoration of the Greek Catholic Church in Czechoslovakia
in 1968, he was appointed pastor of the cathedral parish in Prešov. On
April 2, 1969, the Reverend Hirka became apostolic administrator of
the Prešov eparchy, but the Communist government would not permit

him to be ordained bishop. During his term as an administrator, Msgr. Hirka proved to be a relentless slovakizer of the Prešov eparchy. After the fall of the Communist regime in Czechoslovakia in November 1989, Msgr. Hirka could finally be consecrated bishop; the consecration took place in Prešov on February 17, 1990.

E. Bishops of the Križevci Eparchy

On June 17, 1777, Pope Pius VI issued the *Charitas Illa* bull, by which he canonically erected the independent Križevci eparchy and incorporated into it the parishes of the Bačka (Vojvodinian) Rusyns, who until then had been subordinated to the Hungarian Roman Catholic archbishop of Kalocsa. A list of bishops of the Križevci eparchy follows:

1. VASILIJE BOŽIČKOVIĆ (1777-1785)
2. JOZAFAT BASTAŠIĆ (1787-1793)
3. SILVESTAR BUBANOVIĆ (1794-1810)
4. KONSTANTIN STANIĆ (1814-1830)
5. GABRE SMIČIKLAS (1834-1856)
6. DJURO SMIČIKLAS (1857-1881)
7. ILIJA HRANILOVIĆ (1883-1889)
8. JULIJ DROHOBEC'KYJ (1891-1920), a native of Carpathian Rus'.
9. DIONYSIJ NJARADIJ (1920-1940), first governed the Križevci eparchy as its administrator, and from 1920 onward as its ordinary. He also served as apostolic administrator of the Prešov eparchy (1922-1927) and the apostolic visitator of the Mukačevo eparchy (1938-1939).
10. JANKO ŠIMRAK (1942-1946), who died as confessor for his faith.
11. HAVRYJIL BUKATKO (1952-1981)—governed the eparchy from 1952 to 1960 as apostolic administrator, and from 1960 as its bishop. From 1964 to 1980 he was also the Roman Catholic archbishop of Belgrade. He died on October 19, 1981, and was buried at the parish church in Ruski Krstur.

Auxiliary Bishop JOAKYM SEGEDI (1963-1984)—titular bishop of Gypsaria, retired since 1984.
12. SLAVOMIR MIKLOVŠ (1983—present), established his residence in Zagreb.

F. The Carpatho-Rusyn Hierarchy in the United States

In accordance with a decision of the Apostolic See in 1890, all Greek Catholic parishes in the United States were initially under the jurisdiction of local Roman Catholic ordinaries.

1. ANDREW HODOBAY (1902-1907)—apostolic visitator of the Carpatho-Rusyns but without the powers of a bishop. On March 28, 1907, he was recalled by Rome to the Prešov eparchy, from where he had originally come. He then retired and died in Miskolc, Hungary, on September 24, 1914.

2. SOTER S. ORTYNSKY, OSBM (1907-1916)—at first he governed the Galician and Carpatho-Rusyn parishes as apostolic visitator under the jurisdiction of local Roman Catholic ordinaries, but from May 28, 1913 as an independent bishop of the American "Rusyn-rite" exarchate. He died suddenly on March 24, 1916.

3. GABRIEL MARTYAK (1916-1924)—as apostolic administrator governed only the Carpatho-Rusyn parishes. For the Galicians, Rome appointed the Reverend P. Ponjatyšyn as apostolic administrator. This became the basis for the creation in 1924 of two separate exarchates, one in Pittsburgh for the Carpatho-Rusyns and a second in Philadelphia for the Galicians. The Reverend Martyak died on April 19, 1934 in Landsford, Pennsylvania, where he had served as parish priest.

4. BASIL TAKACH (1924-1948)—the first bishop of the Carpatho-Rusyns in the United States. Born in Vučkove (Máramaros county, now in the Transcarpathian oblast) on October 7, 1879. He obtained his secondary education in Satu-Mare and later in Mukačevo, and then studied theology in Užhorod. He was ordained to the priesthood on December 12, 1902, and until 1911 served as parish priest in Malyj Rakovec' (Ugocsa county). In 1911, he became director of the eparchial funds. The following year he was appointed spiritual director of the eparchial seminary in Užhorod. Nominated bishop for the United States, he was consecrated in Rome on June 15, 1924. He was known as the bishop with a "golden heart," and he suffered a great deal during the struggle over the celibacy issue. He died on May 13, 1948, and was buried at the cemetery of the Basilian nuns at Uniontown, Pennsylvania.

5. DANIEL IVANCHO (1948-1954)—born on March 30, 1908 in Jasinja (Máramaros county, now in the Transcarpathian oblast), where his father was a teacher. After his father's death, he and his mother emigrated in 1914 to the United States and settled in

Cleveland, Ohio. There he completed high school and then college at Lisle, Illinois. He studied theology at Užhorod and was ordained a priest on September 30, 1934 in McKeesport, Pennsylvania. Bishop Takach appointed him to the parish in Minneapolis; then in 1939, he was transferred to Cleveland to organize a new parish. On August 29, 1946, Ivancho was named titular bishop of Europos and auxiliary to bishop Takach with the right of succession. After the death of bishop Takach, on May 13, 1948, bishop Ivancho became the exarch and took over the administration of the Pittsburgh Exarchate. He built the Carpatho-Rusyn theological seminary in Pittsburgh. On December 2, 1954, at the height of his activity, he unexpectedly left the exarchate and at the beginning of September 1955 resigned from the episcopacy. He died in St. Petersburg, Florida on August 2, 1972.

6. NICHOLAS T. ELKO (1955-1967)—born on December 14, 1909 in Donora, Pennsylvania, where he completed his secondary education. After graduation from Duquesne University in Pittsburgh, he went on to study theology in Užhorod. He was ordained to the priesthood together with Daniel Ivancho on September 30, 1930. He served in the parishes of Canonsburg and McAdoo, Pennsylvania, and in Cleveland, Ohio. In 1939-1943, he served as the spiritual director of the Greek Catholic Union (Sojedinenije). In 1952, bishop Ivancho appointed him his vicar-general (with the dignity of papal prelate) and rector of the seminary. In the summer of 1954, Elko was appointed rector of the cathedral in Homestead, Pennsylvania. After bishop Ivancho left (December 2, 1954), Elko was appointed administrator of the Pittsburgh exarchate; then on February 16, 1955, he was named titular bishop, and on March 6 consecrated in Rome. After the resignation of bishop Ivancho, on September 5, 1955 Elko was named exarch, and on July 31, 1963 appointed ordinary of the Pittsburgh eparchy. In 1962-1965, he took part in the Vatican Council II. In 1967, because of difficulties in the administration of his eparchy, he was recalled by the Apostolic See to Rome and appointed ordaining bishop for candidates of the Eastern rite with the title of archbishop of Dara. In 1970, he became auxiliary bishop to the Roman Catholic bishop of Cincinnati, Ohio. Upon turning 75, he retired to Dayton. Ohio, where after a prolonged illness he died on May 18, 1991.

7. STEPHEN J. KOCISKO (1963-1967)—born on July 11, 1915 in Minneapolis, Minnesota. He attended high school in Minneapolis and the Minor Seminary in St. Paul, Minnesota. He continued his priestly formation in Rome, where at College of St. Josaphat he was ordained into the priesthood on March 30, 1941. After his return from

Rome, Kocisko performed pastoral duties in Detroit, Michigan and Lyndora, Pennsylvania. He organized the first of these parishes and built a new church for the second. He was also a professor of patrology at the Pittsburgh seminary. Consecrated auxiliary bishop to bishop Elko in Pittsburgh on October 23, 1956, Kocisko held the post of chancellor, vicar-general, and rector of the seminary. On June 6, 1963, he was appointed the first ordinary of the newly created Passaic eparchy. His installation took place on September 10, 1963 in the presence of the apostolic delegate. After the recall of bishop Elko, in 1967 the Apostolic See appointed bishop Kocisko the ordinary of the Pittsburgh eparchy.

G. The Carpatho-Rusyn Metropolitanate in the United States

On April 2, 1969, the Apostolic See established a metropolitan province for the Carpatho-Rusyns in the United States, and Bishop Stephen J. Kocisko was appointed its first metropolitan. In addition to the Pittsburgh archdiocese, the metropolitanate comprises the Passaic (1963), Parma (1969), and Van Nuys (1981) eparchies. The hierarchy of the Pittsburgh metropolitan province is made up of:

I. The Pittsburgh Archdiocese

1. STEPHEN J. KOCISKO (1969-1991)—transferred from Passaic to serve first as bishop (1967) and later as metropolitan and archbishop of the Pittsburgh See (1969). His installation took place on June 11, 1969. As the metropolitan of the Byzantine Ruthenian Catholics, archbishop Kocisko was a permanent member of the Episcopal Senate of the Apostolic See in Rome and also a member of the Papal Commission for the revision of canon law for the Eastern Churches. He was a dedicated supporter of the church-affiliated and religious press. He retired on June 12, 1991.

2. THOMAS V. DOLINAY (1991-present)—transferred from Van Nuys to Pittsburgh on March 13, 1990, to serve as coadjutor archbishop. On June 12, 1991, he became metropolitan and archbishop of Pittsburgh. (See below, II. The Passaic Eparchy, no.3)

3. JOHN J. BILOCK (1973-present)—born on June 20, 1916 in McAdoo, Pennsylvania, and ordained into the priesthood on February 3, 1946. In addition to zealous pastoral work in several large parishes, he held the posts of secretary to the bishop, notary of the matrimonial tribunal, eparchial consultor, and member of the administrative council. In 1957, he was named a papal chamberlain and

in 1969, a papal prelate. In 1963, Bilock was appointed rector of the cathedral in Munhall, Pennsylvania, and in 1969 became the vicar-general of metropolitan Kocisko. Pope Paul VI named him titular bishop of Pergamum and auxiliary of Pittsburgh. His episcopal ordination was held on May 15, 1973. For many years he has conducted liturgical services on the radio and television for the bedridden. Each year he organizes pilgrimages to Uniontown, Pennsylvania as well as to European shrines and to the Holy Land.

II. The Passaic Eparchy

1. STEPHEN J. KOCISKO (1963-1968)—transferred from his post as auxiliary bishop of Pittsburgh to head the newly created Passaic eparchy. After his appointment as ordinary of Pittsburgh (1967), he acted as apostolic visitator of the Passaic eparchy until the installation of bishop Dudick.

2. MICHAEL J. DUDICK (1968-present)—born on February 23, 1916 in St. Clair, Pennsylvania. After completing his studies in Lisle, Illinois, he was ordained into the priesthood on November 13, 1945. In addition to his pastoral duties, he was also the vice-chancellor of the Pittsburgh exarchate (1946-1955). As pastor at Old Forge, Pennsylvania (1955-1960), he built a new church and parish hall and also restored the church in Freeland, Pennsylvania (1961). In 1963, he became the chancellor of the newly-created Passaic eparchy and was named a papal prelate. He also acted as pastor at Newark, New Jersey, eparchial consultor, and member of the building committee. After the transfer of bishop Kocisko to Pittsburgh, he was appointed the ordinary of Passaic. His episcopal ordination and installation was held on October 24, 1968. He was appointed member of the Sacred Congregation for the Eastern Churches in Rome. Bishop Dudick regulary contributes inspirational editorials to his diocesan paper, *Eastern Catholic Life*. Due to his vision, a new diocesan center and bishop's residence, including a chapel and social center, were constructed in West Paterson, New Jersey and dedicated in 1986.

3. THOMAS V. DOLINAY (1976-1981)—born on July 24, 1923 in Uniontown, Pennsylvania. He completed his theological studies in Lisle, Illinois, and was ordained a priest on April 16, 1948. In addition to pastoral work in various parishes, he was editor of *Prosvita-Enlightenment* (1951-1955) and later assistant editor of Pittsburgh's eparchial paper, *Byzantine Catholic World* (1956-1961). When bishop Kocisko founded the Passaic eparchial weekly, *Eastern Catholic Life*

in 1965, the Reverend Dolinay became its editor. In 1966, he was named a papal chamberlain. In 1976, Pope Paul VI named him titular bishop of Thyatira and appointed him auxiliary of Passaic. Dolinay's episcopal ordination was held in Scranton, Pennsylvania on November 23, 1976. As auxiliary bishop he acted as vicar-general of the eastern Pennsylvania parishes and also edited the diocesan newspaper. At the end of 1981, Dolinay was appointed ordinary of the newly-created Van Nuys eparchy in California.

4. ANDREW PATAKI (1983-1984)—born on August 10, 1927 in Palmerton, Pennsylvania. He studied theology in Lisle, Illinois and in Pittsburgh, Pennsylvania, and was ordained a priest on February 24, 1952. During his pastorate in Lorain, Ohio (1952-1963), he built a school and convent. In 1970-1972, Pataki continued the study of canon law in Rome. Upon his return from Rome, he became rector and professor of canon law at the SS. Cyril and Methodius seminary in Pittsburgh (1973-1979). In 1979, he was assigned to the parish in Weirton, West Virginia, and simultaneously served as the chancellor of the Pittsburgh archdiocese. In 1973-1978, he was a member of the Papal Commission for the revision of canon law for the Eastern Churches. In 1974, he was named a papal prelate. In 1983, Pope Paul VI named Pataki titular bishop of Thelmessus and appointed him auxiliary bishop of Passaic. His episcopal ordination took place in Scranton, Pennsylvania, on August 23, 1983. The following year he was appointed ordinary of Parma.

5. GEORGE M. KUZMA (1987-1990)—born July 24, 1925 in Windber, Pennsylvania. During World War II, he served in the U.S. Navy in the Phillipines (1943-1946). He received his priestly formation at St. Procopius Seminary in Lisle, Illinois and at SS. Cyril and Methodius Seminary in Pittsburgh, Pennsylvania, and was ordained a priest on May 29, 1955. Besides his pastoral work in various parishes, he was also involved in diocesan activities, first in the Pittsburgh and then in the Parma eparchies. At the time of the establishment of Van Nuys eparchy in 1982, Kuzma was pastor of the Anaheim, California parish. He soon became involved in the organization of the newly-created eparchy as treasurer and diocesan consultor, and was working as a member in various eparchial commissions. In 1984, he was raised to the rank of domestic prelate by Pope John Paul II, and two years later he was named auxiliary bishop of Passaic, New Jersey. His episcopal ordination took place in Passaic on February 4, 1987. As the episcopal vicar for the Pennsylvania vicariate, he resided in Con-

yngham, Pennsylvania. On October 23, 1990, he was appointed ordinary of Van Nuys.

III. The Parma Eparchy

1. EMIL I. MIHALIK (1969-1984)—born February 6, 1920 in Pittsburgh. He graduated from the St. Procopius Seminary in Lisle, Illinois, and was ordained to the priesthood on September 30, 1945. As a pastor, he built a new church and residence in Struthers, Ohio; a central school in Youngstown, Ohio; and a magnificent church and social center in Rahway, New Jersey. In 1968, bishop Michael Dudick appointed him chancellor and consultor of the Passaic eparchy. When Pope Paul VI created a new eparchy in Parma, Ohio, he appointed Mihalik its first ordinary. His consecration and installation were held in Parma on June 12, 1969. Bishop Mihalik set about organizing and expanding the new eparchy with great zeal, establishing 18 new parishes and missionary stations. He was the first of the Carpatho-Rusyn bishops to convoke a diocesan synod in 1970. In 1975, he founded the eastern branch of the Sisters of St. Clare with a seat in North Royalton, Ohio, and in January 1979 began a bi-weekly called *Horizons.* After assuring the potential for the development of new parishes in the mid-West, he contributed to the formation of the Van Nuys eparchy in California (1981). He died prematurely of lung cancer on January 27, 1984, and was buried at Mount St. Macrina in Uniontown, Pennsylvania.

2. ANDREW PATAKI (1984-present)—appointed the ordinary of Parma by Pope John Paul II in 1984, while serving as auxiliary bishop of Passaic. His installation was held at the cathedral of St. John the Baptist in Parma on August 16, 1984.

IV. The Van Nuys Eparchy

1. THOMAS V. DOLINAY (1982-1990)—auxiliary bishop of Passaic, appointed bishop of the newly-established Van Nuys, California eparchy on December 3, 1981. His installation took place in Van Nuys on March 9, 1982. In December of that same year, he began publishing the bi-monthly *Newsletter.* In a short time he managed to organize the newly-established eparchy and opened new parishes and missionary stations. On March 13, 1990, he was appointed coadjutor archbishop of the Pittsburgh archdiocese.

2. GEORGE M. KUZMA (1991-present)—appointed ordinary of Van Nuys on October 23, 1990. His installation took place in North Hollywood, California on January 15, 1991.

Notes

Abbreviations

APF   Archivum Sacrae Congregationis de Propaganda Fide
ASV   Archivum Secretum Vaticanum
ČSVV   Čyn sv. Vasylija Velykoho
OSBM   Ordo Sancti Basilii Magni

Preface

1. E. de Csáky, *La question ruthène* (Paris and Budapest, 1920), p. 3.
2. The work was published: Julius Kubinyi, *The History of Prjašiv Eparchy* (Rome, 1970).
3. See the bibliography below.
4. See the bibliography below.
5. The work did appear: Basil Boysak, *Ecumenism and Manuel M. Olshavsky, Bishop of Mukachevo (1743-1767)* (Montreal, Que., 1967).
6. Kubinyi, *History of Prjašiv Eparchy*, esp. p. 156-164.
7. See the bibliography below.

Introduction

1. This description of the extent of Carpathian Rus' reflects the views of S. Zerkal', *Nacional'ni i relihijni vidnosyny na Zakarpatti* (New York, 1956), pp. 1-2.
2. It is not our purpose to discuss the various theories regarding the settlement of Carpathian Rus'. An extensive bibliography on this subject is found in O. Pricak, "Chto taki avtochtony Karpats'koji Ukrajiny?" *Nova zorja* (Stanyslaviv), January 7, 1939, pp. 15-16. In addition to the materials mentioned by Pricak, see A. Duchnovič, "Istinnaja istorija Karpato-Rossov ili Ugorskich Rusinov," in Oleksandr Duchnovyč, *Tvory*, Vol. II (Prešov, 1967), pp. 529-566; Jador N. Strypskij, *Hdî dokumentŷ staršej ystoriy Podkarpatskoj Rusy?* (Užhorod, 1924); Dr. Julij Hadžega, *Dva istoričeskich voprosa*

208 NOTES TO PAGES 10-14

(Užhorod, 1928); G. Gerovskij, "Istoričeskoe prošloe prjaševščiny," in *Prjaševščina* (Prague, 1948), pp. 57-93; and Zerkal', *Nacional'ni i relihijni vidnosyny.*

3. Only after the second Hungarian occupation [1939] did [part of] Carpathian Rus' constitute the so-called Subcarpathian Territory headed by a regent commissioner. See V. Markus, "Carpatho-Ukraine under Hungarian Occupation (1939-1944)," *The Ukrainian Quarterly*, X, 3 (New York, 1954), pp. 252-256.

4. Hungary was divided into administrative units called *comitats* (counties), or, as they were called in Carpathian Rus', *župy*. The Carpatho-Rusyns lived in compact groups or were dispersed in the following counties (Rusyn names are in parentheses): Máramaros (Maramoroš), Ugocsa, (Ugoča), Bereg (Bereh), Szatmár (Sukmar), Szabolcs (Sabolč), Ung (Už), Zemplén (Zemplyn), Abaúj (Abovo-Novhorod), Borsod (Boršod'), Torna (Turnja), Gömör (Gemer), Sáros (Šaryš), and Szepes (Spiš).

5. Prešov is the Slovak form, which is in Rusyn—Prjašev; in Hungarian—Eperjes; in Latin—Fragopolis.

6. Oradea is the Romanian form, which is in Rusyn—Velykyj Varadyn; in Hungarian—Nagyvárad; in Latin—Magno-Varadinum.

7. Gherla is the Romanian form, which is in Hungarian—Számosújvár; in Latin—Armenopolis.

8. After the establishment of new national borders, in 1923 the Apostolic See created the so-called Miskolc exarchate out of 22 parishes belonging to the Mukačevo and Prešov eparchies. After the death of archbishop Antonij Papp in 1945, the Miskolc exarchate was placed under the jurisdiction of the bishop of Hajdúdorog.

1. The Beginnings of Religious Life

1. For example, the Przemyśl (Peremyšl') eparchy—see J. Pelesz, *Geschichte der Union der ruthenischen Kirche mit Rom,* Vol. II (Vienna, 1880), p. 110.

2. *Schematismus Cleri Graeci Ritus Catholicorum Dioecesis Munkácsensis ad A.D. 1908* (Užhorod, 1908), p. 19.

3. D. Bartolini, *Memorie storico-critiche dei SS. Cirillo e Metodio* (Rome, 1881), p. 153.

4. Aleksej Petrov, *Drevnejšija gramoty po istorii karpatorusskoj cerkvy i ierarchii 1391-1498 g.* (Prague, 1930), pp. 102-118 and 151-155.

5. Antal Hodinka, ed., *A munkácsi görög szertartású püspökség okmánytára* (Užhorod, 1911), p. 5. A. Baran, *Metropolia Kioviensis et Eparchia Mukačoviensis* (Rome, 1960), pp. 31-40, tries to prove that the Mukačevo eparchy was created by metropolitan Izydor of Kiev circa 1448, and that Ivan was its first bishop. He interprets the phrase "in accordance with ancient custom" in bishop Ivan's decree of nomination to mean "in accordance with the ancient custom of the Eastern Church," rather than as a reference to the existence of the Mukačevo eparchy. In contrast, I accept the traditional view that the beginnings of the Mukačevo eparchy should be dated to the very dawn of Christianity in Carpathian Rus' as indicated in the *Schematismus a. 1908,*

pp. 18-19: "The eparchy of Mukačevo . . . established *since immemorial times* was because of harsh times and its exposure to various misfortunes administered for several centuries only in a provisional way. This historical fact is deeply rooted in our hearts and will always remain as our inveterate and sacred tradition (*inveterata et sacra traditio semper permanebit apud nos*)."

6. Hodinka, *A munkácsi okmánytára*, pp. 12-13.

7. *Ibid.,* p.16.

8. See the article by O. Pricak, "Mukačiv—hnizdo rebeljantiv i kul'turnyj centr, " *Nova zorja* (Stanyslaviv), March 26, 1939, pp. 6-7; and April 2, 1939, p. 6, which also contains a comprehensive bibliography.

9. See the charter in Hodinka, *A munkácsi okmánytára,* pp. 12-13.

10. *Ibid.,* p. 16.

11. *Ibid.,* pp. 16-17.

12. *Ibid.,* pp. 17-18.

13. *Ibid.,* p. 20.

14. *Ibid.,* pp. 23-24.

15. Some historians refer to him as Vasylij III.

16. See documents of the trial of Zsigmond Rákóczi in Hodinka, *A munkácsi okmánytára,* pp. 30-42.

2. The Movement for Union with Rome

1. Péter Pázmány, S.J., was born in 1570 in Oradea into a Calvinist noble family. In 1584, he converted to Catholicism and joined the Jesuit order. After completing his studies in Rome, he became a professor of philosophy at Graz, but soon turned to missionary work among the Protestant aristocracy. In 1616, Pázmány became the archbishop of Esztergom and the primate of Hungary. He was elevated to the rank of cardinal in 1629 and died in 1637.

2. A. Baran, *Metropolia Kioviensis et Eparchia Mukačoviensis* (Rome, 1960), p. 52.

3. M. Lacko, *Unio Užhorodensis Ruthenorum Carpathicorum cum Ecclesia Catholica* (Rome, 1955), pp. 34-40.

4. "They resisted not only Protestantism, but also Roman Catholicism, regarding their rite the only treasured possession of a poor people." *Ibid.,* p. 34.

5. PP. Clemens VIII, "Benedictus sit Pastor," in A. Welykyj, *Documenta Pontificum Romanorum historiam Ucrainae illustrantia,* Vol. I (Rome, 1953), p. 258.

6. For the most part in Zemplén and Ung counties.

7. On November 25, 1613, bishop Siecziński reported to Rome about bishop Krupec'kyj's mission: "The Hungarian nobleman György of Humenné [!], who has converted from the heretical to the Catholic faith, motivated by the zeal of his Catholic belief and a desire to spread union among the Greek-rite populace in his counties, appealed to me in a letter to send the same Krupec'kyj to his domain in order to bring about union among his subjects. Several days ago, I did so." Cf. A. Theiner, *Vetera Monumenta Poloniae et Lithuaniae gentiumque finitimarum historiam illustrantia,* Vol. III (Rome,

1863), p. 357.

8. The origins of the Monastery of the Holy Spirit in Krásny Brod near Medzilaborce (Zemplén county) date to the fourteenth century. While still a Calvinist, count Drugeth in 1603 burned down the monastery, but after his conversion in 1605, he rebuilt both the monastery and its church. In 1706, during the uprising against the emperor led by Ferenc Rákóczi II, the monastery was plundered and then burned down together with its church. In 1729, the Basilian monks returned to Krásny Brod and rebuilt the monastery. In 1752, they erected a beautiful stone church and, in 1759, a stone monastery. During World War I, in 1915, the monastery and church were destroyed. On its ruins, the Basilians erected a small wooden chapel, which served as the site of pilgrimages every year at Pentecost. See M. Vavryk, *Po Vasylijans'kych Manastyrjach* (Toronto, 1958), pp. 249-251.

9. For this eyewitness account see Lacko, *Unio,* pp. 48-50.

10. Petronij is first mentioned as bishop of Mukačevo in documents from the summer of 1600. That same year, the Romanian voivode Mihail expelled him from Mukačevo and appointed the Romanian hieromonk Serhij (1600-1619, with intervals) to take his place. Bishop Petronij lived in exile among the Basilians in what was then Poland. There, he and his colleague in exile, the monk I. Hryhorovyč, first became acquainted with the pro-union ideas of Josyf V. Ruts'kyj and Josafat Kuncevyč. Owing to the intervention of metropolitan Ruts'kyj (through his relations with the Polish and Hungarian nobility), Petronij was re-installed as bishop of Mukačevo in 1623, but he died soon after in 1627. *Ibid.*, pp. 40-45, 53-54.

11. I. Duliškovič, *Istoričeskija čerty Ugro-Russkich,* Vol. II (Užhorod, 1875), pp. 83-85.

12. Although no documents have so far been found describing the relationship between the two, circumstances indicate that: (1) Hryhorovyč waited a whole year to be consecrated (he was nominated on January 12, 1627, but not ordained until December), most likely while establishing contacts with Ruts'kyj; (2) on Ruts'kyj's advice, Hryhorovyč wrote to patriarch Lucaris of Constantinople, just as bishop M. Smotryc'kyj had done before him; (3) the meeting between Ruts'kyj and Hryhorovyč would have had to be arranged in advance.

13. T. Haluščynskyj and A. Welykyj, eds., *Epistolae Josephi V. Rutskyj, metropolitae Kioviensis catholici (1613-1637)* (Rome, 1956), p. 207.

14. Patriarch Cyril Lucaris occupied the Constantinople see with several interruptions between 1612-1638. This letter was written at the time of his third term as patriarch (1623-1630).

15. See the copy of his letter, dated December 16, 1627, inserted in Ruts'kyj's letter. Cited in Lacko, *Unio,* pp. 196-197.

16. A. Hodinka, ed., *A munkácsi görög szertartású püspökség okmánytára* (Užhorod, 1911), p. 64.

17. Lacko, *Unio,* p. 57.

18. The signature of Krupec'kyj appears on a charter from king Mátyás Corvinus (reigned 1458-1490), which bishop Tarasovyč probably brought back with him. See A. Petrov, *Drevnejšija gramoty po istorii karpatorusskoj cerkvi*

i ierarchii, 1391-1498 gg. (Prague, 1930), p. 159n.

19. At the time, Tarasovyč administered only the central portion of the Mukačevo eparchy; the western portion was administered by bishop Krupec'kyj and the eastern part (the Máramaros region) was under the jurisdiction of bishop Dositej (1628-1637).

20. For documents relating to the imprisonment, charges, and release of Tarasovyč, see Hodinka, *A munkácsi okmánytár,* pp. 94-112.

21. The document containing the verdict has not been found, but the verdict can be reconstructed from the letter of emperor Ferdinand III, dated April 5, 1642, to prince György Rákóczi I. *Ibid.,* p. 133.

22. See the correspondence of the nuncio with Rome in this affair in Lacko, *Unio,* pp. 202-207.

23. See the emperor's charter in Hodinka, *A munkácsi okmánytára,* pp. 143-144.

24. See Jakusics's report in *ibid.,* pp. 137-138, 142.

25. See the charter of nomination of Jus'ko in *ibid.,* pp. 146-148.

26. Lacko, *Unio*, pp. 83-86.

27. A. Hodinka, *A munkácsi görög-katholikus püspökség története* (Budapest, 1909), p. 319.

28. There are some disparities in documents regarding the date of the Union of Užhorod. The accepted date is April 24, 1646—see Gy. Papp, "Az ungvári unió időpontja," *Keleti Egyház,* Nos. 7 and 8 (Miskolc, 1941), pp. 162-167 and 184-188.

29. For the text of the Union of Užhorod, see Lacko, *Unio,* pp. 97-105.

30. Hodinka, *A munkácsi okmánytára,* pp. 154-155.

31. C. Peterffy, *Sacra Concilia Ecclesiae Romano-Catholicae in Regno Hungariae Celebrata,* Vol. II (Vienna, 1742), pp. 382-383.

32. Hodinka, *A munkácsi okmánytára,* p. 158.

33. The certificate of chirotony is in *ibid.,* pp. 158-159.

34. Princess Zsuzsanna Lorántffy, a Calvinist, was the widow of prince György Rákóczi I. After the death of her husband, she governed the Mukačevo domain (1648-1660).

35. Joannykij Zejkan' (Orthodox bishop, 1651-1687) was of noble birth. A priest, he built a monastery on his family estate in Imstyčevo, after the death of his wife, and installed several monks there. He enjoyed the favor of the Protestant lords because of his opposition to the union. For more about him, see Duliškovič, *Istoričeskija čerty,* Vol. II, pp. 122-123; and A. Petruševyč, *Dopolnenie k Svodnoj halycko-russkoj lîtopysy s 1600 po 1700 h.* (L'viv, 1891), pp. 393-394.

36. By allowing an Orthodox metropolitan to consecrate him, bishop Partenij hoped to be permitted to occupy the Mukačevo see. After his return to Užhorod, however, he had to appeal for a lifting of censures and for confirmation from Rome. Rome confirmed him on June 8, 1655 through the intercession of the primate of Hungary, György Lippay. See the papal brief in Welykyj, *Documenta,* Vol. I, pp. 559-560.

37. For a description of an incident that allegedly decided the fate of bishop Partenij, see Basil Boysak, *The Fate of the Holy Union in Carpatho-Ukraine* (Toronto and New York, 1963), p. 51.

38. See excerpts from the Chronicle of the Jesuits for 1652 in Hodinka, *A munkácsi okmánytára*, pp. 167-168.

39. A. Welykyj, ed., *Acta S. Congregationis de Propaganda Fide Ecclesiam Catholicam Ucrainae et Bielarusjae spectantia*, Vol. I (Rome, 1953), pp. 239-240; A . Welykyj, ed., *Litterae S. Congregationis de Propaganda Fide Ecclesiam Catholicam Ucrainae et Bielarusjae spectantes*, Vol. I (Rome, 1954), pp. 203-204.

40. For the documents in this case see Lacko, *Unio*, pp. 209-215. Lacko gives an interesting explanation of Kosovyc'kyj's bi-ritualism, but the fact remains that both the bishop of Eger and Kosovyc'kyj disobeyed the orders of Rome. As late as 1665, bishop Suša complained in Rome that Kosovyc'kyj refused to return to the monastery and was continuing to celebrate liturgy in both rites. See Welykyj, *Acta*, Vol. I, p. 313, n. 14.

41. Welykyj, *Acta*, Vol. I, p. 303: "Si supplica di rimedio, acciò gli permettano di vivere conforme gli usi del loro rito."

42. The issue pertained not to calendar style, but to the observance of Roman Catholic rather than Greek Catholic holy days. This is a question of rite and discipline.

43. See the regulations for Greek Catholics issued in 1692 by the bishop of Eger in Hodinka, *A munkácsi okmánytára*, p. 333, nn. 1-2.

44. In a decree issued on August 23, 1692, emperor Leopold I did not insist on the celebration of Roman Catholic holy days, although he did require the observance of the new calendar. *Ibid.*, pp. 347-350.

45. For the letter of the Carpatho-Rusyn clergy to the Congregation and the pope see *ibid.*, pp. 651-659.

46. Welykyj, *Acta*, Vol. III, pp. 161-162.

47. Welykyj, *Litterae*, Vol. III, p. 124.

48. See letter from the Hungarian primate to the bishop of Eger, dated May 18, 1718, in Duliškovič, *Istoričeskija čerty*, Vol. III, p. 59. For the charges against bishop Bizancij lodged in Rome, see *ibid.*, pp. 59-61 and Welykyj, *Acta*, Vol. III, pp. 164-166.

49. The bishop of Eger once again made the observance of Roman Catholic holy days the key issue. See Welykyj, *Acta*, Vol. III, p. 167.

50. Welykyj, *Litterae*, Vol. III, pp. 127-128.

51. J. Basilovits, *Brevis Notitia Fundationis Theodori Koriathovits*, Vol. I, pt. 2 (Košice, 1799), pp. 152-153.

52. The question of the calendar and holy days in Carpathian Rus' was raised again in 1748 and in 1771. See V. Hadžega, "Dva najdavnîjšî našy pryvyleî," in *Naukovyj zbirnyk t-va 'Prosvita'*, VI (Užhorod, 1929), pp. 267-274. The forcible imposition by the Hungarians of the Gregorian calendar in Carpathian Rus' in 1916 will be discussed in Chapter 6 below.

53. For bishop Esterházy's denunciation of bishop Bradač to Rome see

Miscellanea Valachorum Graeci Ritus, Generalia, Vol. I, folia 48-50, APF, Rome.

54. On the latinization of the Byzantine rite, see M. Solovij, *De reforma tione liturgica H.Lisowskyj* (Rome, 1950); A. Raes, "Le rituel ruthène depuis l'Union de Brest," *Orientalia Christiana Periodica,* I (Rome, 1935), pp. 361-392; his "Le Liturgicon ruthène depuis l'Union de Brest," in *ibid.,* VIII (1942), pp. 95-143; and C. Korolevsky, "Liturgical Publications of the Congregation for the Eastern Church," *The Eastern Churches Quarterly,* V, 3 (London, 1945), pp. 87-96; and VI, 7 (1946), pp. 388-399.

55. W. Ploechl, "The Church Laws for Orientals of the Austrian Monarchy in the Age of the Enlightenment," *Bulletin of the Polish Institute of Arts and Sciences in America,* II, 3 (New York, 1944), p. 756.

56. See the letter of Maria Theresa to the pope, dated November 6, 1770, in *Archivum Nuntiaturae Vindobonensis,* Vol. 79, folia 204-205, ASV.

57. The Sacred Congregation declared that the Ruthenian united priests and clerics enjoy the same privileges, i.e., of canon, forum, immunity, and liberty, which Latin priests enjoy and possess. Welykyj, *Acta,* Vol. I, p. 20.

58. See I.M. Kondratovič, "Očerki iz istorii Mukačevskoj Eparchii," in *Karpatorusskij sbornik* (Užhorod, 1930), pp. 109-110. Bishop Ol'šavs'kyj actually left Černeča Hora only in 1766, when construction of the new monastery began there.

59. See O. Markov, "Materijaly dlja social'noj istorii Podkarpatskoj Rusi v XVIII vjeke," in *ibid.,* pp. 137-145; O. Mycjuk, *Narysy z socijal'no-hospodars'koji istoriji Pidkarpats'koji Rusy* (Prague, 1938), Vol. II, pp. 84-109; M. Lelekač, "Štolovi dochody hreko-katolyckych svjaščenykiv u buvšij Užhorods'kij župi," *Naukovyj zbornyk t-va 'Prosvita',* XII (Užhorod, 1937), pp. 138-140.

60. Hodinka, *A munkácsi okmánytára,* pp. 347-350.

61. See the decree in Duliškovič, *Istoričeskija čerty,* Vol. III, p. 161.

62. See the decree in Basilovits, *Brevis Notitia,* Vol. II, pt. 4 (1804), pp. 228-229.

63. For the proceedings and documents, see *ibid.,* Vol. II, pt. 6 (1805), pp. 21-53.

64. Andrella, who identified the union with the abuses of the bishop of Eger and the arbitrary conduct of the Catholic magnates, preached schism and attacked the Uniates. He left several polemical works subsequently published by A. Petrov, ed., *Duchovno-polemičeskija sočinenija jereja Michaila Orosvigovskago Andrelly protiv katoličestva i unii: texty* (Prague, 1932). See I. Pan'kevyč, "Mychail Orosveguvs'kyj čy Mychail Teodul?," *Naukovyj zbornyk t-va 'Prosvita',* IV (Užhorod, 1925), pp. 5-16; A. Hončarenko, "Plamennyj borec protiv Vatikana i Unii," *V sim'ji jedynij* (Užhorod, 1954), pp. 213-218; and V. L. Mykytas', *Ukrajins'kyj pys'mennyk-polemist Mychajlo Andrella* (Užhorod, 1960).

65. See acts of the synods in Mukačevo and Szatmár (Satu-Mare) in Hodinka, *A munkácsi okmánytára,* pp. 300-302; Ch. De Clercq, *Histoire des Conciles,* Vol. XI: *Conciles des orientaux, pt. 1* (Paris, 1949), pp. 94-96.

66. Sofronij, a native of Anatolia, had studied in Vienna where he converted to Catholicism. Failing to obtain the appointment as pastor of the St. Barbara Church in Vienna, he reverted to Orthodoxy and began to work against the union. An account of Sofronij's activities is given in A. Petrov, in 'Staraja vjera' i Unija v XVII-XVIII vv., Vol. I (St. Petersburg, 1906), pp. 26-72. For his biography, see N. Nilles, Symbolae ad illustrandam historiam Ecclesiae Orientalis in terris Coronae S. Stephani, Vol. II (Innsbruck, 1885), pp. 868-870.

67. On the granting of privileges to the Orthodox Serbs, see C. Korolevskyj, "Le droit austro-serbe," in Codificazione Canonica Orientale, Fonti (Vatican City, 1932), fasc. VIII, pp. 272-274; Ploechl, "Church Laws," pp. 718-722.

68. See their propaganda leaflet in Petrov, Staraja vjera, Vol. I, p. 31.

69. The Sermon on the Holy Union was published in Latin (1764) in Trnava; in German (1765) in Vienna; in Church Slavonic (1769) in Počajiv under the title, Slovo o svjatom meždu Vostočnoju i Zapadnoju Cerkovju sojedynenii; and in Hungarian (1780) in Pest. On the basis of Olšavs'kyj's sermon, the Reverend I. Lub published his Unijni propovidi (Stanyslaviv, 1938). More recently, the sermon in Latin was reprinted in Basil Boysak, Ecumenism and Manuel Michael Olshavsky, Bishop of Mukachevo (1743-1767) (Montreal, 1967), pp. 203-228.

3. The Canonical Erection of the Mukačevo Eparchy

1. This chapter is a resumé of the author's earlier work on the canonical erection of the Mukačevo eparchy. B. Pekar, De erectione canonica eparchiae Mukačoviensis an. 1771 (Rome, 1956).

2. "The unfortunate jealousy of the Latin rite episcopate and nobility restricted there [in Hungary] as in Poland every attempt by the Rusyn clergy to obtain an independent status that would be worthy of its church." A. Theiner, Histoire du pontificat de Clément XIV, pt. 1 (Paris, 1852), p. 411.

3. Some authors, citing Petrov's earlier work, O podložnosti gramoty kn. F. Korjatoviča 1360 g. (St. Petersburg, 1906), deny that prince Korjatovyč founded the monastery of St. Nicholas. However, upon reconsidering his own earlier work, Petrov later concluded in his Drevnješija gramoty po istorii karpatorusskoj cerkvi i ierarchii 1391-1498 gg. (Prague, 1930), p. 201, that "in repudiating the authenticity of Korjatovyč's charter of 1360, we had no intention of denying the local tradition that prince Korjatovyč . . . had either founded the Orthodox monastery of St. Nicholas on Černeča Hora near Mukačevo, or, at least, had greatly contributed to the material security of the monastery founded there earlier by someone else."

4. Antal Hodinka, ed., A munkácsi görög szertartásu püspökség okmánytára (Užhorod, 1911), pp. 53-54.

5. Ibid., pp. 146-148.

6. For the right of patronage of the Hungarian kings over the Carpatho-Rusyns, see A. Bobák, De jure patronatus supremi quoad Ecclesiam Ruthenicam in Hungaria (Rome, 1943).

7. Hodinka, A munkácsi okmánytára, p. 164.

8. After Zejkan' was ousted from Mukačevo in 1664 by Zsófia Báthory, he settled first in the Imstyčevo monastery and later at the monastery in Uhlja in the Máramaros region.

9. Hodinka, *A munkácsi okmánytára,* pp. 159-160.

10. *Ibid.,* pp. 160-161.

11. A. Welykyj, ed., *Acta S. Congregationis de Propaganda Fide Ecclesiam Catholicam Ucrainae et Bielarusjae spectantia,* Vol. I (Rome, 1953), p. 248.

12. *Ibid.,* p. 249.

13. "Se il luogo di Munkach goda già effettivamente il titolo di vescovato, benchè di Rito Ruteno." See M. Lacko, *Unio Užhorodensis Ruthenorum Carpathicorum cum Ecclesia Catholica* (Rome, 1955), p. 221.

14. Hodinka, *A munkácsi okmánytára,* pp. 168-174.

15. A. Welykyj, ed., *Documenta Pontificum Romanorum historiam Ucrainae illustrantia,* Vol. I (Rome, 1953), pp. 559-560.

16. The so-called "titulus in partibus," which is bestowed on titular bishops who do not have their own eparchy.

17. Hodinka, *A munkácsi okmánytára,* pp. 179-181.

18. *Ibid.,* pp. 186-188.

19. See the letter of the Reverend S. Milley, S.J., the confessor of princess Zsófia Báthory, dated October 3, 1662, regarding the new bishop, in Lacko, *Unio,* pp. 234-237.

20. For a detailed study of this period, see J. Praszko, *De Ecclesia Ruthena Catholica sede Metropolitana vacante 1655-1665* (Rome, 1944).

21. See Szelepcsényi's report to the papal nuncio in Vienna in Hodinka, *A munkácsi okmánytára,* pp. 213-216.

22. She had reverted to Catholicism in 1660.

23. Welykyj, *Acta,* Vol. I, pp. 327-328; *Scritture riferite nelle Congregazioni Particolari,* Vol. 20, f. 208-216; Vol. 21, f. 35-41, APF, Rome.

24. A. Baran, "Quaedam ad biographiam J. Vološynovskyj, Ep-pi Mukačoviensis," *Analecta OSBM,* II, 1-2 (Rome, 1954), pp. 209-227.

25. Welykyj, *Documenta,* Vol. I, pp. 657-659. For a detailed study on de Camillis, see A. Pekar, "Tribute to Bishop Joseph J. de Camillis, OSBM," *Analecta OSBM,* XII, 1-4 (Rome, 1985), pp. 374-418.

26. Hodinka, *A munkácsi okmánytára,* pp. 296-297.

27. *Archivum Nuntiaturae Vindobonensis,* Vol. 79, f. 57b-58b, ASV; Hodinka, *A munkácsi okmánytára,* pp. 319-321.

28. See de Camillis's response, dated March 15, 1692, in Hodinka, *A munkácsi okmánytára,* pp. 334-337.

29. S. Tomašivs'kyj, *Uhorščyna i Pol'šča na počatku XVIII vika* (L'viv, 1909), pp. 139-149.

30. Welykyj, *Acta,* Vol. II, p. 195.

31. Hodinka, *A munkácsi okmánytára,* pp. 464-465.

32. *Ibid.,* pp. 469-470.

33. *Ibid.,* pp. 470-471.

34. *Ibid.,* p. 472.

35. The monk Petronij P. Kamins'kyj was an opportunist who played a very deplorable role in the history of the Church in Carpathian Rus'. He regularly crossed over from Galicia to Carpathian Rus' and back again, conducting himself disgracefully wherever he went. He helped prince Ferenc Rákóczi II oust bishop de Camillis from Mukačevo and in return was named bishop by the prince in 1707. Rome never confirmed his appointment and he died in 1710 (in course of Rákóczi's rebellion) in Mukačevo without having been consecrated bishop. He administered the eparchy as its vicar. See Hodinka, *A munkácsi okmánytára,* pp. 472-483, 517.

36. Welykyj, *Acta,* Vol. II, p. 214; and A. Welykyj, ed., *Litterae S. Congregationis de Propaganda Fide Ecclesiam Catholicam Ukrainae et Bielarusjae spectantes,* Vol. II (Rome, 195), pp. 260-261.

37. Welykyj, *Documenta,* Vol. II, p. 9.

38. Hodinka, *A munkácsi okmánytára,* pp. 479-480.

39. During the 10 years that the episcopate remained vacant (1706-1716), the Orthodox bishop J. Stojka ordained some 50 priests for the Mukáčevo eparchy.

40. Welykyj, *Acta,* Vol. II, pp. 219-221; and *Litterae,* Vol. II, pp. 262-263.

41. Hodinka, *A munkácsi okmánytára,* pp. 480-482.

42. *Ibid.,* pp. 483-484.

43. *Ibid.,* pp. 487-488.

44. *Ibid.,* pp. 489.

45. L. Von Pastor, *The History of the Popes,* Vol. XXXII (St. Louis, Mo., 1940), pp. 659-683; C. Artaud de Montor, *The Lives and Times of the Popes,* Vol. VI (New York, 1911), pp. 198-199.

46. Rákóczi's rebels dominated the imperial troops until the end of 1708, when the tide turned and the rising began to disintergrate.

47. Welykyj, *Acta,* Vol. II, p. 232; Hodinka, *A munkácsi okmánytára,* p. 496.

48. Hodinka, *A munkácsi okmánytára,* pp. 499, 517.

49. Welykyj, *Acta,* Vol. II, pp. 224-227.

50. Ivan Duliškovič, *Istoričeskija čerty ugro-russkich,* Vol. III (Užhorod, 1877), p. 33.

51. Hodinka, *A munkácsi okmánytára,* p. 489.

52. *Ibid.,* pp. 503-504, 508, 510-511.

53. Welykyj, *Documenta,* Vol. II, pp. 18-19.

54. Hodinka, *A munkácsi okmánytára,* pp. 540-543.

55. *Ibid.,* p. 541.

56. *Ibid.,* pp. 543-545. The Hungarians considered a Ukrainian from Galicia a "foreigner."

57. Welykyj, *Litterae,* Vol. III, pp. 27-28.

58. Hodermars'kyj had to defend himself against slander and denunciation on several occasions. His letters to the emperor and to the Hungarian primate are his best defense. See Hodinka, *A munkácsi okmánytára*, pp. 528-532. Additional documents in the case of Hodermars'kyj were published by M. Lacko, "Ad Dipolmatarium eparchiae Mukačevensis A. Hodinka supplementa vindobonensia," *Orientalia Christiana Periodica*, XXIII, 3-4 (Rome, 1957), pp. 332-353.

59. Hodinka, *A munkácsi okmánytára*, pp. 543-545.

60. Welykyj, *Acta,* Vol. III, p. 23-26; and Welykyj, *Litterae*, Vol. III, p. 40.

61. Joannicius Basilovits, *Brevis notitia Fundationis Theodori Koriathovits,* Vol. I, pt. 2 (Košice, 1799), pp. 130-136; Hodinka, *A munkácsi okmánytára*, pp. 563-565.

62. Even Hodinka, a sympathizer of Rákóczi, admits that Hodermars'kyj "loved his faith, his rite, defended the clergy's right to elect their own bishops and therefore commanded the loyalty of the priests." Antal Hodinka, *A munkácsi görög-katholikus püspökség története* (Budapest, 1909), p. 432.

63. Welykyj, *Acta,* Vol. III, pp. 41, 92-93.

64. Hodinka, *A munkácsi okmánytára*, pp. 416-417.

65. *Ibid.,* pp. 463-464.

66. *Ibid.,* p. 507.

67. See charter, dated September 20, 1710, in *ibid.,* p. 535.

68. See Bizancij's letter, dated August 15, 1711, in *ibid.,* pp. 553-554.

69. *Ibid.,* p. 565.

70. *Ibid.,* pp. 586-590.

71. *Ibid.,* pp. 597-598.

72. See Hodermars'kyj's letter and Bizancij's reply in *ibid.,* pp. 631-634.

73. See the primate's letter to the clergy in *ibid.,* pp. 645-646.

74. See letter from the clergy to the pope and the Congregation for the Propagation of the Faith in *ibid.,* pp. 651-659.

75. Welykyj, *Acta,* Vol. III, pp. 127-130; and *Litterae*, Vol. III, pp. 109-110.

76. See Bizancij's oath in Duliškovič, *Istoričeskija čerty*, Vol. III, p. 47, n. 2.

77. See the letter from the bishop of Eger to the monks and clergy in *ibid.,* pp. 44-45.

78. *Archivum Nuntiaturae Vindobonensis*, Vol. 79, f. 65a-b, ASV; Basilovits, *Brevis notitia*, Vol. I, pt. 2, p. 137.

79. Welykyj, *Acta,* Vol. III, p. 141; *Acta S. Congregationis de Propaganda Fide,* Vol. 86, f. 27a, APF, Rome.

80. Welykyj, *Acta,* Vol. III, p. 143.

81. Welykyj, *Documenta,* Vol. II, p. 33.

82. *Scritture originali riferite nelle Congregazioni Generali,* Vol. 610, f. 567a-b, APF, Rome.

83. Hodinka, *A munkácsi okmánytára*, pp. 268-273.

84. *Ibid.*, pp. 296-297.

85. Welykyj, *Documenta*, Vol. I, pp. 658-659.

86. *Archivum Nuntiaturae Vindobonensis*, Vol. 79, f. 64a-b, ASV.

87. Welykyj, *Documenta*, Vol. II, p. 19.

88. *Archivum Nuntiaturae Vindobonensis*, Vol. 79, f. 64b-65a, ASV. Bizancij later admitted that he had had to oppose Hodermars'kyj "on the orders of the late bishop of Eger," see Hodinka, *A munkácsi okmánytára*, p. 626.

89. Welykyj, *Documenta*, Vol. II, p. 33.

90. *Archivum Nuntiaturae Vindobonensis*, Vol. 79, f. 65a-66b, 69a-70a; and *Acta S. Congregationis Consistorialis a. 1771*, 20 Marzo, no. 29, ASV.

91. See Bizancij's letter to the Congregation in Welykyj, *Acta*, Vol. III, p. 161.

92. *Ibid.*, p. 162.

93. *Archivum Nuntiaturae Vindobonensis*, Vol. 79, f. 72b, ASV; Welykyj, *Acta*, Vol. III, pp. 164-167.

94. *Archivum Nuntiaturae Vindobonensis*, Vol. 79, f. 72b-73b, ASV; *Scritture riferite nei Congressi-Greci di Croazia, Dalmazia, Schiavonia, Transilvania ed Ungheria*, Vol. II, f. 12a-13a, APF.

95. In a charter dated November 8, 1716, the emperor had also placed Bizancij under the jurisdiction of the bishop of Eger. See Duliškovič, *Istoričeskija čerty*, Vol. III, pp. 49-51.

96. Welykyj, *Acta*, Vol. III, p. 173.

97. The attitudes of Hodermars'kyj and Bizancij toward the bishop of Eger underwent changes. Hodermars'kyj had been a supporter of the emperor and his candidate, as a result of which the bishop of Eger supported Bizancij, a sympathizer of Rákóczi. However, when Bizancij became aware of the Eger prelate's determination to take complete control of the Mukačevo eparchy, he used the opportunity of his episcopal ordination by the Kiev metropolitan Lev Kiška to make an attempt to place the Mukačevo eparchy under the jurisdiction of the Kiev metropolitanate. Hodermars'kyj took advantage of this to "get even" with Bizancij and began to inform the bishop of Eger about everything. Without investigating Hodermars'kyj's charges, the Eger ordinary accused Bizancij in Rome of "abusing his authority," thereby attempting to justify his own interference in the affairs of the Mukačevo eparchy. In this manner, he extended his control over Bizancij. See Duliškovič, *Istoričeskija čerty*, Vol. III, pp. 51-63; A. Baran, *Metropolia Kioviensis et Eparchia Mukačoviensis* (Rome, 1960), pp. 235-240.

98. For a detailed discussion of this dependence, see Hodinka, *A munkácsi története*, pp. 582-596; K. Žatkovič, *Jagerskoje vlijanije i bor'ba protiv toho v istoriji Mukačevskoj diocezii* (Homestead, Pa., n.d.).

99. Duliškovič, *Istoričeskija čerty*, Vol. III, pp. 129-130.

100. Basilovits, *Brevis notitia*, Vol. I, pt. 3, pp. 6-8.

101. Welykyj, *Documenta*, Vol. II, pp. 85-86.

102. A subsequent example of this goal was the so-called Hungarian Haj-dúdorog Greek Catholic eparchy, established in 1912 as a result of magyarization. For details, see below, Chapter 6.

103. *Archivum Nuntiaturae Vindobonensis,* Vol. 79, f. 18b, ASV.

104. Like Hodinka, Irinej Kondratovič, "Očerki iz istorii mukačevskoj eparchii," *Karpatorusskij sbornik* (Užhorod, 1930), pp. 101-102, is incorrect in giving as the reason for Ol'šavs'kyj's visit to Eger in 1747 "the complaints of the Mukačevo Basilians." Earlier, Bazylovyč had clearly stated that the misunderstanding arose because of "the stole fees to the clergy." Basilovits, *Brevis notitia,* Vol. II, pt. 4, *Archivum Nuntiaturae Vindobonensis,* Vol. 79, f. 86a-87b, ASV.

105. Ol'šavs'kyj protested against taking the oath because it was unlawful. Nevertheless, he was eventually compelled to do so. *Archivum Nuntiaturae Vindobonensis,* Vol. 79, f. 13a, 85a-b, ASV.

106. *Ibid.,* f. 87b.

107. For an account of the visitation see Duliškovič, *Istoričeskija čerty,* Vol. III, pp. 137-149.

108. See the letter to pope, dated February 6, 1749, in *ibid.,* Vol. III, pp. 151-152.

109. *Ibid.,* Vol. III, pp. 152-153.

110. Bárkóczy charged Ol'šavs'kyj with the following: (1) that the priests were uneducated; (2) that they were preaching false teachings; (3) that they used "strange ceremonies" (his "understanding" of the Eastern rite); (4) that there were abuses in the administration of the Sacraments; (5) that Latin holy days were not being observed, and so forth. *Archivum Nuntiaturae Vindobonensis,* Vol. 79, f. 89a-b, ASV.

111. The reports of Ol'šavs'kyj served as the basis for V. Hadžega's "Dodatky k ystoriy rusynov i rus'kych cerkvej v Maramoroší," *Naukovyj zbôrnyk tovarystva 'Prosvita',* I (Užhorod, 1922), pp. 140-266; "Dodatky k ystoriî . . . v Užanskoj župi," *ibid.,* II (Užhorod, 1923), pp. 1-64; *ibid.,* III (1924), pp. 155-239; "Dodatky k ystoryî . . . v župî Ugoča," *ibid.,* IV (1925), pp. 117-176; V (1927), pp. 1-62; and "Dodatky k ystoryî . . . v buvšij župî Zemplynskôj," *ibid.,* VII-VIII (1931), pp. 1-167; IX (1932), pp. 1-67; X (1934), pp. 17-120; XI (1935), pp. 17-182; XII (1937), pp. 37-83.

112. Thus, for example, the Roman Catholic parish priest in Korytnjany refused to allow a Carpatho-Rusyn priest to hear confessions, while in the village of Onokovci the Roman Catholic pastor did not allow the Rusyns to ring church bells, etc. See Hadžega, "Dodatky . . . v Užanskoj župî," pp. 60, 64.

113. Hodinka, *A munkácsi története,* p. 603.

114. At the Viennese court, Ol'šav'skyj gave a clear exposition of the rights of an apostolic vicar and declared his independence. *Ibid.,* p. 605.

115. *Ibid.,* p. 605.

116. See Bárkóczy's letter, dated September 20, 1763, in *Archivum Nuntiaturae Vindobonensis,* Vol. 79, f. 95a, 96b, ASV.

117. E. Winter, "Die Kämpfe der Ukrainer Oberungarns um eine nationale

Hierarchie im Theresianischen Zeitalter," *Kyrios,* IV, 2 (Königsberg, 1939-40), pp. 129-141.

118. *Archivum Nuntiaturae Vindobonensis,* ASV; Basilovits, *Brevis notitia,* Vol. II, pt. 4, pp. 32-33.

119. Cited in A. Petrov, *'Staraja vjera' i unija v XVII-XVIII vv.,* Vol. II (St. Petersburg, 1905), pp. 79-80.

120. Earlier, Ol'šavs'kyj had written to Maria Theresa: "Subordination to the Latin bishop and dependence on him is one of the principal obstacles to spreading and maintaining the Holy Union." See Basilovits, *Brevis notitia,* Vol. II, pt. 4, p. 41.

121. Duliškovič, *Istoričeskija čerty,* Vol. III, p. 174.

122. For a complete account of the correspondence between Ol'šavs'kyj, Esterházy, and the Austrian imperial court, see B. Pekar, *De erectione canonica eparchiae Mukačoviensis* (Rome, 1956), pp. 62-69. Cf. J. Fiedler, "Beiträge zur Geschichte der Union der Ruthenen in Nord-Ungarn und der Immunität des Clerus derselben," in *Sitzungsberichte der kaiserlichen Akademie der Wissenschaften: Philosophisch-historische Classe,* XXXIX, 4 (Vienna, 1862), pp. 481-524.

123. See the pope's letter to Maria Theresa, dated June 11, 1766; R. de Martinis, *Iuris Pontificii de Propaganda Fide,* Vol. IV, pt. 1 (Rome, 1892), p. 154.

124. See the nuncio's letter to the Vatican's secretary of state, dated June 26, 1766, in *Archivum Nuntiaturae Vindobonensis,* Vol. 381, f. 443, ASV.

125. See the nuncio's letter, dated October 11, 1766, in *ibid.,* Vol. 172, f. 218.

126. See the letter to the nuncio, dated December 6, 1766, in *ibid.,* Vol. 85, f. 192a.

127. Esterházy makes mention of his procurator Merenda in a letter to the pope, dated August 8, 1770. See *Archivum Nuntiaturae Germaniae,* Vol. 723, no pagination, ASV.

128. See nuncio Visconti's letter to the secretary of state, dated December 13, 1766. *Archivum Nuntiaturae Vindobonensis,* Vol. 85, f. 196-197, ASV.

129. Esterházy sent his long report, consisting of 113 points, to Rome on March 31, 1767. It was published in Eger in 1770 under the title, *Opinio de episcopatu G.R. Munkácsiensi non erigendo,* a copy of which is in *Archivum Nuntiaturae Vindobonensis,* Vol. 79, f. 39a-52b, ASV.

130. See the secretary of state, cardinal Torrigiani's memorandum to papal nuncio Visconti in *ibid.,* Vol. 86, f. 227a-228b.

131. Welykyj, *Documenta,* Vol. II, pp. 195-196; Basilovits, *Brevis notitia,* Vol. II, pt. 4, pp. 125-127; De Martinis, *Iuris Pontificii,* pp. 154-155.

132. See Esterházy's letter to the papal nuncio, dated December 16, 1767, in *Archivum Nuntiaturae Vindobonensis,* Vol. 79, f. 160b-161a, ASV.

133. Welykyj, *Documenta,* Vol. II, pp. 196-197.

134. See pope's letter to Maria Theresa dated April 21, 1768, "Promemoria," in *Archivum Nuntiaturae Vindobonensis,* Vol. 79, f. 170, ASV.

135. See a description of baron Nenni's audience with the secretary of state

on April 2, 1768, in *ibid.,* Vol. 87, f. 87a-88a.

136. For cardinal Albani's appeal, see *ibid.,* Vol. 87, f. 104a-105a; "Motiva reintegrationis Episcopatus Munkacsiensis," *ibid.,* Vol. 79, f. 113a-120b; and Basilovits, *Brevis notitia,* Vol. II, pt. 4, pp. 44-75.

137. It is clear that the pope did not take into account either Nenni's "Memorandum" or Albani's "Motives." See *Archivum Nuntiaturae Germaniae,* Vol. 392, f. 46b-47a; Vol. 642, f. 247-248, ASV.

138. See the letter from imperial council to the papal nuncio, dated June 6, 1678, in *Archivum Nuntiaturae Vindobonensis,* Vol. 79, f. 179-180, ASV.

139. See the nuncio's letters, dated June 11 and August 20, in *Archivum Nuntiaturae Germaniae,* Vol. 392, f. 90a-b, 459a, ASV.

140. Welykyj, *Documenta,* Vol. II, pp. 198-200.

141. See report of count F. Blümegen in *Archivum Nuntiaturae Germaniae,* Vol. 387, f. 1036, ASV; and the description of nuncio's audience with Maria Theresa on August 27, 1768, in *ibid.,* Vol. 382, f. 461a-b.

142. See the letter from the papal secretary of state to the papal nuncio in Vienna, dated October 1, 1768, in *Archivum Nuntiaturae Vindobonensis,* Vol. 87, f. 238a, ASV.

143. See the nuncio's letter, dated June 21, 1766, to the secretary of state: "Patriotism always plays an important role for the Hungarians; it enters into all their affairs." *Archivum Nuntiaturae Germaniae,* Vol. 381, f. 441a, ASV. Bishop Bradač studied at the Jesuit College in Trnava, where he completed his philosophical and theological studies with honors.

144. See the instructions to Esterházy in *ibid.,* Vol. 388, f. 241a-242b; and for Bradač in *Archivum Nuntiaturae Vindobonensis,* Vol. 79, f. 188a-b, ASV. Maria Theresa asked the papal nuncio to order bishop Esterházy to treat the Carpatho-Rusyns "humanely" and not to provoke them. *Archivum Nuntiaturae Germaniae,* Vol. 382, f. 461a-b, ASV.

145. At that time, archdeacons substituted for canons. The Mukačevo chapter of canons was not established until 1776.

146. Bradač's visit to Eger was described by vicar-general A. Bačyns'kyj in his "Diary," which survived in the Užhorod eparchial archive. The description was published by Duliškovič, *Istoričeskija čerty,* Vol. III, pp. 194-211. The nuncio had been informed earlier that bishop Esterházy "under the pretext of religion . . . conceals strong ambitions and an unrestrained desire to dominate and hold the Greek Catholics under his yoke." *Archivum Nuntiaturae Germaniae,* Vol. 387, f. 119a-b, ASV. Chancellor W. A. von Kaunitz reported to the nuncio: "The harsh and despotic treatment of the Greek Catholics by the Latin bishop constantly and strongly provokes them!" When the nuncio asked if Kaunitz meant bishop Esterházy when he used the phrase "Latin bishop," the chancellor replied: "I did not wish to use the name of the bishop of Eger in order not to compromise him." *Ibid.,* Vol. 392, f. 272b-273a. Maria Theresa wrote to the nuncio: "Personally I am not of a bad opinion about the bishop of Eger . . . What I condemn in him is his unyielding, difficult, and domineering character, which is causing the Greek Catholics to be increasingly repelled by him!" *Ibid.,* Vol. 387, f. 102.

147. See Bradač's Memorandum in Basilovits, *Brevis notitia,* Vol. II, pt. 4,

pp. 131-142.

148. See her letter, dated May 12, 1770, in *Archivum Nuntiaturae Vindobonensis,* Vol. 79, f. 195, ASV; and in V. Fraknói, *Oklevéltár a magyar királyi kegyuri jog történetéhez* (Budapest, 1899), p. 491.

149. See the nuncio's letter to the secretary of state, dated June 9, 1770, in *Archivum Nuntiaturae Germaniae,* Vol. 384, f. 316a-b, ASV.

150. Duliškovič, *Istoričeskija čerty,* Vol. III, p. 214, erroneously places Bradač's visit in September. The papal nuncio informed Rome of bishop Bradač's visit already on July 21, 1770. See *Archivum Nuntiaturae Germaniae,* Vol. 384, f. 353-354, ASV.

151. The reconciliation between the two bishops in the imperial court office on August 4, 1770 is described by the papal nuncio. See *Archivum Nuntiaturae Vindobonensis,* Vol. 79, f. 29a-30b, ASV.

152. See Esterházy's letter to the pope, dated August 8, 1770, in *Archivum Nuntiaturae Germaniae,* Vol. 723, n. pag, ASV. For the pope's reply to Esterházy, see Welykyj, *Documenta,* Vol. II, p. 211.

153. See the nuncio's letter to the papal secretary of state, dated September 1, 1770, in *Archivum Nuntiaturae Germaniae,* Vol. 387, f. 101-102, 106b, ASV.

154. A. Theiner, *Clementis XIV Epistulae et Brevia selectioria* (Paris, 1852), pp. 115-118; Welykyj, *Documenta,* Vol. II, pp. 208-210.

155. Maria Theresa's letter to the pope, dated November 6, 1770, in *Archivum Nuntiaturae Germaniae,* Vol. 387, f. 120, ASV.

156. Fraknói, *Oklevéltár,* pp. 348-350; *Archivum Nuntiaturae Vindobonensis,* Vol. 89, f. 246-247, ASV.

157. See the papal briefs, dated November 17 (at the insistence of the nuncio) and November 24, 1770 (in response to Maria Theresa), in Basilovits, *Brevis notitia,* Vol. II, pt. 4, pp. 196-197; Welykyj, *Documenta,* Vol. II, pp. 211-213.

158. *Archivum Nuntiaturae Vindobonensis,* Vol. 90, f. 54-55, ASV.

159. See "Reflexiones Curiae Imperialis," in *ibid.,* Vol. 79, f. 226a-b, 229a; and *Archivum Nuntiaturae Germaniae,* Vol. 654-5, f. 131a-b, ASV.

160. *Acta Congregationis Consistorialis, d. 20. VII. 1771,* n. pag., ASV; *Scritture riferite nei Congressi: Greci de Croazia etc.,* Vol. II, f. 351-353, APF.

161. On the case of Bradač's "heresy," see Theiner, *Histoire,* pt. 2, pp. 19-23; Pekar, *De erectione,* pp. 110-115; and A. Pekar, "Bishop John Bradač, the Last Basilian in the Mukačevo See," *Orientalia Christiana Periodica,* XLIV (Rome, 1983), pp. 130-152.

162. Subsequently, bishop A. Bačyns'kyj was released from the obligation of making an annual profession of faith on April 9, 1777. See Basilovits, *Brevis notitia,* Vol. II, pt. 4, pp. 206-207.

163. The Apostolic See attempted to incorporate the Mukačevo eparchy into the Galician metropolitanate on two occasions: in 1774 (see Pelesz, *Geschichte,* Vol. II, pp. 655-675 passim); and in 1888 (see E. Winter, *Vizantija ta Rym u borot'bi za Ukrajinu* [Prague, 1944], p. 178). Both attempts ended in failure.

164. Officially, the Apostolic See moved the seat of the Mukačevo eparchy to Užhorod only on July 24, 1817. See V. Hadžega, "Papska bulla o pereloženju osîdka Mukačîvs'koî eparchiî," *Naukovyj zbornyk t-va 'Prosvita'*, XI (Užhorod, 1935), pp. 1-7. For the text of the bull of Pope Pius VII, see Welykyj, *Documenta*, Vol. II, pp. 326-327.

165. The ancient Benedictine abbey in Tapolcza (Borsod county) had been in the hands of secular clergy since the fifteenth century. Along with the monastery's possessions, the bishop of Mukačevo was granted the title of archimandrite. The solemn installation of Bačyns'kyj as archimandrite took place on October 23, 1776. A detailed history of the abbey is found in M. Beszkid, *A sz. Péter és sz. Pál Apostolokról Tapolcai apátság története* (Užhorod, 1903).

166. Basilovits, *Brevis notitia*, Vol. II, pt. 5, pp. 1-32.

167. O. Baran, *Jepyskop A. Bačyns'kyj i cerkovne vidrodžennja na Zakarpatti* (Yorkton, Sask., 1963).

4. The Fate of the Máramaros Eparchy

1. See the charter in A. Petrov, *Drevnjejšija gramoty po istorii karpatorusskoj cerkvi i ierarchii, 1391-1498 gg.* (Prague, 1930), pp. 102-114, 126-128, 151-155.

2. *Ibid.*, pp. 171-173.

3. *Ibid.*, pp. 131-133, 174-175.

4. Antal Hodinka, ed., *A munkácsi görög szertartásu püspökség okmánytára* (Užhorod, 1911), pp. 12-13.

5. *Ibid.*, p. 16.

6. *Ibid.*, pp. 53-54.

7. *Ibid.*, pp. 57-60.

8. In Hungarian: Gyulafehérvár; in Rusyn: Bilhorod.

9. Hodinka, *A munkácsi okmánytára*, pp. 63-65.

10. See the founding charter of the Imstyčevo monastery in Joannicius Basilovits, *Brevis notitia Fundationis Theodori Koriathovits*, Vol. II, pt. 6 (Košice, 1805), appendix 2.

11. See Ivan Duliškovič, *Istoričeskija čerty ugro-russkich*, Vol. III (Užhorod, 1877), pp. 3-4; Hodinka, *A munkácsi okmánytára*, pp. 297-298; *Scritture riferite nei Congressi Greci di Croazia*, etc., Vol. I, f. 117b, APF.

12. Hodinka, *A munkácsi okmánytára*, p. 383.

13. *Ibid.*, p. 346.

14. For the legislation of Leopold I on clerical privileges, see W. Ploechl, "The Church Laws for Orientals of the Austrian Monarchy in the Age of Enlightenment," in *Bulletin of the Polish Institute of Arts and Sciences in America*, II, 3 (New York, 1944), pp. 718-730.

15. On the investigation against bishop Stojka, see Hodinka, *A munkácsi okmánytára*, pp. 425-463.

16. See the report of the apostolic administrator Fylypovyč in *ibid.*, pp. 565-566.

17. See bishop de Camillis's letter, dated April 7, 1691, in *Keleti egyház,*

VII, 5 (Miskolc, 1941), pp. 113-114.

18. See the papal nuncio's letter, dated October 3, 1711, in Hodinka, *A munkácsi okmánytára*, pp. 563-564.

19. A. Welykyj, ed., *Acta S. Congregationes de Propaganda Fide Ecclesiam Catholicam Ucrainae et Bielarusjae spectantia*, Vol. III (Rome, 1954), pp. 46-47.

20. The Orthodox bishop of Máramaros, Serafim Petrovan, was then on trial and the eparchy was governed by its administrator Ivan Mojsenij. On Petrovan's work see A. Baran, *Eparchia Maramorošiensis eiusque unio* (Rome, 1962), pp. 39-56.

21. See the emperor's decree in S. Cziple, *A máramarosi püspökség kérdése* (Budapest, n.d.), pp. 125-126.

22. See Duliškovič, *Istoričeskija čerty*, Vol. III, pp. 62-63. Bishop Bizancij's campaign in favor of the union was supported by the Apostolic See. See Welykyj, *Acta*, Vol. III, pp. 199-200; and A. Welykyj, ed., *Litterae S. Congregationis de Propaganda Fide Ecclesiam Catholicam Ucrainae et Bielarusjae spectantes*, Vol. III (Rome, 1956), pp. 210-211.

23. See the complaint from the Romanian synod of 1728 in N. Nilles, *Symbolae ad illustrandam historiam Ecclesiae Orientalis in terris Coronae S. Stephani*, Vol. I (Innsbruck, 1885), p. 494. Bishop Bizancij also lodged complaints against Teodorovyč on several occasions; see Duliškovič, *Istoričeskija čerty*, Vol. III, pp. 77-78. Bishop Ol'šavs'kyj complained in 1733; see *Archivum Nuntiaturae Vindobonensis*, Vol. 79, f. 80b, ASV.

24. Duliškovič, *Istoričeskija čerty*, Vol. III, pp. 61-62, note.

25. See bishop Bizancij's letter, dated January 30, 1722, in *ibid.*, p. 63, note.

26. Welykyj, *Acta*, Vol. III, pp. 228-229; and Welykyj, *Litterae*, Vol. III, pp. 267-268.

27. See his letter in *Scritture riferite nei Congressi Greci di Croazia* etc., Vol. I, f. 193a-194b, APF.

28. *Ibid.*, f. 195a-b.

29. Welykyj, *Acta*, Vol. III, p. 242.

30. *Ibid.*, pp. 254-258; and Welykyj, *Litterae*, Vol. IV, p. 18.

31. See Duliškovič, *Istoričeskija čerty*, Vol. III, pp. 103-104; *Scritture riferite nei Congressi Greci di Croazia* etc., Vol. I, f. 214-215, APF.

32. Duliškovič, *Istoričeskija čerty*, Vol. III, p. 231.

33. For a biography and pastoral letter of Bulko, see *Zapysky ČSVV*, VIII (Žovkva, 1931), pp. 205-210. For his decree of nomination, see Basilovits, *Brevis notitia*, Vol. I, pt. 2 (1799), pp. 171-173.

34. In Hungarian: Máramarossziget; in Rusyn: Maramoroš'kyj Sihot.

35. A. Baran, *Jepyskop Andrej Bačyns'kyj i cerkovne vidrodžennja na Zakarpatti* (Yorkton, Sask., 1963), p. 35; Basilovits, *Brevis notitia*, Vol. II, pt. 5, pp. 17-18.

36. See the "Introduction" to this work, note 7.

37. In Hungarian: Nagy Bánya; in Rusyn: Velyka Banja. See the Apostolic

Constitution, "Solemni Conventione," in *Acta Apostolicae Sedis,* Vol. XXII (Vatican City, 1930), pp. 381-386.

38. See *Dušpastyr',* VIII, 12 (Užhorod, 1931), p. 285. On the death of the last vicar of Máramaros, A. Sabov, see *ibid.,* IX, 1-2 (1932), pp. 33-34.

39. See *Dušpastyr',* XIV, 9-10 (Užhorod, 1937), pp. 235-238; *Dobryj pastyr,* VII (Stanyslaviv, 1937), p. 192. Cf. "Ad Ecclesiasticii Regiminis," *Acta Apostolicae Sedis,* Vol. XXIX (Vatican City, 1937), pp. 366-369.

5. The Creation of the Prešov Eparchy

1. These Romanian parishes were later ceded to newly established Romanian eparchies.

2. His original name was Ivan Kovač. See the nomination charter, dated July 27, 1789, in Joannicius Basilovits, *Brevis notitia Fundationis Theodori Koriathovits,* Vol. II, pt. 5 (Košice, 1805), p. 61.

3. *Ibid.,* p. 62.

4. Kövesfalva in Hungarian; Kamjonka in Rusyn.

5. *Schematismus Gr. Ritus Cath. dioecesis Eperjesiensis pro A.D. 1898* (Prešov, 1898), p. 8.

6. Alexander Duchnovič, *The History of the Eparchy of Prjašev* (Rome, 1971), p. 15.

7. For Bradač's canonical process, see *Archivum Nuntiaturae Vindobonensis: Processi Canonici,* fasc. 687 (n.p.), ASV.

8. A. Welykyj, ed., *Documenta Pontificum Romanorum historiam Ucrainae illustrantia,* Vol. II (Rome, 1954), p. 323.

9. See "Reflexiones Bacsinszky de non facienda avulsione Cott. uum Szathmár et Szabolcs," in *Archivum Nuntiaturae Vindobonensis,* Vol. 79, f. 272-276, ASV.

10. Imre de Jósika-Herczeg, *Hungary after a Thousand Years* (New York, 1934), pp. 62-64.

11. *Archivum Nuntiaturae Germaniae,* Vol. 704, n.p., September 17, 1808; ASV; and *Scritture riferite nei Congressi Greci di Croazia* etc., Vol. II, f. 805a-b, APF.

12. Duchnovič, *History,* p. 23.

13. See the bull in Welykyj, *Documenta,* pp. 337-339.

14. *Ibid.,* p. 325.

15. See Pócsy's consent in *Acta S. Congregationis Consistorialis a. 1818,* pt. 2, f. 274-275, ASV.

16. See the letter, dated May 17, 1816, in *ibid.,* f. 163a-b.

17. *Archivum Nuntiaturae Germaniae,* Vol. 704, n.p., June 30, 1807, ASV.

18. The Hungarian court chancery informed the Mukačevo consistory about the creation of the Prešov eparchy on February 6, 1816. *Acta S. Congr. Consistorialis a. 1818,* pt. 2, f. 237a-b, ASV.

19. See Austrian emperor's letter to the pope, dated March 1, 1816, in *ibid.,* f. 164a-167a.

20. See the decree in Duchnovič, *History,* pp. 35-36.

21. Tarkovyč was then only 62 years old.

22. See the letter of the papal nuncio dated November 23, 1816, in *Archivum Nuntiaturae Vindobonensis: Processi Canonici,* fasc. 706, n.p., ASV.

23. *Acta S. Congr. Consistorialis a. 1818,* pt. 2, f. 250-251, 280-281, ASV.

24. See the bull, "Romanos Decet," in Welykyj, *Documenta,* Vol. II, pp. 326-327.

25. *Acta S. Congregationis Consistorialis anno 1818,* pt. 2, f. 197-199, ASV. The decree is in *ibid.,* f. 193-194, 232a-b.

26. The question of attaching the parishes to the Oradea eparchy was not resolved finally until 1823. See O. Baran, "Podil Mukačivs'koji Eparchiji v XIX storičči," *Zapysky ČSVV,* IV, 3-4 (Rome, 1963), pp. 534-569.

27. *Acta S. Congregationis Consistorialis anno 1818,* pt. 2, f. 244a-247b, ASV.

28. *Ibid.,* f. 152a-159a.

29. A. Welykyj, ed., *Litterae S.C. de Propaganda Fide Ecclesiam Catholicam Ucrainae et Bielarusjae Spectantes,* Vol. VII (Rome, 1957), pp. 142-146.

30. Welykyj, *Documenta,* Vol. II, pp. 327-333.

31. See the documents pertaining to the question of funds in *Acta S. Congregationis Consistorialis anno 1818,* pt. 2, f. 304-308, ASV.

32. The bull lists only 193 parishes, but Duchnovič, *History,* p. 45, insists that there were 194.

33. Duchnovič, *History,* pp. 104 and 140.

34. Until then the patron of the church had been St. John the Evangelist.

35. A sixth chair of canon was added in 1858 to which M. Starec'kyj was appointed on April 20, 1858. See *Cerkovnaja hazeta* (Vienna), no. 10, April 10/22, 1858, p. 79.

36. From the Latin expression: "Pro *congrua* sustentatione cleri."

37. The reign of bishop Gaganec' (1842-1875) coincided with the so-called "spring of nations." See S. Baran, *Vesna narodiv v Avstro-Uhors'kij Ukrajini* (Munich, 1948), pp. 30-31.

6. Attempts to Magyarize the Church

1. Known as the Ausgleich, which was negotiated between the Austrian imperial government in Vienna and the Hungarian government in Budapest, it gave the Hungarians complete freedom in domestic affairs. The agreement transformed the Austrian empire into a dualist monarchy—Austria-Hungary. Cf. W.E. Lingelbach, *Austria-Hungary* (New York, 1928), pp. 398-399.

2. As early as 1655, bishop Jakiv Suša lobbied in Rome to have the Mukačevo eparchy placed under the jurisdiction of the Kiev metropolitan. His efforts were not successful. See A. Baran, *Metropolia Kioviensis et Eparchia Mukačoviensis* (Rome, 1960), pp. 65-75.

3. See O. Baran, *Jepyskop Andrej Bačyns'kyj i cerkovne vidrodžennja na Zakarpatti* (Yorkton, Sask., 1963), pp. 42-47; W. Chotkowski, *Historya*

polityczna kościoła w Galicyi za rządów Maryi Teresy, Vol. II (Cracow, 1909), pp. 411-415; *Archivum Nuntiaturae Germaniae,* Vol. 393-394, f. 328 and *Archivum Nuntiaturae Vindobonensis,* Vol. 175, f. 541, ASV.

4. In the end, a Greek Catholic metropolitanate for Romanians in Transylvania was created in 1853.

5. For the Hungarian memorandum see M. Harasiewicz, *Annales Ecclesiae Ruthenae* (L'viv, 1862), pp. 667-669. M. Stasiw, *Metropolia Haličiensis* (Rome, 1960), p. 113, is incorrect in claiming that the L'viv chapter of canons opposed Bačyns'kyj's nomination "on political grounds."

6. Julian Pelesz, *Geschichte der Union der ruthenischen Kirche mit Rom,* Vol. II (Vienna, 1880), p. 661.

7. As early as 1800, the Ukrainian episcopate had been in favor of incorporating the Mukačevo eparchy into the Galician metropolitanate. See Harasiewicz, *Annales,* p. 580; Stasiw, *Metropolia,* p. 127.

8. O. Baran, "Pytannja ukrajins'koho patrijarchatu," *Lohos,* XIII, I (Yorkton, Sask., 1962), pp. 26-36. A Baran, "Progetto del Patriarcato Ucraino di Gregorio XVI," *Analecta OSBM,* III (Rome, 1960), pp. 454-475 with documents.

9. A. Pekar, "Cerkovna polityka madjariv na Zakarpatti," *Svitlo,* XXVII, 4 (Toronto, 1965), pp. 170-173. E. Vinter, *Vizantija ta Rym u borot'bi za Ukrajinu, 955-1939* (Prague, 1940), p. 178.

10. *Acta Apostolicae Sedis,* Vol. XX (Vatican City, 1928), pp. 65-66; A. Perugini, *Concordata vigentia* (Rome, 1934), pp. 71-75.

11. This action has been described very aptly and objectively by René Martel, *La Ruthénie subcarpathique* (Paris, 1935), pp. 156-178.

12. *Acta Apostolicae Sedis,* Vol. XXIX (1937), pp. 366-369; *Nyva,* XXV (L'viv, 1931), p. 194; *Blahovîstnyk,* XIV, 9 (Užhorod, 1934), pp. 143-144; *Dušpastyr',* XIV, 9-10 (Užhorod, 1937), pp. 235-238.

13. S. Sipos, *Enchiridion Iuris Canonici* (Pécs, 1940), pp. 787-802; A. Bobák, *De Iure Patronatus Supremi quoad Ecclesiam Ruthenican in Hungaria* (Rome, 1943).

14. For bishop Pankovyč's role in magyarization, see Julij Gadžega, *Istorija O-va sv. Vasilija Velikago* (Užhorod, 1925), pp. 18-26; and also Ivan A. Silvaj (Uriil Meteor), *Izbrannije proizvedenija* (Prešov, 1957), pp. 129-138.

15. See the address that bishop Valij was to have read before Pope Leo XIII concerning the Hungarian liturgy in Gyula Grigássy, *A magyar görög katholikusok legujabb tőrténete* (Užhorod, 1913), pp. 127-133. On the exploitation of bishop Valij by the Hungarians, see J. Kubinyi, *The History of Prjašiv Eparchy* (Rome, 1970), pp. 122-125.

16. See the articles in *Lystok,* VIII, 13 (Užhorod, 1892), pp. 149-152; and XI, 11 (1895), pp. 128-129. Concerning forcible magyarization at the Esztergom seminary, see "Zapysky na Služebnyku v Ostryhomi," *Ameryka* (Philadelphia), January 23, 1951, p. 3. One of the annotations of the Carpatho-Rusyn seminarian is the prayer: "Save us, O Lord, from these *ljachy* [actually Poles, but in the Carpathian context read: Magyars]. Amen!"

17. The "Religious Fund" was established in Hungary from church and

monastery possessions that had previously been confiscated by the state, primarily during the reign of Joseph II (1780-1790).

18. P.S. Fedor, *Kratkij očerk djejatel'nosti A.P. Dobrjanskago* (Užhorod, 1926), pp. 14-15. Cf. Dobrjans'kyj's address of 1871 in Peter I. Zeedick, *Back in Eighteen Seventy-One* (Homestead, Pa., 1933), pp. 43-52.

19. A. Vološyn, *Spomyny* (Philadelphia, 1959), pp. 29-30.

20. L. Farkas, *Egy nemzeti küzdelem története* (Budapest, 1896), tried to prove that the "Hungarian Greek Catholics" traced their origins to the presence of Eastern Christianity in Hungary during the reign of St. Stephen, who used Hungarian as a liturgical language as early as the eleventh century. Gyula Grigássy argues that Hungarian had never before been used in the liturgy and that the so-called Hungarian Greek Catholics were magyarized Rusyns and Romanians. The full text of the 1863 memorandum is also given in Grigássy, *A magyar görög katholikusok,* pp. 103-105.

21. Ju. P. Rusak, "Mukačevskaja eparchija i eja borba za prava russkago jazyka i narodnosti vo vremja ep. V. Popoviča," in *Karpatorusskij sbornik* (Užhorod, 1930), pp. 50-68.

22. See *Libellus Memorialis Hungarorum gr. rit. Catholicorum ad SS. Patrem Leonem XIII* (Budapest, 1900), p. 92: "To remove all suspicion, I order that until it will be otherwise decided, i.e. until the Hungarian translation will not be properly approved, sanctioned, and promulgated by a legitimate authority, that you do not celebrate the Holy Liturgy in any other language but Slavonic and only in that language."

23. Vološyn, *Spomyny,* p. 20.

24. A congress of so-called Hungarian Greek Catholics was held on April 16, 1868 in Hajdúdorog. The congress resolved to create a separate Hungarian Greek Catholic eparchy and to introduce the Hungarian language into the liturgy. See their resolutions in *Libellus Memorialis,* pp. 112-116; for their appeals to the emperor and primate see Grigássy, *A magyar görög katholikusok,* pp. 106-112.

25. "The government supported the issue of a Hungarian liturgy, but it was unable to obtain Rome's approval. As far as creating a Hungarian eparchy was concerned, the government believed that it was better not to separate the magyarized Carpatho-Rusyns from the Mukačevo and Prešov eparchies, but rather leave them there to continue the campaign on behalf of Hungarian as the liturgical language." Vološyn, *Spomyny,* p. 20.

26. In a letter dated September 20, 1873, minister Ágoston Trefort ordered the bishop of Mukačevo to make Hungarian mandatory throughout the entire Hajdúdorog vicariate, which at the time encompassed Hajdú, Szabolcs, and Szatmár counties. See his letter in Grigássy, *A magyar görög katholikusok,* pp. 57-58.

27. *Ibid.,* pp. 65-66. On Hungarian liturgical books, see *ibid.,* pp. 60-63.

28. The attempt to impose Hungarian in the liturgy has been described by C. Korolevsky, *Living Languages in Catholic Worship* (Westminster, Md., 1957), pp. 23-45. The agenda of the National Committee was to gain more supporters for the movement advocating the Hungarian liturgy; to compel the Apostolic See to approve the use of Hungarian in the liturgy; and to introduce

the Gregorian calendar. See Grigássy, *A magyar görög katholikusok,* pp. 71-75; *Libellus Memorialis,* pp. 99-101.

29. Vološyn, *Spomyny,* pp. 21-22.

30. Grigássy, *A magyar görög katholikusok,* p. 78, only mentions the decrees of the Congregation for the Propagation of the Faith of September 26, 1899 and of the Vatican State Secretariat of September 30, 1899; he does not provide the texts.

31. Bishop Valij had been blackmailed to undertake this mission by the government under threat of exposure of some of his actions. For an account of the audience, see Vološyn, *Spomyny,* pp. 23-24. For Valij's speech, see Grigássy, *A magyar görög katholikusok,* pp. 127-133.

32. See I. Vančyk, "Madjars'ka mova v cerkovnomu bohosluženju a rus'ke duchovenstvo na Uhorščyni," *Nyva,* V (L'viv, 1907), pp. 227-230; Vološyn, *Spomyny,* p. 23.

33. Korolevsky, *Living Languages,* p. 32.

34. See one such letter in *Nyva,* IX (L'viv, 1911), pp. 301-302.

35. For metropolitan Šeptyc'kyj's appeal to the Hungarian primate, see *Nyva,* IX (L'viv, 1911), p. 300.

36. Korolevsky, *Living Languages,* p. 33.

37. W. de Vries, *Der Christliche Osten in Geschichte und Gegenwart* (Würzburg, 1951), p. 178; Grigássy, *A magyar görög katholikusok,* pp. 85-88.

38. Korolevsky, *Living Languages,* p. 36.

39. Bulla "Christifideles Graeci Ritus" in *Acta Apostolicae Sedis,* Vol. IV (1921), pp. 430-435; Grigássy, *A magyar görög katholikusok,* pp. 133-142. When in March 1912, the Romanian bishop Basil Hossu of Gherla (1912-1916) described the hypocrisy of the Hungarian government in matters of religion, Pope Pius X exclaimed: "They deceived me!" and ordered the bull revised. But it was too late. Korolevsky, *Living Languages,* p. 37.

40. F.C., "Création d'un diocèse de rite greco-catholique en Hongrie," *Echos d'Orient,* XV (Paris, 1912), pp. 553-555; R. Janin, "Diocèse d'Hajdu-Dorogh," *ibid.,* XVII (1914-1915), p. 499, concludes that "the Hungarian government gained much more by the erection of this eparchy than did the Church." The first bishop of Hajdúdorog, István Miklósy, settled at first in Miskolc. Following an attempt on his life in 1914, he transferred his residence to Nyíregyháza and remained there permanently. On bishop Miklósy, see *Nauka,* XVII, 6, 8 and 10 (Užhorod, 1913), pp. 28, 30 and 30. For the attempt on the bishop's life see *Nyva,* XII (L'viv, 1914), p. 142.

41. *Acta Apostolicae Sedis,* Vol. IV (Vatican City, 1912), pp. 432-433.

42. *Ibid.,* p. 433.

43. Korolevsky, *Living Languages,* p. 38. Cf. A. Catoire, "L'Evêche de Hajdudorogh," *Echos d'Orient,* XVI (Paris, 1913), p. 454.

44. See *Nyva,* XII (L'viv, 1914), p. 142.

45. In bishop Miklósy, a magyarized Carpatho-Rusyn from the village of Rakovec nad Ondavou (Zemplén county), the government found itself a "loyal" patriot and magyarizer. Bishop Papp of Užhorod and bishop Novak of Prešov held similar convictions.

46. "Lettre morte" in the words of R. Janin, *Les églises orientales et les rites orientaux* (Paris, 1926), p. 324.

47. On the liturgical reforms of that period, see Vološyn, *Spomyny,* pp. 45-52; and his "Oborona kyrylyky," *Naukovyj zbirnyk t-va 'Prosvita',* XII (Užhorod, 1936), pp. 85-117.

48. See the plan for liturgical reform in *ibid.,* pp. 102-112.

49. For the complete text, see *ibid.,* pp. 99-102.

50. A reform of the Basilian order began in Galicia in 1882, but the Hungarians would not allow these reforms to extend to Carpathian Rus'. There the reforms began only after the war in 1923. See M. Vajda, "Pryčynok do istoriji Vasylijan na Zakarpatti," *Kalendar Syrits'koho domu na 1954 r.* (Philadelphia, 1954), pp. 91-97.

51. Vološyn, "Oborona," p. 88.

52. *Ibid.,* p. 91.

53. Vološyn, *Spomyny,* p. 49.

54. *Ibid.,* p. 50. See the memorandum, dated December 4, 1915, in Vološyn, "Oborona," pp. 113-115, in which a complaint is made to the Apostolic See that the Hungarian authorities are interfering in such purely ecclesiastical affairs as liturgical books, the modification of rituals, changes of the calendar, the education of the clergy, the reform of the Basilian order, etc.

55. Vološyn, "Oborona," p. 97.

56. For the alphabet issue, see Vološyn, *Spomyny,* p. 51; for the forcible introduction of the Gregorian calendar, see Volodymyr Birčak, *Na novych zemljach* (L'viv, 1938), pp. 147-158.

57. See the statement to the Hungarian government by the ministerial commissioner Eduard Egan in 1897, in *Kalendar o-va Ruskych Bratstv u S.Š.A. na 1924 r.* (Philadelphia, 1924), p. 112: "A people, who have no land, no cattle, whose fate rests in the hands of usurers; a people dependent on the mood and arbitrariness of the usurer; a people who have been deliberately driven to drink and demoralized, whom neither the priest nor the magistrate can help and whom every administrative official exploits and wrongs; a people to whom no one in the world extends a helping hand—such a people will decline morally and materially until it ceases to exist altogether."

58. I. O. Panas, "Karpatorusskie otzvuky russkago pochoda v Vengriju 1849 g.," in *Karpatorusskij sbornik* (Užhorod, 1930), pp. 209-229.

59. The Orthodox movement in Carpathian Rus' is discussed below, in Chapter 7.

60. See the memoirs of Toth in *Kalendar' Russkago Pravoslavnago o-va vzaimopomošči na 1938 g.* (Wilkes Barre, Pa., 1938), pp. 141-143.

61. See the comprehensive article on the beginnings of Orthodoxy in Carpathian Rus' by M. Kušnirenko, "Pobut sela Izy—pravoslavije i moskvofil'stvo," in *Zbirnyk Ukrajins' koho Naukovoho Instytutu v Ameryci* (St. Paul and Prague, 1939), pp. 175-184.

7. The Orthodox Movement
1. S. Baran, *Vesna narodiv v avstro-uhors'kij Ukrajini* (Munich, 1948), p. 30.

2. A. Duchnovyč also had contacts with Kustodiev and Raevskij. See *Karpatskij svjet*, II, I (Užhorod, 1929), p. 460.

3. I.S. Svencickij, *Obzor snošenij Karpatskoj Rusi s Rossiej v l-uju polovinu XIX v.* (St. Petersburg, 1906); M. Andrusjak, *Geneza j charakter halyc'koho rusofil'stva v XIX-XX st.* (Prague, 1941), pp. 4-7. For the relationship between Russophilism and Orthodoxy, see Julij Gadžega, *Stat'i po voprosam 'pravoslavija', narodnosti i katoličestva* (Užhorod, 1921), pp. 3-11.

4. See A.I. Dobrjanskij, "Otryvki iz političeskich statej," in *Prjaševščina* (Prague, 1948), pp. 178-179.

5. Pobedonoscev expressed his religious policies as follows: "Russia derives its vital force from Orthodoxy, which is the essential condition of her life." Cited in Gadžega, *Stat'i*, p. 11.

6. Dobrjanskij, "Otryvki," p. 182; and A.I. Dobrjanskij, *O sovremennom religiozno-političeskom položenii Avstro-Ugorskoj Rusi* (Moscow, 1885).

7. See Dobrjans'kyj's statement at the trial: "I do not admit any wrongdoing on my part." Dobrjanskij, "Otryvki," pp. 179-180.

8. For Rakovs'kyj's Russophilism see V.A. Francev, "Iz istorii bor'by za russkij lit. jazyk v Podk. Rusi," in *Karpatorusskij sbornik* (Užhorod, 1930), pp. 5-38.

9. See Julij Gadžega, *Istorija 'O-va sv. Vasilija Velikago'* (Užhorod, 1925).

10. Cited in M. Kušnirenko, "Pobut sela Izy—pravoslavije i moskvofil'stvo," in *Zbirnyk Ukrajins'koho Naukovoho Instytutu v Ameryci* (St. Paul, Minn. and Prague, 1939), p. 176.

11. *Ibid.*, pp. 176-177.

12. F. Tichý, *Vývoj současného spisovného jazyka na Podkarpatské Rusi* (Prague, 1938), pp. 60-98.

13. See A. S. Šlepeckij, "Karpatorossy v Amerike," *Al'manach O.K.S. Vozroždenie* (Prague, 1936), pp. 81-86; and his "Prjaševcy v Amerike," in *Prjaševščina* (Prague, 1948), pp. 255-262. The Reverend Toth's memoirs were published on the 50th anniversary of his death in *Svjet* (Wilkes Barre, Pa.), Nos. 18-19 (May 2, 1952), pp. 1-5; Nos. 20-21 (May 16, 1959), pp. 1-3.

14. The villages in which the Orthodox movement in Carpathian Rus' began were Iza and Velyki Lučky in the Mukačevo eparchy and Becherov in the Prešov eparchy.

15. The first group of so-called "Orthodox" in the village of Iza consisted of: J. Vakarov, M. Plyška, and V. Lazar. They were soon joined by H. Plyška, A. Oros, and I. Andrij. Vakarov died during the trial, providing the Iza group with a "martyr for the Orthodox faith." See P. Charlampov, "K istorii pravoslavnago monašestva v Zakarpate," *Žurnal Moskovskoj Patriarchii,* XIII, 5 (Moscow, 1957), pp. 61-65.

16. Such is the explanation of the beginnings of Orthodoxy offered by D. Pantelejmonovskij, *Povest' ob obraščenii i prisojedinenii na Afone ugro-russa unijata v Pravoslavie* [about A. Kabaljuk] (Šanordino, 1913), pp. 66-69; Konstantin M. Beskid, *Maramorošský proces* (Chust, 1926), p. 12.

17. V.A. Bobrinskoj gives a detailed account of his action in *Pražskij s"jezd (Čechija i Prikarpatskaja Rus')* (St. Petersburg, 1909), pp. 113-127. For the activities of the Gerovskij brothers in Carpathian Rus', see *Vtorŷj videnskij process v 1916* g. (Philadelphia, 1924), pp. 50-55ff.

18. Pantelejmonovskij, *Povest'*, pp. 5-14. For Kabaljuk's biography, see G. Stankaninec, "Schiarchimandrit Aleksij (Kabaljuk)," *Žurnal Moskovskoj Patriarchii*, IV, 2 (Moscow, 1948), pp. 69-70.

19. Metropolitan Evlogij mentions his contacts with Kabaljuk in his memoirs; see T. Manuchina, *Put' mojej žizni* (Paris, 1947), pp. 254-256.

20. There are several works on the Máramoros trial. The more important espousing different points of view are: M. Grabec, *K istorii maramorošskago processa* (Užhorod, 1934); K. Beskid, *Maramorošský proces* (Chust, 1926); V. Aradi, *A ruthén skizmapör* (Budapest, 1914); W. Kuschnir, "Zum ungarischen Hochverratsprocess—Graf Bobrinskij als Zeuge," *Ukrainische Rundschau*, IX (Ödenburg, 1914), pp. 6-12; R. Martel, "La politique slave de la Russie d'avant guerre—le procès ukrainien de Maramorosz-Sziget," *Affaires étrangères*, VI, 10 (Paris 1936), pp. 623-634 and VII, I (1937), pp. 58-64. Bobrinskoj's activities in Carpathian Rus' were condemned by his compatriot, M. Žučenko, in "Ugorskaja Rus'," *Ukrainskaja žizn'*, no. 5-6 (Moscow, 1914), pp. 33-38: "Count Bobrinskoj and his associates [. . .] indulged shamelessly in political agitation among the non-Magyar inhabitants of Hungary, exploiting their difficult circumstances, ignorance, and backwardness. This agitation was readily used by the patriots of the Hungarian motherland at the political trial" (p. 33). The view of the Hungarian government is presented by E. de Csáky, *La question ruthène* (Paris and Budapest, 1920), pp. 9-10.

21. Foreign minister E. Beneš in his *Reč o podkarpatorusskoj probleme* (Užhorod, 1934), p. 13, states that more than 100 Rusyn priests were imprisoned and half of them were deported deep into Hungary.

22. See M. Tvorydlo, "Z krasšych dniv na Pidkarpattju," *Kalendar t-va Prosvity na 1923 r.* (Užhorod), pp. 40-51; Vološyn, *Spomyny*, pp. 53-56; I. Borščak, *Karpats'ka Ukrajina u mižnarodnij hri* (L'viv, 1938), pp. 5-38; V. Pačovs'kyj, *Sribna Zemlja* (L'viv, 1938), pp. 61-66; I. Kondratovyč, *Ystorija Podkarpatskoj Rusy* (Užhorod, 1930), pp. 100-106.

23. See *Blahovîstnyk*, VII, I (Užhorod, 1927), pp. 13-14.

24. See *Žurnal Moskovskoj Patriarchii*, III, 5 (Moscow, 1947), pp. 63-64.

25. For Masaryk's religious policy, "Away from Rome!," see L. Němec, *Church and State in Czechoslovakia* (New York, 1955), pp. 96-145.

26. F. Nemec and V. Moudry, *The Soviet Seizure of Subcarpathian Ruthenia* (Toronto, 1955), pp. 38-39.

27. The Reverend A. Vološyn described this campaign very aptly: "Under Hungary we were dangerous Russophiles, today we are treasonous Magyarones. Where does the truth lie?" See his speech, "Relihijni vidnosyny na Pidkarpats'kij Rusy," in *Acta Conventus Pragensis pro Studiis Orientalibus a. 1919 celebrati* (Olomouc, 1930), pp. 218-221.

28. In particular, the yearly contribution of grain from each family to the pastor known as the *koblyna,* to be discussed in the following chapter.

29. Vološyn, "Relihijni vidnosyny," pp. 218-219.

30. For a discussion of the spread of Orthodoxy in the Máramaros region, see the excellent article by P. Chomyn, "Cerkovne pytannja na Pidkarpats'kij Rusy," *Nyva*, XII (L'viv, 1922), pp. 2-7, 46-52, 123-128. For the Orthodox view, see V. Grigorič, *Pravoslavná církev ve státě Československém* (Prague, 1927), pp. 141-146.

31. For an account of the beginnings of Orthodoxy in the Prešov Region in the vicinity of Bardejov (the village of Becherov), see B. Krpelec, *Bardejov a jeho okolie dávno a dnes* (Bardejov, 1935), pp. 176-181; Grigorič, *Pravoslavná církev*, pp. 46-149.

32. See statistics in S. Zerkal', *Nacional'ni i relihijni vidnosyny na Zakarpatti* (New York, 1956), p. 16.

33. For a discussion of the origins of the Czechoslovak National Church, see František Cinek, *K náboženské otázce v prvních letech naši samostatnosti 1918-1925* (Olomouc, 1926), pp. 27-219.

34. M. Pavlik, later bishop Gorazd, was one of 66 Czech Catholic apostate priests who left the Catholic Church after the Apostolic See had censured their radical organization, Jednota. Cf. *Acta Apostolicae Sedis*, Vol. XII (Vatican City, 1920), p. 37.

35. Archimandrite Savvatij, whose real name was Antonín Vrabec, was born in 1880 in Prague. Attracted by pan-Slavism, in 1900 he went to Russia where he entered a monastery. After completing his theological studies at the Pečers'ka Lavra (Monastery of the Caves) in Kiev, he was ordained to the priesthood in 1907 and sent to Volhynia. There he was elevated to the rank of archimandrite and for a time administered the Kovel' eparchy. In 1921, Červinka summoned him to Prague to head the Czech Orthodox congregation. See Grigorič, *Pravoslavná církev*, pp. 50-51. For an account of the Orthodox movement in Czechoslovakia, see *ibid*, pp. 81-89; and Cinek, *K náboženské otázce*, pp. 221-287.

36. M. d'Herbigny and A. Deubner, *Évêques russes en exil (1918-1930)* (Rome, 1931); *Echos d'Orient*, XXVI (Paris, 1927), pp. 116-117.

37. See the diploma of Savvatij's chirotony in *Pravoslavnyj russkij kalendar na g. 1926* (Vyšní Svidník, 1925), pp. 84-85. For the history of the Orthodox movement in Czechoslovakia, see *ibid.*, pt. 3, pp. 1-27.

38. For the "Tomos" of the canonical erection of the ecclesiastical Orthodox province in Czechoslovakia, dated March 7, 1923, see *ibid.*, p. 65. An analysis of the "tomos" is in *Echos d'Orient*, XXVI (Paris, 1927), pp. 116-117.

39. The Little Entente was comprised of Romania, Czechoslovakia, and Yugoslavia.

40. W. de Vries, *Der christliche Osten in Geschichte und Gegenwart* (Würzburg, 1951), pp. 168-175.

41. Based on data from the *Pravoslavnij russkij kalendar na god 1926*, archimandrite Bogolep headed some 60 priests and monks under the jurisdiction of bishop Savvatij, while archimandrite Kabaljuk governed some 33 under the jurisdiction of Serbia. Because the names of some priests appear under both jurisdictions, this data cannot be regarded as reliable. Cf. *Blahovîstnyk*, VIII,

9 (Užhorod, 1928), pp. 129-130.

42. See *Dušpastyr'*, IV, 2 (Užhorod, 1927), pp. 109-110; *Blahovîstnyk*, VII, 6 (Užhorod, 1927), pp. 81-84.

43. *Dušpastyr'*, IV, 2 (Užhorod, 1927), p. 110; *Blahovîstnyk*, VII, 5 (Užhorod, 1927), p. 80.

44. V. Bušek, "Poměr státu k církvim v ČSR," in *Československá vlastivěda*, Vol. V (Prague, 1931), pp. 351-355 ("pravoslavné vyznání").

45. Bishop Damaskin (Grdanički), of Serbian birth, completed his study of theology in St. Petersburg. Returning after the war to his native Serbia [then part of Yugoslavia], he became a professor of theology at Belgrade University. He was interested in the Orthodox movement in Carpathian Rus' from the very beginning. See the article by the hieromonk Aleksij (Dechterov), "Pravoslavie na Podkarpatskoj Rusi," in *Podkarpatskaja Rus' za gg. 1919-1936* (Užhorod, 1936), pp. 97-100; and N. de Vries, *Der christliche Osten*, pp. 173-175.

8. A Religious Revival

1. While talks between the delegates of Carpathian Rus' and Czechoslovakia were under way in early 1919, president Tomáš Masaryk sent his emissary Captain F. Pisecký to meet with representatives of the higher clergy gathered at the theological seminary in Užhorod. Members of the clergy included: canon S. Sabov, rector; canon P. Gebej, later bishop; canon Ju. Šuba, professor at the seminary; canon V. Hadžega, professor at the seminary; and the Reverend A. Vološyn, a professor at the teachers' college. For an account of this meeting, see F. Cinek, *K náboženské otázce v prvních letech naši samostatnosti 1918-1925* (Olomouc, 1926), p. 242.

2. Cf. T. H. Masaryk, *Svitova revoljucija* (L'viv, 1930), p. 58. See Masaryk's description of "religious evolution," as he called the change in his religious views, in *ibid*, pp. 478-479.

3. T. G. Masaryk, *Los von Rom* (Boston, 1902).

4. Masaryk, *Svitova revoljucija*, p. 482.

5. Bishop Novak died in extreme poverty on a Budapest street on September 6, 1932. See *Nyva*, XXVI (L'viv, 1932), p. 343; and his obituary in *Dušpastyr'*, IX, 10 (Užhorod, 1932), pp. 284-285.

5a. Finally, under pressure from the papal nuncio in Prague, bishop Papp took an oath of loyalty to Czechoslovakia (August, 1923), but it was too late.

6. For an account of the eparchial synod held in Užhorod in 1921, see Ch. de Clercq, *Histoire des Conciles*, Vol. XI: *Conciles des Orientaux catholiques*, Vol. II (Paris, 1952), p. 955.

7. By that time the Orthodox had already seized nearly 40 Greek Catholic churches.

8. See V. Lar', "Orhanyzujme narod," *Dušpastyr'*, III, 5 (Užhorod, 1926), pp. 248-251.

9. *Acta Apostolicae Sedis*, Vol. XX (Vatican City, 1928), pp. 65-66; A. Perugini, *Concordata vigentia* (Rome, 1934), pp. 71-75; "Exposé ministra Dr.

Beneše o Modu Vivendi," *Zahraniční politika,* VII (Prague, 1928), pp. 200-203.

10. Cf. "Ad Ecclesiastici Regiminis," *Acta Apostolicae Sedis,* Vol. XXIX (Vatican City, 1937), pp. 366-369. The explanation of these changes by the bishop of Mukačevo, A. Stojka, is in *Dushpastyr',* XIV, 9-10 (Užhorod, 1937), pp. 235-238.

11. See "Nova era v žyttju mukačivs'koji eparchiji," *Nyva,* XVIII (L'viv, 1924), pp. 209-211.

12. See "Petro Gebej—jepyskop mukačevs'kyj," *Dobryj pastyr',* I (Stanyslaviv, 1931), pp. 230-233.

13. For the text and explanation of the law see *Dušpastyr',* II, 6 (Užhorod, 1925), pp. 274-280.

14. *Ibid.,* VIII, 5 (1931), p. 117.

15. Henceforth we will speak only of the *koblyna,* since by the end of the nineteenth century the *rokovyna* was no longer in force.

16. See *ibid.,* II, 1-2 (1925), p. 68.

17. Cited in Cinek, *K náboženské otázce,* pp. 277-279.

18. On legislation concerning the *congrua,* see A. Stojka, "K uporjadkovanju svjaščennyčeskych deržavnych žalovanij," *Dušpastyr',* IV, 2 (Užhorod, 1927), pp. 103-106; and his "Deržavnoje žalovanie duchovenstva," *ibid.,* pp. 5-9, V, 1 (1928), pp. 5-9.

19. *Dušpastyr',* III, 1 (Užhorod, 1926), pp. 10-13.

20. The so-called "Circle of Clergy of the Christian People's Party" was founded on January 10, 1928 with the participation of bishop Gebej. *Ibid.,* V, 2 (1928), pp. 45-46.

21. *Ibid.,* V, 12, p. 300.

22. *Ibid.,* V, 3, pp. 61-73.

23. See his first pastoral letter, dated August 28, 1924, in *ibid.,* I, 7 (1924), pp. 320-330.

24. Only one Greek Catholic priest, M. Mejheš, went over to the Orthodox faith.

25. See his appeal to the clergy in *ibid.,* III, I (1926), pp. 49-50.

26. *Ibid.,* III, I, p. 13.

27. See the ratification of the by-laws in *ibid.,* II, 4 (1925), pp. 159-162; and S. Rešetylo, "Informaciî v dîlî Narodnych Missij," *ibid.,* pp. 280-282.

28. Cited in *ibid.,* III, I (1926), p. 13.

29. Cited in *ibid.,* III, 7 (1926), p. 384. A full description of the installation of the icon is found in S. Rešetylo, "Obraz Presv. Bohorodyci darovanyj Sv. Otcem Mukačivs'komu monastyrevi," *Zapysky ČSVV,* II, 3-4 (Žovkva, 1926), pp. 411-416.

30. For a history of the Central Office for the Defense of the Faith, see *Kalendar' Blahovîstnyka na 1927 r.* (Užhorod, 1927), pp. 139-143.

31. It should be mentioned that the onset of Hungarian influences and intrigues in Carpathian Rus' began in 1930. See René Martel, *La Ruthénie subcarpathique* (Paris, 1935), pp. 156-163.

32. Cf. his obituary in *Dušpastyr'*, VIII, 5 (Užhorod, 1931), pp. 113-119.

33. See the speech of the apostolic nuncio delivered on September 30, 1931 in *ibid.*, VIII, 10, pp. 240-241. For a more detailed study, see A. Pekar, "Bishop Peter Gebey—Champion of the Holy Union," *Analecta OSBM,* IV (Rome, 1963), pp. 293-326.

34. See "Pro čužincev," *Russkoje slovo* (Prešov), February 20, 1930, p. 4.

35. See the bull in A. Welykyj, ed., *Documenta Pontificum Romanorum historiam Ucrainae et Bielarusjae illustrantia,* Vol. II (Rome, 1957), pp. 548-549.

36. *Blahovîstnyk* (Prešov, 1946), No. 7, p. 17. For a more detailed study of bishop Gojdyč see A. Pekar, *Vasylijanyn-ispovidnyk—žyttja jep. P. Gojdyča, ČSVV* (New York, 1961), and his *Bishop P. Gojdich, OSBM—Confessor of Our Times* (Pittsburgh, Pa., 1980).

37. Cited in *J.E. Pavel Gojdič, ČSSV—Jepiskop Prjaševskij (1927-1947)* (Prešov, 1947), pp. 51-52.

38. G.N. Shuster, *Religion Behind the Iron Curtain* (New York, 1954), p. 72.

39. See *Zorja halyc'ka*, I (L'viv, 1848), pp. 90-92.

40. Vološyn, *Spomyny,* p. 46; R.K., "Slovaky hreko-katolyky v prjaš. eparchiji," *Ameryka* (Philadelphia), No. 170, September 12, 1956, p. 3.

41. See the bishop's order, in *Dušpastyr'*, VI, 8-9 (Užhorod, 1929), "Dodatok," p. II.

42. *Ibid.,* "Dodatok," p. I.

43. See "Pered narodo-sčytaniem," *Russkoe slovo* (Prešov), January 4, 1930, p. 5, which includes the speech of the regional official Baško at a meeting of the Slovak League in Michalovce on November 23, 1929: "Since Rusnaks do not wish to identify with the Slovak people, in the census of 1930 it is necessary to be careful and certain that the Rusyns are entered as Slovaks, that is, give them such questions that they will respond they are Slovaks."

44. See the letter of the School Department and bishop Gojdyč's protest in *ibid.,* January 30, 1930, pp. 2-3.

45. The reference is to the so-called Apponyi Law 27, which the Slovaks had been the first to protest against: "Taking away their mother tongue from children? It amounts to the same as depriving infants of their mothers' milk!" Cited in B. Bjernson, *Ponevoleni narody ta ukrajins'ka sprava* (Winnipeg, 1939), pp. 13-21.

46. For the School Department's response, see *Russkoje slovo,* April 30, 1930, p. 2.

47. From the bishop's letter, cited in *ibid.,* p. 3.

48. There were nearly 240 parochial schools in the Prešov Greek Catholic eparchy at the time.

49. Cf. *J.E. Pavel Gojdič,* pp. 92-94.

50. This is an allusion to a meeting of Rusyn clergy held on October 26, 1937 in Humenné, at which a decision was adopted to use Carpatho-Rusyn as the official language in the Rusyn districts of Humenné, Spiš, Vranov, and Medzilaborce, even in dealings with representatives of the government. See

"Zažerlyvist' maloho susida," *Nova svoboda* (Chust) January 14, 1939, pp. 1-2.

51. *J.E. Pavel Gojdič,* p. 57.

52. See the full text of this letter written in Slovak, in *ibid.,* pp. 57-58.

53. This is how an eyewitness described the incident to me: "When Tiso arrived on an official visit to Prešov, he was welcomed by bishop Pavlo, the Latin-rite bishop, J. Čársky, the Lutheran bishop, and the Jewish rabbi among others. Dr. Tiso shook hands with each of them, but pointedly ignored our bishop. What is more, our bishop was forced to stand on the platform reserved for high officials, because 'there was no chair' for him."

54. The same eyewitness cites the words of Halan: "Bishop, we have another place for people like you!," alluding to the notorious prison in Ilava where many so-called "enemies" of the Slovak people were already incarcerated.

55. See the bishop's letter to the pope in *J.E. Pavel Gojdič,* pp. 103-104, which reads in part: "in place of the undersigned, let a man of a stronger hand be appointed who would enjoy the complete trust of the government."

56. See the letter of premier Béla Tuka, dated January 31, 1940, in *ibid.,* p. 104.

57. See the brève of the Apostolic See in *ibid.,* pp. 105-106.

57a. Even the Latin-rite bishop Jozef Čársky of Košice (1925-1962), who because of the Hungarian occupation of Košice (Kassa) was residing in Prešov at that time, refused to come to bishop Gojdyč's installation. See Ludvík Němec, *Church and State in Czechoslovakia* (New York, 1955), pp. 410-411.

58. See his pastoral letter, dated October 21, 1940, in *ibid.,* p. 137.

59. Based on an account of an eyewitness.

60. See the ministry's order, dated December 18, 1940, in *J.E. Pavel Gojdič,* p. 52.

61. See I. Židovskij, "Prjaševskaja Rus' v bor'be za svoj prava," *Podkarpatskaja Rus' v gg. 1919-1936* (Užhorod, 1936), pp. 89-91; I. Peščak, "Iz prošlago našich škol'nich del," *Kalendar Ukrainskoj Narodnoj Rady Prjaševščiny na 1946 g.* (Prešov, 1945), pp. 50-55.

62. See *Nauka,* VII, 18 (Užhorod, 1903), p. 7.

63. Welykyj, *Documenta Pontificum,* Vol. II, p. 458.

64. Rome's decision came from the Congregation for the Eastern Churches on April 6, 1921. See *Nyva,* XV (L'viv, 1921), p. 311.

65. See Rešetylo, "Učast' Karpats'koji Provinciji ČSVV v misijnim rusi," *Zapysky ČSVV,* I, 2-3 (Žovkva, 1925), pp. 368-377. During the tenure of bishop Gebej, the Basilian Fathers conducted 110 missions, 132 closed retreats, and heard more than 120,000 confessions.

66. Between 1925 and 1935, the Basilian Order's publishing house in Užhorod printed 181,250 copies of the monthly *Blahovîstnyk*; 150,920 copies of various religious periodicals; 76,767 copies of religious books; 78,100 prayer books, 26,800 copies of calendars; 20,000 copies of scholarly works and 173,250 copies of religious brochures. *Blahovîstnyk,* XV, 12 (Užhorod, 1935), p. 181.

67. For an account of the creation of the Carpatho-Rusyn province of the Basilian Order, see *Dušpastyr'*, IX, 10 (Užhorod, 1932), p. 302.

68. M. Vavryk, *Po vasylijans'kych monastyrjach* (Toronto, 1958), p. 223. On the Basilian Fathers in Carpathian Rus', see A. Stankanynec', "Pjat'desjatlittja vidnovy Čyna sv. Vasylija Velykoho," in *Blahovîstnyk*, XII (Užhorod, 1932), no. 8, pp. 113-116; no. 9, pp. 129-131; no. 10, pp. 145-149; no. 11, pp. 161-163; no. 12, pp. 177-179; XIII (1933), no. 1, pp. 3-5; no. 2, pp. 17-18; and A. Pekar, "Vasylijans'ka provincija sv. Mykolaja na Zakarpatt'i," *Zapysky ČSVV*, XI, 1-4 (Rome, 1982), pp. 131-164.

69. See I. Djurkan', "OO. Redemptorysty schidnoho obrjadu na Zakarpatti i v Schidnij Slovaččyni," *Juvilejna knyha OO. Redemptorystiv Schidn'oho Obrjadu (1906-1956)* (Yorkton, Sask., 1955), pp. 202-208.

70. See *Dušpastyr'*, II, 1-2 (Užhorod, 1925), pp. 62-63; *Blahovîstnyk*, XVII, 4 (Užhorod, 1937), p. 62; *J.E. Pavel Gojdič*, pp. 88-92.

71. *Dušpastyr'*, V, 6-7 (Užhorod, 1928), pp. 152-158; *J.E. Pavel Gojdič*, pp. 77-83.

72. Cf. Fr. Vassili (Ch. Bourgeois), "The Podcarpathian Schism," *Pax* (Prinknash, Glos., England), January 1934, pp. 228-234; April 1934, pp. 1-8.

73. See *Dušpastyr'* (Užhorod, 1933), pp. 197-198; K.P., "OO. Jezujity v Užhorods'kij eparchiji," *Nova zorja* (L'viv), September 14, 1933, p. 5. For the fate of these monastic communities, see A. Pekar, "Dolja monachiv i monachyn' na Prjašivščyni," *Svitlo*, XXI, 6 (Toronto, 1958), pp. 15-16.

74. A. Pekar, "Episkop Stojka, 'Otec' bidnych," *Byzantine Catholic World* (Pittsburgh), July 7, 1957, p. 6; A. Pekar, *The Bishops of the Mukachevo Eparchy* (Pittsburgh, Pa. 1979), pp. 66-69.

75. *Dušpastyr'*, IX, 1-2 (Užhorod, 1932), pp. 22-23.

76. *Ibid.*, IX, 3, pp. 53-59.

77. *Ibid.*, IX, 4, pp. 101-102.

78. *Ibid.*, IX, 11-12, pp. 322-331.

79. See the bishop's appeal in *ibid.*, X, 7-8 (1933), p. 202.

80. *Ibid.*, p. 143.

81. See bishop Stojka's first pastoral letter in *ibid.*, IX, 8-9 (1932), pp. 193-206, in which he set forth the program for his episcopacy.

82. *Ibid.*, p. 205.

83. The First Congress of Marian Sodalities was held on May 25, 1931; see *ibid.*, VIII, 6-7 (1931), pp. 174-175.

84. See N. Vajda, "Prečysta Diva Marija na Zakarpatti," *Karpats'kyj holos*, no. 1-4 (Philadelphia, 1954), pp. 8-17.

85. Observator, "Z vražin' na Zakarpatti," *Nova zorja* (L'viv), September 18, 1932, p. 5.

86. This was most likely for personal reasons, because Vološyn had opposed his candidacy to the episcopate. I have several letters from Vološyn to bishop Njaradij concerning this matter; but the time has not yet come to publish them. The Hungarian authorities also demanded that the populist campaign of the Reverend Vološyn be neutralized.

87. In particular, this occurred after Fencyk, the secretary of the Duchnovyč Society and the leader of the Russophile movement in Carpathian Rus', was in 1934 suspended from the priesthood for canonical insubordination; suspicion of schism; and unworthy performance of clerical duties. See *Dušpastyr'*, XI, 12 (Užhorod, 1934), p. 237. Since Fencyk was at the time visiting the United States, bishop Takach [of Pittsburgh] informed him of his suspension in a "Confidential Letter" dated December 6, 1934 and entered under the number G-294/1934. See *Keleti Egyház*, I (Miskolc, 1935), p. 24.

88. The editor-in-chief of the weekly was the Reverend Emilijan Bokšaj (1889-1976), catechist of the Užhorod *gymnasium* and a former collaborator of the Reverend Vološyn. See Bokšaj's biography in the *Byzantine Catholic World* (Pittsburgh), April 19, 1970, pp. 14 and 19, and his necrology in *Blahovîstnyk*, XII, 8 (Prešov 1976), p. 15.

89. See the section, "Le révisionisme hongrois et ses alliés," in Martel, *La Ruthénie subcarpathique*, pp. 163-178.

90. The Czechs refused to recognize the name "Carpatho-Ukraine." It was not until November 30, 1938 that they issued a ministerial order permitting the parallel use of this name with "Podkarpatskaja Rus'." The change in name was officially announced at the first session of the diet of Carpatho-Ukraine on March 15, 1939. See S. Rosocha, *Sojm Karpats'koji Ukrajiny* (Winnipeg, 1949), statutes 1 & 2, p. 80.

91. The Hungarians received 1,586 square kilometers of territory with 181,609 inhabitants.

92. See "Pro hreko-katolyc'ku eparchiju," *Nova svoboda* (Chust), March 10, 1939, p. 2.

93. The decree of nomination in Ukrainian translation was published by Petro Sterčo in *Vil'ne slovo* (Toronto), December 8, 1962, p. 4; and in English in A. Pekar, *The Bishops of the Mukachevo Eparchy* (Pittsburgh, 1979), pp. 70-73.

94. See *Blahovisnyk,* XIX, 1-2 (Chust, 1939), p. 9.

95. See "Preosv. Njaradij i svjaščenstvo na Karp. Ukrajini," *Misionar,* XXXIX (Žovkva, 1939), p. 50; "Intervju z Preosv. Njaradijem red. Revaja," *Nova svoboda* (Chust), January 7, 1939, p. 4.

96. See "Bohoslovy v Olomovci," *Nova svoboda* (Chust), February 19, 1939, p. 4-5. The official opening of the seminary was held on February 5, 1939.

97. *Ibid.,* January 14, 1939, p. 3.

98. See bishop Njaradij's appeal: "Bat'kivs'ke zyčlyve slovo do Vpr. OO. Dušpastyriv," *ibid.,* January 14, 1939, p. 3.

99. See *ibid.,* February 9, 1939, p. 5; *Misionar,* XXXIX (Žovkva, 1939), p. 77; *Nova zorja* (L'viv), January 26, 1939, p. 7.

100. See A. Pekar, "Čolovik Provydinnja—Vlad. D. Njaradij," *Svitlo,* XXVIII, 10 (Toronto, 1965), pp. 354-357; C. Gatti and C. Korolevskij, *I Riti e le Chiese Orientali,* Vol. I (Genoa, 1942), pp. 706-707.

9. The Calvary of the Union

1. *Sovetsko-čechoslovackie otnošenija vo vremja velikoj otečestvennoj vojny 1941-1945 gg: dokumenty i materijaly* (Moscow, 1960); F. Němec and V. Moudry, *The Soviet Seizure of Subcarpathian Ruthenia* (Tornoto, 1955); V. Markus, *L'incorporation de l'Ukraine subcarpathique á l'Ukraine soviétique (1944-1945)* (Louvain, 1956).

2. After the death on May 15, 1942 of patriarch Sergej of Moscow, the metropolitan of Leningrad Aleksej (Šimanskij) succeeded him as administrator and was later elected "patriarch of Moscow and all Russia."

3. See *Dijannja Soboru hreko-katolyc'koji Cerkvy u L'vovi 8-10 bereznja 1946* (L'viv 1946). For a critical study of the synod, see S.V., *Bol'ševyc'kyj Cerkovnyi Sobor u L'vovi 1946 r.* (New York, 1952).

4. After the death of bishop Stojka (May 31, 1943), the Mukačevo eparchy was governed temporarily by the capitular vicar A. Il'nyc'kyj. Because of opposition from the Hungarian government to the appointment of a Rusyn bishop, on January 1, 1944 the Apostolic See named the bishop of Hajdúdorog, Miklós Dudás, OSBM, administrator of the Mukačevo see. As the Soviet front approached, on September 8, 1944, Rome appointed Teodor Ju. Romža auxiliary bishop to Dudás with the right to govern the Mukačevo eparchy. His episcopal ordination was held on September 24, 1944 at the Užhorod cathedral. For bishop Romža's biography, see O. Pun'ko, "Preosv. Teodor Romža (24. IX. 1944—1. XI. 1947)" (Rome, 1949, manuscript); A. Pekar, *Vladyka-Mučenyk T. Romža* (New York, 1962); and A. Pekar, *Our Martyred Bishop Romzha (1911-1947)* (Pittsburgh, Pa., 1977).

5. For an account of the attempts to appoint an Orthodox bishop in Hungary, see W. de Vries, *Der christliche Osten in Geschichte und Gegenwart* (Würzburg, 1951), pp. 178-180.

6. See "Prebyvanie v Moskve delegacii pravoslavnoj Cerkvi Zakarpatskoj Ukrainy," *Žurnal Moskovskoj Patriarchii*, I, 1 (Moscow, 1945), pp. 5-10.

7. See "Prebyvanie v Moskve ep. Mukačevskago Vladimira," ibid., I, 11 (1945), pp. 20-21.

7a. As quoted by A. Punyko, *Bishop Theodore G. Romzha and the Soviet Occupation* (New York, 1967), p. 49.

8. Most of the defendants were Carpatho-Rusyn deputies to the Hungarian parliament in 1939-1944, including one priest, the archdeacon E. Ortutaj. The principal Hungarian collaborators—the archpriest Aleksander Il'nyc'kyj, canon Julij Maryna, and Dr. Stefan Fencyk—were tried separately (the Reverend Maryna managed to escape to the West), contrary to V. Markus's claim in "Nyščennja hreko-katol. cerkvy v Mukačivs'kij Jeparchiji," *Zapysky Naukovoho tovarystva im. Ševčenka*, CLXIX (Paris, 1969), p. 16.

9. See "Odna storinka z istoriji voz"jednannja," *Kalendar Dobroho Pastyrja na 1952 r.* (New York, 1952), pp. 110-113. Upon receiving the news that the Mukačevo monastery had been seized, patriarch Aleksei congratulated bishop Nestor: "I rejoice on account of this event. God's blessing on the monastery." See bishop Nestor's article, "Iz Zakarpattja," in *Žurnal*

Moskovskoj Patriarchii, III, 8 (Moscow, 1947). pp. 35-38.

10. *Ibid.*, III, 10 (1947), pp. 38-41, gives the figure of pilgrims as 30,000, but eyewitnesses dispute this number as false.

10a. Cf. the eyewitness description of bishop Romža's death by S. Karpatskij (pseudonym) in A. Pekar, *"You Shall Be Witnesses Unto Me": The Martyrology of the Byzantine Catholic Church in Subcarpathian Ruthenia* (Pittsburgh, Pa., 1985), pp. 31-35.

11. *Ecclesia*, no. 10 (Vatican City, 1949), p. 539. On the liquidation of the Mukačevo eparchy, see *Žurnal Moskovskoj Patriarchii*, V, 10 (Moscow, 1949), pp. 5-11; R.N., "Holhota uniji v Karpats'kij Ukrajini," *Žyttja i slovo,* no. 3-4 (Innsbruck, 1948-49), pp. 327-346; *Perši zakovani* (Buenos Aires, 1956), pp. 34-40; and G. de Vries, "Suppressione della Chiesa greco-cattolica nella Subcarpazia," *La Civilitá Cattolica*, II (Rome, 1950), pp. 391-399.

12. Close to 20,000 people attended bishop Romža's funeral, despite rainy weather.

13. See archbishop Makarij's biography in *Jeparchijal'nyj visnyk,* no. 4 (L'viv, 1946), pp. 5-7.

14. *Žurnal Moskovskoj Patriarchii*, V, 10 (Moscow, 1949), pp. 5-6. The following quotations are taken from this source.

15. They came "at night" because they were brought there "for conversations" by NKVD agents.

16. See archbishop Makarij's pastoral letter of August 28, 1949 in *ibid.*, pp. 7-9.

17. Former Greek Catholic priests from Galicia, A. Pel'vec'kyj and M. Mel'nyk, whom metropolitan Ivan of Kiev had ordained bishops in 1946. See *Perši zakovani*, p. 30.

18. *Žurnal Moskovskoj Patriarchii*, V, 10 (Moscow, 1949), p. 6.

19. *Ibid*, p. 11.

20. The Mukačevo monastery had been the repository of a miraculous icon of the Blessed Virgin that had been a gift of pope Pius XI in 1926. The patriarch sent another icon in its place as a gift from himself.

21. That is, Irynej Kondratovyč and two Hungarian priests, Papp and Becza.

22. We know from reports submitted to Rome that of 354 priests of the Mukačevo eparchy only 35 went over to Orthodoxy (cf. de Vries, "Suppressione," p. 398), even though archbishop Makarij claims that they constituted "a significant, overwhelming majority." *Žurnal Moskovskoj Patriarchii*, V, 10 (Moscow, 1949), p. 8.

23. For a history of Užhorod University, see V.A. Anučin, *Geografija Sovetskogo Zakarpat'ja* (Moscow, 1956), pp. 140-142.

24. See the decree of the papal nuncio in Budapest, dated April 13, 1939, in *Schematismus Dioeceseos Prešovensis pro A.D. 1944* (Prešov, 1944), p. 173.

25. For bishop Hopko's nomination, see *Blahovîstnyk* (Prešov), January 25, 1947, pp. 1-4; on his chirotony, see *ibid*, May 25, 1947, pp. 1-5, and the papal brief in Welykyj, *Documenta Pontificum*, Vol. II, pp. 594-595; for his

biography, see A. Pekar, *Bishop B. Hopko—Confessor of Faith* (Pittsburgh, Pa., 1979).

26. *Žurnal Moskovskoj Patriarchii*, II, 12, (Moscow, 1946), pp. 33-36.

26a. S. Sabol, *Holhota Hreko-katolyc'koji Cerkvy v Čechoslovaččyni* (Toronto and Rome, 1978), p. 112.

27. See R.N., "Nastup na ukrajins'ku Cerkvu na Prjašivščyni," *Chrystyjans'kyj holos* (Munich), May 15, 1949, p. 6.

28. Just as forcible magyarization in neighboring Carpatho-Ukraine, so forcible slovakization in the Prešov Region laid the groundwork for conversion to Orthodoxy. There is little cause for astonishment on the part of Dr. M. Lacko, who writes in his "Liquidation of the Diocese of Prešov," *Slovak Studies: Historica*, I (Rome, 1961), p. 152: "The Orthodox movement was working at that time among the Ruthenian people in upper Šariš and Zemplín counties." On the same page, Dr. Lacko accuses the Ukrainian National Council of having been the "principal collaborator" in the liquidation of the Greek Catholic Church in the Prešov Region, even though as the *Žurnal Moskovskoj Patriarchii*, VI, 7, (Moscow, 1950), p. 48, as well as *Svetlo Parvoslávia* II, 3, (Prague, 1951), p. 44 and the Reverend Lacko himself puts it, two members of the Slovak National Council and only one member of the Ukrainian National Council were members of the Central Committe for the return to Orthodoxy. It would appear that for the purposes of Slovak propaganda "one" Ukrainian outnumbers "two" Slovaks when it is a matter of determining the responsibility for the liquidation of the Prešov eparchy. Here the Reverend Lacko follows in the steps of Slovak nationalist propaganda, as does, for example, Th. Zubek, *The Church of Silence in Slovakia* (Passaic, N.J., 1956), pp. 220-221.

29. *Žurnal Moskovskoj Patriarchii*, VI, 7, (Moscow, 1950), p. 47.

30. *Ibid.*, p. 49.

30a. His original name was Biharij. The son of a Byzantine Catholic priest, he slovakized his name in order to appear a Slovak patriot.

31. Although 100 priests took part in the congress (as *ibid.*, p. 50 claims), this figure is questionable. Nonetheless, even that figure did not constitute the "overwhelming majority of the clergy," since there were 311 priests in the Prešov eparchy at the time.

32. *Ibid.*

33. The union was concluded in 1646; see above, Chapter 2, note 28.

34. The full text of the resolution appeared as a separate brochure: *Manifest gréckokatolickych duchovnych a veriacich, prijaty na sobore dňa 28. IV. 1940 v Prešove* (Prešov, 1950); and in *Svetlo Pravoslávia*, I, 1-2 (Prague, 1950), pp. 22-24.

35. For full text of the government decree, see *Žurnal Moskovskoj Patriarchii*, VI, 7 (Moscow, 1950), pp. 37-39. The Vatican's response to the Prešov synod is contained in an article entitled "Gli Uniati di Slovacchia," *L'Osservatore Romano* (Vatican), June 13, 1950. p. 1.

36. See S. Sabol, "Mučenyc'kyj šljach Preosv. P. Gojdyča, ČSVV," *Svitlo*, XXIII, 10 (Toronto, 1960), pp. 417-418. The record of the trial was

published by the Communists: *Proces proti vlastizradným biskupom J. Vojtaššakovi, M.Buzalkovi a P. Gojdičovi* (Bratislava, 1951), pp. 33-37, 115-139, 168-175, 203-210, 221-223. See also "Jak sudili Prjaševskoho Episkopa P. Gojdiča?," *Byzantine Catholic World* (Pittsburgh, Pa.), April 21-July 21, 1957, Nos. 16-29, p. 7 in all issues; J.A. Mikuš, *Three Slovak Bishops* (Passaic, N.J., 1953); and A. Pekar, *Bishop P. Gojdich, OSBM—Confessor of Our Times* (Pittsburgh, Pa., 1980), pp. 28-31.

37. S. Baran, "U Bratislavi ne sudovyj vyrok, ale sudovyj zločyn," *Chrystyjans'kyj holos* (Munich), January 28, 1951, p. 1.

38. See "Dolja Kyr Pavla Gojdyča," *Ameryka* (Philadelphia), March 8, 1951, p. 1: "The Communist court in Bratislava intended to condemn Bishop P. Gojdyč, OSBM, to death, but due to world public opinion it mitigated the sentence to life imprisonment."

39. "L'Ultimo Vescovo Ucraino condannato all'ergastolo," *L'Ora dell'Azione* (Rome), June 27, 1951, p. 9.

40. *L'Osservatore Romano,* September 17, 1960, p. 1.

41. On the founding of the Michalovce eparchy, see *Svetlo Pravoslávia*, I, 5-6 (Prague, 1950), pp. 49-76.

42. See P. Karnaševič, "Avtokefalija pravoslavnoj cerkvi v ČSSR," *Ežegodnik pravoslavnoj cerkvi v Čechoslovakii* (Prague, 1962), pp. 38-52.

10. In the Immigration

1. The Latin-rite Svidnik diocese (whose seat is not to be confused with the town of Svidník in the Prešov Region) had been part of the ecclesiastical province of the archbishop of Kalocsa, but it ceased to exist after the Turkish invasions in the sixteenth century. The first bishop of Marča to receive the title of bishop of Svidnik from the emperor was Gabre Predović in 1642. See Havryjil Kostel'nyk's article in *Nyva* (L'viv, 1932), p. 210.

2. *In partibus infidelium* is a technical expression used by the Roman Curia to designate former episcopal sees that were occupied and liquidated by "the infidels." Platea, now in Greece, was at that time occupied by the Ottoman Turks.

3. See A. Welykyj, ed., *Documenta Pontificum Romanorum historiam Ucrainae illustrantia*, Vol. II (Rome, 1954), pp. 254-255; and "S. Congregazione per la Chiesa Orientale," *Oriente Cattolico* (Vatican City, 1962), pp. 240-242.

4. See M. Vajda, "Kryževac'ka eparchija," *Kovčeh*, VII (Stamford, Conn., 1952), pp. 124-125; H. Kostel'nyk, "Kryživs'ka Eparchija," *Nyva, XXVI* (L'viv, 1932), pp. 134-139, 168-179, 209-215; XXVII (1933), pp. 143-147, 175-181; the statistical data is taken from *Annuario Pontificio 1965*, p. 222.

5. A. Pekar, "Čolovik provydinnja" [on the occasion of the 25th anniversary of the death of Bishop D. Njaradij], *Svitlo*, XXVII, 10 (Toronto, 1965), pp. 354-357; M. Firak, "Pokojni Vladika dr. D. Njaradij (1874-1940)," *Ruski kalendar za rusinoch u Jugoslavii na r. 1941* (Ruski Krstur, 1940).

6. M. Vajda, "Smert' herojs'koho jepyskopa," *Kovčeh*, II, 5 (Stamford,

NOTES TO PAGES 165-168
Conn., 1947), pp. 89-90.

7. "Msgr. dr. Gabriel Bukatko," in *Jubilarni Šematizam Križevačke Eparhije* (Zagreb, 1962), pp. 15-20.

8. M.M., "Kryževac'ka eparchija i jiji novyj Vladyka, Preosv. Kyr Joakym," *Ameryka* (Philadelphia), August 23, 1963, p. 2.

8a. Cf. *Servizio Informazioni per le Chiese Orientali*, Vol. XXXVIII, No. 443-444 (Rome, 1983), pp. 10-12.

9. N. Bachtin, *Ugorskaja Rus'* (Petrograd, 1915), pp. 23-30; V. Hnatjuk "Najnovijši visty z Uhors'koji Rusy," in *Peršij rusko-amerykanskij kalendar'* (Mount Carmel, Pa., 1897), pp. 27-39; René Martel, *La Ruthénie subcarpathique* (Paris, 1935), p. 151, wrote: "Thus, it was to pursue methodically the material ruin of the Rusyn nation, a status that was necessary and a precursor to its political subjugation. . . . magyarization followed the evolution of Rusyn economic decline."

10. A. Kudryk, *Vid Popradu po Tysu* (L'viv, 1939), p. 37.

11. Immigrants from Galicia called themselves "Galician Rusyns," while those from Carpathian Rus' referred to themselves as "Hungarian Rusyns" (*uhrorusyny*).

12. For the history of the parish in Shenandoah, see *Peršij rusko-amerykanskij kalendar'*, pp. 134-139; and Bohdan Procko, *Ukrainian Catholics in America* (Washington, D.C., 1982), p. 2-4.

13. See *Ukrajins'ka Katolyc'ka Mytropolija v ZDA* (Philadelphia, 1959), p. 202.

15. I. Konstankevyč and A. Bončevs'kyj, *Unija v Amerycî* (New York, 1902), pp. 24-26; *Peršij rusko-amerykanskij kalendar'*, pp. 51-53.

16. *Ukrajins'ka Katolyc'ka Mytropolija*, pp. 206-207.

17. Of the 10 Greek Catholic priests then in the United States, eight attended the consultation: A. Toth (from the eparchy of Prešov); I. Zapotocky (Prešov); T. Obushkevych (Przemyśl); A. Dzubay (Mukačevo); G. Hrushka (L'viv); E. Volkay (Mukačevo); H. Vysloc'kyj (Prešov); and S. Jackovics (Mukačevo). The other two clergymen, C. Andrukhovych (L'viv) and K. Gulovych (a Basilian from the Mukačevo eparchy), refused to take part in the meeting on the grounds that it was being held in the parish house instead of a hotel.

18. For the minutes of the Wilkes-Barre consultation, see P. Kochanik, *Rus' i Pravoslavije v Sievernoj Amerike* (Wilkes-Barre, Pa. 1920), p. 12-19; and E. Volkay, "Sobor hreko-kat. svjaščennikov v Vilkes Barre," *Lystok*, VII, 2 (Užhorod, 1891), pp. 15-17. The Reverend Volkay was the secretary at the consultation. The minutes were sent to the Metropolitan of L'viv and to the bishops of Mukačevo and Prešov.

19. Kochanik, *Rus' i Pravoslavije*, pp. 20-29.

20. See A. Pekar, "Cerkovna polityka madjariv na Zakarpatt'i," *Svitlo*, XXVIII, 4 (Toronto, 1965), pp. 170-173. At the time the leader of the magyarization process, parliamentary representative Jenő Szabó, told the Reverend Vološyn: "Rusyn culture under the Carpathian Mountains, in the vicinity of the Metropolitan of L'viv, poses a threat to us." Vološyn, *Spomyny* (Philadelphia, 1959), p. 15.

21. The Carpatho-Rusyn historian, Nikolaj Beskid, known for his Russophilism, claimed that the Hungarian authorities sent "special agitators" to the United States, and that the priests were compelled to take "a special oath of loyalty to the Hungarian government" before their departure. Cf. *Karpatskij svjet*, II, 4 (Užhorod, 1929), p. 515. The efforts of the Hungarian government to control Carpatho-Rusyn immigrants in the United States through their clergy were recently revealed in full, based on the documents in the Budapest and Vienna archives, by Marija Majer, "Zakarpats'ki ukrajinci na perelomi stolit'," *Žovten' i ukrajins'ka kul'tura: zbirnyk* (Prešov, 1968), pp. 65-73; and more thoroughly in her book, M. Mayer, *Kárpátukrán (ruszin) politikai és társadalmi törekvések, 1860-1910* (Budapest, 1977), pp. 180-204.

22. A history of the Greek Catholic Union is found in *Zoloto-jubilejnyj Kalendar' Greko-Kaft. Sojedinenija v S.S.A.* (Munhall, Pa., 1942), pp. 39-74.

23. From 1914, its name was changed to the Ukrainian National Association. Its history is provided by L. Myšuga, *Propamjatna knyha Ukrajins'koho Narodnoho Sojuza* (Jersey City, N.J., 1936), pp. 193-207.

24. Konstankevyč and Bončevs'kyj, *Unija*, pp. 35-41; "Vizytator i jeho perši kroky," *Svoboda* (Jersey City, N.J.), June 12, 1902, p. 4; "Z vysokoj polityky," *ibid.*, June 19, 1904, p. 2; "O. Andrij Hodobaj Jepyskopom," *ibid.*, June 30, 1904, p. 4. J. Sekerak, "Naša religijna obščestvennost'," in *Zoloto-jubilejnyj kalendar'*, p. 189, commented: "He [Hodobay] was a political exponent of Hungarian interests."

25. L. Sembratovyč, "Jak pryjšlo do imenuvannja našoho peršoho Jepyskopa v Ameryci," in *Kalendar Provydinnja na 1956 r.* (Philadelphia, 1956), pp. 71-74.

26. Welykyj, *Documenta Pontificum*, Vol. II, pp. 496-502; *Poslanije pastyrs'koje S. Ortyns'koho, jepyskopa, z nahody Bully* [January 11, 1908] (Philadelphia, 1908) and the response in *Svoboda*, February 6—March 26, 1908: "Protest proty Paps'koji Bulli" signed by 78 priests.

27. Quoted from "Jak pryvytaly nominaciju o. S. Ortyns'koho," *Nyva*, II (L'viv, 1907), pp. 230-232.

28. Bishop Ortynsky arrived in the United States on August 29, 1907. For an account of his welcome, see *Kalendar Provydinnja na 1932 r.* (Philadelphia, 1932), pp. 118-120.

29. A. Pekar, "Ternystym šljachom Vladyky-Pionera," *Svitlo*, XXIX, 3 and 4 (Toronto, 1966), pp. 100-102 and 147; V. Vavryk, *Jepyskop Soter Ortyns'kyj, ČSVV* (New York, 1956), pp. 33-52; H. Lužnyc'kyj, *Jepyskop-Pioner Kyr Soter z Ortynyč Ortyns'kyj, ČSVV* (Philadelphia, 1963), pp. 65-70.

30. See the letter from the apostolic delegate of September 8, 1908, in *Dušpastyr'*, I, 9, (New York, 1909), p. 142.

31. More than 40 priests who were also joined by several Russophile Galician priests.

32. See *Protokol Všeobecnoho Kongressu Amerikanskich greko-katol. Uhro-Russkich Farnoscoch, 11-12 januara 1910 v Johnstown, Pa.* (Homestead, Pa., 1910).

33. A. Papp, "Korotkij perehl'ad istoriji Sobranija za 1903-1928r.," in

Kalendar' Sobranija na 1929 r. (McKeesport, Pa., 1929), pp. 136-152.

34. *Dušpastyr'*, I, 5, (New York, 1909), p. 79.

35. For the announcement of the creation of the "Ruthenian rite" eparchy in the United States, see *American Ecclesiastical Review*, XLIX (Washington, 1913), pp. 473-474; for the Apostolic decree of the erection, see *Acta Apostolicae Sedis*, Vol. VI (Vatican City, 1914), pp. 458-463. These documents are copied in W. Paska, *Sources of Particular Law for the Ukrainian Catholic Church in the United States* (Washington, D.C., 1975), pp. 157-162.

35a. Cited from a copy of the letter in the author's possession.

36. See their letter to the apostolic delegate, dated September 11, 1913, in *Kalendar' Sojedinenija na 1914 hod* (Munhall, Pa. 1914), pp. 199-202.

37. *Ibid.*, pp. 206-207.

38. For materials on the nomination of the vicar-general and the consistory, see *Eparchijal'nyj vistnyk* (Philadelphia), March 15, 1914, pp. 1-2. On the reconciliation between the Carpatho-Rusyns and bishop Ortynsky, see *Nauka*, XVII, 11 (Užhorod, 1913), p. 30.

39. Cf. *Acta Apostolicae Sedis*, Vol. VI (Vatican City, 1914), pp. 458-463; and Bohdan Procko, *Ukrainian Catholics in America* (Washington, D.C., 1982), pp. 30-33.

40. *Ukrajins'ka Katolyc'ka Mytropolija v ZDA*, p. 225.

41. For an account of his apostasy and ordination, see *Kalendar Obščestva Vzaimopomošči na 1917 g.* (Wilkes-Barre, Pa., 1917), pp. 182-200. Dzubay's apostasy was widely discussed in *Rusin*, VIII, nos. 30-40 (Pittsburgh, 1916). Cf. Procko, *Ukrainian Catholics*, pp. 37-41.

42. See *Nyva*, XVIII (L'viv, 1924), pp. 291-292. Dzubay's obituary appeared in *Dušpastyr'*, X (Užhorod, 1933), p. 159.

43. The consecration of both bishops was held in Rome on June 15, 1924; see *Dušpastyr'*, I (Užhorod, 1924), pp. 151-153. In the bulls of nomination, Philadelphia was designated as the seat of bishop C. Bohachevsky and New York (later moved to Pittsburgh) as the seat of bishop B. Takach. But bishop Takach settled in a suburb of Pittsburgh, in Homestead, where the principal headquarters of the Greek Catholic Union were located, in order to be able "to hold his finger on the pulse of the Union," as he informed his priests. See Welykyj, *Documenta Pontificum*, Vol. II, pp. 541-543.

43a. From a copy of the letter in the author's possession.

43b. From a copy of the letter in the author's possession.

44. See bishop Takach's pastoral letter of January 14, 1926, p. 4.

45. *Acta Apostolicae Sedis*, Vol. XXI (Vatican City, 1929), pp. 152-159; T.L. Bouscaren, *The Canon Law Digest*, Vol. I (Milwaukee, Wisc., 1933), pp. 6-16.

46. The beginnings of the battle over the celibacy issue are described in *Nyva*, XXV (L'viv, 1931), pp. 426-429; *Dobryj pastyr'*, I (Stanyslaviv), 1931, pp. 306-307; II (1932), pp. 57-61; V (1935), pp. 138-139. The first protest against celibacy came from the local branch of the Greek Catholic Union in Bridgeport, Connecticut, in the form of a letter dated September 18, 1929.

This letter was later published in the *Leader-Vožd*, II, 11 (Cleveland, 1930), p. 16. Cf. M.Z., "Za čto my borimesja?," in *Kalendar' Sobranija na 1935 r.* (McKeesport, Pa., 1935), pp. 111-122; *Amerikansky Russky Viestnik* (Homestead, Pa.), July 7, 1932 and following issues; "Petition to Pope," *ibid.*, August 14, 1933; "Resolution of K.O.V.O.," *ibid.*, October 5, 1933; and *Protocollum Conferentiae Cleri* (Pittsburgh), August 30, 1933, a copy of which is in the possession of the author.

47. See bishop Takach's pastoral letter of August 3, 1936, p. 1.

48. Cf. *Silver Anniversary of the American Carpatho-Russian Orthodox Greek Catholic Diocese of USA* (Johnstown, Pa., 1963), *passim*; O. Koman, "Jak nastala independencija?," in *Kalendar' Sojedinenija na 1951 r.* (Munhall, Pa., 1951), pp. 46-48. For extensive details, see Lawrence Barriger, *Good Victory* (Brookline, Mass., 1985).

49. P. Zeedick and A. Smor, *Naše stanovišče* (Homestead, Pa., 1934).

50. Welykyj, *Documenta Pontificum*, Vol. II, pp. 592-593; for a brief biography of bishop Daniel Ivancho (1946-1954), see Basil Shereghy, *A Historical Album on the Occasion of the 75th Anniversary of the United Societies* (McKeesport, Pa., 1978), pp. 34-36.

51. Obituary in *Amerikansky Russky Viestnik*, May 13, 1948, pp. 1-2 and May 20, 1948, pp. 1, 4-5. See also Basil Shereghy, *Bishop Basil Takach* (Pittsburgh, Pa., 1979).

52. Cf. B. Shereghy and A. Pekar, *The Training of Carpatho-Ruthenian Clergy* (Pittsburgh, 1951), pp. 121-126.

53. In 1910, bishop Ortynsky bought land for a seminary in Yorktown, Virginia. But it soon became clear that the location was unsuitable because it was malarious. Since the number of seminarians was small and funds were unavailable, the construction of a seminary was postponed to an unspecified time in the future. For information about the Pittsburgh seminarians in Baltimore, see *Kalendar' Sobranija na 1921 r.* (McKeesport, Pa., 1921), pp. 189-191.

54. Cf. *Diocesan Pastorals and Communications,* June 14, 1950, p. 1.

55. Cf. *Nebesna Carica,* XXVI, 10 (McKeesport, Pa., 1951), *passim*. This entire issue was dedicated to the seminary. See also Shereghy, *Historical Album*, pp. 129-138.

56. S. Sabol, "Hreko-katolyc'ka jeparchija v ZDA, pro jaku malo znajemo," *Kalendar Slova Dobroho Pastyrja na 1952 r.* (New York, 1952), pp. 99-100. For a historical description of the Uniontown pilgrimages, see Basil Shereghy, *Fifty Years of Piety* (Pittsburgh, Pa., 1985).

Bibliography

I. PRIMARY SOURCES

A. Archival Collections

1. **Archivum Secretum Vaticanum (ASV):**
   Archivum Sacrae Congregationis Consistorialis:

   Acta S. Congregationis Consistorialis anni 1771; Acta S. Congregationis Consistorialis anni 1818; Acta S. Congregationis Consistorialis anni 1823; Acta S. Congregationis Consistorialis anni 1853; Processi Canonici, Vol. 239 (m. Julio a. 1837).

   Archivum Nuntiaturae Vindobonensis—Vols. 79, 85, 86, 87, 89, 90, 172, 175, 381; *Processi Canonici*—fasc. 515, 687, 706, 828, 921, 956, 966.

   Archivum Nuntiaturae Germaniae—Vols. 381, 382, 384, 387, 388, 392, 393-4, 646, 654-5, 704, 723.

2. **Archivum Sacrae Congregationis de Propaganda Fide (APF):**

   Acta S. Congregationis de Propaganda Fide, Vol. 86.

   Miscellanea Valachorum Graeci Ritus—Generalia, Vol. 1.

   Miscellanea Valachicorum Graeci Ritus a. 1773, Vol. I.

   Scritture Originali riferite nelle Congregazioni Generali, Vol. 610.

   Scritture riferite nelle Congregazioni Particolari, Vols. 20, 21.

   Scritture riferite nei Congressi—Greci di Croazia, Dalmazia, Schiavonia, Transilvania ed Ungheria, Vol. I (1642-1760); Vol. II (1761-1845).

B. Published Works

Baran, A. "Archiepiscopus Raphaël Havrilovič eiusque activitas in eparchia Mukačoviensi." *Orientalia Christiana Periodica, XXXI* (Rome, 1965), pp. 119-134.

————"Archiepiscopus Theophanes Maurocordato eiusque activitas in eparchia Mukačoviensi." *Orientalia Christiana Periodica,* XXVII (Rome, 1961), pp. 115-130.

————"Documenta inedita de confirmatione Parthenii Petrovyč, eppi. Mukačoviensis." *Analecta OSBM,* III (Rome, 1960), pp. 440-448.

_____"Progetto del Patriarcato Ucraino di Gregorio XVI." *Analecta OSBM,* III (Rome, 1960), pp. 454-475.

_____"Quaedam ad biographiam J. Vološynovskyj, eppi. Makačoviensis (1667)." *Analecta OSBM,* II (Rome, 1954), pp. 209-227.

Basilovits, J. *Brevis notitia fundationis Theodori Koriathovits,* 2 vols., 6 pts. Košice, 1799-1804.

Beneš, E. *Reč o podkarpatorusskoj probleme.* Užhorod, 1934.

Bouscaren, T. L. *The Canon Law Digest,* 5 vols. Milwaukee, Wisc., 1933-63.

Bušek, V.; Hendrych, J.; Laštovka, K.; and Muller, V. *Československé církevní zákony* Prague, 1931.

De Clercq, Ch. *Histoire des Conciles,* Vol. XI: *Conciles des Orientaux catholiques,* 2 vols., Paris, 1949-52.

Dijannja Soboru hreko-katolyc'koji cerkvy u L'vovi, 8-10 bereznja 1946. L'viv, 1946.

Duchnovič, A. *The History of the Eparchy of Prjašev.* Translated with notes by A. Pekar. Rome, 1971.

Duliškovič, I. *Istoričeskija čerty ugro-russkich,* 3 vols. Užhorod, 1874-77.

Džudžar, Ju. *Katolyc'ka Cerkva vyzantijs'ko-slovjans'koho obrjadu v Jugoslaviji.* Rome, 1986.

Fraknói, V. *Oklevéltár a magyar királyi kegyuri jog történetéhez, Budapest, 1899.*

Grigássy, J. "O ungvarskom unional'nom dokumenti," in *Kalendar' Sobranija 1935.* McKeesport, Pa., 1935, pp. 102-110.

Haluščynskyj, T., and Welykyj, A., eds. *Epistolae, Josephi V. Rutskyj, metropolitae Kioviensis catholici (1613-1637).* Rome, 1956.

Harasiewicz, M. *Annales Ecclesiae Ruthenae.* L'viv, 1862.

Hodinka, A., ed. *A munkácsi görög szertartásu püspökség okmánytára.* Užhorod, 1911.

Holoweckyj, D. *Fontes Juris Canonici Ecclesiae Ruthenae.* Vatican City, 1932.

Lacko, M. "Ad Diplomatarium eparchiae Mukačevensis A. Hodinka supplementa vindobonensia." *Orientalia Christiana Periodica,* XXIII (Rome, 1957), pp. 332-353.

_____. "New Documents About M. M. Olšavsky, Bishop of Mukačevo." *Orientalia Christiana Periodica,* XXV (Rome, 1959), pp. 53-90.

_____. *Unio Užhorodensis Ruthenorum Carpaticorum cum Ecclesia Catholica.* Rome, 1955.

Libellus Memorialis Hungarorum Graeci Ritus Catholicorum ad SS. Patrem Leonen XIII. Budapest, 1900.

Niles, N. *Symbolae ad illustrandam historiam Ecclesiae Orientalis in terris Coronae S. Stephani,* 2 vols. Innsbruck, 1885.

Pekar, A. "Some Documents Concerning the 'Bradač Affair', " *Analecta OSBM,* X (Rome, 1979), pp. 221-228.

Perugini, A. *Concordata vigentia.* Rome, 1934.

Peterffy, C. *Sacra Concilia Ecclesiae Romano-Catholicae in Regno Hungariae celebrata aa. 1016-1715.* Vienna, 1742.

Petrov, Aleksei L. *Drevnejšija gramoty po istorii karpatorusskoj cerkvi i ierarchii 1391-1498 gg.* Prague, 1930.

————. *Duchovno-polemičeskija sočinenija jer. M. Orosvigovskago Andrelly protiv katoličestva i unii.* Prague, 1932.

————. *Národopisná mapa Uher podle uředního lexikonu osad z roku 1773.* Prague, 1924.

Petruševyč, A. *Dopolnenija ko Svodnoj halycko-russkoj litopysy s 1660 po 1700 h.* L'viv, 1891.

Ploechl, W. "The Church Laws for Orientals of the Austrian Monarchy in the Age of Enlightenment." *Bulletin of the Polish Institute of Arts and Sciences in America,* II, 3 (New York, 1944), pp. 711-756.

Proces proti vlastizradným biskupom—Jánovi Vojtaššákovi, Michalovi Buzalkovi, Pavlovi Gojdičovi. Bratislava, 1951.

Sacra Congregazione Orientale. *Codificazione Canonica Orientale—Fonti,* Facs. VIII: *Studi Storici.* Vatican City, 1932.

————. *Oriente Cattolico.* Vatican City, 1962.

————. *Statistica con cenni storici della gerarchia e dei fedeli di Rito Orientale.* Vatican City, 1932.

Slivka, John. *Historical Mirror: Sources of the Rusin and Hungarian Greek Rite Catholics in the U.S.A., 1884-1963.* Brooklyn, N.Y., 1978.

Svencickij, I. *Materijaly po istorii vozroždenija Karpatskoj Rusi.* L'viv, 1906.

Strypskij, Ja. N. *Hdî dokumentŷ staršej ystoriy Podkarpatskoj Rusy?* Užhorod, 1924.

Theiner, A., ed. *Clementis XIV: Epistulae et brevia selectiora.* Paris, 1852.

————. *Vetera monumenta historiam Hungariae sacram illustrantia,* 2 vols. Rome, 1859-1860.

————. *Vetera monumenta Poloniae et Lithuaniae gentiumque finitimarum historiam illustrantia,* Vol. III. Rome, 1863.

Welykyj, A., ed. *Acta S. Congregationis de Propaganda Fide Ecclesiam Catholicam Ucrainae et Bielarusjae spectantia,* 5 vols. Rome 1953-55.

————. *Congregationes Particulares Ecclesiam Catholicam Ucrainae et Bielarusjae spectantes,* 2 vols. Rome, 1956-57.

————. *Documenta Pontificum Romanorum historiam Ucrainae illustrantia,* 2 vols. Rome, 1953-54.

————. *Litterae S.C. de Propaganda Fide Ecclesiam Catholicam Ucrainae et Bielarusjae spectantes,* 7 vols. Rome, 1954-57.

II. SECONDARY SOURCES

Aleksij. "Pravoslavie na Podkarpatskoj Rusi," in *Podkarpatskaja Rus' za gg. 1919-35.* Užhorod, 1936, pp. 97-100.

Aradei, V. *A ruthén skizmapör.* Budapest, 1914.

A.V. "Vizantijs'ko-madjarskyj obrjad?" *Ameryka* (Philadelphia), May 18, 1957, p. 3.

Bača, Jurij and Rudlovčak, Olena, eds. *Chrestomatija novoji zakarpats'koji ukrajins'koji literatury (XIX st.).* Bratislava, 1964.

Bachtin, N. *Ugorskaja Rus'.* Petrograd, 1915.

Balogh, M. *A mármarosi görög szertartású orosz egyház és vikáriátus története.* Užhorod, 1909.

Baran, Alexander. *Eparchia Maramorošiensis eiusque unio.* Rome, 1962.

————. *Metropolia Kioviensis et Eparchia Mukačoviensis.* Rome, 1960.

————. *Jepyskop Andrej Bačynskyj i cerkovne vidrodžennja na Zakarpatti.* Yorkton, Sask., 1963.

————. "Podil mukačivs'koji eparchiji v XIX storičči." *Zapysky ČSVV,* IV, 3-4 (Rome, 1963), pp. 534-569.

————. "Pytannja ukrajins'koho patrijarchatu v polovyni XIX st." *Lohos,* XIII, 1 (Yorkton, Sask., 1962), pp. 26-36.

————. "Synod u Vidni 1773-ho r." *Zapysky ČSVV,* III, 3-4 (Rome, 1960), pp. 394-403.

Baran, Stepan. *Vesna narodiv v avstro-uhors'kij Ukrajini.* Munich, 1948.

Barriger, Lawrence. *Good Victory: Metropolitan O. Chornock and the American Carpatho-Russian Orthodox Greek Catholic Diocese.* Brookline, Mass., 1985.

Barvins'kyj, Bohdan. *Nazva 'Ukrajina' na Zakarpatti.* Winnipeg, 1952.

Beskid, Konstantin M. *Maramarošský proces.* Chust, 1926.

Beskid, Nikolaj. *Iz minuvšaho odnoj krest'anskoj semji (Židik-Olšavsky),* Homestead, Pa., n.d.

————. "Prjaševskaja eparchija," in *Kalendar' Sojedinenija na 1933 h.* Homestead, Pa., 1933, pp. 67-103.

————. [Beszkid, M.] *A sz. Péter és Pál nevezett tapolcai apátság története.* Užhorod, 1903.

Birčak, V. *Literaturni stremlinnja Pidkarpats'koji Rusy.* Užhorod, 1937.

————. *Na novych zemljach.* L'viv, 1938.

Bobák, A. *De iure patronatus supremi quoad Ecclesiam Ruthenicam in Hungaria.* Rome, 1943.

Bočkovs'kyj, O.I. *B.Bjerson, ponevoleni narody ta ukrajins'ka sprava.* Winnipeg, Man., 1939.

Borščak, I. *Karpats'ka Ukrajina u mižnarodnij hri.* L'viv, 1938.

Boruch, I.G. *Naše cerkovno-narodne dilo v Ameryky.* New York, 1950.

Boržava, Ju. *Vid Uhors'koji Rusy do Karpats'koji Ukrajiny.* Philadelphia, 1956.

Boysak, Basil. *Ecumenism and Manuel M. Olshavsky, Bishop of Mukachevo.* Montreal, 1967.

————. *The Fate of the Holy Union in Carpatho-Ukraine.* Toronto and New York, 1963.

Bušek, V. "Poměr státu k církvim Č.S.R.," in *Československá vlastivěda,* Vol. V: *Stát.* Prague, 1931, pp. 324-361.

Catoire, A. "L'évêché de Hajdudorogh." *Echos d'Orient,* XVI (Paris, 1913), p. 454 ff.

252 BIBLIOGRAPHY

Chaloupecký, V. "Dvě studie k dějinám Podkarpatska." *Sborník Filosofické Fakulty,* III (Bratislava, 1925), pp. 131-142.

Charlampov, P. "K istorii pravoslavnogo monašestva v Zakarpat'e." *Žurnal Moskovskoj Patriarchii,* XIII, 5 (Moscow, 1957), pp. 61-65.

Chira, A. "De statu conaminum unitatem promoventium in Podkarpatska Rus'," in *Acta V. Conventus Velehradensis a. 1927.* Olomouc, 1927, pp. 202-207.

Chomyn, P. "Cerkovne pytannja na Pidk. Rusy." *Nyva,* XVI (L'viv, 1922), pp. 2-7, 46-52, 123-128.

Cinek, F. *K náboženské otázce v prvních letech naší samostatnosti 1918-1925.* Olomouc, 1926.

Csáky, E. *La question ruthène.* Paris and Budapest, 1920.

Cziple, S. *A máramorosi püspökség kérdése.* Budapest, n.d.

Dampier, M. G. *History of the Orthodox Church in Austria-Hungary.* London, 1905.

De Martinis, R. *Iuris Pontificii de Propaganda Fide,* Vol. IV, pt. 1. Rome, 1892.

De Vries, G. "Suppressione della Chiesa greco-cattolica nella Subcarpazia," in *La Civiltá Cattolica.* Rome, 1950, pp. 391-399.

De Vries, W. *Der christliche Osten in Geschichte und Gegenwart.* Würzburg, 1951.

Djurkan', I. "Čes'ki OO. Redemptorysty na Zakarpatti," in *Marijs'kyj juvilejnyj kalendar-al'manach na 1939 r.* L'viv and Stanyslaviv, pp. 57-62.

————. "OO. Redemptorysty schidn'oho obrjadu na Zakarpatti," in *Juvilejna knyha OO. Redemptorystiv schidn'oho obrjadu 1906-1956.* Yorkton, Sask., 1955, pp. 202-208.

Dobrjanskij, A.I. *O sovremennom religiozno-političeskom položenii Avstro-Ugorskoj Rusi,* Moscow, 1885.

————. "Otryvki iz političeskich statej," in Ivan Šlepeckij, ed. *Prjaševščina.* Prague, 1948, pp. 177-182.

Dorošenko, D. *Die Namen 'Rus', 'Russland' und 'Ukraine' in ihrer historischen und gegenwärtigen Bedeutung.* Berlin, 1931.

————. *Uhors'ka Ukrajina.* Prague, 1919.

Duker, Russell A. *The Byzantine Catholic Synod of Vienna of 1773.* Rome, 1982.

Egan, E. *Ekonomične položennja rus'kych seljan v Uhorščyni.* L'viv, 1922.

Farkas, L. *Egy nemzeti küzdelem története.* Budapest, 1896.

F.C. "Création d'un diocèse de rite greco-catholique en Hongrie." *Echos d'Orient,* XV (Paris, 1912), pp. 553-555.

Fedeleš, V.I. *Učebnik istorii Podkarpatskoj Rusi.* Mukačevo 1922.

Fedor, P.S. *Kratkij očerk djejatel'nosti A.I. Dobrjanskago.* Užhorod, 1926.

Fencik, E. "Monastyr' Hruševskij," in *Kalendar' Sobranija na 1923 r.* McKeesport, Pa., 1923, pp. 141-142.

Fiedler, J. "Beiträge zur Geschichte der Union der Ruthenen in Nord-Ungarn und der Immunität des Clerus derselben." *Sitzungsberichte der kaiserlichen Akademie der Wissenschaften: Philosophisch-Historische Classe,* XXXIX, 4 (Vienna, 1862), pp. 481-524.

Firak, M. "Pokojni Vladika dr. D. Njaradi (1874-1940)," in *Ruski kalendar za Rusinoch u Jugoslavi na r. 1941.* Ruski Kerestur, 1940.

Francev, V.A. "Iz istorii bor'by za russkij literaturnyj jazyk v Podkarpatskoj Rusy," in *Karpatorusskij sbornik.* Užhorod, 1930, pp. 5-38.

_____. *Obzor važnejšich izučenij Ugorskoj Rusi.* Warsaw, 1901.

Gerovskij, Georgij. "Istoričeskoe prošloe Prjaševščiny," in Ivan Šlepeckij, ed. *Prjaševščina.* Prague, 1948, pp. 47-93.

Gatti, C. and Korolevskyj, C. *I Riti e le Chiese Orientali.* Genoa, 1942.

Grabec, M. *K istorii maramorosškago procesa.* Užhorod, 1934.

Grigássy, Gyula. *A magyar görög-katholikus legujabb története.* Užhorod, 1913.

Grigorič, V. *Pravoslavná církev v Republice Československé.* Prague, 1926.

Gulovich, Stephen C. "The Rusin Exarchate in the United States." *Eastern Churches Quarterly,* VI (London, 1946), pp. 459-486.

Hadžega, Vasylij. "Dodatky k ystoriy rusynov y rus'kych cerkvej v Maramoroší." *Naukovyj zbornyk tovarystva 'Prosvita',* I (Užhorod 1922), pp. 140-266.

_____. "Dodatky k ystoriy rusynov y rus'kych cerkvej v Užanskoj župî." *Naukovyj zbornyk t-va 'Prosvita',* II (1923), pp. 1-64; III (1924), pp. 155-239.

_____. "Dodatky k ystoriy rusynôv y rus'kych cerkvej v župî Ugoča." *Naukovyj zbornik t-va 'Prosvita',* IV (1925), pp. 117-176; V (1927), pp. 1-62.

_____. "Dodatky do ystoriî rusynôv y rus'kych cerkvej v buv. župî Zemplynskôj." *Naukovyj zbornyk t-va 'Prosvita',* VII-VIII (1931), pp. 1-167; IX (1932), pp. 1-67; X (1934), pp. 17-120; XI (1935), pp. 17-182; XII (1937), pp. 37-83.

_____. "Dva najdavnîjšî našy pryvyleî." *Naukovyj zbornyk tovarystva 'Prosvita',* VI (Užhorod, 1929), pp. 267-274.

_____. "Josyf Vološynovs'kyj, jepiskop Mukačivs'kyj i I. Malachovs'kyj, jepiskop peremys'kyj, jak jepiskop mukačivs'kyj." *Zapysky ČSVV,* IV, 1-2 (Žovkva, 1932), pp. 161-170.

_____. "Papska bulla o pereloženju osîdka hreko-kat. mukačîvskoî eparchiî z Mukačeva do Užhorodu." *Naukovyj zbornyk tovarystva 'Prosvita',* XI (Užhorod, 1935), pp. 1-7.

_____. "Perva sproba istoriî hreko-katoličeskoî mukačevs'koî eparchiî." *Naukovyj zbornyk t-va 'Prosvita',* III (Užhorod, 1924), pp. 1-27.

_____. "Přehled církevnîch dějin na Podkarpaské Rusi," in J. Zatloukal, ed. *Podkarpatská Rus.* Bratislava, 1936, pp. 270-278.

Hadžega, Ju. Julij [Gadžega, Julij]. *Dva istoričeskich voprosa.* Užhorod, 1928.

————. *Istorija O-va sv. Vasilija Velikago.* Užhorod, 1925.

————. *Istorija užgorodskoj bogoslovskoj seminarii v jeja glavnych čertach.* Užhorod, 1928.

————. *Naša pravda v viri.* Užhorod, 1920.

————. *Stat'i po voprosam 'pravoslavija', narodnosti i katoličestva.* Užhorod, 1921.

Halecki, Oscar. *From Florence to Brest (1439-1596).* Rome, 1958.

Hanak, Walter K. *The Subcarpathian-Ruthenian Question, 1918-1945,* Munhall, Pa., 1962.

Haraksim, L'udovít. *K sociálnym a kultúrnym dejinám Ukrajincov na Slovensku do r. 1867.* Bratislava, 1961.

Hartl, A. *Die litterarische Renaissance der Karpathoruthenen.* Prague, 1932.

Heisler, J.B. and Mellon, J.E. *Under the Carpathians: Home of a Forgotten People.* London, 1946.

Hnatjuk, V. "Najnoviši visti z Uhors'koji Rusy," in *Peršij ruskoamerikanskij kalendar'.* Mount Carmel, Pa., 1897, pp. 27-39.

Hodinka, A. *A munkácsi görög-katholikus püspökség története.* Budapest, 1909.

Hončarenko, A. "Plamennyj borec protiv Vatikana i unii," in *V sim"ji jedynij.* Užhorod, 1954, pp. 213-218.

Hopko, V. *Greko-katoličeskaja cerkov (1646-1946).* Prešov, 1946.

Hryhorijiv-Naš, N. *T.H. Masaryk, joho žyttja ta dijal'nist'.* Prague, 1925.

Il'nyc'kij, A. *Pamjatna knyha po juvylejnomu rymskomu palomnyčestvu podk. rusynov sv. hoda 1925 r.* Užhorod, 1926.

"Jak sudili Prjaševskoho ep. P. Gojdiča?." *Byzantine Catholic World* (Pittsburgh), Nos. 16-24, April 21-July 21, 1950.

J.E. Pavel Gojdič, ČSSV, jepiskop prjaševskij (1927-1947). Prešov, 1947.

Jósika-Herczeg, Imre de. *Hungary After a Thousand Years.* New York, 1934.

Kadlec, Karel. *Podkarpatskaja Rus'.* Užhorod, 1922.

Karnaševič, P. "Avtokefalia pravoslavnoj cerkvi v ČSSR," in *Ežegodnik Pravoslavnoj Cerkvi v Čechoslovakii.* Prague, 1962, pp. 38-52.

Kochanik, P. *Rus' i pravoslavie v Sjevernoj Amerikje.* Wilkes Barre, Pa., 1920.

Kochannyj-Goralčuk, Kiril. *Podkarpatská Rus v minulosti a přitomnosti.* Prague, 1931.

Kolomiec, I.G. *Očerki po istorii Zakarpatja,* 2 vols. Tomsk, 1953-59.

Koman, O. "Jak nastala independencija?" in *Kalendar' Sojedinenija na h. 1951.* Munhall, Pa. 1951, pp. 46-48.

Kondratovič, I. *Istorija Podkarpatskoji Rusy.* Užhorod, 1930.

————. "Očerki iz istorii mukačevskoj eparchii," in *Karpatorusskij sbornik.* Užhorod, 1930, pp. 91-111.

————. "The Olšavsky Bishops and Their Activity." *Slovak Studies,* III (Rome, 1963), pp. 179-198.

Konstankevyč, I. and Bončevskyj, A. *Unija v Amerycî*. New York, 1902.

Kopal-Stěhovský, L.K. *Co vede Čsl. Církev ku krest'ânskému východu?* Olomouc, 1921.

Korolevsky, C. *Living Languages in Catholic Worship*. Westminster, Md., 1957.

Kostel'nyk, H. "Kryživs'ka eparchija." *Nyva*, XXVI (L'viv, 1932), pp. 134-139, 168-179, 209-215; XXVII (1933), pp. 143-147, 175-181.

Krajnyák, G. "A görög-katholikus egyház Magyarországon és sz. Unió." *Keleti Egyház*, III, 5-6 (Miskolc, 1937), pp. 135-146.

Kralickij, A. "Monastyri Uhorskoj Rusy," in *Vremennyk Stavropihijskaho Instytuta na h. 1872*, VIII (L'viv, 1871), pp. 114-120.

Krofta, C. *Carpathian Ruthenia and the Czechoslovak Republic*. London, 1934.

Kubinyi, Julius. *De cleri educatione in Ucraina Carpatica*. Dissertation, Urban University. Rome, 1953.

_____. *The History of Prjašiv Eparchy*. Rome, 1970.

Kupčanko, G. *Ugorska Rus' i jei russki žiteli*. Vienna, 1897.

Kurdydyk, A. *Vid Popradu po Tysu*. L'viv, 1939.

Kuschnir, W. "Zum ungarischen Hochverratsprocess—Graf Bobrinskij als Zeuge," *Ukrainische Rundschau*, I (Ödenburg, 1914), pp. 6-12.

Kušnirenko, M. "Pobut sela Izy—Pravoslavije i moskvofil'stvo," in *Zbirnyk Ukrajins'koho Naukovoho Instytutu v Ameryci*. St. Paul, Mn. and Prague, 1939, pp. 175-184.

Lacko, M. "A Brief Survey of the History of the Slovak Catholics of the Byzantine Slavonic Rite." *Slovak Studies*, III (Rome, 1963), pp. 199-224.

_____. "Die Užhoroder Union." *Ostkirchliche Studien*, VIII, i (Würzburg, 1959), pp. 3-30.

_____. "Liquidation of the Diocese of Prešov." *Slovak Studies*, I (Rome, 1961), pp. 158-185.

_____. "The Destruction of the Mukačevo Diocese." *Slovak Studies*, I (Rome, 1961), pp. 145-157.

_____. "Pastoral Activity of M.M. Olšavsky, Bishop of Mukačevo." *Orientalia Christiana Periodica*, XXVII (Rome, 1961), pp. 150-161.

_____. *Synodus Episcoporum Ritus Byzantini Catholicorum ex Antiqua Hungaria Vindobonae a. 1773 celebrata*. Rome, 1975.

Lingelbach, W.E. *The History of Nations*, Vol. XVII: *Austria-Hungary*. New York, 1928.

Liscová, M. *The Religious Situation in Czechoslovakia*. Prague, 1925.

Lukan', R. "Vasylijans'ki monastyri v Karp. Ukrajini." *Nova zorja*, 1 (L'viv, 1939), p. 21.

Lužnyc'kyj, H. *Jepyskop-Pioner, Kyr Soter z Ortynyč-Ortyns'kyj, ČSVV*. Philadelphia, 1963.

_____. *Ukrajins'ka cerkva miž schodom i zachodom*. Philadephia, 1954.

Macartney, C.A. *Hungary*. Chicago, 1962.

Magocsi, Paul Robert. *Our People: Carpatho-Rusyns and their Descendants in North America.* Toronto, 1984.

————. *The Shaping of a National Identity: Subcarpathian Rus', 1848-1948.* Cambridge, Mass., 1978.

M.M. "Kryževac'ka eparchija i jiji novyj vladyka Kyr Joakim." *Ameryka* (Philadelphia), August 23, 1963, p. 2.

Manuchina, T. *Put' moej žizni: vospominanija mitropolita Evlogija.* Paris, 1947.

Markus, Vasyl. *L'incorporation de l' Ukraine subcarpathique à l' Ukraine soviétique.* Louvain, 1956.

————. "*Nyščennja hreko-katolyc'koji, cerkvy v mukačivs'kij eparchiji v 1945- 1950 rr.*" *Zapysky Naukovoho tovarystva im. Ševčenka,* CLXIX (Paris and New York, 1962), pp. 386-405.

Martel, R. "La politique slave de la Russie d'avant guerre—Le procès ukr. de Maramorosz-Sziget." *Affaires Étrangères,* VI, 10 (Paris, 1936), pp. 623-634; and VII, 1 (1937), pp. 58-64.

————. *La Ruthénie subcarpathique,* Paris, 1935.

Masaryk, T.G. *Los von Rom.* Boston, 1902.

————. *Modern Man and Religion.* London, 1938.

————. *Svitova revoljucija za vijny j u vijni 1914-1918.* L'viv, 1930.

Mastyl'ak, G. "I Redentoristi di Rito Orientale," in *Acta Academiae Velehradensis,* III-IV (Olomouc, 1948), pp. 262-284.

Mayer, Mária. *Kárpátukrán (ruszin) politikai és társadalmi törekvések, 1860-1910.* Budapest, 1977.

Mikuš, J. *The Three Slovak Bishops.* Passaic, N.J., 1953.

Moioli, G. "Dietro il sipario di ferro," *Ecclesia,* no. 10 (Vatican City, 1949), pp. 534-539.

————. "Sl'ozy u Sribnij Zemli," in *Kalendar Holosu Chrysta Čolovikoljubcja na 1951 r.* Louvain, 1951, pp. 34-37.

Mol'nar, M. *Slovaky i ukrajinci.* Bratislava and Prešov, 1965.

Mondok, J. *Brevis historica notitia dioecesis Munkácsiensis.* Užhorod, 1878.

————. "De episcopatu et episcopis Maramorosiensibus," in *Schematismus dioecesis Munkácsiensis a. 1878.* Užhorod, 1878, pp. 146-162.

Mosolygó, J. *A keleti egyház Magyarországon.* Budapest, 1941.

Mycjuk, O. *Narysy z socijal'no-hospodars'koji istoriji, b. uhors'koji, nyni Pidkarpats'koj Rusy,* 2 vols. Užhorod and Prague, 1936-38.

Mykytas', Vasyl' L. *Ukrajins'kyj pys'mennyk-polemist Mychajlo Andrella.* Užhorod, 1960.

Myšanyč, O.V. *Literatura Zakarpattja XVII-XVIII st.* Kiev, 1964.

Myšuga, L. *Pidkarpats'ka Rus'.* Vienna, 1921.

Nahajevs'kyj, I. *Kyrylo-Metodijivs'ke chrystyjanstvo v Rusi-Ukrajini.* Rome, 1954.

Nazarijiv, O. "Etnohrafična teritorija uhors'kych ukrajinciv-rusyniv." *Zapysky Naukovoho tovarystva im. Ševčenka,* CII (L'viv, 1911), pp. 165-191.

Nazarko, I. "Jepyskop-Svjatytel' (spohad pro Preosv. P. Gojdyča, ČSVV)," in *Kalendar Svitla na 1953 r.* Toronto, 1953, pp. 58-60.

Nedzelskij, E. *Očerk karpatorusskoj literatury.* Užhorod, 1932.

Němec, F., and Moudry, V. *The Soviet Seizure of Subcarpathian Ruthenia.* Toronto, 1955.

Němec, L. *Church and State in Czechoslovakia.* New York, 1955.

Nestor. "Iz Zakarpat'ja." *Žurnal Moskovskoj Patriarchii,* III, 8 (Moscow, 1947), pp. 35-38.

Pačovs'kyj, Vasyl'. *Istorija Zakarpattja.* Munich, 1946.

————. *Sribna Zemlja.* L'viv, 1938.

Pan'kevyč, Ivan. "Mychail Orosveguvs'kyj čy Mychayl Teodul: dva polemyčni traktaty proty uniji." *Naukovyj zbornyk tovarystva 'Prosvita',* IV (Užhorod, 1925), pp. 5-16.

Pantelejmonovskij, D. *Povest' ob obraščenii i prisoedinenii na Afoni ugrorussaunijata v Pravoslavie.* Šanordino, 1913.

Pap, Stepan. *Počatky chrystyjans'tva na Zakarpatti.* Philadelphia, 1983.

Papp, A. "Korotkij perehl'ad istoriji Sobranija za 1903-1928 rr," in *Kalendar' Sobranija na r. 1929.* McKeesport, Pa., 1929, pp. 136-152.

Papp, Gyula. "Adalékok De Camilis J. munkácsi püspök müködéséhez." *Keleti egyház,* VII, 5 (Miskolc, 1941), pp. 110-124.

————. "A munkácsi püspökség eredete." *Keleti egyház,* VI, 9, 10, 11 (Miskolc, 1940), pp. 175-183; 204-212; 221-224.

————. "Az ungvári unió idöpontja." *Keleti egyház,* VII, 7, 8 (Miskolc, 1941), pp. 162-167; 184-188.

————. *Magyarország primásának joghatósága és a görög-katholikus egyház.* Miskolc, 1943.

Pekar, Athanasius B. "Basilian Reform in Transcarpathia." *Zapysky ČSVV,* VII (Rome, 1971), pp. 143-226.

————. *Bishop Basil Hopko, STD (1904-1976).* Pittsburgh, Pa., 1979.

————. "Bishop John Bradač, the Last Basilian in the Mukačevo Episcopal See (1732-1772)." *Orientalia Christiana Periodica,* XLIX (Rome, 1983), pp. 130-152.

————. "Bishop P. Gebey, Champion of the Holy Union." *Analecta OSBM,* IV (Rome, 1963), pp. 293-326.

————. *Bishop Paul P. Gojdich, OSBM.* Pittsburgh, Pa., 1980.

————. *The Bishops of the Eparchy of Mukachevo with Historical Outlines.* Pittsburgh, Pa., 1979.

————. "Cerkovna polityka madjariv na Zakarpatt'i." *Svitlo,* XXVIII, 4 (Toronto, 1965), pp. 170-173.

————. "Čolovik Provydinnja—Vladyka D. Njaradij." *Svitlo,* XXVIII, 9 (Toronto, 1965), pp. 354-357.

————. "Dolja monachiv i monachyn' na Prjašivščyni." *Svitlo,* XXI, 6 (Toronto, 1958), pp. 15-16.

————. *De erectione canonica eparchiae Mukačoviensis.* Rome 1956.

————. "First Byzantine Bishop in America—S.S. Ortynsky, OSBM."

Eastern Catholic Life (Passaic, N.J.), March 20, 1966, p. 8.

_____. *Historic Background of the Eparchy of Prjashev.* Pittsburgh, 1968.

_____. "Historical Background of the Carpatho-Ruthenians in America." *Ukrajins'kyj istoryk,* XIII and XIV (New York, Toronto, and Munich, 1976-77), pp. 87-102 and 70-84.

_____. *Our Martyred Bishop Romzha (1911-1947).* Pittsburgh, 1977.

_____. *Our Past and Present: Historical Outlines of the Byzantine Ruthenian Metropolitan Province.* Pittsburgh, 1974.

_____. *Our Slavic Heritage.* Pittsburgh, 1969.

_____. "Ternystym šljachom Vladyky-Pionera (S. Ortyns'kyj, ČSVV)." *Svitlo,* XXIX, 3 and 4 (Toronto, 1966), pp. 100-102 and 147.

_____. "Tribute to Bishop Joseph J. de Camillis, OSBM." *Analecta OSBM.* XII (Rome, 1985), pp. 374-418.

_____. "Vasylijans'ka provincija sv. Mykolaja na Zakarpatt'i." *Zapysky ČSVV,* XI (Rome, 1982), pp. 131-164.

_____. *Vasylijanyn-ispovidnyk: žyttja jep. P. Gojdyča, ČSVV.* New York, 1961.

_____. *Vladyka-mučenyk, T. Ju. Romža (1911-1947).* New York, 1962.

_____. *"You Shall Be Witnesses Unto Me": Contribution to the Martyrology of the Byzantine Catholic Church in Subcarpathian Ruthenia.* Pittsburgh, 1985.

Pelesz, Julian. *Geschichte der Union der ruthenischen Kirche mit Rom,* 2 vols. Vienna, 1878-80.

Pereni, J. *Iz istorii zakarpatskich ukraincev (1894-1914).* Budapest, 1957.

Perfeckij, E. "Obzor ugro-russkoj istoriografii." *Izvjestija Imperatorskoj Akademii Nauk,* XIX, 1 (St. Petersburg, 1914), pp. 291-341.

_____. "Vasylij Tarasovyč, jepyskop mukačevs'kyj," *Naukovyj zbornyk tovarystva 'Prosvita',* II (Užhorod, 1923), pp. 84-92.

Perhach, George. *Married Priests in the Catholic Church.* Brooklyn, N.Y., 1933.

Petrov, Aleksej L. "Kanoničeskija vizitacii 1750-67 gg." *Naukovyj zbornyk tovarystva 'Prosvita',* III (Užhorod, 1924), pp. 104-135.

_____. "K istorii 'russkich intrig' v Ugrii v XVIII v.," in *Karpatorusskij sbornik.* Užhorod, 1930, pp. 123-133.

_____. *'Staraja vjera' i unija v XVII-XVIII vv.,* 2 vols. St. Petersburg, 1905-06.

Perši zakovani: pro peresliduvannja viry v Ukrajini. Buenos Aires, 1956.

Praszko, J. *De Ecclesia Ruthena Catholica sede metropolitana vacante 1655-1665.* Rome, 1944.

Pricak, O. "Chto taki avtochtony Karpatskoji Ukrajiny," *Nova zorja,* no. 1 (Lviv and Stanyslaviv, 1939), pp. 15-16.

_____. "Mukačiv—hnizdo rebeljantiv i kul'turnyj centr." *Nova zorja,* nos. 23 and 24 (L'viv and Stanyslaviv, 1939), pp. 6-7 and 6.

Procko, Bohdan P. *Ukrainian Catholics in America: A History.* Washington, D.C., 1982.

Punyko, A. *Bishop Theodore G. Romzha and the Soviet Occupation.* New York, 1967.

Rath, Ignác. *Náboženské dějiny Podkarpatské Rusi do r. 1498.* Prague, 1933.

Rešetylo, S. "Obraz Presv. Bohorodyci darovanyj Sv. Otcem mukačivs'komu monastyrevi," *Zapysky ČSVV,* II, 3-4 (Žovkva, 1926), pp. 411-416.

_____. "Učast' Karpats'koji Provinciji ČSVV v misijnomu rusi," *Zapysky ČSVV,* I, 2-3 (Žovkva, 1925), pp. 327-346.

Roman, Michael. *Short Biographies of Famous Carpatho-Russians.* Munhall, Pa., 1962.

Rosocha, Stepan. *Sojm Karpatskoji Ukrajiny.* Winnipeg, 1949.

Rusak, Ju. P. "Mukačevskaja eparchija i eja bor'ba za prava russkago jazyka i narodnosti vo vremja ep. V. Popoviča," in *Karpatorusskij sbornik.* Užhorod, 1930, pp. 50-68.

Sabol, Sevastijan S. *Holhota hreko-katolyc'koji cerkvy v Čechoslovaččyni.* Toronto and Rome, 1978.

_____. "Hreko-katol. jeparchija v ZDA, pro jaku malo znajemo," in *Kalendar Slova Dobroho Pastyrja na 1952 r.* New York, 1952, pp. 99-100.

_____. "Mučenyc'kyj šljach Presov. P. Gojdyča, ČSVV," *Svitlo,* XXIII, 10 (Toronto, 1960), pp. 417-418.

Sabov, E., ed. *Christomatija cerkovno-slavjanskich i ugro-russkich literaturnych pamjatnikov.* Užhorod, 1893.

Schaguna, I. *Geschichte der griechisch-orientalischen Kirche in Oesterreich.* Hermannstadt, 1862.

Scrimali, A. *La Ruthénie subcarpathique et l'état tchécoslovaque.* Paris, 1938.

Šeluchyn, S. "Nazva Pidkarpattja Ukrajinoju," in *Juvilejnyj al'manach Sojuzu pidkarpats'kych studentiv.* Prague, 1931, pp. 40-52.

Sembratovyč, L. "Jak pryjšlo do imenuvannja našoho peršoho Jepyskopa v Ameryci," in *Kalendar Provydinnja na 1956 r.* Philadelphia, 1956, pp. 71-74.

Shereghy, Basil. *Fifty Years of Piety: A History of the Uniontown Pilgrimages.* Pittsburgh, 1985.

_____. ed. *A Historical Album: On the Occasion of the 75th Anniversary of the United Societies.* McKeesport, Pa., 1978.

Sheregy, V. and Pekar, V. *The Training of the Carpatho-Ruthenian Clergy.* Pittsburgh, 1951.

Shuster, G.N. *Religion Behind the Iron Curtain.* New York, 1954.

Šimrak, J. *De relationibus Slavorum Merid. cum S. Romana Sede Apostolica ss. XVII et XVIII,* Vol. I. Zagreb, 1926.

_____. *Graeco-Catholica Ecclesia in Jugoslavia.* Zagreb, 1931.

Šlepeckij, Andrej S. "Karpatorossy v Amerike," in *Al'manach O.K.S. Vozroždenie.* Prague, 1936, pp. 81-86.

_____. *Stručny prehl'ad vývinu ukrajinskej literatúry na Východnom Slovensku.* Prešov, 1959.

_____. "Prjaševcy v Amerike," in Ivan Šlepeckij, ed. *Prjaševščina.*

Prague, 1948, pp. 255-262.

Šlepeckij, Ivan. "Stara vira i unija." *Družno vpered,* XV, 6 and 7 (Prešov, 1965), pp. 18-20 and 22.

Slivka, John. *The History of the Greek Rite Catholics in Pannonia, Hungary, Czechoslovakia and Podkarpatska Rus', 863-1949.* [Brooklyn, N.Y.], 1974.

S[tankanynec', A.] "Desjat'-ročnyj juvilej reformy Vasylijanov na Podkarpats'koj Rusi." *Dušpastyr',* VII, 12 (Užhorod, 1930), pp. 334-337.

————. "Pjat'desjat'littja vidnovy Čyna sv. Vasylija Velykoho." *Blahovîstnyk,* XII (Užhorod, 1932), no. 8, pp. 113-116; no. 9, pp. 129-131; no. 10, pp. 145-149; no. 11, pp. 161-163; no. 12, pp. 177-179; XIII (1933), no. 1, pp. 3-5; no. 2, pp. 17-18.

Stankaninec, G. "Archimandrit Aleksij (Kabaljuk)." *Žurnal Moskovskoj Patriarchii,* IV, 2 (Moscow, 1948), pp. 68-70.

Stasiw, M. *Metropolia Haliciensis.* Rome, 1960.

Stefan, A. *From Carpatho-Ruthenia to Carpatho-Ukraine.* New York, 1954.

Stojka, A. "Deržavnoe žalovanie duchovenstva," *Dušpastyr',* V, 1 (Užhorod, 1928), pp. 5-9.

————. "K uporjadkovanju svjaščeniče's'kich deržavnych žalovanij." *Dušpastyr',* IV, 2 (Užhorod, 1927), pp. 103-106.

Svencickij, I.S. *Obzor snošenij Karpatskoj Rusi s Rossiej v l-uju polovinu XIX v.* St. Petersburg, 1906.

Theiner, A. *Histoire du Pontificat de Clément XIV.* Paris, 1852.

"The Orthodox Church in America." *St. Vladimir's Seminary Quarterly,* V, 1-2 (New York, 1961).

Tichý, František. *Vývoj současného spisovného jazyka na Pokdarpatské Rusi.* Prague, 1938.

Tomašivs'kyj, Stepan. "Pryčynky do piznannja etnografičnoji teritoriji Uhors'koji Rusy." *Zapysky Naukovoho tovarystva im. Ševčenka,* LXVII (L'viv, 1905), pp. 1-18.

————. *Uhorščyna i Pol'šča na počatku XVIII v.* L'viv, 1909.

Trajnin, I.P. *Nacional'nye protivorečija v Avstro-Vengrii i ee raspad.* Moscow and Leningrad, 1947.

Trojckij, S.I. *Pravoslavie, unija i katoličestvo u slavjan i rumyn v Avstro-Vengrii.* St. Petersburg, 1914.

Ukrajins'ka Katolyc'ka Mytropolija v ZDA. Philadelphia, 1959.

Urban, R. *Die slavisch-nationalkirchlichen Bestrebungen in der Tschechoslowakei.* Leipzig, 1938.

V. "Edward Egan, martir podkarpatorusskoho naroda," in *Kalendar' Sobranija na 1929 r.* McKeesport, Pa., 1925, pp. 85-88.

Vajda, M. "Kryževac'ka jeparchija," *Kovčeh,* VII, 8-9 (Stamford, Conn., 1952), pp. 124-125.

————. "Pryčynok do istoriji Vasylijan na Zakarpatti," in *Kalendar Syrits'koho Domu na 1954 r.* Philadelphia, 1954, pp. 91-97.

_____. "Smert herojskoho jepyskopa." *Kovčeh,* II, 5 (Stamford, Conn., 1947), pp. 89-90.

Vančyk, I. "Madjars'ka mova v cerkovnomu bohosluženju i rus'ke duchovenstvo na Uhorščyni." *Nyva,* I (L'viv, 1907), pp. 227-230.

Vassily [Ch. Bourgeois, S. J.]. "The Podcarpathian Schism," *Pax,* nos. 147 and 150 (Prinknash Abbey, 1934).

Vavryk, M. *Po Vasylijans'kych monastyrjach.* Toronto, 1958.

Vavryk, V. *Jepiskop S. Ortynskyj, ČSVV.* New York, 1956.

Vedernikov, A. "Prekraščenie unii v Čechoslovakii," *Žurnal Moskovskoj Patriarchii,* VI, 7 (Moscow, 1950), pp. 40-52.

_____. "Zrušenie únie v Československu," *Svetlo Pravoslávia,* II, 2 (Prague, 1951).

Velykyj, A. *Bol'ševyc'kyj cerkovnyj sobor u L'vovi 1946 r.* New York, 1952.

Vološyn [Voloshyn], Avhustyn. "Carpathian Ruthenia." *The Slavonic Review,* XIII (London, 1934-35), pp. 372-378.

_____. *"Oborona kyrylyky."* *Naukovyj zbirnyk tovarystva 'Prosvita',* XII (Užhorod, 1937), pp. 85-117.

_____. "Religijni vidnosyny na Pidk. Rusi," in *Acta Conventus Pragensis pro Studiis Orientalibus a 1929 celebrati.* Olomouc, 1930, pp. 237-243.

_____. *Spomyny.* Philadelphia, 1959.

Vrchovecký, J. *T. G. Masaryk a náboženství.* Prague, 1937.

Warzeski, Walter C. *Byzantine Rite Rusins in Carpatho-Ruthenia and America.* Pittsburgh, 1971.

Winter, E. "Die Kämpfe der Ukrainer Oberungarns um eine nationale Hierarchie im Theresianischen Zeitalter," *Kyrios,* XI (Königsberg, 1939-40), pp. 129-141.

_____. "Der Kampf der Ecclesia Ruthenica gegen den Rituswechsel," in *Festschrift E. Eichmann zum 70 Geburtstag.* Paderborn, 1940, pp. 237-243.

_____. *Vizantija ta Rym u borot' bi za Ukrajinu 955-1939.* Prague, 1944.

Žatkovyč, Ju. "Duchovnaja Semynarija (1877-1881)," in *Kalendar' Sobranija na 1927 r.* McKeesport, Pa., 1927, pp. 133-148.

_____. [Žatkovič, K.]. *Jagerskoje vl'ijanije i bor'ba protiv toho v istoriji Mukačevskoj diocezji.* Homestead, Pa., n.d.

_____. "Jepyskopy maramoroskije." *Lystok,* VII (Užhorod, 1891), pp. 158-159, 172-173, 182-183, 196-197, 209-211, 225-226, 232-233, 243-244, 256-257.

_____. "Narys istoriji hrušivs'koho monastyrja na Uhors'kij Rusy," in *Naukovyj zbirnyk prysvjačenyj pamjati M. Hruševs'koho.* L'viv, 1906, pp. 155-157.

Zeedick, P. and Smor, A. *Naše stanovišče.* Homestead, Pa., 1934.

Zeller, A. *A magyar egyházpolitika.* Budapest, 1894.

Zerkal, S. *Nacional'ni i relihijni vidnosyny na Zakarpatti.* New York, 1956.

Zubek, Th. *The Church of Silence in Slovakia.* Passaic, N.J., 1956.

Žučenko, M. "Ugorskaja Rus'." *Ukrainskaja žizn'*, no. 5-6 (Moscow, 1914), pp. 33-38.

Žydovskij, I. "Prjaševskaja Rus' v borot'bi za svoji prava," in *Podkarpatskaja Rus' za gg. 1919-1936*. Užhorod, 1936, pp. 89-91.

Index

Abaúj county (Abovo-Novhorod), 78, 81, 208n.4
Abramovce, 199
Agnus, 186
Alba Iulia (Bilhorod), 26, 63-66, 180, 223n.8
Albani, A., 55, 221n.136
Albania, 184
Aleksander, Bishop (Viktor Mychalyč), 161
Aleksei (Dechterev), Bishop, 157, 159, 161, 234n.45
Aleksei of Moscow, Patriarch, 146, 149, 158
Aleksej (Šimanskij), Patriarch, 240n.2,9
Alexander VII, 26, 39, 41, 182
Alexander VIII, 184
Almanac (*Kalendar*), xiii
Alphabet issues, 97-98, 107, 128, 135, 230n.56
Alumneum, 127, 192
America, xii-xv, 104, 169
American Carpatho-Russian Orthodox Greek Catholic Diocese of U.S.A., 173, 247n.48
American "Rusyn-rite" Exarchate, 201
American Rusyns, 162

Americanization of the Church, xvi, 166, 174
Anaheim, California, 205
Analecta Ordinis Sancti Basilii Magni, xii
Anastasia, 13
Anatolia, 214n.66
Ancyra (Ankara), 183
Anderko, Peter, 71
András I, 13
Andrella, Mychajlo, 34, 65, 213n.64
Andrij, I., 231n.15
Andrukhovych, C., 244n.17
Anhelu, Athanasius, 66
Ankara (Ancyra), 183
Anti-Austrianism, 116
Anti-Catholicism, 99, 116-117, 119, 147
Anti-Czech agitation, 113
Anti-Hungarianism, 98-99, 107
Anti-Uniatism, 66, 104, 146, 157-158, 184, 187
Antonij, Bishop, 151, 153
Antonij, Metropolitan, 111
Antony IV, 62
Apafi, M., 70, 181
Apostolate of Prayer, 124, 133
Apostolate of SS. Cyril and Methodius in Subcarpathian Rus', 122